Trek Indian Himalaya

a Lonely Planet walking guide

Garry Weare

D0428266

Trekking in the Indian Himalaya

3rd edition

Published by
Lonely Planet Publications
Head Office: PO Box 617, Hawthorn, Vic 3122, Australia
Branches: 155 Filbert St, Suite 251, Oakland, CA 94607, USA
10 Barley Mow Passage, Chiswick, London W4 4PH, UK
71 bis rue du Cardinal Lemoine, 75005 Paris, France

Printed by
Colorcraft Ltd, Hong Kong

Photographs by
Garry Weare
Lindsay Brown
Front cover: Dhirdham Temple, Darjeeling (Richard I'Anson)

First Published
April 1986

This Edition
April 1997

National Library of Australia Cataloguing in Publication Data

Weare, Garry
Trekking in the Indian Himalaya
3rd ed.
Includes index.
ISBN 0 86442 357 8.

1. Hiking - Himalaya Mountains - Guidebooks. 2. India, Northeastern - Description and travel - Guidebooks.
3. Himalaya Mountains - Guidebooks.
I. Title. (Series : Lonely Planet walking guide).

915.40452

Garry Weare

Garry has spent most of his working life organising and leading treks in the Indian Himalaya since he first trekked in Kashmir in 1970. In the last 20 years he has covered the best part of 20,000 km trekking in this part of the Himalaya. He is a Director of World Expeditions (formerly Australian Himalayan Expeditions) and returns to India regularly to research and lead treks.

From the Author

Trek contributions for this edition came from a number of sources. In Ladakh and Kashmir the route descriptions were compiled by Garry Weare with assistance from Wangchuk Shamshu, Rigzin Jowa, Padam Singh, Meraj Din, Rouf Tramboo and Manzor Ahmed in Himachal Pradesh; with Iqbal Sharma, Judy Parker, Dr Jim Duff, Rejane Belanger and Almos Khan in Uttarakhand; and Arun Kumar in Darjeeling and Sikkim. In Delhi, Harsh Vardhan and Wangchuk Shamshu, as always, provided invaluable logistic support and great friendship.

I would like to thank Dr Jim Duff for the time spent writing the medical section. Thanks also to Nick Kostos for not making me feel too guilty after lengthy absences from the office. A special thanks to Judy Parker for her editorial advice and invaluable contribution to the natural history section, and for her company on the treks – always appreciated (in spite of her constant berating of my need for a Scotch after the day's trek).

Closer to the workface at Lonely Planet in Melbourne, thanks to Andrew Smith for the time he spent producing the trekking maps from my base maps; and to Frith Luton for her constant encouragement and advice throughout the project.

Dedication This book is dedicated to Narpat Singh (1956-94), co-founder of World Expeditions (India), a firm friend and trusted guide; my mother, Mrs D Power (1911-95), for all her encouragement; and my daughter, India Weare, who may also experience the delights of Himalayan trekking.

From the Publisher

This edition of *Trekking in the Indian Himalaya* was edited by Frith Luton and Nick Tapp with assistance from Rob van Driesum and Sharan Kaur. Cartography and design were by Andrew Smith, and Chris Klep took the book through the final stages of production. Steve Womersley proofed the book and Paul Piaia, Chris Love and Michael Signal assisted with the maps. Margaret Jung and Reita Wilson did the illustrating, Kerrie Williams assisted with the index. David Kemp designed the cover with cartography by Adam McCrow. Thanks everyone.

Thanks

Thank you to Rob Stevenson, Roddy McKenzie, Huw Kingston, Margriet Katoen & Erik Meijer, Eugene Clerkin and Mark Thompson for their letters and contributions.

Acknowledgments

The extract from *The Nanda Devi Affair* by Bill Aitken is reproduced courtesy of the author and publishers (Penguin Books Pvt Ltd). Garry would also like to acknowledge *Exploring the Hidden Himalaya* by Soli Mehta and Harish Kapadia, published by Hodder & Stoughton, and *Abode of Snow* by Kenneth Mason, published by Diadem Books, London, and The Mountaineers,

Seattle – two classics on the Himalaya that have inspired him.

Trekking Disclaimer

Although the author and publisher have done their utmost to ensure the accuracy of all information in this guide, they cannot accept any responsibility for any loss, injury or inconvenience sustained by people using this book.

They cannot guarantee that the tracks and routes described here have not become impassable for any reason in the interval between research and publication.

The fact that a trip or area is described in this guidebook does not necessarily mean that it is safe for you and your trekking party. You are ultimately responsible for judging your own capabilities in the light of the conditions you encounter.

Warning & Request

Things change – prices go up, schedules change, good places go bad and bad places go bankrupt – nothing stays the same. So, if you find things better or worse, recently opened or long since closed, please tell us and help make the next edition even more accurate and useful.

We value all of the feedback we receive from travellers. Julie Young coordinates a small team who read and acknowledge every letter, postcard and email, and ensure that every morsel of information finds its way to the appropriate authors, editors and publishers.

Everyone who writes to us will find their name in the next edition of the appropriate guide and will also receive a free subscription to our quarterly newsletter, *Planet Talk*. The very best contributions will be rewarded with a free Lonely Planet guide.

Excerpts from your correspondence may appear in updates (which we add to the end pages of reprints); new editions of this guide; in our newsletter, *Planet Talk*; or in the Postcards section of our Web site – so please let us know if you don't want your letter published or your name acknowledged.

Contents

Map Legend

BOUNDARIES

International Boundary
Province Boundary
Disputed Boundary

ROUTES

Freeway
Highway
Major Road
Unsealed Road or Jeep Road
City Road
City Street
Railway
Underground Railway
Walking Track
Route
Ridge
Ferry Route

AREA FEATURES

Parks
Built-Up Area
Pedestrian Mall
Market
Building
Glacier, Icecap
Beach or Desert
Rocks

HYDROGRAPHIC FEATURES

Coastline
River, Creek
Intermittent River or Creek
Rapids, Waterfalls
Lake, Intermittent Lake
Canal, Swamp
River flow

SYMBOLS

✪ CAPITAL .... National Capital
◉ Capital ...... Province or Regional Capital
⬤ CITY .... Major City
● City .... City
● Town .... Town
• Village .... Village
■ ▼ ....Place to Stay, Place to Eat
☕ ☕ .... Cafe, Pub or Bar
✉ ☎ .... Post Office, Telephone
ℹ ⑨ .... Tourist Information, Bank
◉ ◉ Bus Station or Terminal, Bus Stop
🏛 ⌂ .... Museum, Youth Hostel
🚐 🅰 Caravan Park, Camping Ground
✝ ✚ .... Church, Cathedral
☪ ✡ .... Mosque, Synagogue
卍 ✛ .... Temple, Hospital
★ ...... Police Station or Check Post

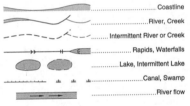

○ 🅿 .... Embassy, Petrol Station
✈ ✚ .... Airport, Airfield
⊟ ✿ .... Swimming Pool, Gardens
❖ 🐘 .... Shopping Centre, Zoo
🍇 🖼 ...Winery or Vineyard, Picnic Site
← A25 One Way Street, Route Number
🏛 ⚱ .... Stately Home, Monument
🏰 ▣ .... Castle, Tomb
⌒ ⌂ .... Cave, Hut or Chalet
▲ ☀ .... Mountain or Hill, Lookout
🗼 ⚓ .... Lighthouse, Shipwreck
)(◎ .... Pass, Spring
⚐ ⚑ .... Beach, Surf Beach
⁂ ...... Archaeological Site or Ruins
.... Ancient or City Wall
⟹ ⟸ ...... Cliff or Escarpment, Tunnel
.... Railway Station

Note: not all symbols displayed above appear in this book

Introduction

The Indian Himalaya provides some superb possibilities for trekking. While the numbers visiting the Indian Himalaya are small in comparison with the numbers trekking in Nepal, there is nonetheless a steady, growing interest. Trekkers are discovering that the Himalaya Range does not end on the border of Nepal and, that there are many opportunities for treks which are as long and demanding as those to Everest or the Annapurna Range.

The Indian Himalaya is undoubtedly one of the most spectacular and impressive mountain ranges in the world. To appreciate this fully, there is no substitute for undertaking a trek. Trekking is an unforgettable experience. It brings you direct contact with the country and its people, and helps to foster an appreciation of the mountain environments.

There are many reasons for trekking the Indian Himalaya. In the space of a week or

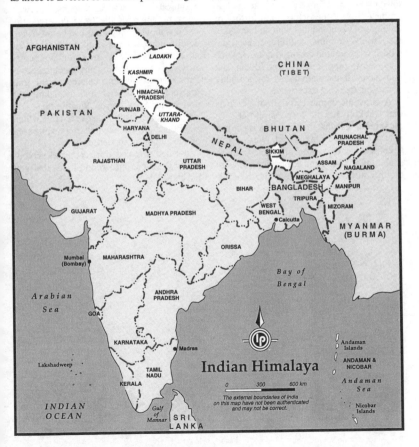

Indian Himalaya

0   300   600 km

The external boundaries of India on this map have not been authenticated and may not be correct.

two you may trek through Hindu settlements and past temples, isolated Buddhist monasteries, camp beside shepherd encampments or visit villages that support traditional Islamic culture. On a typical trek you may traverse the Great Himalaya Range and appreciate the sheer geographic diversity – from the verdant, forested valleys and the flowered meadows carpeted with wildflowers to the arid and rugged terrain of the Trans Himalaya that extends north and east to the Tibetan plateau. While crossing the high passes it is also salutary to note the many pilgrims, traders and armies who have followed these trails for generations and whose journeys reflect the rich cultural history of the region. Combine this with an interest in the variety of birds, wildlife, forests and wildflowers and the opportunity to view the many snow-capped peaks over 7000m, and you have all the ingredients for a highly rewarding trekking experience.

A constant theme throughout guide is that trekking has its responsibilities. We must recognise that the Himalaya is not just a vast adventure playground. We need to acknowledge these concerns and aim to share and evolve simple, practical ways to ensure a minimum impact on both the environment and the local culture and traditions.

It is also acknowledged that the Indian Himalaya has been beset by political problems over the past five years and the small trekking section on Kashmir has been included in the hope that the situation will eventually improve. For the present there are, however, many attractive alternatives.

This guide has been classified into the regions of Ladakh, Kashmir, Himachal Pradesh, Uttarakhand, Darjeeling and Sikkim. In each area there is an overall assessment of the trekking possibilities. The regions are introduced with a description of their geographical and historical features, followed by a rundown of the treks covered, the seasons in which the trails can be followed, details about where to buy supplies and an assessment of local trekking agencies. Advice is also given on any potential problems that may be encountered on the trail together with the cost and availability of porters and pack horses. Finally, there is a stage by stage description of each trek which is outlined on accurate trekking maps based on the author's experience.

It's then up to you to select the trek according to the time, interest and funds that you have available.

Facts about the Region

HISTORY

From near the Nun Kun mountains and from no other spot in Asia, we go westwards through countries entirely Mohammedan, eastward among none but Buddhists, and southwards over lands where the Hindu religion prevails to the extremity of the Indian peninsula.

Frederick Drew, *The Northern Barrier of India*, 1877

History & Culture

The Indian Himalaya marks the crossroads of Asia's three main cultures. The Kashmir Himalaya is the cultural boundary of Islam; the foothills of Jammu, Himachal Pradesh and the regions of Garhwal and Kumaon in Uttarakhand define the northern limits of Hinduism; while Ladakh is predominantly Buddhist.

From the earliest records, the Himalaya has been revered as the abode of the gods. Since the time the Aryans migrated to northern India between 2500 and 1500 BC, the mountains have been held in awe. In about 1000 BC these people composed the *Vedas*, a set of hymns devoted to the gods: Agni the god of fire, Surya the god of the sun, Vago the god of the wind, and Indra the mighty god of the sky. All resided in the Himalaya, an arena where immortal beings could determine the destiny of the world.

The power of these gods was revealed in an elaborate system of ritual and sacrifice. For the Aryan warriors the sacrifice was of paramount importance, particularly when needed to secure the favour of the gods in times of war. The ceremonies of sacrifice were taken as sacrosanct, with the priests – the Brahmans – assuming a crucial role. The sacrificial rites naturally increased the power of the Brahmans, and gradually they were able to dominate the village and local communities with their interests. A caste system was instituted which has remained an integral part of life in India until the present day.

The powerful position of the Brahmans and their exclusive rituals gave rise to alternatives which became popular. The teachings of the Buddha spread, and had a wide appeal across northern India from the 5th century BC. Two centuries later, the Emperor Ashoka patronised the third Buddhist congress in Kashmir, while the Emperor Kanishka also encouraged the discussion of Buddhist fundamentals during the fourth congress in Kashmir in the 1st century AD. During this time Buddhist teachings spread well beyond the Himalayan foothills, and as far as China.

The spread of Buddhism did not undermine the position of the Brahmans. Although some Vedic gods fell out of favour, others, such as Shiva, Vishnu and Brahma, came to the fore. Brahma was seen as the creator, Vishnu the preserver and Shiva the destroyer.

In the 1st century AD, two epic poems were composed to commemorate the history and heroes of India, the *Mahabharata* and the *Ramayana*. They were not written as religious treatises, but as they gained popularity these works were revised by the Brahmans and given a religious status. Their heroes, including Rama and Krishna, became associated with incarnations of Vishnu. Shiva was linked with the popular fertility cults of the bull and the worship of the *lingam* (phallic symbol). It was an association which gained wider appeal with the spread of Tantric cults (embedded in magic and mystery) and the worship of the mother goddess.

The cult of sexual union was raised to divine status, with each god being assigned a female partner. For example, Shiva was associated with Parvati and Vishnu with Lakshmi. Pilgrimages were undertaken to the Himalaya, the home of the gods. Pilgrims trekked to the Amarnath Cave (which symbolises the essence of the mother goddess), inside which the ice statue represents the divine lingam. This sign of cosmic creation has become part of the Himalayan tradition.

The traditional Hindu values were not undermined until the coming of Islam. In the

11

11th century the Mahmud of Ghanzi over-threw the local Hindu rulers of a small principality just south of Kabul. From this base Islam spread across the Hindukush and north-west India, with the sultanate of Delhi being established a century or so later. Kashmir was converted to Islam during the 14th century. Essentially this conversion was peaceful, and independent of the Turkish forces which had by then assumed power across the north Indian plains.

Despite these religious changes, Ladakh remained Buddhist, and continued to trace its cultural origins to the time when the Tantric sage Padmasambhava wandered from India to Tibet in the 8th century. From that time on, the animistic Bon Po beliefs fell into decline, and by the 10th century the kings of western Tibet and Ladakh had been fully converted.

While the wave of Islam was to spread to other nearby Himalayan regions, such as Baltistan, the hill kingdoms from Jammu across the foothills to the Garhwal were able to maintain their cultural heritage. The three distinct cultural worlds of Buddhist Ladakh, Islamic Kashmir and the Hindu hill states had almost evolved into their present-day situation.

The founding of the Moghul empire re-aligned cultural boundaries. After consolidating his power over the Indian plains and the territories of the Rajputs, the Moghul emperor Akbar invaded Kashmir in 1588. During Akbar's time the local administration was upgraded, and more equitable systems of land tenure were introduced. Akbar's son Jahangir and his grandson Shah Jehan were responsible for the famous Moghul gardens. They also extended Moghul influence to the Indian hill states, with Jammu, Kangra, Chamba and the rulers of Garhwal and Kumaon paying tribute to the Moghul courts.

To the north, Ladakh had carved out a sizeable empire for itself, having managed to secure its borders from the Islamic rulers of both Kashmir and Kashgar. In the early 16th century, however, the kingdom was subject to the rule of Ali Mir, the ruler of Baltistan.

Yet Ladakh's fortunes were forever chang-ing, and during the time of one of its most illustrious rulers, Singge Namgyal (1570-1642), it was able to secure its independence and expand its territories to include Guge, Zanskar and Spiti. But not long after this Ladakh was drawn into a war with the Tibet-Mongol army under the 5th Dalai Lama, and its boundaries were confined again to the Indus Valley. This war would have reduced the Ladakhi borders even further had it not been for the intervention of the Moghuls. Aurangzeb, the last of the great Moghul emperors, called for the Ladakhi king to pay a nominal tribute to his court – to build a mosque at the end of the Leh bazaar.

Following the decline of the Moghuls, a complex political situation evolved. Kashmir was invaded by the much-feared Afghani forces while Jammu gradually secured a position of autonomy in the foothills. The nearby state of Kangra also extended its influence across the Kullu Valley as far as the Sutlej River, while the Gurkhas of Nepal expanded their borders over the Kumaon and the Garhwal as far as the Shimla hill states. To complete the picture, by the second half of the 18th century the Sikhs had established an empire across the Punjab, while the East India Company was setting its sights far beyond the established trading posts of Calcutta.

The state of Kangra, the Sikhs and the Gurkhas all had ambitions to control the Punjab Himalaya. The Gurkhas sought the assistance of the Sikhs, but the Sikhs had their own plans to extend their territory beyond Lahore. The Gurkhas therefore led a united front with the deposed hill rajahs against the Kangra army. These forces retreated to the Kangra Fort, and called on the Sikhs for assistance. The Sikhs complied, the Gurkhas withdrew to the Sutlej, and the Sikhs took control of most of the hill states, which were soon to include Kashmir.

The British were wary of the extent of Sikh influence, and equally aware that any combined Gurkha-Sikh empire stretching from Sikkim to Kashmir would be a formi-dable force to deal with. The British were determined to forge a neutral zone between the Sikhs and the Gurkhas, which they achieved as a result of the Gurkha wars of 1814-16. The Gurkhas were restricted to the eastern banks of the Karnali River, the present boundary between India and Nepal – leaving the districts of Garhwal, Naini Tal, Kumaon and Dehra Dun under British control.

By the 1830s the Sikhs, with assistance of the Dogras of Jammu, had taken Kishtwar, Ladakh, and Baltistan. After the death of the noted Sikh ruler Ranjit Singh, the British gained control of the Punjab during the Sikh wars in the mid-1840s. Under their leader, Gulab Singh, the Dogras remained neutral. The political evolution of north-west India was almost complete.

On 9 March 1846, following the Treaty of Amritsar, the Sikh Durbar agreed to cede to the British 'the hilly and mountainous country' between the Beas and Indus rivers. The British in fact owned Kashmir for one week. A week later, a separate treaty was entered into between the British and the Dogra leader, Gulab Singh. Essentially, this treaty transferred the whole region between the Ravi and Indus rivers to the Dogras.

For the next 101 years Kashmir was ruled by four Dogra maharajahs. The first, Gulab Singh, died in 1857 and was succeeded by Ranbir Singh, who ruled until 1888. Following his death, the British installed a Resident and formed a Council of Regency until 1905 when Pratap Singh, the heir to the throne, was deemed to be a competent ruler.

He remained maharajah until 1923 when he was succeeded by Hari Singh, the last of the Dogra rulers. During Hari Singh's rule, the majority of the Muslim population of Kashmir continued to live in poverty with little in the way of educational or religious facilities. Eventually, in opposition to the rule of the Dogra leaders, a National Conference party was formed.

In 1947 Hari Singh was forced to choose between joining India or Pakistan. On paper the choice was clear. Kashmir was predominantly Muslim, so Pakistan was the natural cultural choice. However, Hari Singh remained indecisive. As a Hindu, he had little feeling for Pakistan, while as a maharajah he had even less inclination to lose his kingdom to India. His true desire was for an independent maharajah's kingdom – an impossible dream.

Pakistan seized upon the urgency of the situation, and 'organised' a coup by dispatching Pathan tribesmen to capture Srinagar. Hari Singh called on India for support, and paid the political price – a full-scale war which was not settled until 1 January 1949, and the division of Kashmir between India and Pakistan.

The Kashmir line of control became a matter of constant dispute between India and Pakistan, and further conflicts arose in 1965 and 1971. Meanwhile, in Ladakh, India and China went to war with each other in 1962 following a dispute along the Tibet-India border.

The outcome in India is the state of Jammu & Kashmir (J&K): Jammu is predominantly Hindu and Kashmir, Muslim, while Ladakh, in the north-east of J&K, is Buddhist. It's a state born more out of political accident than cultural design.

The hill states of Chamba, Kangra, Kullu, and Lahaul came under the Punjab administration after 1947. In 1966 the administration was reorganised and Kangra, Kullu and Lahaul were merged with the Shimla hill states to form Himachal Pradesh. In 1971 Himachal Pradesh was given full statehood in the Indian Union. Being essentially a Hindu state, it is devoid of the cultural complexities of Jammu & Kashmir.

To the east of Himachal Pradesh, wedged between the high Himalaya and the kingdom of Nepal, are the regions of Garhwal and Kumaon. In 1947 these hill states were merged with the regions on the upper reaches of the Yamuna and Ganges rivers to form the state of Uttar Pradesh, one of the most geographically diverse states in India.

Recently there has been a movement to form a separate hill region known as Uttarakhand, which would comprise the Himalayan districts within today's Uttar Pradesh state.

European Exploration

While the main trails and passes of the Himalaya had been known to pilgrims and traders for many centuries, it was not until the late 16th century that the earliest sketches were compiled. The Moghul courts employed geographers to help delineate their empires, so the first Jesuit priests attached to Akbar's court had access to the most recent surveys on the West Himalaya.

In 1624 the Jesuits achieved their goal of reaching Tibet. Their route was up the Alaknanda Valley to Badrinath and over the Mana La. It marked the beginning of an era. In the following decade the Jesuits completed a full circuit of the Himalaya, trekking across Tibet to Mt Kailas and thereon following the course of the Indus to Leh in Ladakh. They continued south over the Baralacha La and over the Hampta Pass to the Kullu Valley before completing their ambitious circuit back to Agra. In 1661 the Jesuits Johann Grueber and Albert d'Orville undertook a trek from China across Tibet on their way back to Rome. On this journey they reached Lhasa before heading down the Sun Kosi Valley to Kathmandu and the north Indian plains to Agra.

The Jesuit ambitions to explore new routes to Lhasa continued. In the autumn of 1714 Ippolito Desideri crossed the Pir Panjal Pass to Srinagar where he passed the winter in the Kashmir Valley. The following spring he continued over the Zoji La to Leh and from there up the Indus Valley to Tibet and Lhasa, where he was to spend the next five years.

It was not until the East India Company expanded its influence in the early 19th century that a more detailed knowledge of the West Himalaya evolved. At the turn of the 19th century, the company's representatives realised that the Gurkha expansion across to the Sutlej River could have serious repercussions. The East India Company feared that the Gurkhas would make an accord with the Sikhs and between them establish a formidable Trans Himalayan empire. Such an accord would limit British trade north to the potentially rich markets of Tibet and Central Asia. It was a situation not resolved until the Gurkha wars.

In the decade leading up to the Gurkha wars, the East India Company lost little opportunity to deploy its survey teams in the Garhwal and Kumaon. In 1808 Lieutenant Webb led a Bengal survey team to check whether there was an accessible pass across the Himalaya and Zanskar ranges to Tibet. First they explored the upper Bhagirathi Valley before following the trail up the Alaknanda Valley to assess local reports on the Mana and Niti passes. A year later, in 1809, they returned and gained permission from the Sikh ruler Ranjit Singh to explore the upper Sutlej, where they noted a further route into Tibet.

In 1812, William Moorcroft, an eminent veterinary surgeon employed by the East India Company, undertook the first British expedition to Tibet. He followed the Alaknanda Valley before crossing the Niti Pass (east of the Mana La) and became the first European to reach Tibet since Desideri in 1715.

During this period expeditions were being undertaken for a variety of motives. To the quest for geographical knowledge was now added the need for trade. There was also a pressing need for political information as the realities of the strength and ambitions of the Russian tsars came to the fore. Indeed, the need for intelligence in 'the Great Game' (as this covert struggle between Britain and Russia came to be known) was to be the underlying motive of Himalayan exploration throughout the 19th century.

Exploration was not, however, confined to European travellers. During the time of Moorcroft's first journeys, a local guide, Saiyad Mir Izzet Ullah, was commissioned by the East India Company to recce the route from Srinagar, in the Kashmir Valley, across the Zoji La to Leh. From here he headed north across the Karakoram Pass to Yarkand and Kashgar. It was on the basis of this report that Moorcroft set off, with geologist George Trebeck, on what was to become one of the classic journeys of the 19th century. The pair left the Kullu Valley in 1820 and headed over the Baralacha La to Leh. In Leh they tried to gain permission to travel north over the Karakoram Pass to Kashgar. Permission was not granted so they continued to Kashmir and eventually on to northern Afghanistan, and Bukhara where they both died – oddly, within months of each other – in 1825. Moorcrofts' journals were later recovered and published, providing an invaluable contribution to the understanding of the geography and politics of the West Himalaya.

In the 1830s a number of travellers and explorers crossed the high passes linking Kashmir, Ladakh and Baltistan. Of note were the journeys of GT Vigne, who travelled extensively in the region between 1835 and 1838. Later he recorded his accounts in his *Travels in Kashmir, Ladak, Iskardo, the Countries adjoining the Mountain Course of the Indus, and the Himalaya North of the Punjab*. For the first time detailed information on the routes over the less travelled passes linking Kashmir, Jammu, Ladakh and Baltistan became available.

Following the first of the Sikh wars in 1845 and the Treaty of Amritsar in 1846, the East India Company was able to gain unimpeded access to the passes and ranges along the frontiers of north-west India. A Boundary Commission was established in 1847, and over the next two years men such as Cunningham, Strachey and Thomson were employed to travel extensively throughout the West Himalaya. Cunningham compiled an authoritative text on Ladakh, including an outline of the extent and form of the Zanskar Range. Strachey explored much of western Tibet, while Thomson travelled via Chamba and the Umasi La to Ladakh before becoming the first European to reach the Karakoram Pass – the geographical divide between British India and Central Asia.

The Great Trigonometrical Survey of India was to fill many of the gaps in the knowledge about the complex mountain ranges comprising the Indian Himalaya. In 1855 the survey team reached the Pir Panjal Range immediately south of Kashmir and for the next six years established its plane tables on many high and remote peaks in order to identify the ranges of the Punjab Himalaya and the Karakoram. In the autumn of 1856 the survey ascended the high ridges of the main summit of Harimukh in northern Kashmir. Here the full extent of the Karakoram Range was appreciated, including K2, which, over next the two seasons, was confirmed as the second-highest peak in the world.

The British geologist Frederick Drew spent many seasons in the field under the employ of Ranbir Singh, the second maharajah of Kashmir. Drew is credited with advancing the research into the *karewas* – the series of alluvial deposits found around the Kashmir Valley – which added weight to the legend that the Kashmir Valley was, until recent geological times, a vast inland lake. Drew also travelled to many of the remote valleys in Ladakh and Baltistan, and concluded in his *Northern Barrier of India*, published in 1877, that there were no easily accessible passes across the eastern Karakoram to British India. This conclusion was, however, still to be put to the test, as at the time there were few reliable reports of the terrain north of the Karakoram. That vast area was still a blank on the map.

In 1864, shortly after the Ground Survey of Ladakh was completed, Johnson, one of the team's most able people, was authorised to cross the Karakoram Pass to the Kun Lun mountain range and Khotan. This notable journey indicated for the first time that the Karakoram Range was not the only significant barrier to trade and communication to Central Asia.

In 1868 an expedition was organised to Yarkand and Kashgar. The official party was led by Robert Shaw, whose caravan crossed the Kun Lun a month after setting out from Leh. Shaw's was not the only group to venture into the area. The intrepid traveller George Hayward was also intent on reaching Central Asia, but his motives were quite different. For Shaw, securing commercial concessions with the Kashgar ruler Ayub Beg was of paramount importance, while Hayward's ambition was to continue to the Pamirs. Neither was successful and both eventually returned to the Karakoram the following spring.

The British wanted to subdue Russian influence in the region, and to this end they considered it necessary that eastern Turkestan be a buffer zone between British India and tsarist Russia. With this in mind, two trade missions were mounted, the first in 1870, and the second in 1873. In spite of the high pomp and ceremony of the missions, there was little commercial or political success. Indeed, in 1877, Ayub Beg was assassinated, and the following year the Chinese had again re-asserted their power over the region. Shortly after this, a Russian envoy was installed in Kashgar.

These developments were of great concern, particularly in light of the geographic intelligence gathered by the surveyors who had stayed on after the second mission returned to India. These surveyors succeeded in crossing the Little Pamirs as far as the Wakhan Valley before exploring some of the main Oxus tributaries. They were also able to ascertain that the Pamirs were nowhere as high or as formidable as the Kun Lun or the Karakoram, with the passes leading south from the Pamirs over the Hindukush easily accessible to Chitral, Hunza, Gilgit and Kashmir. Routes for a Russian advance abounded, and the area between the Karakoram, the Hindukush and the Pamirs became the focus for exploration until the end of the century.

Notable in this new era were the exploits of Francis Younghusband. In 1887, after a short period on government business in Manchuria, the budding explorer elected to return to India via Turfan, Kashgar and Yarkand to Srinagar. Instead of taking the standard route from Sinkiang to Leh, he was asked to explore the possibilities of crossing the Mustagh Pass situated to the west of the Karakoram Pass. No prior knowledge could have prepared him for what was one of the most difficult traverses over the Karakoram. Indeed, the traverse is still highly acclaimed today, particularly since neither Younghusband nor his team of local porters had any prior mountaineering skills or equipment.

Francis Younghusband was one of the notable 19th-century explorers of the Indian Himalaya.

His finding put paid to the idea that there was an easier, more accessible pass over the Karakoram to the west of the Karakoram Pass.

In 1889 Younghusband returned to Central Asia. This time he headed further west of the Karakoram Range towards the Shimshal Pass north of the Hunza Valley. In October 1889 he ascended the pass before returning to investigate a rumour that Russian troops were assembled at the base of the Kun Lun mountains. The rumour turned out to be true. Yet Younghusand's meeting with the Russian officer Grombtchevski and his small troop of Cossacks was a dignified encounter and an understanding was reached that the Russians would stay clear of Hunza and Dardistan.

There was, of course, still an uncomfortable belief that a small Russian force could cross the Hindukush and, if undeterred, reach Kashmir in a week. However, such an action would require the cooperation of the various local rulers in Hunza, Gilgit and Chitral. To prevent this, and also to gain a better appreciation of the nature of the passes over the Hindukush, the British re-established the Gilgit Agency in 1888. It was an intriguing situation, and when Younghusband returned to the Pamirs in 1890, a Russian territorial advance over the Hindukush was a distinct possibility. On this expedition he reached Lake Karabal – one of the main sources of the Oxus River – before spending the winter of 1890 in Kashgar. It was during this period that he gained reliable information that the Russians indeed intended to annex the whole of the Pamirs right up to the Hindukush and the passes into Hunza and Gilgit.

Protracted negotiations ensued, and, following the British offensive in Hunza and the establishment of the British-Indian border on the Hindukush, a proposal for a neutral corridor between the Hindukush and the Russian territory was accepted. In 1895 a joint Anglo-Russian Boundary Commission was appointed resulting in the demarcation of the Wakhan Corridor – a tract of land linking Afghanistan and Sinkiang – to separate the British and Russian empires.

Evolution of Exploration & Trekking

By the turn of the 20th century cart roads had been constructed into the Kashmir Valley, and the Public Works Department (PWD) and Forest Departments commenced upgrading the trails into the remoter regions of the Indian Himalaya. Trekking and mountaineering were by this time well under way. It was not uncommon for the British to undertake a trek from Srinagar to Gilgit or to cover the 14 stages from Srinagar to Leh as part of their annual leave. Agencies were established in Srinagar and Shimla to specialise in sport-related activities – hunting, fishing and trekking. Huge canvas tents and collapsible string beds would be carried by a large retinue of porters. Arthur Neve's *The Tourist's Guide to Kashmir, Ladakh & Skardo*, first published in 1911, records this romantic era. It was a time when men such as Francis Younghusband, the newly installed Resident in Kashmir, ascended the forested slopes of the Lidder Valley in search of game; when Auriel Stein, living on an alpine meadow above the Sindh Valley, planned his next expedition to Central Asia;

and Sven Hedin set off from Srinagar in 1906 on his second expedition to Tibet.

Expeditions were mounted to climb the Punjab Himalaya and the Karakoram. Nanga Parbat had been attempted in 1895 by a team of British alpinists, while a recce of Nun and Kun, the highest peaks in the Punjab Himalaya, was conducted by CG Bruce in 1898. In 1902 and 1904 Arthur Neve was able to correct some of the complex topography of the massif. Two years later it was the turn of the American couple William and Fanny Bullock Workman, while Arthur Neve returned again in 1910. Kun was climbed by the Italian Count Calciati in 1914 – but Nun remained unclimbed until 1953. Closer to the Kashmir Valley, Kolahoi was attempted by Ernest Neve a number of times – before the first successful summit attempt with Kenneth Mason in 1911.

The Karakoram also attracted much attention at the turn of the century. The first major expedition was mounted by the Duke of Abruzzi in 1909, setting out from Srinagar with several hundred porters. Although the expedition team was not able to make a serious summit attempt on K2, climbers today still refer to the standard route to its summit as the Abruzzi Ridge.

Many peaks of the Garhwal and Kumaon were also being explored. In particular, the approach to Nanda Devi was examined by WW Graham in 1883 on his attempt to ascend the Rishi Ganga. Longstaff, in 1905, explored the gorge leading to the inner sanctuary. In 1907 Longstaff returned, and after climbing the high col between Dunagiri and Changabang again attempted, without success, to enter the inner sanctuary. He did, however, divert his energies to climbing Trisul (7120m) which at the time set the record for the highest climbed peak in the world. Longstaff also made a recce of Kamet (7756m), the second-highest peak in the Indian Himalaya and not climbed until 1931.

In Sikkim, Claude White, the first British Resident, spent a number of seasons from 1890 exploring the glacial systems below Kangchenjunga and later the remote Lhonak Valley in northern Sikkim. The first attempt to climb Kangchenjunga was made in 1905, while the Scottish doctor AM Kellas spent six seasons exploring the possibilities on Kangchenjunga and climbing a number of peaks along the nearby Singali Ridge.

To assist the exploration and appreciation of the Himalaya, the Himalayan Club was founded in 1927. It established branches in Kashmir, Chamba, Shimla, Almora and Darjeeling. Its initial purpose was to assist with transport and supplies for both trekking and mountaineering teams.

During the 1930s a new style of exploration and climbing evolved in the Himalaya, typified by Eric Shipton, HW Tilman and Frank Smythe. Their expeditions in the Indian Himalaya were initially concentrated in the Garhwal, where Shipton and Smythe were members of the first expedition to climb Kamet in 1931. After the climb they explored many other peaks and passes in the vicinity. The hallmark of the team was travelling lightly, without complicated logistics, and often in the company of just a climbing Sherpa or two.

In 1934, Shipton and Tilman, with three Sherpas, returned to the Garhwal. The small team managed to forge a route up the Rishi Ganga to the base of Nanda Devi. (This was to lead to Tilman's successfully climbing Nanda Devi on a joint Anglo-American expedition two years later.) After completing their foray into the Nanda Devi Sanctuary, Tilman and Shipton and the team of Sherpas completed two challenging traverses: the first between Badrinath and Gaumukh and the second from Badrinath to Kedarnath. The second foray was quite an epic, with the members having little or nothing to eat for most of the expedition. Frank Smythe shared Tilman and Shipton's trekking philosophy when he spent the 1937 season climbing and exploring many of the peaks in the vicinity of the Bhyundar Valley, including Mana (7272m). The successes of these mountaineers underlined the fact that a small, lightweight expedition had a greater chance of achieving its goals than the huge British expeditions mounted to climb Everest in the 1920s and 1930s.

By now trekking had become an established pastime. In 1933 Ernest Neve revised the 15th edition of *The Tourist's Guide to Kashmir, Ladakh & Skardo* to reflect the increasing interest in travelling to higher and more remote valleys. Arrangements out of Kashmir could be left to Cockburns Agency or to a houseboat family and, judging by the reports retained by some houseboat families, a trusted guide and a reliable cook were the most valuable assets to any trekking party. Crossing huge distances was no longer considered extraordinary. Consider the case of Robert Fleming, who trekked for seven months from Peking to Kashmir and received not so much as a nod of acknowledgment from the reservations clerk when he finally checked into Nedou's Hotel in September 1935.

Following Indian independence in 1947, the nature of climbing and trekking the high and remote Himalayan valleys was restructured to accommodate the new political changes. For instance, the India-Pakistan partition meant it was no longer possible to trek from Kashmir to Baltistan. To the north, much of India's border with China was restricted, with the war in 1962 leading to the enforcement of inner line restrictions (pertaining to the restricted areas close to India's sensitive border regions with Pakistan and China) in Ladakh, Himachal Pradesh (at that time part of the Punjab hill states), Uttar Pradesh and Sikkim.

Regions such as Kashmir and the Kullu Valley attracted trekkers and climbers in the 1950s and 60s, although movement was restricted to the main Himalayan Range in Kashmir. The Pir Panjal Range dividing the Kullu Valley and Lahaul was as far as one could trek in Himachal. In Uttar Pradesh similar restrictions applied and only a few of the classic treks could be undertaken without inner line permits.

The gradual lifting of restrictions in 1974 allowed trekkers to visit Ladakh, Zanskar and Lahaul. Permits were no longer necessary to enter the Nanda Devi Sanctuary or trek the upper reaches of the Gangotri Glacier in Uttar Pradesh. In 1988 further restrictions were lifted for travel to Ladakh, and in 1992 the regions of Kinnaur, Spiti and the Johar Valley in Uttarakhand were opened up for trekking. More remote trek options could soon be possible.

GEOGRAPHY

The Himalaya is one of the youngest mountain ranges in the world. Its evolution can be traced to the Jurassic era (80 million years ago) when the world's landmasses were split into two: Laurasia in the northern hemisphere, and Gondwanaland in the southern hemisphere. The landmass which is now India broke away from Gondwanaland and floated across the earth's surface until it collided with Asia. The hard volcanic rocks of India were thrust against the soft sedimentary crust of Asia, creating the highest mountain range in the world.

It was a collision that formed mountain ranges right across Asia, including the Karakoram, the Pamirs, the Hindukush, the Tien Shan and the Kun Lun. The Himalayan mountains, at the front of this continental collision, are still being formed, rising and assuming complex profiles. For the ancient geographer, the complexities of this vast mountain range were a constant source of speculation. From the earliest accounts, Mt Kailas was believed to be the centre of the universe with the river systems of the Indus, the Brahmaputra, and the Sutlej all flowing from its snowy ridges and maintaining the courses which they had followed prior to the forming of the Himalaya.

The Sutlej was able to maintain its course flowing directly from Tibet through the main Himalaya Range to the Indian subcontinent, while the huge gorges on both flanks of the Himalaya reflect the ability of the Indus and the Brahmaputra to follow their original courses. The Indus flows west until it rounds the Himalaya by the Nanga Parbat massif, while the Brahmaputra flows eastwards for nearly 1000 km around the Assam Himalaya and descends to the Bay of Bengal.

It was not surprising, therefore, that 19th century geographers experienced formidable difficulties in tracing the river systems, and defining the various mountain ranges that constitute the Himalaya. Even today, with the advent of satellite pictures and state-of-the-art ordnance maps, it is still difficult to appreciate the form and extent of some of the ranges that constitute the Himalaya.

Main Himalaya Range

This is the principal mountain range dividing the Indian subcontinent from the Tibetan plateau. From Nanga Parbat (8125m) in the west, the range stretches for over 2000 km to the mountains bordering Sikkim and Bhutan in the east. The West Himalaya is the part of this range that divides Kashmir and Himachal Pradesh from Ladakh. The highest mountains here are Nun (7135m) and Kun (7077m). In Kashmir the subsidiary ridges of the Himalaya include the North Sonarmarg, Kolahoi and Amarnath ranges. Further east, the Himalaya extends across to the Baralacha Range in Himachal Pradesh before merging with the Parbati Range to the east of the Kullu Valley. It then extends across Kinnaur Kailas to the Swargarohini and Bandarpunch ranges in Uttarakhand. Further east it is defined by the snow-capped range north of the Gangotri Glacier and by the huge peaks in the vicinity of Nanda Devi (7816m), the highest mountain in the Indian Himalaya. In western Nepal the range is equally prominent across the Annapurna and Dhaulagiri massifs, while in eastern Nepal the main ridgeline frequently coincides with the political boundary between Nepal and Tibet.

The major passes over the main Himalaya Range include the Zoji La, at the head of the Sindh Valley; the Boktol Pass, at the head of the Warvan Valley; the Umasi La in the Kishtwar region; and the Kang La and the Shingo La between Lahaul and the Zanskar region of Ladakh. It also includes the Pin Parbati Pass between the Kullu Valley and Spiti, while in Kinnaur it is traversed when crossing the Charang La in the Kinnaur Kailas Range.

In Uttarakhand, roads are being constructed to the main places of pilgrimage in the heart of the Himalaya. These include Yamunotri and the source of the Yamuna

River, Gangotri at the head of the Bhagirathi Valley, Kedarnath at the head of the Mandakini Valley, and Badrinath in the Alaknanda Valley. There are, however, many trekking possibilities across the mountain ridges and glacial valleys including those bordering the Nanda Devi Sanctuary.

The main Himalaya Range extends east across central Sikkim from the huge Kangchenjunga massif, which includes Kangchenjunga I (8586m), the world's third-highest peak. The East Himalaya is breached by the headwaters of the Tista River, which forms the geographical divide between the verdant alpine valleys to the south and the more arid regions that extend north to Tibet. Trekking possibilities are at present confined to the vicinity of the Singali Ridge, an impressive range that extends south from the main Himalaya and forms the border between India and Nepal.

In Darjeeling the treks include the route along the southern extremity of the Singali Range, while in Sikkim the trails out of Yuksam explore the ridges and valleys to the south of the Kangchenjunga massif.

Pir Panjal Range

The Pir Panjal Range lies south of the main Himalaya at an average elevation of 5000m. From Gulmarg in the north-west it follows the southern rim of the Kashmir Valley to the Banihal Pass. Here the Pir Panjal meets the ridgeline separating the Kashmir Valley from the Warvan Valley. From Banihal the Pir Panjal sweeps south-east to Kishtwar and then to the east, where it forms the divide between the Chandra and Ravi valleys. Further east of the Kullu Valley it merges with the main Himalaya Range. The Pir Panjal is breached only once – at Kishtwar, where the combined waters of the Warvan and Chandra rivers meet to form the Chenab River, one of the main tributaries of the Indus.

The main passes over the Pir Panjal include the Pir Panjal Pass due west of Srinagar, the Banihal Pass which lies at the head of the Jhelum River at the southern end of the Kashmir Valley, and the Sythen Pass

linking Kashmir with Kishtwar. In Himachal Pradesh the main passes are the Sach which links the Ravi and the Chandra valleys, and the Rohtang which links the Beas and Kullu valleys with the upper Chandra Valley and Lahaul. Roads are being constructed over all these passes – the Banihal is now tunnelled and work is in progress on roads over the Sythen Pass in Kashmir and the Sach Pass in Himachal Pradesh. There are plans to tunnel through the Pir Panjal west of the Rohtang Pass, to make Lahaul accessible by road from the outside world within the next decade. However, for trekkers there is still the attraction of the Kugti, Kalicho and Chobia passes between the Ravi Valley and Lahaul, and the Hampta Pass links the Kullu Valley with Lahaul.

Dhaula Dhar Range

The Dhaula Dhar Range lies to the south of the Pir Panjal. It is easily recognised as the snow-capped ridge behind Dharamsala where it forms the divide between the Ravi and the Beas valleys. To the west it provides the divide between the Chenab Valley below Kishtwar and the Tawi Valley which twists south to Jammu. This is the range crossed at Panitop on the Jammu-Srinagar highway. To the east it extends across Himachal Pradesh forming the high ridges of the Largi Gorge and extending south of the Pin Parvati Valley before forming the impressive ridgeline east of the Sutlej River. Thereon it forms the snow-capped divide between the Sangla Valley and upper Tons catchment area in Uttar Pradesh, including the Har ki Dun Valley. Beyond the Bhagirathi River it forms the range between Gangotri and Kedarnath before merging with the main Himalaya at the head of the Gangotri Glacier.

There are many attractive trekking passes over the Dhaula Dhar. These include the Indrahar Pass north of Dharamsala; and in Kinnaur, the Borasu Pass linking the Sangla Valley to Har ki Dun in Uttar Pradesh.

Note Whether the Swargarohini and Bandarpunch ranges form part of the main Himalaya or whether they form part of the Dhaula Dhar

Range is a matter of dispute. Kenneth Mason in his *Abode of Snow* argues that these ranges are part of the lesser Himalaya and continue east to include the peaks to the south of Gangotri Glacier including Kedarnath (6490m) and Kedar Dome (6831m) before merging with the Great Himalaya Range at the head of the Gangotri Glacier.

Siwalik Hills

The Siwalik Hills lie to the south of the Dhaula Dhar, with an average elevation of 1500 to 2000m. They are the first range of hills encountered en route from the plains and are geologically separate from the Himalaya. They include the Jammu Hills and Vishnu Devi, and extend to Kangra and further east to the range south of Mandi. In Uttar Pradesh they extend from Dehra Dun to Almora before heading across the southern borders of Nepal. Most of the range is crossed by a network of roads, linking the northern Indian plains with Kangra, the Kullu Valley, Shimla and Dehra Dun.

Zanskar Range

The Zanskar Range lies to the north of the main Himalaya. It forms the backbone of Ladakh south of the Indus River, stretching from the ridges beyond Lamayuru in the west across the Zanskar region, where it is divided from the main Himalaya by the Stod and Tsarap valleys, the populated districts of the Zanskar Valley. The Zanskar Range is breached where the Zanskar River flows north, creating awesome gorges until it reaches the Indus River just below Leh. To the east of the Zanskar region the range continues through Lahaul & Spiti, providing a complex buffer zone between the main Himalaya and the Tibetan plateau. It continues across the north of Kinnaur before extending west across Uttarakhand, where it again forms the intermediary range between the Himalaya and the Tibetan plateau, which includes Kamet (7756m), the second highest peak in India. The range finally peters out north east of the Kali River – close to the border between India and Nepal.

On the Zanskar Range, the Fatu La, on the Leh-Srinagar road, is considered the most easterly pass; while the Singge La, the Cha Cha La and the Rubrang La are the main trekking passes into the Zanskar Valley. For the hardy Ladakh trader, the main route in winter between the Zanskar Valley and Leh is down the icebound Zanskar River gorges. Further to the east, many of the Zanskar Range passes to the north of Spiti and Kinnaur are close to the India-Tibet border, and are closed to trekkers.

Ladakh Range

The Ladakh Range lies to the north of Leh and is an integral part of the Trans Himalaya Range that merges with the Kailas Range in Tibet. The passes include the famous Kardung La (5606m), the highest motorable pass in the world, while the Digar La to the north-east of Leh is at present the only pass open to trekkers.

East Karakoram Range

The East Karakoram Range is the huge range that forms the geographical divide between India and Central Asia. It includes many high peaks including Teram Kangri (7464m), Saltoro Kangri (7742m) and Rimo (7385m), while the Karakoram Pass (5672m) was the main trading link between the markets of Leh, Yarkand and Kashgar. At present this region is closed to trekkers, although a few foreign mountaineering groups were permitted to climb there in the last decade.

CLIMATE

Climatically, the Indian Himalaya can be divided into the following regions:

Beyond the Monsoon

Ladakh and Zanskar, Spiti, northern Kinnaur and some areas of northern Uttarakhand are isolated from the main brunt of the Indian monsoon. These regions lie to the north of the main Himalaya Range and escape the full impact of the monsoon. Humidity is always low, and rainfall no more than a few centimetres a year. These regions experience some of the coldest temperatures anywhere in the world, and it doesn't warm up till the

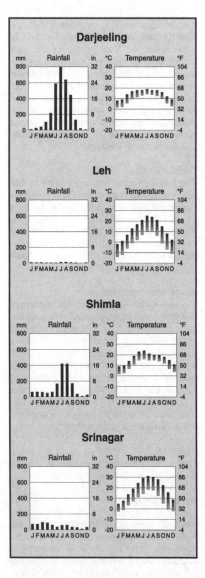

most of the treks can be undertaken from then on until the middle of October. Heavy rain storms can occasionally be experienced in July and August, and river crossing should be undertaken with great care at this time. By September the conditions are ideal, and they normally remain so until late October even though night-time temperatures may fall below freezing. By November, the early winter snows fall on the passes closest to the Himalaya. In winter the villagers still travel, enduring the intense cold, to follow the valley floors where river crossings are no longer a problem.

Modified Monsoon

The Kashmir Valley and the lower Warvan and Chenab valleys in Jammu and Lahaul experience a modified monsoon climate. These regions lie between the Pir Panjal Range and the main Himalaya Range, and although occasional clouds break over the Pir Panjal, this does not normally cause a major disruption to the trekking season, which extends from May till the middle of October. After October the daytime temperatures drop, but the weather is generally settled until the middle of November when the first of the heavy winter snows fall on the high mountain passes. The winter months from December to March are often bleak, with snow falling in Srinagar, although the waters of Dal Lake freeze over on average only once every 15 years. April and May are characterised by heavy precipitation which falls as snow in the mountains, precluding trekking over the passes until the spring snows melt in June.

Monsoon – West Himalaya

Most of the hill states including Kangra and Chamba, the Kullu Valley, Shimla in Himachal and most regions of the Garhwal and Kumaon in Uttarakhand come under the influence of the Indian monsoon.

The first heavy monsoon rains fall by the end of June and continue until the middle of September. The rains tend to become progressively heavier as the monsoon continues, with the heaviest falls lasting

spring in late April or early May. In June, daytime temperatures frequently rise to the mid 20°Cs, the snow on the passes melts and through August till early September. Temperatures at this time of the year rise during the day to the mid-20°Cs while at night they fall to between 5°C and 10°C. The post-monsoon period from mid-September to late October is generally settled with clear, fine days although the daytime temperatures fall considerably towards the end of October. This weather trend continues through to December, although the daytime temperatures are often little above freezing. The winter months bring heavy snowfall that continues till the end of March and early April. The winter snows melt on the lower ridges by May and on some of the higher passes by June during the short pre-monsoon season. Temperatures begin to rise in May and by the middle of June they can reach 20°C during the day before the onset of the first monsoon rainfall.

Monsoon – East Himalaya

Both Darjeeling and Sikkim are subject to the Indian monsoon that sweeps up from the Bay of Bengal, bringing heavy rainfall from early June until the end of September. The post-monsoon months of October and November provide settled conditions, with clear views of the mountains, although night-time temperatures above 3500m frequently fall below freezing. During the pre-monsoon period, which lasts from mid-March until the end of May, the temperatures often rise to 25°C during the day, although storm clouds which occasionally gather by the middle of the morning may preclude good views of the mountains.

ECOLOGY & ENVIRONMENT

Over the last decade there have been numerous reports on the pressures on land use in the Himalayan region. There is now an increasing awareness of the delicate ecological balance in many of the remoter mountain regions, where population growth has led to the clearing of more forest for cultivation and soil erosion has resulted.

The demands on marginal grazing areas are also acute. There are few alpine pastures in the high Himalaya that have not attracted the migration of the Gaddi or the Bakharval with their huge flocks of sheep and goats, while in the forested valleys the Gujar with their herds of buffalo may spend many days carrying supplies of milk and cheese to the local market. Logging policies have also taken their toll with forest officers having neither the time nor resources to check that contractors fell no more than the approved quota of trees. Wildlife officers working under similar budgetary constraints face similar problems, so poachers of rare wildlife species risk little chance of detection.

To counter this, some regions which have been overgrazed or denuded of timber have been designated as national parks or sanctuaries, while there are plans to impose restrictions on many of the other alpine valleys in the Indian Himalaya.

In Ladakh the Hemis High Altitude National Park was created in 1981 to protect the endangered flora and fauna in an area that extends across the Stok Range to the Markha Valley. This has been partially successful, although there are still reports of snow leopards being stoned to death by irate villagers whose domestic sheep and goats have been attacked.

In J&K a vast national park was created in the area north-east of the Warvan Valley and north-west of the Chenab Valley up to the main Himalayan watershed. This ambitious plan has not, however, restricted the movement of the Bakharval goat herders or the Gaddi shepherds grazing their huge flocks on the already fragile alpine hillsides. Closer to the Kashmir Valley the Dachigam National Park legislation has been more strictly enforced. Yet even here, the J&K authorities still need to evolve a practical solution for there is no benefit in excluding the shepherds from one area if it simply means that they overgraze elsewhere.

In Himachal Pradesh there are proposals to extend the Kanawer Sanctuary into a national park which will include the whole of the upper Parbati Valley catchment area above Manikaran. The ambitious scheme would help to preserve one of the state's most beautiful valleys. However, current debate is

NATIONAL PARKS

Region	Name	Location
Ladakh	Hemis High Altitude National Park	Markha & Rumbak valleys
Kashmir & Jammu	Dachigam National Park	20 km from Srinagar
	Kishtwar National Park	Warvan & Chenab valleys
Himachal Pradesh	Great Himalayan National Park	Sainj & Tirthan valleys
	Kanawer Sanctuary	North Parbati Valley
	Manali Sanctuary	Manaslu Nullah
Uttarakhand	Corbett National Park	Ramnagar
	Govind Sanctuary	Tons River and Har ki Dun Valley
	Nanda Devi National Park	Joshimath
	Valley of the Flowers National Park	Joshimath
Sikkim	Kangchenjunga National Park	Yuksam

centred on how this can be reconciled with the need to dam the Parbati River to provide towns in the lower Kullu Valley with hydro-electricity.

In 1983, the Uttar Pradesh (UP) government introduced restrictions on movement in the Bhyundar Valley (Valley of the Flowers) and the Nanda Devi Sanctuary. Both the local shepherds and climbers had damaged the flora and fauna and a suitable period of time was necessary for these regions to regenerate. There were many reports of wild goat and sheep species, and even the snow leopard, being hunted by expeditions. It is unlikely

Wildlife	Trek	Further Information & Permits
bharal, ibex, snow leopard	Spitok to Hemis via Markha Valley	DFO Hemis National Park, Leh, Ladakh
Kashmir stag, black & brown bear, musk deer	extension of Pahalgam to Lidderwat & Tar Sar	Chief Wildlife Warden, Srinagar, Kashmir
Hangul deer, musk deer, forest leopard, markhor, ibex	Pahalgam to Panikhar (Ladakh)	Regional Wildlife Warden, Jammu
black & brown bear, forest leopard, musk deer, bharal	combine with trek out of Manali	Wildlife Director, Kullu, HP
black & brown bear, forest leopard, musk deer, bharal	Manikaran to Spiti	Wildlife Director, Kullu, HP
thar, musk deer, forest & snow leopard, black & brown bear	combine with trek out of Manali	Wildlife Director, Kullu, HP
tiger, elephant, forest leopard, black bear, chital, wild boar, mugger, gharial	combine with spring trek to Dodi Tal or Gaumukh	Field Director, Corbett National Park, Ramnagar, Naini Tal, UP
musk deer, black & brown bear, bharal, forest leopard	Har ki Dun Valley & Ruinsara Lake	ACF Uttarkashi, UP
bharal, musk deer, snow leopard	trekking not permitted within the sanctuary	DCF Nanda Devi National Park, Joshimath, Chamoli, UP
thar, musk deer, forest leopard	Valley of the Flowers & Hem Kund	DCF Nanda Devi National Park, Joshimath, Chamoli, UP
thar, musk deer, forest & snow leopard, bharal	Yuksam to Dzongri	Wildlife Officer, Forest Department, Deorali, Sikkim

that there will be any significant lifting of the restrictions for many years. The UP government has also been involved with the Himalayan Environment Trust in the Gangotri Conservation Project, an ambitious scheme to rectify the environmental problems in the vicinity of Gangotri and Gaumukh, the sacred source of the Ganges. One of the long-term aims of the trust is to create environmental awareness among the many thousands of pilgrims who visit the Bhagirathi Valley.

In the East Himalaya the Sikkim government has recognised the problems of deforestation, and logging in the luxuriant

HIMALAYAN VEGETATION ZONES

In the Indian Himalaya three main regions are identified – the North Himalaya, West Himalaya and the East Himalaya. All three regions contain several vegetation zones.

North Himalaya

This region includes Ladakh, Zanskar, upper Lahaul & Spiti. It includes an alpine zone found generally from 4000m to 5000m and even higher as you move north towards the Karakoram Range. The zone is often virtually devoid of vegetation bar the sage bush and the grassy meadow found alongside a watercourse. The sub-alpine zone extends from 3500m to 4000m and includes stunted juniper. A lower zone, from 3000m to 3500m, includes willows and cultivated poplars. Irrigated barley fields, sprinkled with leguminous plants, geraniums, aquilegias and louseworts, thrive in the depths of the valleys.

West Himalaya

This region includes Kashmir and extends across the regions of Himachal and Uttar Pradesh to the south of the main Himalaya Range. It supports an alpine zone from 3500m to 4500m altitude which includes the open grazing meadows at the higher levels, while birch groves mark the lower level of this zone. The temperate zone extends from 1500m to 3500m. The conifers, including fir, hemlock, pine as well as cedar, are found between 2500m and 3500m, while oak and blue pine are found at the lower elevations. In regions where the forests have been cleared, cornfields are found between 1800m and 3000m; and rice paddies somewhat lower, between 1500m and 2000m, as in the Kashmir and Kullu Valleys.

The tropical and subtropical zone in Himachal and Uttarakhand includes the long-needled pine, sal and oak forests, while thorn scrub is found closer to the Indian plains where much of the original forest belt has been cleared. In the more remote mountain districts the forest floor is covered with more luxuriant cover including bamboo, ferns and shrubs. The upper limit of this zone is 1400m.

East Himalaya

The East Himalaya includes Sikkim and Darjeeling and is, in many respects, a geographic extension of eastern Nepal. The region includes an alpine zone which extends between 3500m and 4500m, while the sub-alpine zone with juniper and dwarf rhododendron extends from 3300m to 4000m. Note that there is an absence of birch trees in this zone. The temperate forest range extends from 1800m to 3500m and includes a band of conifers, magnolias, daphne and rhododendrons at the upper levels, and an oak, bamboo and rhododendron band between 2000m and 3000m, while at the lower elevations there are oak, alder and chestnut trees. This merges with the subtropical forests, which are better preserved than those in the West Himalaya. Among the deciduous and evergreen forests the sal tree is the most easily identified in southern Sikkim. In the tropical zone a variety of shrubs, bamboos, palms and ferns are also found. ■

forests in southern Sikkim is strictly controlled. The creation of the Kangchenjunga National Park, together with effective forest check posts and trekking permits restricting numbers visiting the region, has contributed to the preservation of some of the finest rhododendron and magnolia forests in the Himalaya.

A fuller consideration of these factors is included under Responsible Trekking in the Facts for the Trekker chapter.

FLORA

The Himalaya can be broadly classified into five main vegetation zones.

The permanent snow line is the highest zone – an area of scant vegetation with only the occasional lichen found in the scree and glacial moraine.

Next, the alpine zone consists of meadows of pasture and wildflowers above the tree line.

The sub-alpine zone lies below the alpine and is characterised by birch groves, juniper and frequently rhododendrons – usually pink and white, and a dwarf variety which is often yellow. Its upper bands extend into the alpine zone, while in the lower elevations it overlaps with the temperate forest with occasional fir, pine and spruce trees. The trails are at times lined with clusters of rose shrubs – many five-petalled.

The temperate forest zone is a broad band of mixed forest, with concentrations of conifers at the upper levels and deciduous trees at the lower elevations. Trees include maples, elms, laurels, beeches, oaks, horse chestnuts and walnuts, as well as viburnums, cotoneasters and fruit trees such as apricots and prunus. The zone is also characterised by the common red tree rhododendron. Small flowering plants include begonias, ragworts, salvias, poppies, violets, balsams and wild raspberries and strawberries.

The subtropical to tropical zone is the lowest zone and is found in the foothills bordering the northern Indian plains. Trees in this zone include cassias, figs and coral trees.

The relation between altitude and the vegetation zones can be appreciated within the confines of a particular valley over a very short distance. Descending from the moraine of the upper Jagatsukh Valley, for example, you can cross alpine meadows and then descend through distinct bands of conifer and deciduous forests to the barley fields and rice paddies of the Kullu Valley in one long morning's walk. The descent from Rup Kund to the Pindari Valley in Uttar Pradesh also illustrates the effect of altitude on the vegetation zones.

Wildflowers

The alpine regions of Kashmir, Himachal Pradesh and Uttarakhand provide excellent scope for appreciating the wide range of flora species, many of which are similar to the mountain flora of Europe and the USA. For identifying the hundreds of varieties of wildflowers in the mountainous areas of the subcontinent, consult *Flowers of the Himalaya* by Polunin & Stainton. Briefly, flowers include daisies of many types, wax flowers,

edelweiss, primulas, ajugas, gentians, trefoils, cinquefoils and marsh marigolds.

The flowering season is dependent on the spring snow melt and can vary considerably from year to year. In the regions over 3500m the alpine meadows become clear of snow sometime between mid-June and late July, depending on the harshness of the winter.

In Ladakh the wetter regions to the immediate west of the Himalaya, such as the Pentse La and the grazing grounds en route to the higher passes, support many wildflower species. As you move further away from the Himalaya, however, the alpine zones contain fewer flowering species.

In Kashmir a short trek up the Lidder Valley to the meadows above the Gujar village of Satalanjan will reap rewards for those interested in wildflowers while the trekking trails into the main Himalaya en route to Ladakh pass through alpine meadows which support a wide variety of flora. Flowers include massed irises, delphiniums and euphorbias.

In Himachal Pradesh the alpine plateaus above the Kullu Valley are notable for wildflowers. The higher stages of the trek up the Jagatsukh Valley are particularly recommended, as the flora is subject to monsoon rains and abounds with exotic varieties during the rainy season. The trek up the Pin Parbati Valley is also recommended, particularly in the middle of summer, while the alpine pastures of the Miyar Nullah are appealing from the middle of July until the end of August. The trek stages up to the Sach Pass beyond Chamba and the meadows below the Kugti Pass are also renowned for wildflowers such as saxifrage, anemones, ranunculus and alpine forget-me-nots.

In Uttarakhand the alpine meadows between Yamunotri and Har ki Dun are recommended and anyone who has read Frank Smythe's *The Valley of Flowers* is sure to be attracted to the Bhyundar Valley in the heart of the Garhwal. However, there are many other areas, in particular those south of the Nanda Devi Sanctuary where high-altitude meadows (locally known as *bugyals*) abound in wildflowers throughout the summer and in particular during the monsoon months of July and August. Flowers include a variety of liliums, cobra plants, Kumaon irises, primulas and gentians.

In Sikkim the huge variety of rhododendrons – over 400 different species been recorded – is a superb attraction. The flowers come into bloom from the end of April till the middle of June. There are 453 species of orchid in Sikkim, and nearly 300 different ferns.

FAUNA
Mammals

The sighting of wildlife in the Indian Himalaya, while dependent on the seasons and the respective vegetation zones, has also been influenced considerably by the migration of shepherds and villagers to the mountain regions. As a general rule, the more remote the area, the greater the chance of seeing animals in their natural state. However, there are exceptions to this with the wildlife found in the Dachigam National Park close to Srinagar in Kashmir, and in Hemis High Altitude Park in Ladakh close to the Indus Valley and Leh. Both of these national parks were established by the J&K Wildlife Directorate in the 1980s.

Viewing the wildlife when the seasons are changing is another important consideration. In the West Himalaya, wildlife such as the black and brown bear, the red fox and the forest leopard wander the coniferous forests as soon the winter snows begin to melt in mid to late April. At this time, the animals seem less wary of human encroachment and it is an ideal time to explore the valleys out of Pahalgam or Manali on skis or snowshoes.

By the middle of June the snow begins to melt at the higher alpine elevations. This is the time to see both black and brown bears with their cubs foraging for food above the Lidder Valley or in the coniferous forests above the Kullu Valley. From the middle of summer the black bear is attracted to the valleys by the ripening cornfields. Many tales are told of the destruction they cause and the measures adopted to control them. The rarer brown bear remains at a higher

elevation foraging for food on the alpine pastures.

In Ladakh, the rare sheep and goat species, including the bharal, migrate to the high ridges where the scanty vegetation provides them with their summer feed. The snow leopard and the wolf also roam these higher elevations, while down valley the marmots whistle from the security of their burrows to warn their young of any danger.

Most of the animals commence the descent to their winter pastures in late autumn, after the shepherds have departed down the valleys. North of the Himalayan divide, the wild sheep and goats descend to the shelter of the valleys by mid to late October. They are followed by packs of wolves and the lone snow leopard wandering close to the outlying villages of Ladakh, Zanskar, Lahaul & Spiti. South of the Himalayan Range, in Kashmir and the alpine valleys of Himachal and Uttarakhand, the forest leopards follow a similar migration pattern, descending from the coniferous to the temperate forests close to the villages where they remain throughout the winter months.

The following observations, while by no means comprehensive, will provide an initial point of reference.

Primates The langur, a long-tailed grey monkey with a black face, is found in the temperate forests, often in the vicinity of

Common langur (*Presbytis entellus*)

villages. These monkeys live in large troops and migrate in early spring up from the temperate to the lower coniferous forests. Troops of 50 or more have been seen above the village in Aru in the Lidder Valley migrating down valley in early December. Similar migrations have also been noted moving through the forests of the lower Warvan Valley, and in the valleys of Uttar and Himachal Pradesh.

The rhesus monkey is found at lower elevations. It is brownish red in colour and is often seen close to towns and villages including Shimla, Naini Tal, Dharamsala, Dalhousie and Darjeeling.

Marmots These large rodents of the squirrel family are scattered widely throughout the West Himalaya. They live in large colonies in networks of deep burrows where they hibernate during the winter. Their loud whistles to their young can be heard many km away and alerts all animals in the vicinity to oncoming danger. They are about half a metre long, although far larger individuals are often sighted in Ladakh. In Kashmir they are sometimes trapped for their thick, golden brown fur. While found in Kashmir, Ladakh, Lahaul and Zanskar and Himachal Pradesh, they are not so common in the alpine regions of Uttarakhand.

Red fox *(Vulpes vulpes)*

preying on small rodents. They are of similar size and appearance to the European and North American red fox.

Bears Himalayan black bears are attracted to the cornfields during the summer. At other times of the year they seek refuge in the temperate and coniferous forests before hibernating in the winter. They are widespread in Kashmir, Himachal and Uttarakhand. Brown bears tend to remain on the high alpine pastures foraging for edible roots and grasses. They are easily startled, and like all bears should be given ample room when encountered at close range.

Marmot *(Marmota himalayana)*

Red Foxes Red foxes are rarely seen except in late springtime when their footprints may be followed in the snow. In the summer time they are sometimes observed on a forest trail

Brown Bear *(Ursus isabellinus)*

Cats Also known as swamp cats, jungle cats are larger than the domestic cat on which they prey. They are found in the temperate forests in Uttarakhand, often climbing high up the branches of oak trees, in groups of up to 10 or more.

Snow leopards inhabit the highest and most remote regions of the West Himalaya. They are solitary creatures, the size of a large, sleek dog with a long tail. Although protected, they are still occasionally killed by villagers for preying on domestic animals. They are most elusive as evidenced in the recent film documentary made by the Bedi brothers, two eminent naturalists from Delhi, who spent two full winters in Ladakh before they gained their first sightings in the upper Markha Valley.

Snow leopard *(Panthera uncia)*

The forest leopard is larger than the snow leopard. In India, forest leopards are often called panthers. Some are black so their spots show up only dimly. They inhabit the temperate forests near to villages and towns, such as Naini Tal, Mussoorie and Shimla where they prey on domestic dogs. To combat this, shepherds in Uttarakhand place huge collars with iron spikes around the necks of their dogs to ward off attacks.

Kiang Also known as the Tibetan wild ass, the kiang inhabits the high grassy plateaus in the Rupshu region in the east of Ladakh close to the Tibetan border. They are normally found in herds of 10 to 20.

Tibetan wild ass *(Equus hemionus kiang)*

Wild Yaks These huge animals, in their undomesticated state, are now restricted to the Changdenmo region of Ladakh close to Tibet.

Wild Sheep & Goats With few exceptions, these animals have being seriously depleted over the last two generations. A comprehensive description of the various species, together with their locations, is covered in George Schaller's *Stones of Silence*. The following are some of the more common species found in the West Himalaya.

Blue sheep or bharal *(Pseudois nayaur)*

Ibex *(Capra ibex)*

The Punjab urial is identified by its large, curved horns. It can be found in Ladakh, in the vicinity of Leh and the Indus Valley, and on the remote ridges above the Zanskar gorges.

Not actually classified in the genus *Ovis* along with other sheep, bharal (or blue sheep) are distinguished by their thick, horizontally sprouting horns and the dark blue wool on the rumps of the males. If you are lucky you may sight them on the high arid ridges of Ladakh, Zanskar, Lahaul & Spiti. They are also found in the Nanda Devi Sanctuary.

One of the largest of the Himalayan goats, alpine ibex have impressive serrated, sweep-

Markhor *(Capra falconeri)*

ing horns. Found west of the Sutlej River throughout Himachal, Kashmir and West Ladakh, like the bharal they select the highest crags for protection during summer.

With their distinctive spiralling horns, markhor goats may be found throughout Kashmir and Himachal, generally below the snow line on forested slopes and open meadows.

The Himalayan thar, a heavily built goat with short, curving horns, is distributed throughout the Himalaya although reduced in numbers now like all the wild goats and sheep.

Himalayan thar *(Hermitragus jemlahicus)*

Deer A sub-species of the red deer, the Kashmir stag is nowadays only found in the Dachigam National Park in Kashmir. During the summer they roam the birch groves to around 4000m, before returning to the lower elevations in the early winter. In the 1970s there was great concern regarding their declining numbers – a drop from over 1000 in 1947 to fewer than 150 in 1970. Strong measures backed by the J&K Wildlife Directorate and the World Wild Fund for Nature (WWF) have been responsible for checking this decline and the numbers today have increased to more than 500.

The samdar (barking deer) is short in stature with a brown body, and has a dog-like bark. Samdar are found in the forests of the Garhwal and Kumaon.

Traditionally much sought after for their musk glands, musk deer have curving tusks instead of horns. Their numbers much depleted, they are mainly found in forested areas.

Birdlife

As with the study of plant life and vegetation in the Himalaya, there are broad distinctions between the bird species which inhabit the West and the East Himalaya. The area around the Kali Gandaki in Nepal is cited as the transitional region between bird species originating from Europe and Central Asia (the Palaearctic) and those from South-East Asia (the Indo-Chinese and the Indo-Malay species).

Salim Ali, in his authoritative texts on birdlife in the Indian subcontinent, draws the following threefold distinction:

Species endemic to the Himalaya
This group includes birds migrating to higher altitudes to breed during the summer before returning to the foothills during the winter months. In this category he cites two of the raptors: the bearded vulture or lammergeier with its distinctive cream-coloured neck and head and goatee beard, and the golden eagle; plus the game birds – the most distinctive bird family in the Himalaya – such as pheasant and jungle fowl. The game birds include the Himalayan monal, with their distinctive plumage, which can be found in oak, rhododendron and deodar forest, although they may also be seen above the tree line as high as 4500m, particularly in the Garhwal. The Koklas pheasant is found in the wooded ravines in oak and coniferous forest, while the Chir pheasant is found in oak forest between 1400 and 3500m.

Species which fly over the Himalaya to/from Central Asia
This group can be observed during the spring and autumn migrations. In regard to this category, Salim Ali notes that about 300 of the 2100 species found in the Indian subcontinent migrate to and from Central Asia. Included are the hordes of duck, geese and cranes, many of which inhabit the lakes of the Kashmir Valley and Himachal before continuing to the wetlands of the Indian plains. Also included are a wide assortment of flycatchers, robins, warblers, thrushes, wagtails, pipits, finches and swallows. It is of interest that many of these species fly directly over the Himalayan Range; for example, the Siberian crane flies from Ladakh at altitudes of 6000m. Simi-

larly, some of the smaller species, such as woodcocks and various flycatchers, opt for the direct route south, coasting over the mountain ranges down to the Indian plains during the autumn migration. In the springtime the going is harder for birds, flying against the winds emanating from the Himalayan ranges. The valley routes, particularly up the Indus Valley, are therefore a favoured migratory path to Central Asia.

Species which breed in the Himalayan foothills during summer
These birds return to the south Indian hills during winter. Species include the woodcock, the pied ground-thrush, Indian blue chat and the brown-breasted and blue-throated flycatcher.

To help identify some of the hundreds of hill birds it is recommended you consult Salim Ali's *Indian Hill Birds*; if trekking in Sikkim and Darjeeling, refer to his volume *Birds of the Eastern Himalaya*.

PEOPLE & CULTURE

As the West Himalaya marks the meeting point of three of the world's main religions – Islam, Hinduism and Buddhism – so too it marks the boundaries of the Aryan and Tibetan/Mongoloid races. Complexities arise when considering the relationship between race, religion and people. Frederick Drew, in his book *The Northern Barrier of India* of 1877, set out the following divisions to try to clarify the relationship:

Race	People	Religion
Aryan	Dogra	Hindu
Aryan	Pahari	Hindu
Aryan	Kashmiri	Muslim
Aryan	Dard	Muslim
Tibetan	Balti	Muslim
Tibetan	Ladakhi	Buddhist

This complex relationship between race, religion and people still holds today. There are many regions of the Himalaya where the people of a certain race and ancestry still subscribe to a variant religion.

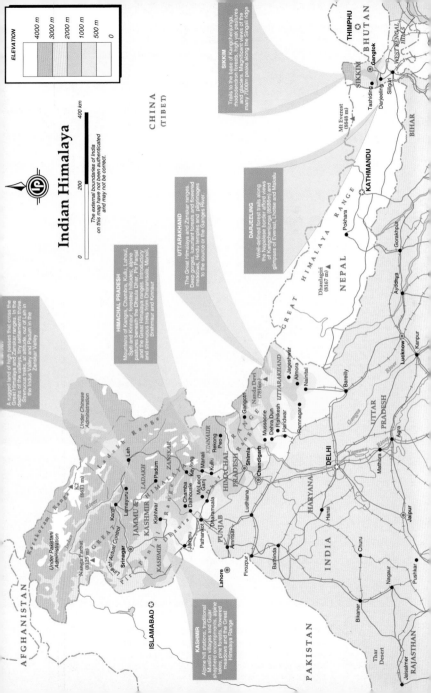

Indian Himalaya

ELEVATION

4000 m
3000 m
2000 m
1000 m
500 m
0

The external boundaries of India on this map have not been authenticated and may not be correct.

0   200   400 km

KASHMIR
Alpine hill stations, traditional Muslim villages and Gujar shepherd encampments, alpine lakes, pine forests, flowered meadows and the Great Himalaya Range.

A rugged land of high passes that cross the Great Himalaya and Zanskar ranges in the depths of the valleys, tiny settlements thrive Strenuous treks, at altitude, out of Leh in the Indus Valley and Padum in the Zanskar Valley.

HIMACHAL PRADESH
Mountains of Kangra, Chamba, Kullu, Lahaul, Spiti and Kinnaur; forested hillsides; alpine pastures beneath the Dhaula Dhar, Pir Panjal and the Great Himalaya ranges. Introductory and strenuous treks around Shimla, Manali, Brahmaur and Kinnaur.

UTTARAKHAND
The Great Himalaya and Zanskar ranges. Deep gorges, luxuriant forests and flowered meadows, Hindu temples and pilgrimages to the source of the Ganges River.

DARJEELING
Well-defined forest trails along the Nepalese border beneath the peaks of Kangchenjunga (8586m) and glimpses of Everest, Lhotse and Makalu.

SIKKIM
Trails to the base of Kangchenjunga, rhododendron forests, high yak pastures and glaciers. Magnificent views of the many 7000m peaks along the Singail ridge

AFGHANISTAN

PAKISTAN

Karakoram Range

K2 (8611 m)

Under Chinese Administration

Under Pakistani Administration

Line of Actual Control

Ladakh Range

Indus River

Lamayuru

Leh

Zanskar River

Padum

Kargil

Nanga Parbat (8125 m)

Line of Actual Control

Kishtwar

JAMMU & KASHMIR

Srinagar

Jammu

Pir Panjal Range

KASHMIR

Dhaula Dhar Range

LADAKH

ZANSKAR RANGE

KINNAUR

Chamba

McLeod Ganj

Dharamsala

Dalhousie

Keylong

Manali

Kullu

Rekong Peo

HIMACHAL PRADESH

Pathankot

Amritsar

Ludhiana

Shimla

Chandigarh

Firozpur

Bathinda

PUNJAB

ISLAMABAD

Lahore

Bikaner

Churu

Hansi

Nagaur

Pushkar

Bhatinda

HARYANA

Jaipur

RAJASTHAN

Thar Desert

Jaisalmer

INDIA

DELHI

Agra

Mathura

Jagestwar

Almora

Nainital

Gangotri

Nanda Devi (7816m)

UTTARAKHAND

GREAT HIMALAYA RANGE

Mussoorie

Debra Dun

Rishikesh

Haridwar

Ramnagar

Bareilly

Yamuna River

UTTAR PRADESH

Lucknow

Kanpur

Ganges River

Ayodhya

Gorakhpur

NEPAL

Dhaulagiri (8167 m)

Pokhara

KATHMANDU

GREAT HIMALAYA RANGE

Mt Everest (8848 m)

Tashiding

Darjeeling

Siliguri

SIKKIM

Gangtok

WEST BENGAL HILLS

THIMPHU

BHUTAN

BIHAR

CHINA (TIBET)

GARRY WEARE

GARRY WEARE

GARRY WEARE

GARRY WEARE

Top: River crossing on birch branches, Uttarakhand
Middle: Pack horses atop the Kanji La, Ladakh (Panikhar to Heniskot trek)
Bottom Left: Lotus flower, Dal Lake, Srinagar, Kashmir
Bottom Right: Barn swallows spotted around Dal Lake, Srinagar, Kashmir

Birds

Black-Headed Sibia (*Heterophasia capistrata*, 20 cm) This lively, light orange bird, with black head and semi crest, is common in oak-rhododendron forests from 915 to 3355m, and familiar around many of the Himalayan hill stations. It jerks its tail up and down when perching and is often acrobatic when searching for insects. Its song is a loud, ringing whistle. When alarmed, its crest is fully raised.

Black-headed sibia

Plumbeous Redstart (*Rhyacornis fuliginsis*, 14 cm) Often perched on boulders even in raging torrents, this charming little bird of the streams of the Himalaya is found at altitudes from 750 to 4110m. The male is slate blue with a broad rufous-maroon tail. The tail is constantly moved up and down and flared out so its white is clearly seen. This bird is forever on the move, flitting from rock to rock. Feeding on fruit and insects from bushes at the water's edge, it actively hunts insects at dusk. It has a ringing song.

Plumbeous redstart

Yellow-Billed Blue Magpie (*Cissa flavirostris*, 64 cm) Although fairly common in oak-rhododendron and coniferous forest from 2135 to 3650m, this shy bird keeps trees between itself and the observer. Its beautiful long tail is flicked up when feeding. In follow-the-leader flight formation across ravines, it intersperses its heavy wingbeats with glides. It has both a wheezy 'peck-pecking' note as well as a high calling tone of 'clear clear'.

Scarlet Minivet (*Pericrocotus flammeus*, 23 cm) Frequently in groups, the sight of a party of these birds with their red, yellow and black plumage flitting through the green foliage is entrancing. Common from 150 to 1830m, they are seen in gardens, and tropical and sub-tropical forests, and are partial to pines. They frequently emit an attractive mellow 'tweet tweet'. Constantly on the move, minivets sidle along branches, hover and drop to the ground for insects.

Black Drongo (*Dicturus adsimilis*, 30 cm) Totally glossy black, with a long, deeply forked tail, this bird is abundant in open areas – fields, villages and the edge of forests from 275 to 1830m. Constantly active, it swoops after insects in the air, returns to its perch and bobs its tail. It is masterly in flight when pursuing its prey or aggressively chasing off an intruder. Bold and noisy in the mating season, it has a loud danger warning note followed by a slow call.

Black drongo

Scarlet minivet

Blood Pheasant (*Ithaginis cruentus*, 38 cm) Often found near water in open scrub and bamboo, rhododendron and juniper forests from 3355 to 4110m, this short-tailed pheasant with pale, streaked plumage and green below, has a red throat and breast. The female is a warm brown. Both sexes have coral red legs. Seen in pairs or small coveys, they work their way through the thickets feeding on berries and other vegetable matter. Apart from their loud, grating alarm screech, their common call is a repeated 'chuk' sound.

Blood pheasant

Lammergeier (*Gypaetus barbatus*, bearded vulture, literally 'lamb hawk') Nesting on inaccessible cliffs, the lammergeier inhabits the entire length of the Himalayan mountain range from 1220 to 7320m. With a superb wingspan of up to 2.8m, this magnificent bird is unique in its method of feeding on bones. Carried in the talons to high altitude, the bones are dropped onto the rocks below; the lammergeier then swoops down to feed on the exposed bone marrow. It also feeds on carcasses and in village rubbish dumps. In flight, its long, wedge-shaped tail distinguishes it from other birds of prey.

Lammergeier

Flowers

Primula Family (*Primulaceae*) Mainly concentrated in the northern temperate zone, primulas are herbaceous, dying down at the end of the year. The leaves commonly form an entire rosette around the stem, the flower stem itself being leafless. The flowers often form branched clusters. Some people become itchy on the fingers after touching the plant. Certain of the larger primula species are unpalatable to animals, so often occur gregariously around shepherd encampments in the Himalayan high meadows where there is much dung. Although very attractive they do not improve the pasture. Right across the Indian Himalaya the *Primula denticulata*, in particular, is very common on open grazing slopes and in shrubberies, at altitudes from 1500m right up to 4500m. It is often called the 'drumstick primula', named for its compact globular head of massed individual flowers. The flowers are purple to mauvish blue, although there is a white form. Each petal is split at the top. The tooth-edged leaves crowd tightly round the plant. Both the leaves and the stem, initially around 10 cm, extend up to 30 cm by the end of the season.

Primula denticulata

Iris Family (*Iridaceae*) This herbaceous family, which includes the crocus genus (cultivated in the Kashmir Valley), is world-wide in distribution. It is distinguished by its six petals and alternate leaves, usually long and narrow. The iris genus is distinguished by the fact that three of the petals on the attractive flowers sit up erect and are fused below into a tube, and the other three petals, known as 'falls', hang down. The rhizomes (the swollen underground stems) creep along to spread. Vast numbers of rhizomes from the Himalayan species have been dug out by plant hunters to take back to cultivate in Europe. The *Iris kemaonensis* is a common species right across the Himalaya in the alpine meadows in early spring, appearing not long after the snow melt. Often in large clumps, this bright lilac to purple flower with dark spots and blotches on its petals can be found way up to 4000m. The flowers are solitary and virtually stalkless. Each of the three 'falls' has a bright yellow-coloured beard. The flowers appear with the young leaves, but in due course the leaves grow longer. The *kemaonensis* thrives where there is heavy stock grazing.

Iris kemaonensis

Saxifrage Family (*Saxifragaceae*) Also a herbaceous family, the *Bergenia* genus has leaves which are simple rather than compound, and large – their blades (the flattened part of the leaf) being five cm or more. These big thick leaves have leaf stalks sheathing at the base, and the stout flowering stems, which are leafless, rise from the strong rootstock. Both the *Bergenia ciliata* and *Bergenia stracheyi*, which are common across the Indian Himalaya, have leaf margins with bristly hairs. The word 'ciliata' actually means bristly. The *Bergenia ciliata*, found in forests and on rock ledges, flowers from March to July. The *stracheyi*, the common alpine species of the western part of the Himalaya, grows on open slopes and flowers later, from June to August. Both are found up to higher than 4000m, but the *ciliata* grows at much lower altitudes, appearing from 1800m. The leaves of the *ciliata* are quite large compared to the individual flower stems of spreading or densely clustered white, pink or purple flowers. These leaves grow larger and turn bright red in the autumn before dying off. The *stracheyi* has shorter leaf stems, and the flowers, which are longer, are only pink in colour and hang in a drooping cluster.

Bergenia stracheyi

Daisy Family (*Compositae*) This large family with world wide distribution is characterised by its distinctive flowerheads which are composed of numerous small florets on a flower stem. There are many differences amongst the actual types of the florets. *Leontopodium*, the edelweiss genus, has 35 different species, many of which are fairly difficult to distinguish. The name Leontopodium comes from *leon* (lion) and *pous* (foot), in reference to the shape of the flower heads. Edelweiss need to be protected from the winter wet when cultivated, so these perennials persist well below the ground between growing seasons under the dry snow of the high alpine areas in their natural habitats. Both the *Leontopodim himalayanum* and *Leontopodium jacotianum* (smaller and more tufted) are quite common in the West Himalaya, above 3000m or more. Both are found on open slopes and flower from July to September/October. The plants are grey, woolly haired

Leontopodium jacotianum

and tufted, with clusters of many small globular white flowerheads which turn brown as they die off before winter. The dense woolly haired leaves, as they dry off, are ideal for their use as tinder by the shepherds who also carry a flint in their pouches for fire making.

Spurge Family (*Euphorbiaceae*) Herbaceous perennials, with rootstock persisting until the next growing season, many of this family including pointsettias are found in Africa. All *Euphorbias* have a milky sap which emerges freely when the plant is damaged. Some people are allergic to this sap when they come into contact with it. The *Euphorbia wallichii* occurs in the western Himalaya and is particularly common on Kashmiri open slopes and grazing grounds. It flowers from April to May. This erect plant has very leafy stems, of 30 to 60 cm in height, which terminate in several yellow flowerheads in virtually flat-topped clusters. The yellow heads are actually the bracts, the flower surrounders which attract the pollinating agents. The insignificant flowers are within. When dry, the smooth, blue-grey seeds burst open.

Euphorbia wallichii

Rose Family (*Rosaceae*) The *Rosa* genus of the rose family, with its prickly shrubs at least a metre high, can be distinguished by the fact that its many hard, one-seeded carpels (the female part of the flower) are enclosed within a hip – the fruit, a fleshy receptacle. The species *Rosa webbiana* is very common in the western Himalaya, naturally occurring at altitudes from 1500 to 4000m. From June to August, on the dry rocky slopes of Lahaul, Ladakh and right across to Pakistan, this cheerful, pink-flowered rose brightens the barren hillsides. It has also been cultivated round many of the villages. Up to 2.5m high, it has slender branches and straight prickles. The small, rounded leaves have prickly leaf stalks. The single, five-petalled flowers, up to seven cm across, are rather densely clustered. The stems and leaves often turn bright pink.

Buttercup Family (*Ranunculaceae*) Many members of the large buttercup family can be found in the Himalaya. The *Aquilegia* genus, for example, commonly known as the columbine or 'Granny's bonnet', has several species in the Himalaya. The Aquilegia is distinguished by the five backward-projecting spurs to the inner petals. The *Aquilegia nivalis*, of the West Himalaya, has deep-purple, solitary, nodding flowers. It can be seen flowering from June to August on high alpine slopes, screes and rocks. The stem, of up to 20 cm long, is unbranched and there are only a few kidney-shaped leaves.

Another genus of the buttercup family is the *Caltha*. The *Caltha palustris* is commonly called the marsh marigold, as 'palustris' means swampy. This flower is very common on open slopes and grazing grounds right across the Himalaya from 2400 to 4000m. A small plant, spread low to the ground, it is distinguished by its relatively large, fleshy, rounded, heart-shaped leaves and its terminal clusters of yellow or white buttercup-shaped flowers, with five or more pointy petals. The *Anemone rivularis* species of the *Anemone* genus of the buttercup family is common in the western Himalaya too – in meadows, shrubberies and grazing grounds from 2100 to 3600m. Like several other alpine flowers, it grows in great profusion on the meadows heavily grazed by the sheep and goats. Its white flowers, of five to eight petals, are often flushed violet outside. The stems can grow up to 90 cm high by the end of the season. The leaves, with three deeply indented lobes and silky-haired on both sides, are at the base of the stem.

Trees
Sal (*Shorea robusta*) Growing up to altitudes of about 1500m, the sal is dominant over much of the lower foothill country of the Indian Himalaya. A large deciduous tree, with smooth, dark-brown bark and large, shining, pale leaves, it is actually rarely without foliage. The most important

hardwood tree of the sub-Himalayan hills and valleys, it yields valuable and durable timber which is used extensively in building. It is also tapped for its resin, used medicinally and in incense. Oil is obtained from the small fruit, and also a flour for cooking. The small, pale-yellow flowers are very fragrant. The large leaves are often used for platters for temple offerings and for dining plates.

Pipal (*Ficus religiosa*) The Bo, Bodhi or pipal tree is widely cultivated in the lower Himalaya up to about 1400m. Revered by both the Hindus and the Buddhists, it is often planted beside small shrines of sacred objects. As the Buddha sat under a pipal tree while gaining enlightenment, branches from the actual parent tree that have been transplanted elsewhere form important places of pilgrimage. A large tree, the pipal is easily distinguished by its heart-shaped, long, pointed leaves on slender stalks. The leaves, bark and fleshy fruit are used for local medicines. The pipal is commonly planted in wayside resting places along with *Ficus benghalensis*, the large spreading

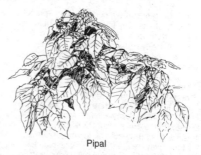

Pipal

banyan tree, with its aerial roots descending from spreading branches to root in the ground, thicken and become trunk-like. Superb for individual shade, these ficus trees do not form forests.

Oak (*Quercus semecarpifolia*) Forming whole forests, this hardwood is common right across the Himalaya, upward from 2100m, and in places is dominant right to the upper treeline. This large evergreen tree is distinguished by its globular (acorn) nuts. The leaves of the young trees have spiny marginal teeth (like the traditional shape of a holly leaf), but on older trees the leaf has entire margins and the upper surface is dark glossy green. It is common on steep, rocky, south-facing slopes from which the snow cover clears quickly. The trees are very important in the hill villages and cultivated areas of the temperate hill forests as they are extensively lopped for cattle fodder. The wood is used locally for building and it also gives good fuel. The bark contains much tannin.

Horse Chestnut (*Aesculus indica*) A large deciduous tree of up to 30m or more in height, the horse chestnut tree is found in forests and shady ravines across the altitude zone from 1800 to 3000m in the Indian Himalaya. The trees are impressive for their large, upright pyramidal clusters of white flowers, the petals often streaked with red at the base. The leaves are distinctive, long-stalked and divided in a palm-like manner. The fruit is a leathery capsule, usually with one large shining seed. Like several trees in the Himalaya, the leaves are lopped as stock fodder. Superb forests of horse

Oak

Horse chestnut

chestnuts, interspersed with maples and the Himalayan walnut tree (*Juglans regia*), can be found towards the upper reaches of the Ganges tributaries in Kumaon and Garhwal. Troops of langur migrate through these forests, enjoying the leafy cover. As with the walnut trees, the wood is often used for turned articles and the bark is used medicinally.

Rhododendron (*Rhododendron*) One of the heath family, this tree/shrub genus comprises over 800 species, most of which are evergreen. Although not unique to the Himalaya, many species are distributed widely across the Indian Himalaya, with some endemic only to the eastern Himalaya and Nepal. The *Rhododendron aboreum* is the most widely distributed in the Himalaya, at a range of altitudes from 1500m. It has many different forms, some reaching a height of 15m. Its flowers range from red and pink to white, usually at the higher altitudes. The mass blooms are superb in early spring. Shallow rooted, rhodendrons virtually always grow in acid soils rich in humus, although the *arboreum* can be found on limestone soil too.

Rhododendron

Towards the upper valleys of Uttarakhand the *aboreum* clings tenaciously to the hillsides in thick, branching clusters of shrubs which are almost impenetrable. Along with the birch trees, it forms the highest treeline vegetation right up to 3600m. The multiple herds of migrating sheep and goats do not eat rhododendrons, and in fact the young leaves are poisonous. The flowers are presented as offerings in hillside temples, and the wood is frequently used for fuel.

Chir Pine (*Pinus roxburghii*) Ancient in terms of geological time, the long-leaved chir pine forms extensive forests in the Indian Himalaya, from 500 to 2700m. A large, slim, triangular tree, up to 40m high, it is distinctive for its very thick and deeply fissured rough bark. The bark drops off in broad, scaly plates. The chir grows on acid or alkaline soil without any apparent discrimination. It can cling to ravines so steep that they are virtually impossible to climb. The chir discourages undergrowth and the forest floor is thick and slippery with the fallen clusters of long, needle-like leaves. The trees are particularly drought tolerant, and occasionally after a very dry spell will lose their leaves for a period before regrowth. Mature trees can withstand forest fires, but the young seedlings are not fire resistant, so repeated burnings make regeneration impossible. The edible seeds from the solitary or clustered deciduous cones are winged, and spiral down to the ground after the hot weather. The sapwood has a sweet smelling resin and the bark yields a tannin used in dyeing. Oil of turpentine, used medicinally, is obtained from the wood. Although the timber is not particularly durable, it is still used for general construction purposes.

Chir pine cone

Himalayan Birch (*Betula utilis*) Growing from 2700m right up to 4300m, the birch marks the upper limit of the treeline right across the Indian Himalaya, particularly in Kashmir. In a few, mainly moister areas, oaks instead of the birch actually give way to the high alpine meadows and scree. The birch tolerates long periods of snow (and therefore dry soil), and frequently can be seen clinging in isolated, small, spindly clusters to slopes of high-altitude gullies where the snow is packed and lasts long into the spring. The Himalayan birch was first botanically described in 1880. Much more recently the *Betula jacquemontii*, also common to the area, has been considered a separate species. The bark on the *jacquemontii* is white, whereas on the *utilis* it is brownish red.

On the young trees in particular, the bark peels off round the tree in thin transverse sheets. It makes excellent kindling for lighting fires, and traditionally has been used as paper for manuscripts. The bark is also used locally for waterproofing and roofing huts. The inconspicuous birch flowers, borne in small catkins, appear before the leaves emerge in spring. The leaves are light green and on the *utilis* have less pronounced teeth margins. Frequently swept down in landslides, the thin, gnarled trunks are often used by the shepherds as supports for their tent shelters when grazing their flocks in the alpine meadows. The Himalayan birch is often commonly mislabelled the silver birch (*Betula pendula*).

Himalayan birch (*Betula utilis*)

The Dogra people from the hills beyond Jammu, the Pahari from Himachal Pradesh and hill people who live elsewhere in the foothills trace their ancestry to the Aryan race and are Hindu. However, the Kashmir people are also Aryan but subscribe to Islam, as do the Dards who live in Gilgit (now in Pakistan). But the Baltis who live in the Suru and the Drass valleys in Ladakh, although Muslim, are from the Mongol Tibetan group of races, while the Ladakhi and the Khampa originate from Tibet and are Buddhist.

The original inhabitants of Ladakh were the Khampa who roamed the vast Tibetan plateau in search of pastures for their yaks and goats. Nowadays they are found on the high grazing plateaus on the present border with Tibet. The Mons, Buddhist missionaries from India, established settlements in the valleys, while later the Dards wandered up valley and introduced irrigation to the upper reaches of the Indus. In the 7th century the migration of Tibetans slowly displaced the Dards. Some of these Tibetans, together with the Dards, were converted to Islam in the 15th century. Since 1947 these Dards have been confined to the upper sections of the Drass, Suru and Bodhkarbu valleys, while outposts of Dardic culture are still found in Gilgit and the Hunza Valley in Pakistan.

The Kashmiri people trace their origins to successive migrations up the Indus Valley. The original inhabitants believed in the Naga, the benevolent half-snake, half-human beings who dwelt in the valley when it was still a large inland lake. With the successive Aryan migrations an accord was made between the Naga and Aryan priests. In spite of the important Buddhist congresses held in the valley there was no long-term conversion to Buddhism. It was a situation that was to remain until the 14th century when the majority of Kashmir people were converted to Islam.

South of the Vale of Kashmir the Dogra and the Pahari villagers gradually settled in the hills, and many of the hill kingdoms such as Jammu, Chamba and Kangra were founded around the 10th century. Like many peoples in northern India their ancestors would have migrated from Asia Minor around the 10th century BC and would have subscribed to Brahmanism and later to Hinduism.

While the various races and peoples have evolved a complex tapestry across the West Himalaya, the high culture of the region was nonetheless determined by the dominant religion.

Islam is the dominant belief in the Kashmir Valley, with some 92% of the population being Muslim. To the east of the Kashmir Valley, in the upper valleys of Drass, Suru and Bodhkarbu, the people are Shia Muslims (followers of the son-in-law of the Prophet), linked with Baltistan until the Indian partition in 1947. There is also a sizeable Muslim community in Leh, some being descendants of trading families which settled in Leh when trade was still undertaken over the Karakoram Pass to Yarkand and Kashmir.

Zanskar has a small community of Muslims in Padum, where they settled after following the armies of Zorawar Singh in the 1830s.

Yet in spite of the Islamic inroads into Ladakh, the high culture remains Buddhism. The Buddhist beliefs extend from the borderlands of Tibet down the Indus Valley and south through Zanskar to the regions of Lahaul and Spiti, which were at times part of the Kingdom of Guge and Western Tibet. There is also the recent addition of the Tibetans who were exiled from Tibet in 1959. Their communities are scattered across the West Himalaya. These include Dharamsala where the 14th Dalai Lama is in residence, Leh, Manali and the Kullu Valley. There is also a small community on the outskirts of Srinagar to the north of the Hari Parbat Fort.

The regions south of the Kashmir, Kishtwar, Lahaul and Spiti are predominantly Hindu. The Hindu culture extends from Jammu to the Kangra and Chamba valleys, through to the Kullu Valley, and beyond to Uttar Pradesh. Hindu pilgrimages play an important part in the cultural fabric of the Himalaya. These include the pilgrimages to Vaishnu Devi north of Jammu and to many sacred sites in Uttarakhand including Yamunotri, Gangotri, Kedarnath and Badrinath. It also includes the annual trek to the Amarnath Cave in Kashmir that is still undertaken today.

In Sikkim and Darjeeling the people are either Hindu or Buddhist, sharing many cultural traditions with both Nepalese and Tibetans. The original inhabitants were the Lepchas who migrated from the Assam Hills to Sikkim around the 10th century. Much later, in the 17th century, Tibetans came across the Himalaya and settled in the valleys while throughout the 19th century Nepalese migrated to Darjeeling and Sikkim. This influx of Tibetans and Nepalese forced the Lepchas to move to more remote regions in Sikkim. A more recent wave of Tibetans arrived after 1959.

RELIGION
Buddhism

The basic teachings of the historical Gautama Buddha date back to the 5th century BC. The Gautama Buddha was a prince who, as a young adult, renounced his standing and riches in order to follow his quest for the means of salvation. After first practising and later rejecting the ascetic lifestyle he eventually reached enlightenment after a long and intense period of meditation. Soon after he preached his first sermon at the Deer Park at Sarnath in north India. He expounded the 'four noble truths' – that the world is full of suffering, suffering is caused by human desires, the renunciation of desire is the path to salvation and this salvation is possible by following the 'eightfold path'. This path included the right views, resolves, speech, conduct, livelihood, effort, recollection, and meditation. Collectively they are known as the 'middle way'. The Buddha taught that by following the eightfold path we would recognise the futility of our desires and commence on the progressive stages to enlightenment, returning from one reincarnation to the next until reaching a state of nirvana, the final release from the round of rebirths. The path through this cycle of rebirths is known as karma, a law of cause and effect, which says that what you do in one life will gain (or lose) you merit in the next.

Gradually monastic orders were introduced and Buddhist monks began to spread the word. The teachings of the Gautama Buddha were not written down, however, so over time doctrinal disputes began to evolve. One of the most significant of these disputes was debated in the 1st century AD during the 4th Buddhist Congress in Kashmir. Essentially two rival schools of thought had evolved – the orthodox monks known as the Hinayana school or 'lesser vehicle', and the reformists referred to as the Mahayana school or 'greater vehicle'. The differences centred on the role of the Bodhisattvas, those who have reached enlightenment during their lifetimes. For the followers of the lesser vehicle this was the ultimate human state necessary for the enlightened monk to pass into the state of nirvana. For the reformists this was not entirely acceptable. They argued that a monk, after achieving enlightenment, could defer his entry into nirvana so that he might help others. Hence the notion of the Compassionate Buddha arose. The orders agreed to differ and to go their own ways in search of patronage and support. The followers of the traditional view eventually flourished in India, Sri Lanka, Burma and Thailand while the reformists were to gain popular following in Tibet, Japan and China.

The sage Padmasambhava (750-800 AD) was to have a remarkable influence on the development of Buddhism in the Himalaya and was one of the foremost proponents of Tantric Buddhism. Like the Gautama Buddha he was said to have been born through immaculate conception and was found as a child floating down the Indus River on a lotus bud. He soon realised that the traditional Buddhist teaching had lost much of its appeal and had little relevance to the peoples of remote mountain villages whose lives were dominated by the elements and who still believed in animism. Padmasambhava acknowledged that the appeal of Buddhism could be widened if the tenets of Tantric Buddhism were adapted to the animistic beliefs. As his fame grew he assumed the role of a magician holding the key to the esoteric,

to the supernatural powers that controlled the universe. He would often appeal to the most spectacular manifestation of the elements – the thunderbolt. He gave rise to the Buddhist school known as Varjrana Buddhism – the Vehicle of the Thunderbolt.

Although Buddhism was to gain favour after the kings of Tibet invaded Ladakh in the 8th and 9th centuries, it took many generations for the Buddhist teachings to capture the local imagination. The sage Naropa is said to have founded one of the earliest monasteries at Lamayuru high above the Indus. Legend has it that the Lamayuru Valley was once filled by a lake that was drained by Naropa to found the monastery. The original building, situated below the main monastery, was built in the 10th century and is one of the oldest sites in west Tibet. The monastery at Sani, close to Padum in the Zanskar Valley, also dates from this period, with its origins again attributed to the miraculous deeds of Naropa. At this time Buddhist monks began migrating over the Himalaya in search of patronage. The artistic designs in monasteries such as the Alchi Gompa, which dates from the 11th century, still provide some of the best surviving examples of Buddhist art of the period.

Yet the tradition of gaining inspiration from India or from the Kashmir Valley was about to close. From then on the movement and inspiration of Buddhist thought would be initiated from the far side of the Himalaya. One of the greatest influences came from Tibet in the 14th century when the saint Tsongkhapa propounded a new order that restored much of the traditional teachings.

The Gelukpa order was to become the dominant cultural force in Tibet, while in Ladakh the monasteries of Thikse, Likir and Spitok were founded by this order in the early half of the 15th century. The order was headed by the Dalai Lama, and even today the 14th Dalai Lama undertakes regular visits to the monasteries in Ladakh and Zanskar.

The teachings of the Tantric sages, too, were revised in the following century. A new monastery at Hemis was founded with the patronage of the Ladakhi royal family. Affiliated monasteries at Stakna and in the king's palace at Leh also date from this period. The traditions of Padmasambhava were revered, and today the annual festival at Hemis during the time of the June-July full moon is held in his honour. Monks from throughout Ladakh trek for many days or even weeks to attend the festival.

Hinduism

While the term Hinduism was coined by Arab traders in the 8th century to denote the faith of those who followed either Vishnu or Shiva, the foundations of the beliefs of the Brahmans (Brahmanism) date back to the 10th century BC. This was the time when the first of the Aryan races migrated across northern India and compiled the Vedic scriptures, a set of devotional hymns to the various gods of nature including many who resided in the Himalaya.

Hinduism's beliefs evolved with the practices of the Brahman priests and incorporated many complex sacrifices and rituals. The teachings did not evolve in terms of a divine revelation or from the teaching of a particular saint or prophet, and gods and beliefs were changed to suit the circumstances. With the introduction of Buddhism and Jainism, the idea of a trinity of gods emerged, with Brahma featuring as the creator; Vishnu, the preserver; and Shiva, the destroyer and reproducer. Further, the devotees of Hinduism adhered to the belief that their god was a manifestation of the absolute, a concept that had been set out in the sacred works of the Upanishads.

Essential to the beliefs of the Brahmans, as it was in the teaching of the Gautama Buddha, was the notion of reincarnation and the doctrine of karma. In this belief we all go through a series of rebirths or reincarnations which will finally lead to spiritual salvation. Karma is a law of cause and effect. Bad actions will lead to a lower reincarnation, while good actions will lead to a higher rebirth and increase the chances of gaining release from the round of rebirths.

The morality of a person's action depends on whether it adheres to the *dharma* – the sacred law set out by the Brahmans and embodied in the *Gita*, a sacred text which sets out the philosophical basis for reincarnation. There are, however, many refinements which basically depend on the emphasis placed on the believer's relationship with their god – for example, on whether it is based on love and devotion or whether it is dependent on intellect and theology.

Various schools placed different emphasis on the importance of devotion or theology and some followed the renowned 8th century philosopher Shankara who subscribed to the belief that the world around us was a *maya* (illusion) and that reality lay beyond this. Asceticism and complex yoga practices going beyond the senses were the way to perceive reality. While Shankara opposed unnecessary ritual, he accepted that there was a need for simplified worship, and a number of centres including those at Badrinath in Uttarakhand and Puri in Orissa were established in his name.

Most Hindus profess to being either a Vaishnava (a follower of Vishnu) or a Shaivist (a follower of Shiva).Yet it is never an exclusive arrangement. Temples devoted to Vishnu will portray a statue of Garuda, the divine eagle and Vishnu's vehicle of transport throughout the universe. Relief carvings will demonstrate the sanctity of nature – the trees, mountains and animals which roam the nearby hillsides, while along the bases of the main temple the gods of Yamuna and Ganga will be carved, as recognition of the rivers that drain the Indian subcontinent. Shiva, on the other hand, is less prone to rich embellishments. His presence was often associated with fertility cults and the worship of the stone lingam. The annual pilgrimage to the Amarnath Cave in Kashmir, for example, still attracts up to 20,000 pilgrims at the time of the August full moon.

Whatever the belief, the caste system has remained as integral a part of Hinduism since it was instituted by the high priests in the times of the *Vedas*. The four main castes include the Brahman or the priest caste, the

Kshatriyas or the soldiers and governors, the Vaishyas or tradespeople, and the Shudras which includes the menial workers and crafts people. Beneath these castes are the Harijans or untouchables – the most menial workers. Non-Hindus and westerners are regarded as being unclean and outside the caste system.

Islam

The fundamental Islamic beliefs are set out in the *Koran*, a record of the formal utterances and discourses which Mohammed and his followers accepted as divinely inspired. It includes the famous profession of faith 'There is but one god, and Mohammed is the apostle of god'. This declaration evolved in the Arabian desert in the 7th century. For Mohammed the essential tenet was belief in one supreme god (Allah being Arabic for 'god'). This god was the Being, Creator and Sustainer of the universe, the all-knowing and all-powerful arbiter of good and evil, and the final judge of all humankind.

Muslims believe that god has sent messengers or prophets to preach the unity of god and to warn them of the day of Judgement, when, it is said, those who have acted in god's faith will enter the Garden of Paradise, while the non-believers will be forever damned. These prophets, who are not workers of miracles, have included Abraham, Moses and Jesus. The last of the prophets is believed to be Mohammed – a man with no special knowledge apart from that revealed to him during his life and times in the Arabian desert.

To gain a favourable hearing on the day of Judgement, acts of devotion must be made, including the observance of ritual prayers which are performed in set order five times a day – at daybreak, noon, mid-afternoon, after sunset and in the early part of the night. The acts of devotion also include ritual ablution, the giving of alms, fasting during the month of Ramadan and a pilgrimage to Mecca. In addition, a system of social conduct is set down regarding marriage, divorce, the consumption of alcohol and the making of images. These were all later embodied in the Islamic law.

From the time that the call to Allah was first heard in the deserts of Arabia, it took nearly 700 years for it to gain acceptance in the Kashmir Valley. The Arab traders who settled in the Sind in the 8th century introduced Islam to the Indian subcontinent. For them, trade was of prime concern; they had little time for conversion. By the 10th century a powerful group of Turkish nobility had settled in the region of Ghanzi, a small province of Afghanistan. In 1014 AD, the Mahmud of Ghanzi made an unsuccessful bid to cross the high passes of the Pir Panjal into Kashmir. It took a further three centuries before Kashmir was converted peacefully to Islam. By then there would already have been a significant number of Muslims living in the valley.

The cultural impetus of Islam was to spread throughout Kashmir. Many sacred sites were designated for Sufi meditation and the temperate climate made it a popular haven for Sufis (ascetic Muslim mystics) keen to pursue their studies. These included the famed Sufi teacher Sheikh Nur ur Din known as the patron saint of Kashmir. His teachings are even today revered by the local people. His famous shrine, at the village of Charir Sharif on the road to Yusmarg, was greatly venerated. In early 1995 it was destroyed by fire. Beyond the Kashmir Valley much of Baltistan, including Gilgit, Hunza, Skardu and nearby Drass and Kargil was gradually converted to Islam. Yet this was the limit of Islam and these valleys mark the present boundaries between the Islamic and Buddhist worlds.

LANGUAGE

Hindi and Urdu are the most widely understood languages in northern India. As spoken languages there is little difference between them. However, Hindi is a Sanskrit-based language written in Devanagiri script, while Urdu is essentially a Persian language written in Arabic script.

In all of the main towns of northern India English is widely spoken; in the mountains, however, this is not the case and any attempt to speak a little of the local language will be to your advantage. In Darjeeling and Sikkim, and most areas of Uttarakhand and Himachal Pradesh, Hindi is widely understood. It is also the language of the Gujar and Bakharval shepherds who roam the Kashmir mountains throughout the summer months. In the outlying villages of the Kashmir Valley the people only speak and understand Kashmiri. Similarly Ladakhi, a Tibetan-based language, is the only language understood in the more remote valleys of Ladakh and Zanskar. In Himachal and Uttarakhand, Pahari and Garwhali, respectively, are widely used in the village areas. For a full introduction to the language and pronunciation refer to Lonely Planet's *Hindi/Urdu phrasebook*.

Greetings

The traditional greeting when meeting a Hindu is to hold your palms together and say *Namaste*. The reply is the same. Muslims, on the other hand, give the greeting *Salaam alekum* – literally, 'Peace be on you'. The reply is either the same or *Valekum as salaam*, meaning 'And also on you'.

With goodbyes, Hindus again say *Namaste*, while the Muslims say *Khuda hafiz*, which means, literally, 'May god bless you'.

When addressing a stranger, particularly if the person is of some standing, then the suffix *ji* is a very polite expression, almost like 'sir'. This term may also be used as 'Yes' in reply to a question.

Basics

Excuse me.	*Zara suniye*
Thank you.	*Shukriya*
OK/That's fine.	*Theek hai*
What's your name?	*Aap ka nam kya hai?*
My name is	*Mera nam ... hai*
How are you?	*Aap kaise hain?*
I know.	*Mujhe pata hai*
I don't know.	*Mujhe nahi pato*
Where is ...?	*... kahan hai?*
How much is ...?	*... kitne ka hai?*

Unfortunately, the first greeting from many village children in well-trekked areas is of

the 'give me' variety, while older villagers will ask for medicine as a cure-all. It is useful, therefore, to know the following words.

I have ...	*Mere pas ... hai*
I don't have ...	*Mere pas ... nahi hai*
chocolate	*chauklet*
money	*paisa*
medicine	*davai*

Hiring Porters & Horsemen

You will have little need to negotiate for porters or horsemen using their own language, as at the trailhead or town there is bound to be someone who can assist with the arrangements. However, the following terms may be useful.

Will you come with me?
Aap mere sath chalenge?
How many horses do you have?
Aap ka pas kitne ghore hai?
I have to go to ...
Mujhe ... jana hai
What do you charge per day?
Ek din ka kitna kiraya hoga?
Do I provide your food?
Kya aap ka khana mujhe dena hoga?
What food do you need?
Aap ke liye kya khana lena hoga?
What weight do you carry?
Aap kitna vajan uthate hai?
What weight does your horse carry?
Aap ghore par kitna yajan lete hai?

Equipment

It is imperative to check with porters at the outset of the trek whether they have the right clothing and equipment.

Do you have ... ?	*Kya aap ka pas ... hai?*
backpack	*backpack*
boots	*joota*
gloves	*dastane*
jacket	*jacket*
kerosene	*kerosin*
knife	*chhuri*
tent	*tambu*

sunglasses	*chasma*
stove	*stove*

Directions

When asking directions and timings in remote villages it is a mistake to ask a closed question, such as 'Does it take four hours to reach...?'. The answer will invariably be in the affirmative as the villager does not want to disappoint you with a negative reply! Likewise, the villager will more often than not shorten the number of km or hours it takes to reach a particular camp on the assumption that is what you wish to hear.

How far is...?
  ... kitna dur hai?
Which trail goes to ?
  Kon sa rasta ... ko jata hai?

far	*dur*
near	*nazdik*
right	*dahina*
left	*bayen*
north	*uttar*
south	*dakshin*
east	*purab*
west	*pashchim*
level	*samtal*
uphill	*charai*
downhill	*utrai*

Accommodation

While the use of tea stalls-cum-hotels for accommodation is not as common as in Nepal, there are times when trying to find the Forest Rest House (which is often a km or so out of the village) or the *chowkidar* (care-taker) can necessitate a few questions:

Where is the ...?	*... khai hai?*
rest house	*rest house*
hotel	*hotal*
shop	*dukan*
caretaker	*chowkidar*

Do you have a ...?	*Kya aap ka pas ... hai?*
bed	*bistar*

room	*kamra*
blanket	*kambal*

How much is ...?	*... kya dam hai?*
food	*khana*
lodgings	*kamra*

Family

Being invited into a family house is one of the delightful aspects of trekking the Himalaya.

Is this your ...?	*Kya ye aap ke ... hai?*
sister	*behin*
mother	*mataji*
father	*pitaji*
son	*beta*
daughter	*beti*
elder brother	*bhaiya*
elder sister	*didi*
friend	*dost*
married	*shadishuda*
unmarried	*shadinahin*

Food

This is not normally provided in most Public Works Department (PWD) houses or Forest Rest Houses in India. You either have a cook with you, buy your food and cook it yourself, or find a *dhaba* (local restaurant) or eating house.

Do you have ...?
  kya aap ka pas ... hai?
I am hungry.
  Mujhe bhookh lagi hai
I am thirsty.
  Mujhe pyas lagi hai
I like hot and spicy food.
  Muje mirch masale vala khana acha lagta hai
I don't like hot and spicy food.
  Mujhe mirch masle vala khana acha nahi lagta hai

tea	*chai*
sugar	*chini*
water	*pani*
cold water	*thanda pani*

boiled water	*ubla pani*
chicken	*murgi*
bread	*roti*
eggs	*anda*
vegetable	*sabzi*
fruit	*phal*
potato	*aaloo*
rice	*chawal*
dahl	*dal*
curd	*dahi*

Weather

Today is ...	*Aj ... hai*
cloudy	*badal*
windy	*hava*
stormy	*toofan*
rainy	*barish*
sunny	*dhup*
hot	*garam*
cold	*thanda*

Along the Way

bear	*bhalu*
goats (wild)	*bhakri*
leopard	*bagh*
monkey	*bandar*
mountain	*pahar*
lake	*jhil*
peak	*choti*
pass	*jot/khal/la*
river	*nadi*
big river	*bara nadi*
road	*sarak*
rock	*pathar*
sheep (wild)	*bher*
spring	*chasma*
village	*gaon*
Buddhist monastery	*gompa*
Hindu temple	*mandir*
Muslim mosque	*masjid*

Numbers

1	*ek*
2	*do*
3	*tin*
4	*char*
5	*panch*
6	*chha*
7	*sat*
8	*ath*
9	*nou*
10	*das*
11	*gyarah*
12	*barah*
13	*terah*
14	*choudah*
15	*pandrah*
16	*solah*
17	*satrah*
18	*aththarah*
19	*unnis*
20	*bis*
25	*pachchis*
30	*tis*
40	*chalis*
50	*pachas*
60	*sath*
70	*sattar*
80	*assi*
90	*nabbe*
100	*ek saw*
1000	*ek hazar*

Time & Dates

What time is it?	*Kya vakt ho gha hai?*
It's ... o'clock.	*Abhi ... baze hai*
day	*din*
night	*rat*
morning	*subah*
evening	*sham*
today	*aj*
yesterday	*kal (jo gaya)*
tomorrow	*kal (jo ane vala hai)*
day after tomorrow	*parso*
now	*ab*
week	*hafta*
month	*mahina*
year	*sal*

Useful Words

big	*bara*
cheap	*sasta*
clean	*saaf*
dirty	*ganda*
expensive	*mehanga*
far	*dur*
fast	*tez*
go	*jana*
good	*acha*

happy	*kush*	mine	*mera*
here	*yahan*	small	*chhota*
heavy	*bhati*	that	*vo*
his	*uska*	there	*vahan*
hers	*uski*	tired	*thak*
light (weight)	*halka*	this/these	*ye*
load	*vajan*	yours	*tumhara*

Facts for the Trekker

General Information

PLANNING

There are three main questions when considering a trek in the Himalaya. The first is where to go, and for this it is necessary to check out maps of the Himalaya and read up relevant books, pamphlets and brochures. Secondly, you need to decide when to go. The climate and geography of the Himalaya is very complex and it is no use setting your heart on trekking out of Darjeeling, for instance, if your holidays are restricted to July and August. Thirdly, check your budget. Decide what you can afford and whether you intend to trek through an adventure travel company or prefer to make your own arrangements.

A few words of advice: firstly, if making your own arrangements, work out your budget for the trek and double it. Secondly, never be too ambitious about your plans particularly if you have not trekked in the Himalaya before. Delays are inevitable and should be built into your plans.

Books, Maps & Brochures

Study an overall map of the Himalaya. The Bartholomew map of the Indian subcontinent, the Nelles Verlag on the Himalaya and the Lonely Planet *India & Bangladesh – travel atlas* include details of many of the Himalayan regions. Check out exactly where the different trekking regions are and get a general idea of where you want to go to.

Read as much as you can. Consult the bibliography in this section and cross reference this with any particular interest books, whether they be on Buddhist monasteries, wildlife or wildflowers. At this initial stage consult the Government of India Tourist Office (GITO) and check through their pamphlets. They are always keen to promote the Indian Himalaya and will do their best to

assist you. Also consult some of the adventure travel companies which specialise in Himalayan trekking. Study their brochures and attend a film night. Even if you are not considering trekking with an organised company, the evenings are generally informative and can answer many of your initial questions.

When to Trek

There is an explanation of the various climatic regions in the first chapter of this book, while a more detailed description of the various trekking seasons is included in the introduction to the main trekking regions. Further advice about when to undertake a trek is included in the introduction to each trek described in this book. In summary, however, the trekking seasons in the Indian Himalaya are as follows:

Region	Season
Ladakh & Zanskar	May to October
Kashmir	May to October
Himachal Pradesh	May and June, September and October
Uttarakhand	May and June, September and October
Darjeeling	October to May
Sikkim	October, or April and May

Broadly, the India Himalaya is divided into two distinct geographic regions: the West Himalaya, which includes Ladakh, Kashmir, Himachal Pradesh and Uttarakhand; and the

East Himalaya, which includes Darjeeling and Sikkim.

The West Himalaya lies to the north-west of Nepal. It is subject to far colder winter temperatures than many regions of Nepal, with heavy winter snows that preclude trekking from November until the following May. The trekking season for the West Himalaya is from May to October, while the trekking season in Darjeeling and Sikkim extends from October to the following May.

However, there is also the influence of the monsoon to consider. Sikkim and Darjeeling are subject to the full brunt of the monsoon that sweeps up from the Bay of Bengal and across the East Himalaya in early June. The monsoon is falling across most parts of Nepal by June and continues until the middle of September. The monsoonal influence also extends across many of the regions of Uttarakhand and Himachal Pradesh. It affects these regions in July and August through to early September, making the short pre and post-monsoon periods in May and June, and September and October, respectively, the times to trek. The Kashmir Valley is not subject to the Indian monsoon, and for this reason it enjoys an uninterrupted trekking season from May until October. Ladakh and the Zanskar Valley also lie outside the influence of the monsoon and offer a similar trekking season.

Style of Trek

Decide on your budget. Check what trekking gear you have. Decide what you need to purchase and whether it is sufficient for the region in which you intend to trek. If you do not already have or wish to purchase a high-quality sleeping bag and tent, then it is not advisable to undertake an extended trek across the main Himalaya Range. However, a lighter sleeping bag is quite sufficient for a trek up an alpine valley where there are tea houses and Forest Rest Houses in which to spend the night. Assess your level of fitness and your ability to carry a backpack for a week to 10 days at a time. Consider whether you want to (and can afford to) hire local

porters or horsemen and whether you want to hire local cooks and assistants.

Consider then whether to go on an organised trek or whether to make your own arrangements. Check again what time you have available. Waiting for days at a trailhead for horsemen to materialise can be fun if you have time at hand, but it can be very frustrating if you are on a tight schedule. Each of these options is outlined in the Trekking Information section later in this chapter.

TOURIST OFFICES
Tourist information

The Government of India Tourist Office (GITO) maintains a number of overseas branches where you can obtain brochures, leaflets and general information about India. The tourist office leaflets contain plenty of detail and are worth getting hold of. There are also smaller 'promotional offices' in Osaka (Japan) and in Dallas, Miami, San Francisco and Washington, DC (USA).

Australia
    Level 1, 17 Castlereagh Street, Sydney, NSW 2000 (☎ (02) 9232-1600; fax 9223-3003)
Canada
    60 Bloor Street West, Suite No 1003, Toronto, Ontario M4W3B8 (☎ (416) 962-3787; fax 962-6279)
France
    8, Blvd de la Madeleine, 75009 Paris (☎ 01-42-65-83-86; fax 01-42-65-01-16)
Germany
    Kaisertrasse 77-III, D-6000 Frankfurt-am-Main (☎ (069) 23-5423)
Italy
    Via Albricci 9, 20122 Milan (☎ (02) 80-4952; fax 7202-1681)
Japan
    Pearl Building, 9-18 Ginza, 7-Chome, Chuo ku, Tokyo 104 (☎ (03) 571-5062; fax 571-5235)
Malaysia
    Wisma HLA, Lot 203, 2nd floor, Jalan Raja Chulan, 50200 Kuala Lumpur (☎ (03) 242-5285; fax 242-5301)
Netherlands
    Rokin 9-15, 1012 KK Amsterdam (☎ (020) 620-8991; fax 38-3059)
Singapore
    United House, No 20 Kramak Lane, 01-01A, Singapore 0922 (☎ 235-3800; fax 235-8677)

Spain
    c/o The Embassy of India, Avenida Pío XII 30-32, Madrid 28016 (☎ 3457339)
Sweden
    Sveavagen 9-11, S-111 57, Stockholm 11157 (☎ (08) 21-5081; fax 21-0186)
Switzerland
    1-3 Rue de Chantepoulet, 1201 Geneva (☎ (022) 732-1813; fax 731-5660)
Thailand
    Kentucky Fried Chicken Building, 3rd floor, 62/5 Thaniya Rd, Bangkok 10500 (☎ (020) 35-2585)
UK
    7 Cork St, London WIX 2AB (☎ (0171) 437-3677; fax 494-1048)
USA
    30 Rockefeller Plaza, 15 North Mezzanine, New York, NY 10112 (☎ (212) 586-4901; fax 582-3274)
    3550 Wilshire Blvd, Suite 204, Los Angeles, CA 90010 (☎ (213) 380-8855; fax 380-6111)

Within India there are several GTIO branches which should be useful for general information, and these are listed below. Avoid dealing with touts operating near some of these offices.

Calcutta
    Sandozi Bldg, 26 Himayat Nagar, Hyderabad (☎ 63-0037)
Delhi
    88 Janpath, New Delhi (☎ 332-0005)
Jammu
    Gulab Bhavan (☎ 5121)
Madras
    154 Anna Salai (☎ 852-4295)
Mumbai (Bombay)
    123 M Karve Rd, opposite Churchgate (☎ 203-2932)
Srinagar
    Residency Rd

VISAS & DOCUMENTS
Passport
When obtaining a visa for India, your passport should have at least six months of validity left. Be sure that it has enough blank pages for any visa extensions as it is a hassle trying to get your embassy to insert extra pages when you are away.

Should you lose your passport, first report the loss to the local police and then return to New Delhi, as it is practically impossible to travel anywhere in India without your passport. Most embassies will issue a temporary passport, valid for one year, to get you home. A photocopy of your lost passport, either carried with you or left with friends at home, should help to speed up the process. Upon receiving your new passport you will then have to contact the Foreigners' Registration Office in New Delhi (see address below). Some proof of when and where you entered the country will help matters.

Visas
People of all nationalities, including British Commonwealth citizens, require a valid passport and a visa. Visas are issued at Indian embassies. They are valid for 120 days and must be obtained no more than six months before your arrival in India. If you are planning to visit a neighbouring country such as Nepal, then a double/multi-entry visa is necessary so that you can return to India on the same visa.

Note that if you apply to visit Sikkim, Arunachal Pradesh or other politically sensitive regions, your application can take up to three months, and sometimes longer, to process. If you are travelling independently, and have any doubts at all about whether this will fit into your plans, forget it. Once you have applied to visit one of these regions you cannot reapply for an ordinary tourist visa until your original application has been cleared.

Visa Extensions
Within India, visas can be extended at the Foreigners' Registration Office in Delhi, Srinagar or Darjeeling, or at any office of the Superintendent of Police – in Leh, Manali or Mussoorie, for example. The application is usually straightforward, and no particular problems are encountered. The address in Delhi of the Foreigners' Registration Office (☎ 331-9489) is Hans Bhavan, Tilak Bridge, New Delhi.

If you stay in India for more than 120 days, hold on to your bank exchange certificates as you will need a tax clearance before leaving the country. The clearance certificate is issued by the Foreigners' Section, Income Tax Office (☎ 331-7826), Indraprastha Estate, Delhi. Allow a day to complete formalities.

Travel & Trek Permits

There are no special travel permits required for visiting the Indian Himalaya, but there are restrictions on travelling close to the sensitive borders with Pakistan and China. These inner line restrictions have been eased in the last few years making it possible for foreigners to travel and trek in hitherto restricted regions in Ladakh, Himachal Pradesh and Uttarakhand.

Trekking permits are not necessary in India. However, you should carry your passport with you at all times as a means of identification. For further details regarding local regulations refer to the sections on the various trekking regions.

Travel Insurance

Whether you're going alone or with a trekking agency, it is imperative to take out some insurance cover against sickness, injury and loss of baggage. Most policies also cover the reimbursement of cancellation fees and other non-recoverable expenses if you are forced to cancel your booking because of an accident or illness of a close family member. If you are trekking to a more remote location, more than a few days from the nearest trailhead, then you must also seriously consider evacuation cover. Evacuation by helicopter can be very expensive – US$3000 or more – and a helicopter will not be sent unless the Indian Air Force has some guarantee of payment. Most reputable agencies which run treks to the Himalaya can organise policies to cover emergency evacuation; indeed, many insist that this be taken out as a condition of booking. Do not rely on your consulate or embassy in Delhi to help in an emergency.

Most insurance companies will cover a trekking trip for a premium equal to, or only slightly more than, the insurance for a normal holiday in India. A substantially higher premium is involved if you are intending to go mountaineering or skiing.

If you purchase insurance and lose baggage or personal items, you must submit proof of this in order to make a claim. If you have a medical problem it is important that you save all your bills and have a doctor's letter stating that you were sick. If you lose something covered by insurance you must file a police report and obtain a copy to send to the insurance company, no matter how remote the location. Insurance companies will generally not consider claims without this documentation. Read your policy carefully and make sure you understand all the conditions.

International Health Certificate

This certificate provides a record of the vaccinations you have had prior to travelling to India. It is a useful record but is not required by authorities in India. India no longer requires immunisation against smallpox and cholera. However, a yellow fever certificate is required for all travellers who have been in Africa, South America or Papua New Guinea in the six days prior to arrival in India.

Other Documents

It is worthwhile keeping a photocopy of your passport, including the Indian visa page, your airline ticket, travellers' cheques and credit cards in a safe place. It can save any amount of hassles should these documents be stolen.

EMBASSIES
Indian Embassies Abroad

India's embassies and consulates include:

Australia
    3-5 Moonah Place, Yarralumla, ACT 2600
    (☎ (06) 273-3999; fax 273-3328)
    Level 27, 25 Bligh St, Sydney, NSW 2000
    (☎ (02) 9223-9500; fax 9223-9246)
    13 Munro St, Coburg, Melbourne, Vic 3058
    (☎ (03) 9386-7399; fax 9384-1609)
    The India Centre, 49 Bennett St, Perth, WA 6004
    (☎ (09) 221-1485; fax 221-1206)

Bangladesh
    120 Road 2, Dhamondi, Dhaka
    (☎ (02) 50-3606; fax 86-3662)
    1253/1256 OR Nizam Rd, Mehdi Bagh,
    Chittagong (☎ (031) 21-1007; fax 22-5178)
Belgium
    217 Chaussee de Vleurgat, 1050 Brussels
    (☎ (02) 640-9802; fax 648-9638)
Bhutan
    India House Estate, Thimpu, Bhutan
    (☎ (0975) 22-162; fax 23-195)
Canada
    10 Springfield Rd, Ottawa K1M 1C9
    (☎ (613) 744-3751; fax 744-0913)
China
    1 Ri Tan Dong Lu, Beijing
    (☎ (01) 532-1908; fax 532-4684)
Denmark
    Vangehusvej 15, 2100 Copenhagen
    (☎ (045) 3118-2888; fax 3927-0218)
Egypt
    5 Aziz Ababa St, Zamalek, Cairo 11511
    (☎ (02) 341-3051; fax 341-4038)
France
    15 rue Alfred Dehodencq, 75016 Paris
    (☎ 01-40-50-70-70; fax 01-40-50-09-96)
Germany
    Adenauerallee 262, 53113 Bonn 1
    (☎ (0228) 54-050; fax 54-05154)
Israel
    4 Kaufman St, Sharbat House, Tel Aviv 68012
    (☎ (03) 58-4585; fax 510-1434)
Italy
    Via XX Settembre 5, 00187 Rome
    (☎ (06) 488-4642; fax 481-9539)
Japan
    2-2-11 Kudan Minami, Chiyoda-ku, Tokyo 102
    (☎ (03) 3262-2391; fax 3234-4866)
Jordan
    1st Circle, Jebel Amman, Amman
    (☎ (06) 62-2098; fax 65-9540)
Kenya
    Jeevan Bharati Bldg, Harambee Ave, Nairobi
    (☎ (02) 22-2566; fax 33-4167)
Myanmar (Burma)
    545-547 Merchant St, Yangon (Rangoon)
    (☎ (01) 82-550; fax 89-562)
Nepal
    Lainchaur, GPO Box 292, Kathmandu
    (☎ (071) 41-1940; fax 41-3132)
The Netherlands
    Buitenrustweg 2, 252 KD, The Hague
    (☎ (070) 346-9771; fax 361-7072)
New Zealand
    180 Molesworth St, Wellington
    (☎ (04) 473-6390; fax 499-0665)
Pakistan
    G5 Diplomatic Enclave, Islamabad
    (☎ (051) 81-4371; fax 82-0742)

India House, 3 Fatima Jinnah Rd, Karachi
    (☎ (021) 52-2275; fax 568-0929)
Russia
    6 ulitsa Obukha, Moscow
    (☎ (095) 297-0820; fax 975-2337)
Singapore
    India House, 31 Grange Rd
    (☎ 737-6777; fax 732-6909)
South Africa
    Sanlam Centre, Johannesburg
    (☎ (011) 333-1525; fax 333-0690)
Sri Lanka
    36-38 Galla Rd, Colombo 3
    (☎ (01) 421-605; fax 44-6403)
Sweden
    Adolf Fredriks Kyrkogata 12, 11183 Stockholm
    (☎ (08) 10-7008; fax 24-8505)
Switzerland
    Effingerstrasse 45, CH-3008 Berne
    (☎ (031) 382-3111; fax 382-2687)
Syria
    40/46 Adnan Malki St, Yassin, Damascus
    (☎ (011) 71-9581; fax 71-3294)
Tanzania
    NIC Investment House, Samora Ave, Dar es
    Salaam
    (☎ (051) 28-198; fax 46-747)
Thailand
    46 Soi 23 (Prasarnmitr), Sukhumvit Rd, Bangkok
    (☎ (02) 258-0300; fax 258-4627)
    113 Bumruangrat Rd, Chiang Mai 50000
    (☎ (053) 24-3066; fax 24-7879)
UK
    India House, Aldwych, London WC2B 4NA
    (☎ (0171) 836-8484; fax 836-4331)
    8219 Augusta St, Birmingham B18 6DS
    (☎ (0121) 212-2782; fax 212-2786)
USA
    2107 Massachusetts Ave NW, Washington, DC
    20008 (☎ (202) 939-7000; fax 939-7027)
    3 East 64th St, Manhattan, New York, NY 10021-
    7097 (☎ (212) 879-7800; fax 988-6423)
    540 Arguello Blvd, San Francisco, CA 94118
    (☎ (415) 668-0662; fax 668-2073)

Foreign Embassies & High Commissions in India

If you should come into difficulties in India
then your embassy may assist you with your
problem, but it cannot, under any circumstances, circumvent the Indian legal system.
If you lose your passport it will take some
time for it to be replaced, generally with an
emergency passport to get you home. If you
or a friend require an emergency evacuation
then the embassy will generally contact your

next of kin, who will have to guarantee payment. This is a regulation that some embassies may dismiss if it is a case of life or death but not otherwise. Should you run out of money while you are in India most embassies will repatriate you after contacting next of kin for a guarantee.

However, this should only be considered as a last resort. Embassies generally do not hold onto mail, but forward it to the local foreign mail post office for collection.

Most foreign diplomatic missions are in the nation's capital, Delhi, but there are also quite a few consulates in the other major cities of Mumbai (Bombay), Calcutta and Madras. Embassies and consulates in Delhi and Calcutta are as follows (telephone area codes are 011 for New Delhi and 033 for Calcutta):

Afghanistan
    5/50-F Shantipath, Chanakyapuri, New Delhi (☎ 60-3331; fax 687-5439)
Australia
    1/50-G Shantipath, Chanakyapuri, New Delhi (☎ 688-8223; fax 687-4126)
Austria
    EP-13 Chandergupta Marg, Chanakyapuri, New Delhi (☎ 60-1238; fax 688-6929)
Bangladesh
    56 Ring Rd, Lajpat Nagar-III, New Delhi (☎ 683-4668; fax 683-9237)
    9 Circus Ave, Calcutta (☎ 247-5208)
Belgium
    50-N Shantipath, Chanakyapuri, New Delhi (☎ 608-295; fax 688-5821)
Bhutan
    Chandragupta Marg, Chanakyapuri, New Delhi (☎ 60-9217; fax 687-6710)
    48 Tivoli Court, Pramothesh Barua Sarani, Calcutta (☎ 241-301)
Canada
    7/8 Shantipath, Chanakyapuri, New Delhi (☎ 687-6500; fax 687-0031)
China
    50-D Shantipath, Chanakyapuri, New Delhi (☎ 60-0328; fax 688-5486)
Denmark
    11 Aurangzeb Rd, New Delhi (☎ 301-0900; fax 301-0961)
    3 N S Rd, Calcutta (☎ 248-7478)
Finland
    E-3 Nyaya Marg, Chanakyapuri, New Delhi (☎ 611-5258; fax 688-6713)

France
    2/50-E Shantipath, Chanakyapuri, New Delhi (☎ 611-8790; fax 687-2305)
    26 Park St (inside the courtyard on the right-hand side of Alliance Française), Calcutta (☎ 29-0978)
Germany
    6/50-G Shantipath, Chanakyapuri, New Delhi (☎ 60-4861; fax 687-3117)
    1 Hastings Park Rd, Calcutta (☎ 479-1141)
Indonesia
    50-A Chanakyapuri, New Delhi (☎ 611-8642; fax 688-4402)
Iran
    5 Barakhamba Rd, New Delhi (☎ 332-9600; fax 332-5493)
Iraq
    169-171 Jor Bagh Rd, New Delhi (☎ 461-8011; fax 463-1547)
Ireland
    13 Jor Bagh Rd, New Delhi (☎ 461-7435; fax 469-7053)
Israel
    3 Aurangzeb Rd, New Delhi (☎ 301-3238; fax 301-4298)
Italy
    50-E Chandragupta Marg, Chanakyapuri, New Delhi (☎ 611-4355; fax 687-3889)
    3 Raja Santosh Rd, Calcutta (☎ 479-2426)
Japan
    4-5/50-G Shantipath, Chanakyapuri, New Delhi (☎ 687-6581)
    12 Pretoria St, Calcutta (☎ 242-2241)
Kenya
    66 Vasant Marg, Vasant Vihar, New Delhi (☎ 687-6540; fax 687-6550)
Malaysia
    50-M Satya Marg, Chanakyapuri, New Delhi (☎ 60-1297; fax 688-1538)
Myanmar (Burma)
    3/50-F Nyaya Marg, Chanakyapuri, New Delhi (☎ 60-0251; fax 687-7942)
Nepal
    Barakhamba Rd, New Delhi (☎ 332-8191; fax 332-6857)
    19 Sterndale Rd, Calcutta (☎ 479-1003)
The Netherlands
    6/50-F Shantipath, Chanakyapuri, New Delhi (☎ 688-4951; fax 688-4856)
    18-A Brabourne Rd, Calcutta (☎ 26-2160)
New Zealand
    50-N Nyaya Marg, Chanakyapuri, New Delhi (☎ 688-3170; fax 687-2317)
Norway
    50-C Shantipath, Chanakyapuri, New Delhi (☎ 687-3532; fax 687-3814)
Pakistan
    2/50-G Shantipath, Chanakyapuri, New Delhi (☎ 60-0603; fax 637-2339)

Russia
  Shantipath, Chanakyapuri, New Delhi (☎ 687-3799; fax 687-6823)
  31 Shakespeare Sarani, Calcutta (☎ 247-4982)
Singapore
  E-6 Chandragupta Marg, Chanakyapuri, New Delhi (☎ 688-5659; fax 688-6798)
South Africa
  B-18 Vasant Marg, Vasant Vihar, New Delhi (☎ 611-9411, 611-3505)
Spain
  12 Prithviraj Rd, New Delhi (☎ 379-2085; fax 379-3375)
Sri Lanka
  27 Kautilya Marg, Chanakyapuri, New Delhi (☎ 301-0201; fax 301-5295)
Sweden
  Nyaya Marg, Chanakyapuri, New Delhi (☎ 687 5760; fax 688-5401)
Switzerland
  Nyaya Marg, Chanakyapuri, New Delhi (☎ 60-4225; fax 687-3093)
Syria
  28 Vasant Marg, Vasant Vihar, New Delhi (☎ 67-0233; fax 687-3107)
Thailand
  56-N Nyaya Marg, Chanakyapuri, New Delhi (☎ 60-5679; fax 687-2029)
  18B Mandeville Gardens, Calcutta (☎ 76-0836)
UK
  50 Shantipath, Chanakyapuri, New Delhi (☎ 687-2161; fax 687-2882)
  1 Ho Chi Minh Sarani, Calcutta (☎ 242-5171)
USA
  Shantipath, Chanakyapuri, New Delhi (☎ 60-0651)
  5/1 Ho Chi Minh Sarani, Calcutta (☎ 242-3611)

CUSTOMS
Arrival
The usual duty-free regulations apply for India – that is, one bottle of spirits and 200 cigarettes. If you bring in more than US$10,000 in cash and/or travellers' cheques you are required to fill in a currency declaration form.

You are also allowed to bring in any number of electrical goods, but high-value items, including video cameras, are likely to be entered on a Tourist Baggage Re-Export (TBRE) form to ensure that you export the goods with you. The entry is made inside your passport and is checked when you leave. Occasionally you are also required to enter your camera on the TBRE form, although this depends on the customs officer you encounter. Similarly, some customs officers may want to record sports goods including ice axes, crampons and even sleeping bags. However, no duty is levied provided they are re-exported.

Departure
Upon departure, your passport will be checked for any TBRE entries. Customs officials do not take kindly to police reports stating that the goods have been stolen and are just as likely to charge you duty, which can be prohibitive.

Warnings
Although soft drugs such as marijuana are available in some regions of the Indian Himalaya there are serious penalties for possession or if caught smuggling drugs out of India. This can involve being held in an Indian prison for up to a year before trial – well worth avoiding.

MONEY
Carrying Money
After you have made an accurate estimate of the amount of money you require for your trek, there are a number of options for carrying your money. Cash is the simplest, preferably in US dollars, which can be changed at a bank or hotel before undertaking your trek. Travellers' cheques have the advantage of replacement if they are stolen or lost.

Again, select cheques in US dollars if you are planning to change money in banks in more remote areas. Credit cards, such as Diners Club, MasterCard, American Express and Visa, are widely accepted when paying for services in Delhi. Some also provide a cash advance in US dollar travellers' cheques or Indian rupees on a personal cheque. ATM cards are at present not generally accepted in India.

An alternative is to have money transferred to you while you are in India. This can take time and a lot of chasing around. Banks that have been recommended include Bank of America, Chartered Bank, Banque

Nationale de Paris, Citibank and ANZ Grindlays. American Express and Thomas Cook are also efficient organisations to transfer money through. They can save you days and the expense of waiting in Delhi or Calcutta for funds to arrive.

It is advisable to carry as much cash as you will need for your trek with you. Cash payments are still the norm for porters and horsemen. There are many areas where it is not possible to change money. When in doubt, change money in one of the major towns: for example, in Leh for trekking in Ladakh and Zanskar; in Srinagar for trekking in Kashmir; in Manali for trekking out of the Kullu Valley; and in Dharamsala before trekking out of McLeod Ganj. In Uttarakhand change money in Mussoorie, Dehra Dun or Naini Tal. Alternatively, change money in Delhi before you head out. In Darjeeling there is no problem changing money and similarly in Gangtok.

Don't be too concerned about ensuring that you are carrying low-denomination notes. Hundred-rupee notes can normally be changed at tea stalls and dhabas along the trail, and the total bill for porters and horsemen is likely to run into many hundreds of rupees. However, ensure that the notes are in good condition. Torn or dirty notes are not generally acceptable in many places in India, especially remoter regions.

Currency

The Indian rupee (Rs) is divided into 100 paise. There are coins of 5, 10, 20, 25 and 50 paise, and Rs 1, 2, and 5. Notes cover Rs 1, 2, 5,10, 20, 50,100 and 500. The rupee was once divided into 16 annas, and you may occasionally hear prices quoted in annas in bazaars and markets: 4 annas equalled 25 paise.

Currency Exchange

Current approximate exchange rates follow:

Australia	A$1	=	Rs 25.0
Canada	C$1	=	Rs 25.0
France	FF1	=	Rs 6.5
Germany	DM1	=	Rs 26.0
Japan	¥100	=	Rs 32.5
New Zealand	NZ$1	=	Rs 22.0
United Kingdom	UK£1	=	Rs 52.0
USA	US$1	=	Rs 33.0

Changing Money

The most relevant consideration when changing money in India is time. Waiting in two or three bank queues – first to sign a travellers' cheque, then to encash the money token and finally to wait to receive an encashment certificate – is generally not worth the time unless you are changing a large amount of money. Hotels are a good alternative.

Black Market

With financial liberalisation in India in the early 1990s there is no longer any significant black market for US dollars in India. Besides being illegal, using the black market is risky with counterfeit notes being exchanged and the chances of being short changed in the street. It is well worth avoiding.

Tipping

After a trek it is standard procedure to tip the porters and staff. The amount will vary, but 10 to 15% of the trek wages is normal. Of course, if the trek was unduly difficult or if the porters performed tasks not normally in their line of duty, such as helping the cook, then the tip should be on the more generous side. This should also apply when a particular porter goes out of his way on the trail to help rather than just carrying his load.

In order to ensure that the tips are distributed to the right people, try whenever possible to tip each porter individually rather than giving the total sum to the contractor or head porter to distribute.

Items of clothing and equipment, including boots and sandshoes, are also appreciated.

Finally, don't forget to include in your budget the tips to room boys and helpers who take you around the market before the trek and the host of other people forever coming out of the woodwork to help. Do note that tipping is the custom in India.

Trekking Budget

When compiling a budget for expenses, it is best to break down expenses into a number of categories.

Travel This includes the cost of travelling from Delhi or Calcutta to the trekking region and from there the cost of travelling to the trailhead. An estimate of these costs is made in the Getting Around chapter and also in the Getting There & Away and Access sections in each trekking chapter. These costs may vary enormously depending on whether you decide to fly or drive by private vehicle to the region.

Accommodation The price of accommodation can also vary enormously depending on how much time you spend in Delhi or Calcutta. Trekking in India often requires an night or two at a hotel, be it in Manali, Mussoorie, Leh or Srinagar, before travelling on to the start of the trek. Allow up to Rs 1000 per double per night, including food.

Porters in the Miyar Nullah, an area of high summer pastures near the Kang La in Lahaul.

Porters & Horsemen An estimate of the daily rate for porters or horsemen is included in each trek section. Much, however, will depend on your negotiation skills. You may, for instance, think you have a good deal with the porters until you discover that they require payment for relocation at the end of the trek, or that they will only carry 15 kg each, or that they require an allowance for new boots and waterproof jackets and also an additional food allowance. Ensure that you spell things out or your budget will blow out.

Food This is generally not an expensive item as most basic foods in India such as rice, flour and potatoes are quite inexpensive compared to western prices. However, other items such as tinned cheese and tinned fish cost similar to what you would pay at home. Good dried fruit may be even more expensive than you would normally pay in your local health food store, and a bottle of beer may set you back more than you would pay in your local bottle shop.

Your budget should also include kerosene and cooking oil. You may need to include the provision of pots and pans together with a stove if you have not brought one with you. It may, in fact, be worth considering hiring a cook and assistant rather than paying the additional expense for these cooking items.

Equipment There are a number of outlets in India now renting out sleeping bags, down jackets, tents and sleeping mats. A deposit roughly equivalent to the replacement cost will normally be required. An estimate of what is involved and what is available is outlined in the trekking sections. A medical kit should also be compiled; see the Health, Safety & First Aid chapter.

The Bottom Line The total of all the above categories is still a conservative budget estimate and is likely to fall well short of the actual cost. There will always be extras, whether it be tipping the porters, discovering that the local bus is out of action and that you have to hire a very expensive jeep, or that all the available porters have just been recruited for an expedition.

POST & COMMUNICATIONS
Postal Rates
Aerograms cost Rs 6.50, postcards Rs 6 and air-mail letters Rs 11 to send from India. Air-mail letters to Australia, Europe and the USA take between a week and 10 days to arrive.

Sending Mail
Sending letters in India can be a time-consuming process. You first need to queue to purchase the stamps, then join a second queue to ensure they are franked. In spite of its time-consuming nature, the system works and the vast majority of letters reach their destination safely.

Posting Packages When sending packages, the tedious system of packing, insurance and paperwork does ensure that most arrive without undue delay. The system is somewhat complicated. First you take the parcel to a tailor and get it stitched up for sending overseas. Then you go to the post office and fill out the necessary customs declaration. To avoid duty, state the goods are a gift and the value is less than Rs 1000. Then it's on to the weighing and franking queues before the transaction is completed.

Parcels that are sent by air take approximately two weeks. Surface mail can take somewhere in the vicinity of three months. An alternative to consider is air freight. Most airlines are prepared to offer attractive discount rates provided that you already hold a ticket with the carrier and that you send the goods before travelling home.

Receiving Mail
To receive mail in India you need to find the poste restante counter, which is usually in some obscure room in the main post office. Most post offices ask you to produce your passport or a similar means of ID before letting you check through the mail corresponding to the alphabetical letter of your surname. When informing friends about where to send mail, emphasise that they underline your surname, Poste Restante, and the city in question. Many lost letters are simply filed under given (Christian) names, so always check under both your names. Note, mail is normally held for three months and is then sent back to the sender by surface mail.

Alternatively, companies such as American Express will hold mail for their card-holders (and American Express will hold mail for you if you are using their travellers' cheques). Hotels may also hold mail, although many will automatically return mail to the sender if the guest is not at the hotel when the mail arrives.

Telephone & Fax
Nowadays, the telephone system in India has improved to the point where you can be reasonably assured of making an international or interstate phone call without undue delay. In most towns you'll come across private STD/ISD call booths with fax facilities and direct dialling for both interstate and overseas. They are quick and efficient, and are connected with a digital meter so that you can keep an eye on what the call is costing. Direct international calls cost around Rs 70 per minute depending on the country you are calling, while an interstate call from, for example, Manali to Delhi would cost around Rs 30 per minute.

If calling from your hotel, check the rates beforehand as the billings may be anything up to 300% more than the standard call charge. Reverse-charge (collect) calls also attract a service charge from most hotels. The best alternative is to book a call for just the minimum three minutes and get your friends or family to call you back.

BOOKS
Bookshops
Most books are published in different editions by different publishers in different countries. As a result, a book might be a hardcover rarity in one country while it's readily available in paperback in another. Fortunately, bookshops and libraries search by title or author, so your local bookshop or

library is best placed to advise you on the availability of the books recommended.

The many bookshops around Janpath and Connaught Circle in New Delhi provide India's largest stock of books on the Indian Himalaya, including many of the reprints listed below. Closer to the hills, the Artou Bookshop in Leh stocks many books on the history and culture of Ladakh and Tibet, while the Kashmir Bookshop on Sharvani Rd, Srinagar, has a comprehensive selection on Kashmir and Ladakh. In Shimla and Darjeeling, the Oxford Bookshop provides a good selection although by no means as wide as the selection available in Delhi.

Guidebooks

Trekking in Pakistan and India by Hugh Swift (1990) gives an overview of trekking possibilities in the Himalaya.

India – travel survival kit (Lonely Planet) is recognised as *the* guide to travel in India.

Indian Himalaya – travel survival kit (Lonely Planet) is the perfect companion to this book.

Himalaya – Playground of the Gods by Mohan Kolhi (Vikas, Delhi, 1983) is also worth consulting.

The Himalayan Experience by Jonathan Chester (1989) provides a comprehensive overview of the trekking possibilities, including a section on the Indian Himalaya.

The Tourist's Guide to Kashmir, Ladakh & Skardo revised by Arthur Neve (Civil & Military, Lahore, 15th edition, 1933). If you are fortunate enough to come across this book, hang on to it. The guide ran to 17 editions between the wars and has interesting information about the state of the trails 50 years ago.

Hiking in Zanskar and Ladakh (1987) is a useful trekking guide.

Garhwal by G & M Thukral (Frank Bros, Delhi, 1987) is a well illustrated book on the region.

Sikkim, Darjeeling and Kalimpong by Wendy Brewer Lama (Insight Pocket Guides, 1993) provides details of sightseeing and the Kangchenjunga trek in Sikkim.

India's Western Himalaya (Insight Guides, 1992) illustrates and describes some of the more popular treks in the West Himalaya.

Indian Wildlife (Insight Guides, 1987) is a comprehensive record of wildlife, which includes a section on the wildlife of the Himalaya.

Culture & Religion – Ladakh

Ladakh by Heinrich Harrer (1980) is the best of the many illustrated books on Ladakh.

The Cultural History of Ladakh Volumes 1 and 2, by Snellgrove & Skorupski (Vikas, Delhi, 1977 & 1980), provides the most comprehensive cultural background.

The Lion River by Jean Fairly and *A Journey into Ladakh* by Andrew Harvey (1975) are also recommended.

Himalayan Art by Madanjeet Singh (1968) is an excellent guide to the various art styles that have evolved in the Himalaya, and includes sections on Ladakh and Lahaul.

Ladak: Physical, Statistical and Historical, &c. by Alexandra Cunningham (Sagar Publications, Delhi, reprint 1977), written in the mid-19th century, provides a comprehensive survey of all things Ladakhi and is a wealth of information.

A History of Ladakh by Francke (Sterling Publications, Delhi, reprint 1977) is a standard history on Ladakh.

Culture & Religion – Kashmir

Kashmir by Rughubir Singh (1983) is the best illustrated book on the Kashmir Valley, followed by *Kashmir* by Francis Brunel (Rupca & Co, Delhi, 1979).

This is Kashmir by Pearce Gervis (Universal Publications, Delhi, 1974) is a storehouse of historical information.

Travels in Kashmir by Bridgid Keenan (1989) provides a highly readable account of the history and handicrafts of the Kashmir Valley.

An Area of Darkness by VS Naipaul (1968) includes a section on the annual trek to the Amarnath Cave.

India, the Siege Within by MJ Akbar (1985) includes a section on the contemporary development of Kashmir.

History and Culture of the Himalayan States, Volumes 1 to 3 on Himachal Pradesh, and Volumes 4 & 5 on Jammu, by Charak (Light & Life Publications, New Delhi, 1978), provide historical accounts of the West Himalayan states.

Culture & Religion – Himachal Pradesh & Uttarakhand

Himalayan Hill Districts of Kooloo, Lahaul & Spiti by Harcourt (Vivek Publications, Delhi, reprint 1982) was the first account of the rich history of the Kullu Valley.

Himalayan Circuit by GD Khosla (Delhi, 1989) provides some interesting details of the valleys of Lahaul & Spiti during a trek by an Indian judge in the 1950s.

Kulu – the End of the Habitable World by Penelope Chetwode (Allied Publications, Delhi, 1980) is a marvellously idiosyncratic account written in the 1960s.

Over the High Passes by Christina Noble (1987) also picks up on the background of the Kullu and Kangra valleys, while tracing the migration of the Gaddi shepherds.

At Home in the Himalayas by Christina Noble (1991) is a highly readable account of the author's times and experiences in organising treks in the Kullu Valley.

The Nanda Devi Affair by Bill Aitken (Delhi, 1994) describes in detail the author's love of, and wanderings in, the vicinity of Nanda Devi.

History & Exploration – 19th Century

Travels in the Himalayan Provinces of Hindustan and the Panjab by Moorcroft & Trebeck (OUP, Delhi, reprint 1979) is indispensable background reading on travels in the western Himalaya in the 1820s.

Travels in Kashmir, Ladak, Iskardo, the Countries adjoining the Mountain Course of the Indus, and the Himalaya North of the Punjab by GT Vigne (Sagar Publications, Delhi, reprint 1978) documents the author's journeys in Kashmir, Ladakh and Baltistan in the 1830s.

Western Himalaya and Tibet by Thomson (Cosmo Publications, Delhi, reprint 1978) and *Ladak: Physical, Statistical and Historical, &c.* by Alexandra Cunningham (Sagar Publications, Delhi, reprint 1977) are both references from the Ground Commission established in 1847.

The Northern Barrier of India by Frederick Drew (Light & Life Publications, Delhi, reprint 1971) contains interesting geological and geographical information of many of the then remote regions of Jammu & Kashmir.

The Valley of Kashmir by Lawrence (Kaser Publications, Srinagar, reprint 1967). Lawrence was the Land Reform Commissioner in Kashmir in the 1880s.

History & Exploration – 20th Century

Kashmir by Francis Younghusband (Sagar Publications, Delhi, reprint 1970) includes a description of the Kashmir Valley at the turn of the century.

Kashmir in Sunlight and Shade by Tyndale Biscoe (Sagar Publications, Delhi, reprint 1971) is a readable account of Kashmir between 1890 and 1920.

Thirty Years in Kashmir by Arthur Neve (Asia Publications, Lucknow, reprint 1984) describes the life and times of an eminent doctor and mountaineer who spent most of his working life in Kashmir.

When Men and Mountains Meet (1977) and *The Gilgit Game* (1979), both by John Keay are two indispensable books on the history of exploration in the West Himalaya during the 19th century.

Foreign Devils on the Silk Road (1980), *Trespassers on the Roof of the World* (1982) and *Setting the East Ablaze* (1984), a trilogy by Peter Hopkirk, are good background reading on the areas bordering the Himalaya.

The Great Game by Peter Hopkirk (1990) is a comprehensive and highly readable account of the development of British and Russian territorial ambitions throughout the Himalaya in the 19th century.

Mountains of the Gods by James Cameron (1984) is a well-written account of the history of Himalayan exploration.

Plain Tales from the Raj (1980) and *A Mountain in Tibet* (1983), both by Charles Allen, also provide popular introductions to the history of the region.

The Wonder that was India by Basham (1984) and *The History of India*, Volumes 1 and 2, by Romila Thapar and Percival Spear (Penguin, London, 1966) both offer a general historical introduction to India.

Younghusband by Patrick French (1994), is the definitive biography on one of Britain's most eminent explorers.

Auriel Stein by Annabel Walker (1995) is a recent biography that highlights the extraordinary life of a prodigious explorer.

Trekking & Mountaineering

Abode of Snow by Kenneth Mason (reprint 1987) is the classic on Himalayan exploration and climbs.

Exploring the High Himalaya by Soli Mehta & Harish Kapadia (1990) was written by two prominent members of the Himalayan Club with access to a host of information on the history of climbing in the Indian Himalaya.

HW Tilman – The Seven Mountain-Travel Books compiled by the Mountaineers, Seattle (1985) includes *The Ascent of Nanda Devi*, which records the first successful ascent of Nanda Devi in 1936, and *When Men and Mountains Meet*, which includes exploration of the East Himalaya and Assam in the prewar and war years.

Eric Shipton – The Six Mountain-Travel Books compiled by the Mountaineers, Seattle (1985) includes *Nanda Devi* and records the exploration of the Nanda Devi Sanctuary.

That Untravelled World by Eric Shipton (1969) includes accounts of much of the exploration in the Indian Himalaya in the 1930s.

Kamet by Frank Smythe (Natraj Publications, Dehra Dun, reprint 1991) includes an account of the first ascent in 1931 of Kamet, the second-highest peak in the Indian Himalaya and the alpine-style exploration in the Garhwal that was undertaken after the climb.

The Valley of the Flowers by Frank Smythe (Natraj Publications, Delhi, reprint 1980) highlights a remarkable season of climbing in the Garhwal in 1937.

Himalayan Odyssey by Trevor Braham (1974) records a climbing career that included many ascents and exploration from Sikkim to Himachal Pradesh in the postwar years.

High Himalaya, Unknown Valleys by Harish Kapadia (Indus Publishing, New Delhi, 1993) outlines some of the many treks and expeditions of one of the Himalayan Club's most active members.

Painted Mountains by Stephen Venables (1986) gives a vivid account of the first ascent of Shivling in the Kishtwar Himalaya and an expedition on Rimo in the Indian Karakoram.

The Shining Mountain by Peter Boardman (1978) is an incredible account of the ascent of the West Wall of Changabang.

Rimo by Peter Hillary (1988) describes an arduous and exasperating expedition to the Indian Karakoram.

First Across the Roof of the World by Graeme Dingle and Peter Hillary (1982) is a trekking epic that includes traversing Sikkim and the West Himalaya.

Across the Top by Sorrel Wilby (1992) gives an account of a trekking expedition which included exploits in Ladakh, Himachal and Uttarakhand and also one of the first recorded treks by westerners through the untouched valleys of Arunachal Pradesh.

Natural History

Indian Hill Birds by Salim Ali (OUP, Delhi, 1977) is still the best bird book available.

Flowers of the Himalaya by Polunin & Stainton (1984) is essential for anyone interested in the flora of the region.

Collins Handguide to the Birds of the Indian Sub-continent by Martin Woodcock (1980) is a compact guide.

The Stones of Silence by GB Schaller (Vikas Publishing, New Delhi, 1980) provides a comprehensive, illustrated guide to the wildlife of the region.

Indian Wildlife (Insight Guides, 1987) is a superbly illustrated book, including a section on the national parks in the Indian Himalaya.

Carpet Sahib by Martin Booth (1991) is a highly readable account of the incredible life of Jim Corbett.

Journals

The Himalayan Journal is the annual publication of the Himalayan Club. Copies can be purchased from PO Box 1905, Bombay 400 001, India, and in selected bookshops in India and Nepal.

Indian Mountaineer is the bi-annual publication of the Indian Mountaineering Foundation (IMF). Copies and information can be obtained from the IMF, Benito Juarez Rd, New Delhi 110 021, India.

Himal magazine is published every two months by the Himal Association, PO Box 42, Patan Dhoka, Lalitpur, Nepal. It has informative articles pertaining to the Himalayan region.

PHOTOGRAPHY & VIDEO
Cameras & Equipment

Ideally you should bring two single-lens reflex (SLR) cameras with you – one to use and one as a backup. As far as lenses are concerned, you could bring a wide-angle for village profiles and monastery interiors, a macro lens for wildflowers, a telephoto for dramatic mountain shots and people close-ups and a zoom lens for on-the-move photography. A flash unit, light meter and tripod should also be carried, together with a Polaroid camera so that every mother and child in every village can have a memento of your visit. All this, of course, requires at least 10 rolls of colour film per day to cover the wide variety of interests that abounds when you are trekking.

In practice, most of us have to settle for less, and get by with an compact automatic or SLR camera with a standard 35 or 50 mm lens. If you have never used a camera before, then a trip to the Himalaya is an ideal opportunity to start. If you have previously used a camera, I would advise a reliable SLR body with a wide-angle and zoom lens. A zoom lens is ideal for non-intrusive people photography. You can get full-frame photographs of shy villagers without them noticing that you have taken their picture. If you can afford it, buy a zoom lens that is of the same make as your SLR camera. A wide-angle lens is great for taking shots of interiors, and of camp sites with a full panorama of mountains.

If you are buying new equipment, check it out thoroughly beforehand and make sure you know how to use it. Keep a record of light conditions and compare the results when the photos are developed. If you haven't used your camera for a while, have it serviced before you leave. If your camera breaks when you are trekking then you have problems. The photographic shops in Leh, Srinagar, Manali or Darjeeling do not have the facilities to repair SLR cameras. Companies like Mahatmas on Connaught Circle in New Delhi are able to handle mechanical repairs but don't normally have the necessary spare parts to rectify the more complex electrical faults.

Extra camera and flash batteries are essential. Bring also a change of UV filters plus a blower brush and cleaning equipment. Note that batteries can be purchased in Delhi and in most of the trekking-off points including Leh, Srinagar, Darjeeling and Manali. The temperatures in summer do not necessitate the camera being winterised to withstand very low temperatures. If, however, you have plans to trek in Ladakh in the winter, then this process should be considered. Don't forget, waterproof containers are essential to protect your film and camera gear in prolonged rainy conditions. A lead-lined bag is highly recommended for taking your film through the many airport security checks on the Indian subcontinent (see Airport Security following).

Your camera gear will almost certainly be the heaviest item in your day pack, so don't weigh yourself down with too much gear. Taking photographs should complement the enjoyment of your trek, and not be viewed as an end in itself.

Film

Over the past few years the price of film in India has become very competitive, with good stocks of film available in the reputable camera shops in Delhi. A roll of slide film with 36 exposures can be purchased for around Rs 200. Be aware that it is possible that film may have been stored beyond the use-by date or subjected to hot conditions. If possible, allow about a roll of film per day's trekking. Otherwise try to ration your film so that you don't use half of your supplies before you set off on the trail. One word of advice: it is always useful to calculate the amount of film you need for the trek and then double it. You can't go far wrong, as any film

you have left over can either be sold or taken back to be stored in the fridge until you have another chance to use it. Some fast film, ISO 400, is necessary, especially if you're using a zoom or telephoto lens in low light conditions. A stock of ISO 100 or ISO 64 film is also recommended. Slide film is cheaper than the print variety, and your best slides can be reprocessed as prints. Don't send film back from India by post – it will probably get there but it may be delayed or damaged by heat or opening for customs inspection. Keep it cool and secure until your return home. Colour film can be processed in Bombay and Delhi, but the quality is not always up to standard.

Video

The use of video film has taken off in a big way in India over the last decade. Blank VHS videos are freely available in New Delhi. If you are bringing a standard video recorder into India, then declare it when arriving at customs. If the item is then entered into your passport you can easily take it out of the country when you leave.

If you have not used a video camera before arriving in India try to allocate your video stock evenly throughout your trek. Wait for the best light in the early morning or late afternoon for filming shots around the camp. When filming sequences with good light and a good subject, try to hold the shot for as long as the interest lasts. When using a zoom lens, pan in on the subject slowly, ensuring that the camera is held securely to avoid any camera shudder. Finally, plan the sequences of your video with some semblance of consistency so that the film will be of interest to others when you return home.

Restrictions

Photographing airports before and after you board the plane is strictly prohibited in India, as are military sites and bridges along the main highways. The photography of dams, as well as TV towers, radio towers and other important communication installations, is also banned.

Photographing People

When photographing in remote areas, try to be unobtrusive. Consider the feelings of the local people. In most villages, particularly in Islamic areas, photographing women is normally not acceptable. Indeed, your local guide or porter should check out the feeling of the villagers or shepherds before you even ask about taking photographs. Above all, respect people's privacy and imagine what you would feel like if a group of Indian tourists arrived in your backyard and started photographing you without as much as an acknowledgment.

Airport Security

In some airports, such as Leh and Srinagar, the security authorities may not permit hand baggage on the plane, and that includes cameras. It is advisable to pack them securely in your check-in baggage before departure. Most airports in India also ban all batteries from being carried on the plane and this includes camera batteries.

In India the X-ray machines are film safe, claiming they will not damage unprocessed film unless over ASA 1000. However, given the number of X-rays that your film is subject to, both to and from and within India, it is imperative that you carry your film in a lead-lined bag. Be aware, however, that the X-ray may be strengthened so that security staff can see the bag's contents. So it is preferable to ask to have the film inspected by hand.

TIME

India is 5½ hours ahead of GMT/UTC, 4½ hours behind Australian Eastern Time and 10½ hours ahead of American Eastern Standard Time.

ELECTRICITY

The electric current is 230V to 240V AC, 50 Hz. Electricity is widely available in India, but breakdowns, blackouts, time sharing and load shedding are commonplace in most Himalayan regions. Sockets are of the two round-pin variety and it is worth your while getting a local electrician to make you an adaptor that will fit your plugs to the hotel sockets. Batteries are available everywhere in India while the most common small-cell camera batteries can be bought in Delhi, Calcutta and most towns in the Himalayan region.

WEIGHTS & MEASURES

The metric system was introduced to India in 1966 and is now generally accepted throughout the country. For conversions for temperatures, distances, weight and volume, refer to the inside back cover of this guide.

LAUNDRY

One of the great luxuries of returning from a trek is giving all your gear to the local *dhobi* or laundryman, who will return the clothing the following day in spotless condition. Payment is small in comparison to the sheer delight of not having to do the washing. Expect to pay a maximum of Rs 100 after a three-week trek.

During the trek you are unlikely to be accompanied by a dhobi. How often you wash your own clothes is for you to decide. Once, while trekking in Zanskar for a month during rather cold weather, I did not wash or change most of my clothes and ended with a splendid case of body lice! However, the regular washing of socks and underwear can help prevent blisters and chafing (see the Health, Safety & First Aid chapter). It is advisable to take biodegradable soap and wash all clothes in a bucket away from the river or stream so as not to contaminate the water. A washing line is also useful together with a small supply of pegs, though you should be cautious about leaving washing hanging out overnight in areas where theft is likely to be a problem.

WOMEN TREKKERS

The paradox of worshipping woman as a goddess and yet treating her daily as a beast of burden is central to the religious order of the UP hills. Until this neurotic dichotomy is squarely faced, the petulant spite of males will continue to breed disharmony.
Bill Aitken, *The Nanda Devi Affair*, 1994

While opposition to the inequalities and

injustice perpetuated by the caste system was championed by Mahatma Gandhi, the role of women, particularly in village communities, is still subject to many medieval attitudes. In many Hindu villages in Himachal and Uttarakhand, the traditional attitudes are still prevalent. These attitudes are also found in the Islamic regions of Kashmir, although economic necessity often requires the women in these villages to play a more active role than their counterparts in the towns and cities. By contrast, the women in the Buddhist regions of Ladakh, Zanskar and Spiti enjoy a more equal status and it is to these regions that women trekkers are often attracted when considering a trek in the Indian Himalaya.

Simply put, the traditional attitudes expressed in most remote villages is that there must be something wrong with females who are trekking without male company. Here, your guide – who normally comes from a more educated area – can assist by explaining why you have decided to trek without male company. This can go a long way to assisting women trekkers who want to spend time in the villages, visit the local school and be invited into the houses.

On the trek, the male trekking crew (there are rarely, if ever, women porters, horse handlers or guides) treat women trekkers with more respect although they will always defer to any males for instructions on where to camp, the length of the trekking day or the kind of food to be cooked. It is an attitude to be recognised. It will change as more women undertake treks in India and it can be overcome to some extent with good humour and patience. Women trek leaders are likely to be treated with appropriate respect.

Precautions
While prejudice against women exists, the mountain trails are still a safe place to go. Fortunately, sexual prejudice in the mountains does not translate into acts of violence. Indeed, the traditional attitude of the males is not likely to be anywhere near as harassing as it is when confronting males in a large city such as Delhi or Mumbai.

It is still, however, not advisable to trek on your own (a consideration whether you are male or female). Expressions of friendliness can sometimes be misinterpreted and misunderstandings do sometimes occur. The mention of a fictitious husband or boyfriend can deter some unwanted advances.

Clothing
Common sense will guide you in most situations. It is not advisable to wear tight jeans, high-cut shorts or tight T-shirts. When trekking, a pair of culottes or a long skirt is acceptable, although trekking pants or track suit bottoms should always be worn when entering some of the remoter villages. When entering a temple or mosque it is advisable to cover both legs and arms and wear a head scarf. In short, the more you cover up, the better you are likely to be accepted.

When bathing, go well away from a village or encampment; washing in a river with a bathing costume is generally not acceptable. For calls of nature along the trail, an umbrella to use as a screen is an asset.

TREKKING WITH CHILDREN
Trekking with children is an ideal family holiday. Over the seasons the author has arranged many treks for families and received much positive feedback. A close friend took her three-year-old daughter on a 15 day trek in Kashmir. Since then the daughter has been on a number of treks in Nepal, Himachal and Uttarakhand.

A trek can be an eye-opener for children, especially when they compare the living standards of the children in the villages with their own. After initial adjustment, children quickly break down cultural barriers. Children tend not to feel the same inhibitions as adults when it comes to joining in games and being invited into local houses. It is difficult to specify a minimum age. Some argue that seven is the youngest age at which the child will gain a worthwhile experience; others argue that only much older children should go on treks.

If planning a trek, try to get other families to come with you. It is also necessary that the children understand where they are going, and why they are going, well before departure. Find ways of keeping your children fully occupied; for example, devise checklists for identifying wildflowers and birds.

On the trek do not include too many long stages. Children have boundless energy, but tire easily and do not have the mental fortitude of adults in times of inclement weather or undue delays. Here an obliging porter or horseman may have to carry the child for at least some of the day. This can usually be arranged. For medical considerations, refer to the Health, Safety & First Aid chapter, and Lonely Planet's *Travel with Children*.

DANGERS & ANNOYANCES

It is always advisable to leave a copy of your trek itinerary and your possible time of return with a hotel manager, houseboat owner or friend. Never trek on your own. If an accident occurs you may be many days away from the nearest settlement or village. Always register with the local police or the tourist offices in places like Padum in Zanskar and leave your itinerary.

However, the chances of an accident while trekking are minimal when compared with what can happen on many other more conventional holidays. Sound preparation, both physical and mental, plus a modicum of common sense will prepare you for the majority of situations you encounter. Even though you may be trekking on more remote wilderness trails than elsewhere in the Himalaya, dangers such as avalanches, falling into a crevasse, being swept away while crossing a river, or crossing an ice bridge as it collapses, are minimal. Wild animals also pose minimal danger. I have encountered both black and brown bear at close quarters (well, reasonably close) without incident. They, like all wild animals, will not attack unless they feel threatened. Snakes are also very rare and you can confidently expect poisonous species to move away well before you approach. Yaks can be a little more temperamental and it is not advisable to move too

close to a herd grazing on the high pastures in Ladakh. Buffalo, again, should be avoided. They are nervous of your scent (unless you are with a Gujar shepherd) although there is little chance that they would actually attack.

There have been incidents of monks in Ladakh and the occasional villager in Himachal taking exception to the occasional trekker. But provided you observe the social mores and retain a degree of normality, then the situation is hardly likely to get out of hand. Always observe dress codes in the remoter villages. Women in particular should ensure their heads and shoulders are covered and wear jeans or long trousers when entering a village mosque. The same applies to the more remote monasteries in Ladakh and temples in Himachal and Uttarakhand.

Avoid charcoal-fuelled fires in poorly ventilated hotel rooms: tragically, carbon monoxide poisoning has caused some deaths in the region.

Theft is not commonplace, although it is not advisable to leave a display of valuables unattended at your camp site. The temptation may prove too much for the village children. Boots, together with your washing, should always be brought inside the tent at night.

Some of the Gujar and Bakharval shepherds in Kashmir have gained a reputation for less than honest conduct. A number of tents have been slashed in the middle of the night, particularly those belonging to groups in the Kanital Valley below the Boktol Pass. In one case I was able to apprehend the culprits the following day, the local police were contacted and the culprits arrested. All to no avail. The stolen goods were also appropriated by the police as evidence and they ended up in Kishtwar, where they still remain.

Finally, at present travel warnings have been issued by most governments advising tourists not to visit Kashmir. While this warning also includes Jammu, it does not generally refer to Ladakh, which has not experienced the political unrest in the Kashmir Valley. See also the Kashmir chapter.

GARRY WEARE

GARRY WEARE

GARRY WEARE

Top: Pack goats, Johar Valley, Uttarakhand
Middle: Wanlah village, Ladakh, on the Lamayuru to Chilling trek
Bottom: Pulley-bridge river crossing, Lahaul, Himachal Pradesh

GARRY WEARE

GARRY WEARE

GARRY WEARE

Top Left: Buddhist prayer flags above the Victory Fort, Leh, Ladakh
Top Right: Ladakhi trader. Ladakh is historically at the crossroads of trading routes linking India and Central Asia.
Bottom: Panorama from the Victory Fort, Leh, Ladakh

BUSINESS HOURS

In India, Sunday is the weekly holiday. The working week is from Monday to Friday from 10 am to 5 pm and Saturday morning. These working hours apply to government offices, banks, tourist offices and post offices. Most public holidays and festivals are normally regarded as holidays. Remember to pre-plan money changing and office visits carefully – there are many holidays for festivals in India.

SPECIAL EVENTS

While there are an impressive number of festivals in India throughout the year, most will have little or no effect on your trekking plans. Those that will are listed below.

February-March

Holi This is one of the most colourful (literally) of the Hindu festivals, with people marking the end of winter by throwing coloured water and red powder over one another.

April

Id-ul-Zuhara This is the Muslim festival commemorating Abraham's attempt to sacrifice his son. It is celebrated with prayers and feasts. It will be held around 19 April in 1997 and 11 days earlier in 1998 as the events on the Muslim calendar fall about 11 days earlier each year.

May-June

Buddha Jayanti The Buddha's birth, enlightenment and attainment of Nirvana (earthly release) are all celebrated on this day. On the Hindu calendar it is referred to as Wesak while Tibetans and Ladakhi refer to the date as the Saka Dawa. Both of these festivals are celebrated at the time of the full moon, but since the Ladakhi people keep different calendars, the festivals do not necessarily coincide with the same full moon.

August

Independence Day This holiday, on 15 August, celebrates the anniversary of India's independence from Britain in 1947. The prime minister delivers an address from the ramparts of Delhi's Red Fort and there are parades of military strength. At present it is particularly advisable to avoid the towns of Srinagar and Jammu on these days and head for the hills.

October

Dussehra This is the most important Hindu festival, and takes place in October. It lasts for 10 days and celebrates the *Ramayana*. It commences on the first day of the Hindu month of Asvina. In the Kullu Valley there is a colourful

celebration where normal business stops for a couple of days. Elsewhere shops are closed and it is difficult to get crew to commence a trek until after the festival is over.

October-November

Diwali Diwali is celebrated on the 15th day of the month of Kartika (October-November). At night many oil lamps are lit as a symbol of their original purpose of showing Rama (an incarnation of Vishnu) the way home from his period of exile. In Calcutta the festival is also dedicated to Kali (goddess of destruction) and the festival lasts five days. Particularly relevant is the third day which is spent worshipping Lakshmi, the goddess of wealth and fortune. Most treks in the West Himalaya would be over by this time, but plans for treks out of Darjeeling and Sikkim should take the timing of this festival into consideration.

December-January

Ramadan Ramadan is the most important event in the Muslim year, and consists of a 30 day dawn-to-dusk fast. It was during this month that the prophet Mohammed had the *Koran* revealed to him in Mecca. In Muslim regions, and particularly in Kashmir, this can be a difficult time to organise treks.

Local Festivals

Apart from the main festivals listed above there are a number of other local festivals that may interrupt and enhance your plans.

Ladakh

One of the most famous Buddhist monastery festivals is the Hemis festival held to commemorate Padmasambhava's birthday. The date is calculated as the 10th day of the 6th month of the Tibetan calendar which generally falls between the middle of June and early July.

Kashmir

During the full moon day of the Hindu month of Sravana in July-August the day is celebrated with the pilgrimage of many thousands of Hindus to the Amarnath Cave, where it is said that the Hindu god Shiva expounded his theory of reincarnation to his consort Parvati. The trek commences from Pahalgam four days prior to the full moon night. Many of the pilgrims leave Srinagar a week earlier, walking the complete distance to the cave.

Himachal Pradesh

The Dussehra festival in the Kullu Valley in October celebrates Rama's victory over the demon king Ravana. The festival continues for a week and commences on the 10th day of the rising moon, known as Vijay Dashmi.

The temples at Yamunotri and Gangotri are opened on the religious day of Akshaya-Tritya which falls during the last week of April or the first week of May, and remain open till the Diwali festival in October that marks the end of the pilgrimage season. The temple at Kedarnath is also opened around the same time, on the day of Maha Shivrati, while Badrinath opens a few days later. Both temples normally close around the time of the Diwali festival. In Kedarnath the closing *puja* (prayer session) is conducted by the local priests from Ukhimath, while the head priest from Badrinath together with his staff move down to Joshimath for the winter.

ACCOMMODATION

While tea-house trekking is generally not applicable to most parts of the Indian Himalaya, overnight accommodation can be arranged in the many Public Works Department (PWD) huts, Forest Rest Houses and Dak bungalows that have been established since the middle of the 19th century. Each is run by a local *chowkidar* (caretaker) who lives nearby and faithfully maintains a register of arrivals.

While it is always advisable to carry a tent for stages where there is no bungalow or hut, staying in a rest house allows you to unpack fully and experience a sense of space for the night. The huts are generally sparsely furnished with perhaps a *charpoy* (string bed) or two, a dusty desk and chair. So don't expect luxury. There is normally a kitchen for cooking, with basic facilities, at the back of the hut. With few exceptions, it is not normally necessary to make a reservation. The chances of an official party staying there are minimal and the chowkidar is pleased to assist. Payment is made direct to the chowkidar and costs generally around Rs 20 per person per night. Sometimes it is necessary to pre-book in locations which are popular with Indian trekkers.

In Ladakh there are a number of private lodges in the Suru Valley and at the village of Juldo, close to Rangdum monastery, and there are also some at Padum, the capital of

Zanskar. There are some lodges or tented accommodation on the Markha Valley trek in Ladakh, and on the Padum to Lamayuru and Padum to Darcha treks in the Zanskar region. Rs 10 will cover your stay with the proviso that you purchase an evening meal and breakfast. Note that not every village is serviced by a hotel and there are stages beyond the village network where you will need to bring a tent.

In Himachal and Uttarakhand the Forest Rest House and PWD hut arrangement is quite well developed even in the remoter villages. However, with the exception of the trek to Gaumukh out of Gangotri, where you can stay in very basic style in the *dhabas* (small tea stalls), there is no established system of tea-house trekking. It is the same in Sikkim. However, the trek out of Darjeeling can be completed in true Nepalese style with the tea houses along the trail making it unnecessary to carry a tent or food.

Accommodation before starting out on a trek is outlined in each section with a brief summary of the options available. For more comprehensive details of all the hotels, houseboats and private lodges, refer to Lonely Planet's *India – travel survival kit* or *Indian Himalaya – travel survival kit*.

FOOD

A healthy diet makes for a healthy trek. By adopting the best of the locally available food and using a little imagination or a good local cook, delicious meals can be prepared that will enhance your overall trekking experience.

Available Food

Besides the fruit and vegetables available in the local markets, fresh meat, eggs, pulses or *dhal*, cheese, ghee, flour and rice are widely available across India. Butter and dried milk are available in tins. Nuts and raisins, honey, peanut butter, jams, tea and coffee, sugar, biscuits and chocolate can also be purchased locally. The cost of locally produced food, such as rice, flour, fruit, vegetables and pulses is low; while the meat, tinned goods, butter, cheese, fish and dried fruit are on a par with western prices. However, for daytime snacks when on the trek it is recommended that you bring a stock of dried fruit as Indian dried fruit is both expensive and of a poorer quality. This can then be mixed with a supply of nuts and chocolate. The quality of muesli is also questionable in India and a small quantity brought with you can help liven up the porridge for a while. Other suggested items include packets of dried soup, herbal teas and energy bars. Australian groups often bring Vegemite while British groups often bring Marmite to give that extra dimension to puris, parathas and chapattis (the local breads).

If you are making your own arrangements, don't forget that many of the luxuries may also be shared with the porters or horsemen or villagers on the way. Remember that the tea-house trekking style is by no means as developed as it is in Nepal, and if you intend to live in the houses don't expect any of the gastronomic delights that you find on some of the more popular routes in the Annapurna or Everest regions. Indeed, if you are trekking in Ladakh, then often the only local food available is *tsampa* (roasted ground barley), butter tea, plus a few vegetables and dried apricots. In each trekking chapter there is reference to the food available locally and at the trailhead.

If your arrangements are being handled for you, then try to specify any dietary requirements from the outset. If you have an allergy, then ensure that your leader as well as the cook and his assistant are completely clear on your requirements. A token nod of the head is not good enough. Also encourage the cook not to take too much canned or bottled food on the trek as there is always the likelihood that the containers will be discarded along the way. See Responsible Trekking in the Trekking Information section later in this chapter for suggestions.

It is important to have a balanced diet of carbohydrates, proteins and fats on the trek; it is equally important not to miss the delicacies of Indian cooking. Try delicious puris or parathas with honey for breakfast, instead of white bread and biscuits. A succulent mutton curry, cooked with local vegetables and dhal, is more appetising and interesting than roast mutton and boiled vegetables. Sausage, beans and chips may be OK, but a simple chicken or vegetable *pulao* (savoury rice) for lunch, with chutneys and local curd, tastes so much better. It is usually quite possible to obtain fruit and vegetables which will not perish while being carried – for example, cabbages, cauliflowers, potatoes, onions and carrots. Apples are a speciality in the Kullu Valley, as are apricots in Ladakh.

Eric Shipton, the British explorer who specialised in small, lightweight expeditions in the Himalaya, reduced his requirements to just oatmeal. Food was simply calculated by multiplying the number of days out on a trek by the quantity of oatmeal needed per day. Apparently, he spent considerable time debating whether salt was a luxury that could be dispensed with. For us lesser mortals, it is easy to exist quite happily for three or four weeks at a time on a substantial diet of porridge, puris and honey in the morning; with daytime snacks of nuts, raisins and tea; and an evening meal of rice, dhal and vegetables. On such treks there is little need for freeze-dried, tinned or packaged food.

DRINKS

The adage of not drinking the water is one that should be remembered at all times while trekking in India. Putting iodine in the water, or boiling it at night for use the following day, is the most satisfactory option. Even when you are trekking way above the villages there is a need to be wary of the crystal clear stream. It should always be assumed that shepherds and their animals are above your water source. The only exception is if you discover a spring line – a place where the water comes straight out of the ground high on an alpine pasture. Even there you must ensure that you fill your water bottle straight form the source and not at a lower point where the supply may already be contaminated. It is also necessary to ensure that you do not inadvertently contaminate a local village water supply. This is especially relevant in Ladakh where the water sources are often limited. Do not camp close to the streams, and if you want to have a wash, then take the water in a bowl to an area well away from its source.

While tea is the mainstay on the trek, be prepared to be flexible. Indian *chai*, which is a combination of tea leaves, water, milk and sugar all boiled and mixed in together, is the way Indian crews and *dhaba wallahs* (proprietors of small food stalls) believe tea should be prepared. If you want sugar and milk separate, ask at the outset and your needs may be accommodated. In the Buddhist villages in Ladakh, Lahaul and Spiti butter tea may be offered. It is prepared by mixing tea with rancid butter and salt in a wooden churn. Provided you think of it as soup rather than as tea, it's fine, particularly when mixed with tsampa, the ground barley grain common throughout Ladakh, Zanskar, Lahaul and Spiti.

Soft Drinks & Bottled Water
India has a wide variety of canned and bottled drinks, including the locally produced Thumbs Up and Limca. These are now competing with Cola-Cola following its recent re-introduction to India. Many drinks such as bottled mango juice and apple juice are also available, while small cartons of mango, apple or peach drinks are also becoming popular. Mineral water is also available. Cans and bottles are not yet recycled and need to be disposed of with care.

Alcohol
Alcohol is freely available in all of the Himalayan states with the exception of Kashmir, where it has been banned during the current political situation. Bottled beer, including such brands as Golden Eagle and Rosy Pelican, is quite satisfactory and costs Rs 50 per bottle. Indian whisky, rum and gin and imported vodka cost between Rs 100 and Rs 200 depending on the quality. Imported spirits and wine are not available except in the five-star hotels in Delhi, where a premium price is charged. Alternatively, purchase a duty-free bottle before you arrive in India. Don't forget a hip flask!

Although I'm not advocating overindulgence on the trek, staff and trekkers have been known to appreciate a hot rum toddy. Then again, when trekking in Ladakh a glass of *chang*, a barley beer, can be refreshing. It is drunk by the families when they are harvesting the fields and has a very low alcohol content. More lethal is *tongba*, available in Sikkim. Prepared in a wooden pot and drunk through a special straw, it consists of fermented millet mixed with boiling water.

THINGS TO BUY
The variety of handicrafts available in India can easily upset the most conservative budget. A convenient way to discover what is available is to visit the Government of India Emporium in Janpath, New Delhi, which will also give you an idea of the prices and the various options for sending the goods home. Many of the state governments, too, have their emporiums in Delhi including Rajasthan, Jammu & Kashmir and Himachal Pradesh. There are also many shops in Connaught Circle which stock handicrafts. Payments for more expensive items can often be made by credit card through American Express, Visa or MasterCard or with travellers' cheques or US dollars cash.

The government art emporiums often insist on the production of bank exchange certificates if you elect to pay in rupees. This is not necessary in private showrooms. There are also tales of purchases that have been paid for and then gone astray with unscrupulous dealers. Provided you have the documentation, and the goods are insured for transit, the likelihood is that they will finally reach you. Most delays occur when an item is specially ordered and the time promised for completion is unrealistic. If letters and phone calls do not have the required effect, then making contact with the Government of India Tourist Office (GITO) nearest your home will normally do the trick.

In Ladakh, Manali, Dharamsala and Darjeeling there are specific outlets for the production of Tibetan goods which have flourished since 1959. The carpets may not be to everyone's taste but many of the designs have been modified with subtle colour combinations and designs that have kept abreast of western fashions. Expect to pay US$80 to US$150 for a six foot by four foot woollen carpet. (Note that imperial measurements are still employed in the carpet business.) The Tibetan-made warm wool pullovers are also worth considering. Prices are comparable to the Kashmir alternatives. At the Tibetan refugee handicraft centres in Leh, Dharamsala and Darjeeling you can appreciate how the goods are made.

Many of the handicrafts on display in the Leh bazaar, including copper bowls, butter lamps and Buddhist statues, are made in villages such as Chilling, specifically for the tourist market. This provides valuable local income, while at the same time the important items of Ladakh's cultural heritage remain in Ladakh.

Remember, it is illegal to export antiquities over 100 years old. Customs officials in Delhi and Calcutta will interpret this to include any old-looking artefact. Trekkers in Leh have been stopped at the airport, so it is essential that you obtain the correct documentation before returning to Delhi or home.

The handicrafts in Kashmir are world renowned and include finely knotted carpets, papier-mâché, jewellery, leather goods, shawls, woodcarving and furniture. With the current political situation many Kashmiris have set up shop in Delhi and there are many bargains on offer. Look at paying around 30% to 50% of the asking price with some goods. With carpets, a simple calculation is often a good indication as to whether you are being overcharged. The design is for the most part irrelevant when determining the price. All that matters is the size, say six feet by four feet, and the quality – whether the carpet is wool, silk or a combination of the two. For a six foot by four foot carpet expect to pay US$350 for a woollen one, US$700-plus for silk and US$450 for a silk/wool combination.

Sending handicrafts home can be a problem if you are not fully familiar with the hassles involved. If you want to send the goods yourself you must find a tailor who can pack them in a cotton bag which conforms to government export regulations.

Once this is completed, large items will be sent by ship and can take up to three months to arrive. Air-freighted items take far less time but are much more expensive to send. If you are purchasing an item from a reputable dealer try to get them to include the price of transportation and let them deal with the bureaucracy. Alternatively, take the goods home with you, even if it does entail bargaining at the airline check-in counters. It ensures that you will arrive home with your goods without any fear of delay or loss.

Trekking Information

TYPES OF TREK
Do-It-Yourself

At a hill station or trekking-off point you can arrange your own equipment, food and staff. If you have sufficient time and patience to organise things, either directly or through a local person, this can be a highly rewarding experience, as well as saving you money.

You must, however, be aware of the problems of dealing with a culture that is vastly different from your own. This will colour many of your negotiations. Don't expect things to happen quickly, or expect a straight answer when it comes to times and stages. It's an open bargaining situation. The horsemen will naturally want to go on the less demanding route, and will lose little time in explaining to you that the relevant passes you wish to cross are snowbound, blocked by bears or any number of other obstacles. The result is that you may have to alter your ambitious plans and accept an easier, less challenging, alternative. Generally, staff or horsemen are not prepared to go on an extended trek on their own. They will insist on taking a work companion with them, and this will obviously increase the cost. It is worth considering the possibility of having other people join your party and sharing some of the expenses.

A cook is a valuable asset who will save you the expense of buying pots and pans, and can recommend the food that is most suitable to bring with you. A cook can also bargain hard for you in the market, saving large amounts of otherwise wasted time. In return, he will expect some clothing allowance, normally local walking boots, plus a decent tip at the end of the trek.

Your choice of guide is vital. You are dependent on his experience and reliability, which can either make or break your trek. It is essential that, before hiring a guide, you check his attitude and connections with other staff, and his general knowledge of the region. Once the rate has been fixed, the guide is your representative, and should be reminded of this when negotiating with the cook, the horsemen or the various other suppliers.

Remember, as the contractor of your trek you will also be held in the position of employer should something go wrong. It is particularly necessary that you have additional funds with you to deal with an emergency, and carry a medical kit that can cover most eventualities.

Backpacking

Carrying your own gear and being self-sufficient is not difficult on short treks where the load is light and the stages easy. On a long trek, your backpack may weigh you down to the point where you see more of your feet than of the mountains. In Nepal, tea-house trekking has become popular on the main trekking routes as more and more villagers are realising the potential of the tourist dollar and catering for the trekker's need for cooked food and accommodation.

In India there are few areas where you can undertake a tea-house trek. This is because the demand for these services is still very small. Also much of the trekking in India goes beyond the villages and past shepherd encampments to remote camps where there is no likelihood of gaining food and shelter for the night. In Ladakh and Zanskar,

however, a tea-house system of sorts has evolved in the last decade on the Markha Valley trek, the Padum to Lamayuru trek and also on the Padum to Darcha route. The only problem is that not all the stages are covered all the time and some, particularly in the vicinity of the passes, have no facilities at all. You must therefore come prepared with a tent, stove and a few days provisions at the very least. In the more populated valleys in Kashmir, Himachal and Uttar Pradesh you may come across Forest Rest Houses or PWD huts. These are normally manned by a chowkidar (caretaker) but are often simply furnished. The food supplies en route tend to be unreliable. In Sikkim a series of huts has been constructed to provide basic shelter for porters as the weather can be particularly nasty at any time of the year. Trekkers may also use these huts, although a tent provides by far the best means of availing yourself of the best camp spot and fully appreciating the mountain backdrop.

Remember that it is one thing to carry your own gear for a few days, but quite another to carry it for two weeks or more. Of course this ultimately depends on your level of fitness and your experience of wilderness areas. Many trekkers compromise, hiring a porter or two or a horseman to help carry the load and therefore assist them to complete their trek in some degree of comfort.

Adventure Travel Companies

Most recognised adventure travel companies operate programmes in the Indian Himalaya. The Government of India Tourist Office has a file of recommended organisations. Points to bear in mind when considering these companies include their experience in handling trips to India, the leaders they employ, the type of food, equipment, medical kits and information they provide, their evacuation/insurance cover, and the specialist interests they cater for.

Compare the trip notes and if possible attend a film evening to find whether the type of trek you are considering is appropriate to your interest and ability. Ultimately, any travel company is only as good as its local ground agent, and this should be carefully considered before making any commitment.

Local Agents

You could, of course, try to bypass the overseas travel company, and deal directly with the local agent. See the Information Services section later in this chapter or the Trekking Agents sections in the relevant trekking chapters. You can contact these agents beforehand, or on arrival in India. Get quotes from two or three companies. You will need to ascertain their degree of expertise and competence in dealing with your party. You must, of course, carefully check what is included, particularly with regard to the equipment provided, as there are few places to hire quality gear once you are in India. Check the details of your trek itinerary, so that you end up paying for what you wanted and going where you planned. This takes time, and has to be weighed up against the do-it-yourself option.

Other Considerations

Whatever option you choose, whether it be backpacking, joining an adventure travel company group, or something in between, be sure to share the magic of the Himalaya with the local people.

A local crew can enhance your experience in a way that is sometimes not appreciated by people wary of anything that hints of the Raj. Working with trekking parties is a valuable source of employment for local cooks, guides and horsemen, and their involvement and sense of humour can remain with you for a long time after you return home. Experiences in the Himalaya are shared experiences, and there is nothing finer than having these enhanced by a great crew.

ATTITUDE

A suitable temperament is the most important requirement for anyone undertaking a trek in the Himalaya. If you have any doubts about whether you can cope with the stresses of being away from it all for a period of weeks, then it is advisable to restrict your initial outdoors experience to a shorter trek nearer to home.

I have led many groups over the last 20 years, and I am convinced that if people have the will to complete a trek, then they will do so. Trekking is not an activity exclusively for the young; age is no barrier. In fact, people of more mature years very often do better than the young. It is essential to approach the Himalaya with a tolerant attitude.

Remember that a trek to the Himalaya is not a climbing trip. On 95% of treks there is no need for ice axes and crampons, just the ability to put one foot in front of the other. Since most treks in the Indian Himalaya are undertaken during the summer, you will have between 12 and 14 hours of daylight. This makes it possible for you to commence trekking early in the morning and get to camp by lunch time with the rest of the afternoon free to photograph, visit villages and monasteries or check out the wildflowers. This compares very favourably with weekend bushwalking in Australia, tramping in New Zealand or hiking in Europe, where the norm is to walk for a longer period of the day.

Remember that you can also employ staff to assist you. It is not necessary to spend time cooking or washing up if you employ a cook and crew, while taking porters will ensure that you need carry little more than a day pack – though ardent backpackers can of course carry more.

Choosing the right trek is of course imperative. Select one to begin with that is within your capabilities. A trek is not an endurance test and if you need to prove something to yourself about your strength or fitness it is again better to sort it out on trails closer to home. A summary of the various trek gradings is outlined later in the following sections.

Having made the decision to go to the Himalaya, get fit! Jogging, swimming, cycling (in fact any regular physical exercise) is desirable. Begin your programme at least three months before your trek, and try to exercise daily for at least half an hour. The fitter you are, the more you get out of your trek. If you do nothing beforehand, you will probably finish the trek but will feel completely exhausted during the first week on the trail.

Finally, remember that Himalayan trekking is addictive. Many non-outdoors people, on completing a trek, decide to return the following season. Most people have never felt better than after two or three weeks of continuous walking in the mountains. The rarefied air, exercise and wholesome food are the ideal combination for rejuvenating both mind and body.

PERMITS & FORMALITIES
Trekking Permits

Trekking permits are not necessary in India, although some areas require separate permission for trekking. To date this includes regions like the Milam Glacier in Uttar Pradesh and the region north of Yuksam in Sikkim. In both regions, a minimum of four people must trek together and their arrangements must be made by a locally recognised agency.

Restricted Areas

Special permits are not required for visiting Ladakh, Kashmir, Himachal Pradesh or Uttar Pradesh. However, you must obtain a land permit to visit Darjeeling and a permit for entering Sikkim. Remember, all Himalayan border regions are politically sensitive.

The area of Ladakh from one mile (1.6 km) north of the Leh-Srinagar road is generally regarded as a restricted zone for foreigners, although permission is now granted to visit the Nubra Valley, and the Pangong Lake district north of the Indus Valley. The same restrictions apply to the area one mile east of the Leh-Manali road beyond the Baralacha La. However, the Indian government is now permitting organised groups of foreigners to visit the outlying Rupshu area closer to the disputed India-China border. These regulations are always changing, so check local regulations before making plans. The region of Spiti has been open since 1992, as has the nearby region of Kinnaur. In the Garhwal,

similar restrictions apply as you get closer to the India-China border. It should also be noted that certain other trekking areas, such as the Nanda Devi Sanctuary, are at present closed to trekkers.

In the East Himalaya a land permit is issued on arrival at Bagdogra airport and also at the nearby New Jalpaiguri station. For permits for Sikkim it is necessary to apply either in Delhi or Calcutta, or at the Foreigners' Registration Office in Darjeeling.

It is necessary to carry your passport with you at all times. This is your only bona fide means of identification, and you will need to show it at strategically placed checkpoints in Ladakh, Zanskar, Lahaul, Spiti and Kinnaur.

National Park Fees

A small fee is levied when entering some of the national parks in the Indian Himalaya. Fees range from Rs 20 when trekking to the Hemis High Altitude National Park in Ladakh to Rs 100 for foreigners and Rs 20 for Indian trekkers when trekking into the Valley of the Flowers in Uttar Pradesh.

INFORMATION SERVICES
Government Departments

For more information about specific treks from the state governments within India you can contact the following:

Himachal Pradesh
    Trekking Officer in Charge, Tourist Office, Shimla, Himachal Pradesh
Jammu & Kashmir
    Trekking Officer in Charge, Tourist Reception Centre, Srinagar, Kashmir
Sikkim
    Trekking Officer in Charge, Tourist Office, Gangtok, Sikkim
Uttar Pradesh
    Trekking Officer in Charge, Tourist Office, Dehra Dun, Uttar Pradesh

However, the local agents listed in the trek sections normally have a better idea of what is available. In Himachal Pradesh, the local mountaineering institutes in Manali, Bharmour and McLeod Ganj are staffed by enthusiastic and committed staff. Likewise in Uttar Pradesh, the Garhwal Mandal Vikas Niwas (GMVN) offices in Uttarkashi, Joshimath and Mussoorie and the Kumaon Mandal Vikas Niwas (KMVN) at Naini Tal have staff with first-hand experience of the treks in their region.

Trekking Agents

There are literally hundreds of travel agents in Delhi. The following are members of the Adventure Tour Operators Association, an organisation that focuses on the professional development of adventure sports including trekking. All the following members are recognised by the GITO.

Artou
    13 Hanuman Road, Vasant Vihar, New Delhi 110029 H (☎ 687 5280; fax 688 5188)
EssQee Travexpress
    106 Hanuman Rd, Safdarjang Enclave, New Delhi 110029 (☎ 687-0016; fax 687-5433)
Exotic Journeys
    26, Sector 2 Market, RK Puram, New Delhi 110022 (☎ 67-8658; fax 67-0221)
Far Horizon Tours
    M/57-A Malviya Naga, New Delhi 110017 (☎ 645-0945; fax 647-9320)
High Point
    39 Paschimi Marg, Vasant Vihar, New Delhi 110029 (☎ 60-1224; fax 317-2316)
Ruck Sack Tours
    B45 Som Datt Chambers-1, 5 Bhikaji Cama Place, New Delhi 100066 (☎ 67-3717; fax 687-4377)
Shikhar Travel
    209 Competent House, F14 Middle Circle, Connaught Place, New Delhi 110001 (☎ 331-2444; fax 332-3660)
Snow Leopard Adventures
    Sector C9 Vasant Kunj, New Delhi 110030, (☎ 689-5905; fax 611-3973)
Wanderlust Travels
    M51-52 Palika Bhawan, opposite Hotel Hyatt Regency, New Delhi 110066 (☎ 60-2180; fax 688-5188)
World Expeditions
    Ground Floor, MG Bhawan-1, 7 Local Shopping Centre, Madangir, New Delhi 110062 (☎ 698-3358; fax 698-3357)

TREKKING ROUTES
Route Descriptions

The descriptions outlined in the trekking sections will give you an idea of the terrain and culture covered on each trek, together with an indication of the degree of difficulty and the ease of organisation. The descriptions provide a general route guide. It is important to recognise that many of the routes followed go far beyond the village trails and that the route may vary from season to season.

Local guides can be invaluable for introducing you to the local village culture and the flora and fauna. On shorter valley treks it may be easy to follow a well-established trail; however, a knowledgeable local guide can show you some of the hidden valleys and delights that many do-it-yourself trekkers miss out on. On longer treks a guide is highly recommended, while for treks which require high pass crossings a guide is essential.

True Left, True Right
The most important convention adopted in the trek descriptions is the use of the terms true left and true right. The true side of the valley is defined as the side you are facing when looking down the valley, that is when the river or glacial source is behind you. Hence when trekking up the valley towards the river source the right hand side of the valley is the true left side and vice versa. ■

Level of Difficulty

The trek gradings take a number of factors into consideration including the length of the trek, the height of the pass crossings, the number of river crossings, the condition of the trail and the number of hours per day you are likely to be trekking. Of course, this can vary considerably depending on which time of the year you undertake a particular trek. Passes are far more demanding when under deep snow in the spring, and rivers which require demanding crossings during the summer may have virtually dried up by the end of the season or be crossed by snow bridges in the springtime. Before selecting a trek, check the list of treks in this book and then read the relevant trek stage descriptions. Also consider your level of outdoor experience and fitness and your attitude to trekking in relatively remote areas for perhaps weeks at a time.

Grading System

- **Introductory** treks include walking for up to six hours a day and generally do not exceed 3000m in altitude.
- **Moderate** treks include stages of up to six or seven hours a day. The trek may exceed 4000m.
- **Strenuous** treks include some stages where you may be required to trek for up to 10 hours. The altitude may reach 5000m.
- **Technical** treks include stages where the altitude may exceed 5000m. They may also include stages where ice axes and crampons are required. ■

Route Stages

The daily stages on each trek should give you a basic appreciation of the time necessary to complete a particular trek. The stages have been selected with regard to a number of factors which include camp site convenience and availability, location of supplies, opportunities for local staff to visit families or the fact that the group requires maximum time for acclimatisation. When trekking at high altitude, it is particularly necessary to allow a sufficient number of stages before crossing a high pass or undertaking high-altitude exploration. By the same token any trip can be reasonably extended to include further time for exploratory options or to appreciate an interesting village before continuing. Whatever you do, don't rush. There is nothing worse than having to adhere to a tight schedule with little time to savour the trekking experience.

Times & Distances

The times below the heading of each trek section indicate the approximate time taken by an average trekking group. An average group will cover three to four km an hour along a well-defined trail, but somewhat less, perhaps two km, when climbing to a demanding pass. Therefore, on an average five to six-hour day, a group will average 15 to 18 km.

If you consistently cover the distance in less time, then you can apply the same adjustments to this book as you continue the trek. You should, however, acknowledge that the average villager or shepherd will have little conception of time, and any enquires about the amount of time needed to get to the next village should be crosschecked a number of times. Remember that local people often walk for a very long time each day, so an hour or two is not really important to them. Many seasons ago I planned on trekking from the village of Sanku in the Suru Valley across to Drass. The villagers assured me that if I left at first light I would be in Drass that afternoon. In actuality it took me two full days and their advice, however well meaning, could have left me in difficulty if I had not taken a tent, stove and food supplies with me for the unscheduled overnight stop.

Trek Combinations

In the Indian Himalaya there are few classic or well-established treks that, for instance, go in to a base camp or complete a circuit around a particular mountain massif. A trek from Lahaul in Himachal Pradesh over the Kang La to Padum in the Zanskar Valley could be extended, either by continuing on via Karsha to Lamayuru, or by ascending the high passes of the Cha Cha La and Rubrang La to the Markha Valley and Leh. Or the trek could even be made into an ambitious circuit, returning to Lahaul via the Shingo La or the Phitse La. In Uttarakhand there are many options for combining treks. For instance, the trek out of Uttarkashi to Dodi Tal can be extended to Hanumanchatti or can head over the Yamunotri Pass to the Har ki Dun Valley.

Possible extensions are outlined at the end of each trek description.

Maps

The maps included in this book are compiled with reference to the best available maps of the region and the author's experience. The trekking maps depict the ridgelines which mark the highest level between two valleys. If the trail crosses the ridgeline you will cross a pass. The maps give an indication as to the terrain you will cover on your trek. They will give an idea of the main mountain ranges to be traversed on a longer trek and the extent of the intermediary valleys. These trekking maps should be used in conjunction with some of the map series listed below.

The AMS U502 series of topographical maps covers many of the main trekking regions in India. They can be used in conjunction with the comprehensive Leomann series (1987) and also the recently published Air India trekking maps, which are upgraded versions of the state government trekking maps compiled in the early 1980s. At the beginning of each trek section the relevant map to be consulted is indicated, together with any other useful references.

AMS U502 Series 1:250,000 These are based on the Survey of India and were revised by the US military and published in 1948. The original series were in colour and these have recently been reprinted. The following sheets are now available.

NI 43-06 Srinagar, includes Srinagar and the areas to the north and west

NI 43-07 Kargil, includes the region of Sonamarg and the Amarnath Cave

NI 43-08 Leh, includes the Ladakh Range

NI 44-05 Shyok, includes the Nubra Valley and eastern Ladakh to the Tibet border

NI 43-11 Anantnag, includes the west Zanskar

NI 43-12 Martselang, includes central Ladakh, south of Leh and the Zanskar River

NI 44-09 Pangong Tso, includes east Ladakh, Pangong Lake and the Tibet border

NI 44-16 Palampur, includes the area north and east of Shimla and the Sutlej River

NI 44-13 Tso Morari, includes Lake Morari, Spiti River, east Himachal Pradesh and Tibet

NH 43-04 Shimla, includes the area north and east of Shimla and the Sutlej River

NH 44-01 Chini, includes east Himachal Pradesh, Sutlej River and Tibet

NH 44 -05 Dehra Dun, includes Gangotri, Kedarnath and the Garhwal foothills

NH 44 -06 Nanda Devi, includes east Garhwal, Nanda Devi, Trisul and Dunagiri

Leomann Map Series 1:200,000 This series of ridge and river maps covers most regions of the Indian Himalaya with the trekking routes depicted in three colours. It is best to use these in conjunction with the U502 Series.

Sheet 1 Jammu and Kashmir, includes Srinagar, Kolahoi Glacier and Kishtwar

Sheet 2 Jammu and Kashmir, includes Kargil, Zanskar and the Nun Kun area

Sheet 3 Jammu and Kashmir, includes the Nubra Valley, Leh and the Zanskar area

Sheet 4 Himachal Pradesh, includes Chamba, the Dhaula Dhar, the Pangi Valley and central Lahaul

Sheet 5 Himachal Pradesh, includes the Kullu Valley, the Parbati Valley and central Lahaul

Sheet 6 Himachal Pradesh, includes Kalpa-Kinnaur, Spiti and the Shimla area

Sheet 7 Uttar Pradesh (Garhwal), includes Gangotri, Har-ki-Dun and the Mussoorie area

Sheet 8 Uttar Pradesh (Kumaon), includes Pindari Glacier, Badrinath and Nanda Devi

Air India Map Series 1:250,000 These were produced a few years ago with ridge and river sections useful to trekkers in the Indian Himalaya. They have been produced by veteran Himachal trekker Manmohan Singh Bawa. The sections provide a good introduction and should be used in conjunction with the U502 Series.

Altitude Measurements

Carrying an altimeter at all times has the disadvantage that the trekker cannot unduly exaggerate his or her performance after returning home. However, there is always some leeway. I have experienced Leh rise and fall nearly 100m in one day, not from any strange hallucinations but simply by recording altimeter readings on a stormy day. Barometric pressures change considerably in mountain regions and I am still wary of

THE TREKS

Trek	Stages	Grading	Maximum Elevation	When to Trek	Other Information
Ladakh					
Leh & the Indus Valley					
Spitok to Hemis via Markha Valley	7	moderate to strenuous	5030m	end June to mid-Oct	the most popular trek out of Leh
Lamayuru to Chilling	5	moderate to strenuous	4950m	end June to mid-Oct	along less frequented trails to Lamayuru
Kargil & the Suru Valley					
Panikhar to Heniskot via Kanji La	7	strenuous	5290m	end June to mid-Oct	a traverse over the Zanskar Range
Padum & the Zanskar Valley					
Padum to Lamayuru via Singge La	10	strenuous	5050m	end June to early Oct	the classic trek over the Zanskar Range
Padum to Leh via Cha Cha La, Rubrang La & Markha Valley	10	strenuous	5030m	mid-Aug to early Oct	trek through remote gorges to the Markha Valley and Leh
Padum to Darcha via Shingo La	7	strenuous	5090m	end June to early Oct	established trek over the Himalaya Range to the Kullu Valley
Padum to Darcha via Phitse La & Baralacha La	8	strenuous	5250m	end June to early Oct	an alternative trek out of the Zanskar Valley to Baralacha La
Padum to Manali (Kishtwar) via the Umasi La	9	strenuous	5340m	end June to early Oct	a challenging trek to either Manali or Kishtwar
Kashmir					
Pahalgam					
Pahalgam to Kolahoi Glacier & Tar Sar	5	introductory	3900m	May to Oct	the most popular trek in Kashmir
Pahalgam to Sumbal via Sonamous Pass	5	moderate	4200m	late June to mid-Oct	the normal trek route from the Lidder to the Sindh Valley
Pahalgam to Amarnath Cave via Mahagunas Pass	6	moderate	3960m	late June to mid-Oct	pilgrimage trek to the sacred Amarnath Cave
Pahalgam to Suru Valley (Ladakh) via Boktol Pass	8	moderate to strenuous	4860m	July to late Sept	the classic route from Kashmir to Ladakh
Himachal Pradesh					
Manali & the Kullu Valley					
Manali to Chandra Valley via Hampta Pass	5	moderate	4270m	June to Oct	popular trek across Pir Panjal Range to Lahaul
Jagatsukh to base of Deo Tibba	4	introductory	3900m	June to Oct	wildflowers; spectacular views of Deo Tibba
Nagar to Parbati Valley via Chandrakani Pass	4	moderate	3650m	June to Oct	bird's eye view of the Kullu Valley; ancient culture of Malana village
Manikaran to Spiti Valley via Pin Parbati Pass	9	moderate to strenuous	4810m	mid-Sept to mid-Oct	alpine trails over Himalaya Range to Buddhist villages in Spiti
Lahaul & Spiti					
Batal to Chandra Tal & Baralacha La	4	moderate	4950m	mid-July to late Sept	Chandra Tal lake; wildflowers & Mulkilla Range

Trek	Stages	Grading	Maximum Elevation	When to Trek	Other Information
Himachal Pradesh *continued*					
Udaipur to Padum via Kang La	8	strenuous to technical	5450m	mid-July to late Sept	challenging trek over Himalaya Range to Zanskar Valley
Dharamsala & the Kangra Valley					
McLeod Ganj to Machetar via Indrahar Pass	5	moderate	4350m	late June & mid-Sept to mid-Oct	traverse over the Dhaula Dhar Range to Ravi Valley
Hardsar to Chandra Valley via Kugti Pass	5	moderate	5040m	late June to early Oct	following Gaddi shepherd trails over Pir Panjal Range
Kinnaur & the Sangla Valley					
Kinnaur Kailas Circuit	4	strenuous	5260m	late June to early Oct	traverse Himalaya Range to the Sangla Valley
Uttarakhand					
Mussoorie					
Har-ki-Dun Valley & Ruinsara Lake	6	introductory	3510m	May to end June & mid-Sept to end Oct	well-defined trail through villages & meadows of the Har-ki-Dun Valley
Uttarkashi					
Uttarkashi to Hanuman Chatti via Dodi Tal	4	moderate	4150m	May to end June & mid-Sept to end Oct	wildflowers, Dodi Tal and fine views of the Bandarpunch Range
Gangotri to Gaumukh & Tabovan	3	introductory	4450m	May to end June & mid-Sept to end Oct	ancient pilgrim trail to source of the Ganges
Joshimath					
Valley of the Flowers & Hem Kund	4	introductory	4330m	May to end June & mid-Sept to mid-Oct	wildflowers of Bhyundar Valley, pilgrimage trail to Hem Kund
Joshimath to Ghat via Kuari Pass	5	introductory	3640m	late June & mid-Sept to mid-Oct	spectacular views of the Nanda Devi Sanctuary
Ghat to Mundoli via Rup Kund	7	moderate	4620m	late June & mid-Sept to mid-Oct	alpine trails to sacred lake, impressive views of Trisul
Naini Tal & Almora					
Song to the Pindari Glacier	7	introductory	3650m	May to end of June & mid-Sept to end Oct	impressive views of Nanda Kat & Pindari Glacier
Munsyari to the Milam Glacier	7	moderate	3450m	May to end June & mid-Sept to mid-Oct	spectacular views of Nanda Devi, historic trading ties with Tibet
Darjeeling & Sikkim					
Darjeeling					
Mana Bhanjang to Rimbik via Sandakphu	3	introductory	3640m	Oct to May	village trail affording views of Kangchenjunga, Makalu & Everest
Sikkim					
Yuksam to Dzongri & the Guicha La	6	moderate	4020m	April to May & Oct to mid-Nov	Rhododendron forests to Dzongri, impressive views of Kangchenjunga

committing my records to the scrutiny of professional surveyors.

The spot heights referring to mountain summits in this book have been taken from the Ground Survey of India and are accurate. However, the altitudes given in the trekking stages are mostly based on my own readings and are approximate. In the case of pass heights, the altitude has often been rounded to the nearest 10m, as I have little inclination to dig through the snow to bedrock and then wait at the pass for a few days in order to calculate the exact barometric pressure. The quest to define a village height to the nearest metre has also been avoided. Many of the villages do not have village squares or a main bazaar and houses are often scattered 200m up the hillside. In alpine areas, camp sites are often spread out over a number of km, and to define a camp site down to the last metre is inappropriate. The camp site in the vicinity of the Kauri Pass in Uttar Pradesh is a good example. Here the potential camp sites are spread over two to three km, and there is a difference in height between the lowest and highest camp of over 200m.

It is also acknowledged that there is always room for revision. Indeed, on some treks I have not carried an altimeter, and in the absence of any other references, the heights have been estimated. Feedback from trekkers is therefore always appreciated.

Changes

Many of the trek descriptions in this edition of the book have been changed or modified since the last edition. This has been caused by the developing political situation in the J&K state, by the Indian government reviewing its inner line areas and by road developments which have over the last 20 years changed the character of many Himalayan valleys and villages.

Most of the trek descriptions in Kashmir have been omitted from this edition as the region is not currently safe for trekking. The inclusion of four of the most popular treks out of Pahalgam is in anticipation of an improvement in the current situation. Simi-

larly, the treks out of Kishtwar in the Jammu region have been omitted from this edition.

In the 1990s the Indian government relaxed its regulations regarding the need for inner line permits in a number of regions in the Indian Himalaya. In Ladakh, the Nubra Valley region is now open to travellers although the trekking possibilities are at present restricted to the Digar La, a trekking pass over the Ladakh Range linking Leh to the Nubra Valley. In Himachal the regions of Kinnaur and Spiti have been derestricted allowing trekkers to complete the trek around Kinnaur Kailas and also to trek from the Kullu Valley to Spiti via the Pin Parbati Pass. In Uttarakhand the Milam Glacier region is now derestricted allowing many challenging treks to be made east of the Nanda Devi Sanctuary.

Road developments have also had an impact on trekking routes. In Ladakh there are plans to develop the road from Nimmu up the Zanskar River to the Markha Valley, which will eventually link these villages by road to Leh. It is likely that by the next edition of this book these developments will have reached the lower villages in the Markha Valley making the area less attractive for trekkers. There are also plans to develop a road up the Zanskar Gorge to the Zanskar region. This, however, is easier said than done, for even the inventive Ladakhi trailmakers have not been able to construct a walking trail along the precipitous gorge.

While in some cases road developments over short sections do not totally undermine the trekking experience, in others the development of the road makes the trek no longer viable. In the early 1980s the trek from Chamba to Manali was still a delightful 10-day walk. Today the road has been completed in many stages and the trek, even over the Sach Pass to Chamba, is no longer attractive.

On the other hand there have been some gains for trekkers. Local protest groups in Manali have been able to stop the road leading to the Kun Zum La being extended to beautiful Chandra Tal in Lahaul.

The road tunnel being commenced under

the Pir Panjal, linking Manali and the Beas Valley with Lahaul, although having considerable effect on the development of Lahaul, will eventually undermine the need to maintain the road over the Rhotang Pass, making this route once again attractive for future generations of trekkers.

Place Names & Terminology

There are many variations between the names listed in this book and names in other maps or guides. This is because there is often no universally accepted form of transliteration of Kashmiri, Ladakhi or Hindi names into English.

A number of local terms are used throughout this book. For example, when trekking in Ladakh we frequently pass Buddhist *mani* walls (walls containing stones carved with prayers) and *chortens* (reliquaries or shrines to the memory of a Buddhist saint). In Kashmir we come across Bakharval shepherds while in Himachal the wandering shepherds who come from the region of Kangra are known as Gaddis. Gujar shepherds, on the other hand, frequent many of the less remote valleys in Kashmir, Himachal and Uttar Pradesh. When staying overnight on a trek we sometimes stay in PWD huts, Forest Rest Houses or Dak bungalows where the *chowkidar* (caretaker) may be able to arrange *dhal bhat* (lentils and rice) to eat. In Ladakh we may finish the evening off with a glass of *rakshi* (rice wine) while during the day a bucket of *chang* (barley beer) provides a less intoxicating refreshment. On some stages in Kashmir and Himachal we cross a *nullah* (river bed), while in Ladakh we cross a *la* (pass) in order to traverse a mountain range. A glossary of these and other terms is included at the end of the book.

GUIDES & PORTERS
Guides

A Himalayan trek is not just a question of getting from point A to point B. It provides an opportunity to appreciate the village culture or the flora and fauna or many of the other things that bring trekkers to India. A local guide, for these reasons, can enhance your experience of the region you visit. The task of showing the way is but one of many roles that he can undertake. Clearly guiding is an important role, so it is necessary to ensure that your guide is fully conversant with the route before hiring him. If you decide to go ahead, then it is the guide's job to hire the porters or horsemen for you and to ensure that the trek arrangements are organised smoothly and safely. He can also be invaluable in the case of inclement weather or an accident when outside help may be needed. And he can help you chat with the local villagers.

The cost of hiring a local guide varies considerably. There are many self-styled guides who are worse than useless. In such cases you are better off just hiring a porter who speaks English. On the other hand, a professional guide recommended by a reputable organisation is worth his weight in gold. Expect to pay around Rs 200 per day for a local guide, while more professional guides will expect up to Rs 1000 plus equipment allowance.

Horsemen & Porters

Porters or horsemen are generally hired from the roadhead or a major town before you undertake the trek. They can be organised by a local agency or you can do it yourself. A list of the agencies and the porter rates is given in the introduction to each trek.

Wages The going rate for porters will vary tremendously, depending on where you are trekking and the season. Generally the rates will rise during the harvest season from the middle of August to the middle of September. Also, horsemen and porters will bargain for better rates at the margins of the season. Horsemen in Manali, for instance, are not keen to trek over the Shingo La to the Zanskar Valley after the middle of September for fear that they will be stranded for the winter, and will charge at least double their normal daily rate of Rs 200 per packhorse.

Daily porter rates will vary from Rs 60 to Rs 80 out of Gangotri, while porters hired from Padum will demand up to Rs 2000 to complete the five trekking stages over the Umasi La. In between, expect to pay around Rs 100 to Rs 150 per day for a porter to carry between 20 kg and 30 kg. An estimate of the cost of hiring porters or horsemen is given in the introduction to each trek.

Clothing & Equipment Most porters and horsemen will expect a clothing and equipment allowance before undertaking a trek. This may include buying local rubber boots, woollen gloves and snow goggles in the market. It is your responsibility to ensure that both horsemen and porters are properly equipped. This will include the provision of a mess tent and a cooking stove plus an adequate supply of kerosene. When issuing items of equipment it is important to clarify whether they are to be returned at the end of the trek. Hiring porters through a local agency should minimise related disputes.

Porter Insurance Most reputable trekking companies in India insure all staff including casual staff. It is a legal requirement in India and if you undertake to hire porters directly then you are technically acting as the employer and must assume the responsibilities. The problem is that you can rarely buy insurance at the same time as you are hiring, particularly in remote regions. It is, when all is said and done, easier to pay a higher price through a local agency and let it deal with this problem.

CLOTHING & FOOTWEAR

Clothing considerations differ widely from trek to trek. A short hike to Dodi Tal in Uttar Pradesh could be undertaken with just the basics, as you are likely to trek in shorts, cotton shirt, a warm pullover, sandshoes and a sun hat, plus a good waterproof jacket. However, if you are considering an extended trek involving crossing a number of passes, then it is imperative that you bring along far more comprehensive gear.

One of the most important considerations is the manner in which you trek: clearly, if you are using packhorses then weight is not such a problem as when carrying all your gear in a backpack. The checklist below must therefore be interpreted with a degree of flexibility. Experienced bushwalkers will already have a good idea of what they believe is most suitable, but for those with less outdoor experience the following hints may prove useful.

In all mountain areas you should be prepared for inclement weather. Remember that most of the clothing that you would take on a weekend bushwalk is suitable for trekking the Himalayan foothills. During the period in which you will be walking in India, heat will be just as much a consideration as the cold. For the majority of treks you will not be walking in snow, and it is not necessary to equip yourself with double boots and heavy down gear as if you were about to climb Everest. A sturdy pair of boots is always recommended, as are a good wind and waterproof jacket and a comfortable backpack adequate for your needs.

If you are travelling exclusively in India and are not prepared to carry huge quantities of trekking gear around, you can practically equip yourself in India. A local tailor can make up a pair of shorts and comfortable long trousers in an afternoon. Raw wool pullovers, long johns, string vests, gloves, socks and balaclavas can be purchased in the bazaars; local hunter boots are just about adequate for a short valley trek. The state government tourist offices in Srinagar, Leh and Manali, plus the GMVN offices in Uttarkashi and Joshimath, have some trekking gear for hire, but cannot be compared to the local trekking and clothing shops found in Kathmandu.

Clothing & Footwear Checklist

Walking Boots These are the most important item when considering your trekking gear. Boots must give good ankle support and have a sole flexible enough to cope with the anticipated walking conditions. A sole fitted with a three-quarter length shank is not necessary unless you intend to tackle extensive snow and glacial terrain. Ensure that your boots are well walked-in beforehand, and don't forget to bring spare laces and some waterproofing application such as Dubbin. Some of the high-tech, lightweight boots are recommended although not for the higher treks over 3500m or where you are likely to be walking continually through scree and rocks for days at a time.

Light Footwear Sandshoes or tennis shoes can be purchased locally and are ideal for wandering around camp at night. Try to dry your feet out as much as possible at the end of the day's trekking; a pair of thongs or open sandals will help to get the air circulating around your feet.

Socks Take at least three pairs of woollen outer and cotton inner socks for a 10-day trek or longer. A cotton inner sock liner is useful in taking the rub and sweat out of breaking in a new pair of boots. If wearing liners, heavy outer socks are likely to need less washing than the liner.

Down Vest A down vest is recommended for those chilly mornings. If you already have a down or fibre-filled jacket, there is no harm in bringing it along, although the temperatures on your trek are seldom likely to call for its use, except on some of the higher altitude treks.

Wool Shirt, Pullover or Synthetic Pile Jacket A thick woollen shirt is worth its weight in gold. This is an item that does not cost the earth but can contribute greatly to your total wellbeing. As an alternative, raw wool pullovers can be purchased locally in Srinagar, Leh and Manali for about Rs 150. Synthetic pile or fleece jackets are recommended, being warm and easy to keep clean and very easy to dry after rainfall.

Shorts & Skirts You will probably wear shorts or a skirt for most of the day. They should not be worn in villages, monasteries or others places were they may cause offence to the locals. Ensure they are loose fitting, with plenty of pockets. The skimpy, cut-down variety are inappropriate for both men and women to wear in these areas. Culottes are an alternative to skirts.

Shirts T-shirts are OK, but include cotton shirts with collar and sleeves to give much-needed protection from the sun. Ex-army shirts with plenty of pockets are ideal.

Sunhat A wide-brimmed hat is ideal although it can get carried away in a high wind. Always take an additional sunhat with you as hats are forever being left on walls beside the trail!

Wind & Waterproof Jacket A Gore-Tex jacket will best serve your needs in the Himalaya, and will be an invaluable asset on any outdoor trip you undertake when you return home. Select one that gives protection from the wind as well as the rain, as wind-chill can lead to hypothermia.

Over-Trousers A strong, waterproof pair is indispensable in wet weather.

Trousers A pair of woollen walking breeches is ideal for cold weather. Ex-army woollen pants are another option. Pile trousers provide a satisfactory alternative but are virtually always too hot for the walking part of the day. Tracksuit bottoms are fine if you are not likely to be going above 3500m. Jeans are totally unsuitable in wet conditions as they take the heat away from the body.

Thermal Underwear Both thermal vest and bottoms can make a significant difference to your comfort. A double-layered vest is especially recommended, particularly if you are unsure of the adequacy of your sleeping bag. Also include a normal quantity of regular underwear for the trek.

Gloves & Balaclava Both items can be purchased locally in the Srinagar, Manali and Leh markets. A balaclava is particularly important as considerable body heat is lost through the head. Wear it to bed on cold nights.

Tracksuit A tracksuit is a useful item for sitting round camp in the evening.

Snow Gaiters If you already own gaiters and are undertaking a trek in the early part of the season when the trails can be under soft snow, then they are well worth bringing. If your itinerary only involves one or two high pass crossings later in the season (from August onwards), then gaiters are not so important.

Snow Goggles/Sunglasses Good-quality eyewear such as ski goggles are necessary to combat the glare of the snow. Even if you are not actually walking on snow, the side glare from snow on the ridges can make goggles necessary. For non-snow conditions sunglasses are adequate. You should take a few spare pairs of sunglasses for the porters and staff if you are trekking early in the season before snow melt or intend to traverse high snow passes. These can be purchased in the local bazaar.

EQUIPMENT

Over the last few seasons a number of outlets in Delhi have acquired stocks of lightweight equipment for hire. In Delhi it is best to check with the Government of India Tourist Office in Janpath for up-to-date lists of stockists. However, serious trekkers making their own arrangements are still advised to bring their own tent, sleeping bag, insulated mat, stove and backpack. For those undertaking an inclusive trek, professional agencies usually provide these items, although it is advisable to double check exactly what is provided before you leave for India.

Equipment Checklist

Holdall A strong duffel bag or holdall is necessary for carrying your gear on the packhorses. This is preferable to bringing along an expensive rucksack that may end up in less than pristine condition after it has been tied on horses or yaks for 20 days at a time. The holdall should be large enough to contain all your personal gear. Strong garbage bags are ideal for lining the duffel

bag and ensuring that your gear is protected from the elements.

Stuff Bags Some cloth bags that close with a drawstring are recommended so you can separate your clean gear from the not so clean, and therefore do not have to repack all your gear every day. They are also useful for packing food items which may melt or disintegrate en route.

Backpack An internal-frame backpack is ideal for longer treks and it is recommended that you try it out for a few weekends before your trek to get the feel of what you will be carrying when you are on the trail. If you will not be backpacking, ensure that your day pack is large enough to carry your toilet gear, camera, waterproof jacket and sweater, as the packhorses may not be at hand during a sudden change of weather during the day. Given the cost of good backpacks it is recommended that you invest in a cheap kitbag big enough to hold your backpack for protection when travelling on planes and buses.

Walking Stick A walking stick or ski pole is indispensable for extended walks and river crossings and gives confidence on long downhill walks.

Water Bottle A sturdy aluminium or plastic water bottle is recommended; plastic bottles can be purchased locally.

Swiss Army Knife The pride of any shepherd's possessions, it is always useful for peeling fruit and opening tins; one with a small screwdriver can be invaluable for carrying out camera repairs.

Torch (Flashlight) These are available in India; don't forget spare batteries and bulbs.

Head Torch A head torch is invaluable for reading, attending to camp chores or trekking at night.

Umbrella Available locally, to shield you from the rain and the sun, an umbrella is also handy when making discreet calls of nature.

First Aid Kit Refer to the Health, Safety & First Aid chapter for recommendations on what to include.

Miscellaneous Don't forget toiletries, toilet paper, waterproof matches, sun block, towel, laundry soap, sewing kit, safety pins, a length of cord, and some small plastic bags to carry toilet paper and litter until you can dispose of it properly. A padlock can also come in very handy.

Optional Extras You could consider carrying altimeter, compass, binoculars, notebook and pens.

Equipment for Independent Trekkers

Additional equipment should be carried by trekkers going it alone. This checklist serves as a guide only and must be geared to the trekker's level of experience and expertise in the outdoors.

Tent A dome, tunnel or A-framed tent is necessary on most treks. Select a tent that you can use at home and try it out in inclement conditions before bringing it to India. Ensure that the tent is fully waterproof and that you have spare rods or poles. Also check that the zips are in good repair as on-the-spot repairs are often difficult. Your own tent will give you the flexibility to select the best possible camping spot and allow you to appreciate the scenery with a degree of solitude. However, you must also consider the requirements of the porters or horsemen coming along with you and a mess tent should be hired to accommodate them.

Sleeping Bag Bring along the best sleeping bag that you can afford. Ensure that it gives you a rating of at least minus 5°C, as even during the middle of summer there can be cold and windy nights. Fibrefill bags dry a lot faster in wet conditions, although those filled with down are more compact and lighter.

Insulating Mat A closed-cell foam mat should provide adequate insulation from the ground. A space blanket can double as a ground sheet. A Therm-a-Rest or inflatable foam mat is a bonus and well worth bringing despite what some hardy types may say.

Rope Whatever trek you are undertaking, a 40 metre length of rope is highly recommended for ensuring safe river crossings, particularly in Kashmir, the Kullu Valley and the Garhwal in the early part of the season, and in Ladakh and the Zanskar Valley in the middle of summer.

Cooking Utensils Cooking pots and pans, enamel mugs, plates and cutlery (in fact all kitchen utensils) can be purchased in India. Camping Gaz containers or refills are not available. Local kerosene stoves provide a cheap and efficient alternative, although most locals use wood fires for cooking their evening meals. Remember to take spare parts and an ample supply of stove pins. In fact, practise taking the stove apart before you set off to ensure that you are fully conversant with its operation. If you have hired a cook then you can request he brings all the kitchen gear. It is also preferable to carry your own mug and cutlery during the day. This is particularly important if a trek member is sick, as it lets everyone in the group take responsibility for washing their own utensils.

Miscellaneous Plastic drums for carrying kerosene, mustard oil and the like can be purchased locally. Large canvas mess tents, for your crew to sleep in during the trek, can be hired at some of the trekking-off points such as Leh or Manali. Others may have to be hired further afield or in Delhi before you set out.

Equipment for High-Altitude Treks

For treks which traverse glaciers – for example, over the Boktol Pass on the Pahalgam to Ladakh trek; over the Umasi La on the Zanskar to Manali trek; and over the Kang La on the Udaipur to Padum trek – trekkers must bring basic safety equipment.

This includes rope, ice axe, harness and karabiners as most of these items are not readily available for hire in India. In the early part of the season, from May until the middle of July, many of the other passes over the Pir Panjal, the Great Himalaya or Zanskar Range will be under snow. A length of rope together with an ice axe can be invaluable for cutting steps on the steeper sections and for assisting horsemen or porters along trail sections that might be unduly icy or exposed.

RESPONSIBLE TREKKING

The increasing number of trekkers has highlighted the need for responsible trekking policies in the Indian Himalaya. In the 1970s there was, for instance, only a handful of companies offering the challenging three-week trek between Phalagam or Lehinvan in the Kashmir Valley and Heniskot or Lamayuru in Ladakh. By 1989 over 30 trekking companies throughout the world were offering similar itineraries. The adverse effect on the environment was acknowledged: camp sites were being turned into regular garbage dumps. There was also the very obvious effect on the local culture. Villagers in the Warvan Valley in Kashmir no longer treated trekking groups as honoured guests, Bakharval shepherds in the alpine valleys regularly broke into trekkers' tents, while in Ladakh a generation of children latched onto the 'one pen' mantra. Thoughtless groups selected camp sites close to the villagers' source of water and arguments became the order of the day as packhorsemen were confronted by villagers anxious to protect grazing areas that had until then been set aside for communal use.

There were many other examples of detrimental effects in Zanskar, in Himachal and in the remoter regions of Uttarakhand that undermined the environment, the local culture and the trekking experience.

These developments have led to much discussion as to whether there is a need now for more legislation. The self-regulation that has so far been the norm for trekking companies and individuals needs to be examined and, at the very least, a user-pays concept

introduced to combat some of the worst effects of trekking. In the meantime the following may help to lessen our impact on both the local culture and the environment.

People & Culture

The tradition of hospitality has been an integral part of the way of life of most Himalayan peoples. There would be few villages in the remote valleys where you would not be greeted on arrival and offered tea and a place where you could unpack your sleeping bags for the night. Beyond the villages, the shepherds grazing their herds throughout the summer months accept you as an honoured guest when you reach their encampment. It is essential that this not be undermined, although it is acknowledged that some undesirable developments are already occurring.

While the overwhelming majority of the people we meet on the trail are honest, theft has been a cause for concern, with trekking groups complaining of their camps being raided for boots, socks and other trekking clothing. Medical demands are also a cause for concern, with requests for medications being made on the assumption that most European trekkers are either doctors or have access to cure-all drugs. On the more popular trails the children ask for one rupee, or for their photograph to be taken, or demand sweets or lollies as trekkers pass through the villages.

Some problems arise from curiosity. Many local people are still confused about why you should want to trek. If you are not trading, or on a tour of inspection such as with the local Forest Officers, or en route to see relatives and friends, then there seems no reason to walk for walking's sake. Suspicions arise when no plausible answer is given. Consider how you would feel if a group of Indian trekkers marched into your town or village and set up camp in the village green or park without any plausible reason.

Remember that it is hard to describe to people who have always lived among such magnificent mountain panoramas that there are places in the world where we live that do not have access to such beauty. Try to explain clearly why you have visited their village. Let's face it, trekking is very much an indulgence. Trying to convey our work or lifestyle pressures is difficult, particularly to people who are subject each year to the vagaries of the seasons.

In order to enhance your time on the trail it is also necessary to observe the following social and cultural considerations:

Dress Codes Wear appropriate clothing while in a village or encampment. Neither women nor men should wear high-cut shorts, although long, baggy shorts are sometimes OK for men. Women should wear trekking trousers or tracksuit pants and loose-fitting tops. When entering a home, temple, mosque or monastery always remove your shoes unless specifically told otherwise.

Bargaining Always be fair in bargaining situations and always keep your word. If you have promised to pay a porter for six stages which you discover later you could complete in two, so be it. The porters must be paid the agreed amount. The same applies to staff and horsemen.

Photography Never take photographs until you have secured permission. Never offer money for photographs unless there is a particular sign in a monastery requesting a donation.

Theft Don't encourage theft by leaving high-value items around the camp site.

Washing Nudity is completely unacceptable and a swimsuit must be worn even when bathing in a remote locality; even this is sometimes inappropriate.

Etiquette Never throw food into a fire whether at a camp site or in a home. It is also expedient not to touch food or cooking utensils that local people will use, particularly when trekking through Hindu regions. Also, you should use your right hand for all social interactions, whether passing money or food or any other item.

For religious reasons do not touch local people on the head and similarly never direct the soles of your feet at a person or religious shrine as this may again cause offence.

Overt public displays of affection should be avoided.

Gifts Avoid handing out pens, balloons and sweets to children in the villages, but do take the time to have genuine interactions with them. Indeed, bring photograph albums of your family, bring musical instruments, learn a few local phrases, learn a few folk songs or folk dances. Learn the rudiments of cricket – anything that can help establish a relationship without the need to offer money or presents. Once a relationship is established then the children in the Himalaya are as trusting as anywhere else in the world and experiences can be shared rather than stifled.

Environment

For many seasons the trekking traditions in the Indian Himalaya had only a minimal impact on the environment. Even 20 years ago a trekker would undertake a trek with a minimum of canned or bottled goods, while plastic bags were a novelty. After breaking camp in those days there was a minimum of rubbish which, even if not properly disposed of, was mainly biodegradable (such as vegetable and fruit peels, egg shells and the like). There was also an abundance of dead wood in many of the valleys to gather for a modest fire for cooking and warmth.

Nowadays there is an increasing demand for tinned food and lunches packed in plastic bags. The number of batteries carried, together with glass cordial bottles and plastic bottles for mineral water, is cause for serious concern. Garbage disposal is now high on the list of priorities. Trekkers are advised to carry out what they don't consume.

Toilet trenches need to be dug and maintained, and matches should be carried to burn toilet paper. The increase in the number of trekkers has even led to crews cutting green wood for fires.

The Himalayan Adventure Trust

Since 1990 the Himalayan Trust has sought to gain co-operation from Pakistan, Nepal and India to draw attention to the environmental problems affecting the Himalaya. In doing so it has drawn on worldwide support to help protect the Himalayan environment. The aims and objectives set out by the Trust include:

Support Groups The mobilisation of support from mountaineers, trekkers, alpine clubs, adventure tour operators and the Himalayan region governments for protecting the environment, its flora, fauna and natural resources, as well as the customs and interests of the local people.

Codes of Conduct To evolve a code of conduct and ethics to be followed by all visitors to the Himalayan region, as part of a continuing effort to maintain and sustain the well being of the Himalayan environment.

Promoting Awareness To hold international conferences, seminars and Himalayan tourist meets on problems relating to the Himalayan environment, and focus world attention on such matters.

Information To exchange information, and co-operate with other local, national and international agencies engaged in similar work, such as the International Centre for Integrated Mountain Development in Kathmandu.

Guidelines for Adventure Tourism To evolve necessary guidelines – in consultation with the Himalayan countries – concerning adventure tourism, to avoid the overcrowding of trails and to achieve a fair spread of trekkers and mountaineers throughout the Himalaya. ∎

These environmental problems were for years ignored in many regions of the Indian Himalaya, where the harsh winter conditions and heavy snowfall helped garbage that had been left behind to decompose. With increasing numbers of trekkers this is no longer the case, and many of the more popular camp sites are not able to recover from one season to the next. In Ladakh, in particular, this has become apparent. Large groups are now undermining the delicate environmental balance.

The following guidelines may help to combat this situation:

Rubbish When you arrive at a camp site, begin by clearing up any garbage that has been left by previous trekking groups. This will impress the crew and illustrate a genuine concern to preserve the camp site. It will also, more often than not, help them to see the importance of not leaving non-biodegradable rubbish behind. If trekking with porters ensure that you bring a few bags for carrying out bottles, tin cans and plastic bags. Provide an incentive (a tip in most cases) to ensure that the garbage bags are carried out to the trailhead.

Food Try to ensure that a minimum of non-biodegradable food is brought with you. If you are employing a cook, brief him beforehand. What you don't carry in terms of tins of food you don't have to carry out as empty cans. Also ensure that you buy all major food supplies before undertaking the trek, in particular staples such as rice and flour, so as not to put pressure on the economy of local villages along the trail.

Washing Wash all clothes and equipment in biodegradable soap in a bucket well away from the water supply. This is imperative if the water supply provides drinking water for a local village or settlement.

Fires Limit the use of wood fires by ensuring that you bring ample supplies of kerosene with you. Don't forget a stove and a supply of kerosene for the porters or horsemen. Limit the amount of dead wood collected to that required for a modest camp fire, and never burn wood for this purpose until well beyond the village areas.

Toilet Dig toilet trenches well away from camp sites. Provide a trowel or shovel for the staff to bury their faeces. Burn all toilet paper and ensure all faeces are buried after a call of nature while trekking during the day.

Health, Safety & First Aid

The material on trekkers' health and first aid in this section was prepared by Dr Jim Duff, a doctor with wide experience of medical treatment in remote areas.

A suitable first aid course including cardiopulmonary resuscitation (CPR) is highly recommended.

Good reference books include *The Himalayan First Aid Manual* by Dr Jim Duff & Dr Peter Gormley (available through outdoor equipment shops), and *Medicine for Mountaineering*, edited by James Wilkerson and published by the Mountaineers, Seattle, WA, USA.

Preparations for a Trek

MEDICAL CHECK-UP
It is recommended that you have a physical and dental examination before undertaking your trek. Anyone with long-term symptoms (such as indigestion, chest pain, wheezing or coughing, back or joint problems, recurrent infections, or dental problems) should have them thoroughly investigated before leaving home. All problems are exacerbated by altitude and strenuous exercise, and seem more serious in proportion to your distance from medical help.

IMMUNISATION & PROPHYLAXIS
Some of the diseases that you may encounter in India can be prevented by vaccination and prophylaxis. Plan ahead as some vaccinations require an initial dose followed by a booster.

Tetanus-Diphtheria A booster is recommended if it is more than 10 years since the last shot, especially if you are over 50 years old.

Polio Have a booster if it is more than 10 years since the last one. Primary adult immunisation must be by injection.

Typhoid A primary course or a booster is recommended if it's more than three years since the last one. It can be given orally or by injection.

Hepatitis A Gamma globulin gives prophylaxis against hepatitis A. One five-ml dose lasts four months. This gives passive protection and is administered just before your departure. Longer-term protection is now available by vaccination.

Meningococcal Meningitis The vaccine gives three years protection.

Rabies Optional, pre-exposure vaccination is available. Post-exposure vaccination is available in larger medical centres. It is expensive.

Malaria Prophylaxis Protection is given by chloroquine phosphate or sulphate 500 mg weekly, plus proguanil 200 mg daily. Alternatively, take doxycycline 100 mg daily or Mefloquine* (* indicates a trade name) 250 mg weekly. These should be taken from two weeks before entering until four weeks after leaving the malarial area. Check the latest public health recommendations, as drug resistance changes.

Cholera This vaccination is not currently recommended in Asia.

TRAVEL INSURANCE
A travel insurance policy is vital if you are going trekking. While most general travel insurances cover you against sickness while on a trek, not all cover you for emergency evacuation, which could run into many thousands of dollars if a helicopter were required. Remember that, should evacuation be necessary, some proof of insurance and of your ability to pay will save time, and perhaps even a life. Bear in mind that most embassies in Delhi will authorise evacuation only after

contacting your next of kin, and that, again, can take days.

FIRST AID KIT

The kit to take on your trek will depend on the length of the trek, its remoteness and the number of people going. It will also depend on the degree of confidence and knowledge you have in handling medical situations.

The following list has been prepared as a rough guide, and needs to be varied depending on the above considerations. It is adequate for a group of four to six persons on a moderate trek of two weeks duration.

Drugs are listed under their indications by their generic names, followed, in some cases, by trade names (indicated by *). A description and guide to dosage is given in the medication chart later in this chapter. For more details of dosage and administration of these drugs, follow the instructions of the manufacturer or the doctor who prescribed them. In cases of known drug allergy take the appropriate alternatives.

Instruments
    scissors, tweezers, thermometer, sewing needle, safety pins, scalpel blade plus handle
Dressings
    steristrips (two packets), cotton buds, large roll cotton wool, a minimum of 10 pieces of sterile gauze squares, 10 pieces of 10 cm sq sterile dressing, triangular bandage, Band-Aids, moleskin, 2.5 cm adhesive tape, 10 cm adhesive bandage, 10 cm elastic bandage, two crepe bandages
Antiseptics
    Betadine*, Dettol*, Lugol's solution, burn cream
Analgesics (pain killers)
    paracetamol (30 tablets), aspirin (20 tablets), codeine phosphate (15 tablets), Fortral* (15 tablets)
Antibiotics (infection)
    metronidazole (enough for two courses), ciprofloxacin (enough for two 10 day courses), Bactrim DS* or Septrin Forte* (20 tablets) or amoxycillin (enough for one 10 day course) or erythromycin (enough for one 10 day course)
Ear & eye infection
    ear and eye drops
Diarrhoea medications
    rehydration salt sachet eg Gastrolyte* or Jeevan Jal* (10 sachets)
    Imodium* or Lomotil* (20 tablets or capsules)

Fungal infection
    Canestan*
Nausea & vomiting
    Stemetil* or Maxolon* (10 tablets and 5 suppositories)
Constipation
    Durolax*
Haemorrhoids
    Rectinol* ointment or suppositories
Allergies
    Diphenydramine HCl, Benadryl* (15 tablets), antihistamine cream, Anthisan*, hydrocortisone cream, Hydrocort*
Sore throat
    Strepsil* lozenges (30)
Nasal decongestant
    Dristan* or Drixine*
Indigestion
    Antacid tablets (20 tablets)
Acute Mountain Sickness
    Diamox* (30 tablets)

Hygiene on the Trek

Prevention is better than cure. Careful attention to water purification, food preparation and personal hygiene will prevent many of the diseases encountered while trekking. Read also the sections on diarrhoea and malaria later in this chapter.

Water Purification

The adage 'don't drink the water' applies equally in the Himalaya as elsewhere in India. The following points should be observed:

Boiling Bringing water to the boil sterilises it even at high altitudes. If the water has a lot of sediment or is heavily contaminated boil for two minutes.

Iodine Iodine tablets, or Lugol's iodine solution, are a reliable method for sterilising water for drinking, cooking or washing. Lugol's solution can be purchased locally in India. Add eight drops to a litre of water and wait 30 minutes. Wait longer if the water is very cold or particularly polluted. Iodine tablets are best purchased in your own country. Do not add flavouring crystals or rehydration solution to your drinking water until sterilisation is completed.

Water Filters Lightweight water filters are available. They are only effective if they combine physical and chemical filters. Water filters provide an alternative to those who do not like the taste of iodine. They are not available in India.

Food Preparation
Be particularly careful to ensure everyone washes their hands thoroughly with soap before the preparation of food. All water used in the preparation of food and washing of pots and utensils must be sterilised. Salads should be soaked for half an hour or more in water containing one teaspoon of Lugol's solution for every four litres. Fruit should be peeled before eating.

Stopping at wayside tea shops is part of the trekking experience. Be selective: choose clean premises with happy, healthy owners and freshly cooked food. Consider carrying your own cup and eating utensils.

Personal Hygiene
The best way to prevent the diarrhoeas which plague travellers and trekkers is to break the cycle of faecal-oral contamination by washing one's hands regularly with soap and water throughout the day. This applies particularly while travelling through population centres.

Clean socks, cotton underwear and sweat shirt will prevent skin infections. Chafing should be dealt with as soon as it is noticed. Toenails should be clipped short and one's feet pampered and massaged.

Climatic Extremes
If you lie half in the shade and half in the sun at high altitude it is possible to get sunburn and frostbite at the same time! The best way to describe the trekking environment in the Himalaya is 'extreme'. Sudden changes in the weather are to be expected. To cope with this, layers of clothing, finishing with a wind and waterproof outer shell, are required. Hypothermia is an ever present threat when

wind and rain combine. (See the section on hypothermia later in thhis chapter.)

A broad-brimmed hat, UV-proof glasses with side blinkers and an SPF 15-plus sun block will protect against the increased solar radiation at altitude. The air can be very dry, and a scarf and lip balm are essential. Hard exercise, heat and dry air promote dehydration so carrying a water bottle, and using it, is essential.

Accident & Emergencies

Prompt and effective management of cases of collapse or trauma increases the victim's chances of survival especially in the first hour or so after an accident. A brief outline of the correct response to various emergencies follows:

CARDIOPULMONARY RESUSCITATION
These notes on cardiopulmonary resuscitation (CPR) are a reminder for those with training. If you don't know CPR, a training course is highly recommended.

If a person collapses for whatever reasons, don't panic! Before approaching or handling the victim, be aware of any danger to yourself and take appropriate action.

Determine if the victim is conscious or unconscious: shake the victim firmly by the shoulders, ask for their name, command them to squeeze your hand. If they don't respond, they are unconscious and you must proceed as follows:

The 'ABC' Method
Airway Quickly turn the victim on the side with head tilted backward and face turned slightly down. Clear the mouth of vomit, loose teeth or foreign material.

Breathing Check for breathing by listening and feeling at the victim's mouth and nose. If not breathing, quickly turn the person on their back and tilt the head back, then give five quick breaths, mouth to mouth, with their nose pinched closed. Now feel the carotid pulse in the groove alongside the windpipe. If there is a pulse, give mouth to mouth breathing at the rate of one breath every five seconds.

Circulation If the pulse is absent this means the heart has stopped and that heart compression must be started. This is a specialised technique which requires training on dummies. Do not practise on living persons. Compress the lower half of the breast bone four to five cm (1½ to two inches) slightly faster than once a second. Kneel beside the patient, rock from your hips, with arms locked straight and the heel of the palm on the lower half of the breast bone – one hand on top of the other. After 15 compressions give two full breaths (making sure the head is in full backward tilt). If there are two rescuers the ratio is five compressions to one breath. Stop compression and check for the carotid pulse every two to three minutes. If the heart restarts, continue with mouth to mouth breathing only, at the rate of one breath every five seconds.

Assessment of the Victim
Once airway, breathing and circulation are established do a primary survey of the whole body. This is done to assess quickly the victim's injuries, as one obvious injury may distract from other problems. If the victim is conscious ask them where it hurts. Feel lightly around the head and look for blood. Feel and squeeze the shoulders, arms, and hands, the chest, pelvis, legs and feet. Apply gentle pressure to the belly and finally feel underneath the person for pooling blood. When all injuries have been dealt with, a thorough secondary survey should be performed. Always suspect head, neck or spinal injury (see the following section).

Care of the Unconscious (but Breathing) or Semiconscious Victim
Place the victim on the side with the top leg bent at the hip and knee to stabilise the body (lateral position). Maintain the backward

Vital Signs

Condition	Recognition
Normal temperature	oral 37.0°C (98.4°F), rectal 37.6°C (99.7°F)
normal (adult) pulse rate	60 to 80 beats per minute
normal respiratory rate	12 to 14 breaths per minute
normal urine output	at least 500 ml (one pint) of pale yellow urine per day

head tilt. Monitor the breathing and the pulse, and provide protection from the elements.

HEAD, NECK & SPINAL INJURY
When a neck or spinal injury is suspected, movement of the victim must be kept to an absolute minimum. If the victim must be moved, support the head and keep the pelvis, shoulders and head in alignment to avoid sideways bending or rotation of the spine.

If the patient is unconscious, nurse in the lateral position with the airway open. Stabilise the neck and back using appropriate padding and strapping on a rigid surface. Examine the pupils of the patient's eyes, which may have become unequal in size or unresponsive to light shone in them. Both are signs of cerebral trauma and need urgent medical attention.

Keep the victim under observation as unconsciousness may occur many hours or days after an accident.

BLEEDING & WOUNDS
External bleeding is usually obvious, but check for absorption by clothing or pooling under the body. A pad of anything clean firmly pressed over a wound will stop most bleeding in five minutes. Don't keep dabbing the clot away. It may be necessary to elevate a limb to stop the bleeding. Cuts need to be

cleaned with an antiseptic and closed with steristrips (if necessary), a sterile dressing and a firm bandage. Leave the dressing in place until it becomes dirty. If infection (pain, redness, heat, discharge) sets in, change the bandage daily and give the patient an oral antibiotic.

BURNS

Burns are extremely painful and can cause shock due to the pain or the fluid loss. Cool the burn at once by using cold water or cold compresses for at least 10 to 20 minutes. Cover with a burn cream and a sterile dressing. Do not change the dressing unless it becomes soiled or infection sets in.

The pain may be severe and will need to be controlled using appropriate pain killers. Shock and dehydration occur in extensive burns and will need to be treated (read the section below on shock).

FRACTURES

Fractures may be recognised by deformity, swelling, pain and loss of use of the part. The pain may be severe. If there is deformity it may be possible to straighten the limb by slowly and gently pulling while moving the limb in the required direction. Someone else must stabilise the limb above the break during this manoeuvre. In the first minutes after a fracture there is a period of relative numbness when straightening deformed limbs is much easier. Check the circulation, and readjust the position if a pulse cannot be felt below the fracture.

Apply a well-padded splint, which prevents further injury to the tissues and reduces pain and shock. In a lower leg fracture the good leg may be used as part of the splint.

Check every 20 minutes to make sure the splint is not restricting the circulation. A cold, numb, painful, pulseless, white or purple limb with pins and needles and loss of use will tell you the circulation has been cut off, and you must loosen the splint. Air splints should be partially deflated before air evacuation.

If the fracture is compound (when the bone protrudes or is exposed to the air through a laceration), treat the wound and thoroughly disinfect the bone before proceeding as above. Give an antibiotic (Septrin* or amoxycillin).

SPRAINED ANKLE

Sprains are injuries to joints where the ligaments are partially torn but not completely ruptured. A badly sprained ankle may mimic a fracture. Swelling and bruising occur but limited movement is usually possible.

The general treatment for sprains is RICE (Rest, Ice or cold compresses, Compression and Elevation). Depending on the severity of the injury some degree of support must be provided with elastic or adhesive bandages. Limited weight bearing should be possile within a day or two, unlike with a fracure.

INTERNAL INJURIES

Abdominal organs may rupture or bleed in traumatic accidents in which case pressure on the belly with the flat of the hand will produce pain. The belly will feel rigid because the abdominal muscles are in spasm. Shock will occur and should be treated (see below). Do not give anything by mouth. Urgent evacuation is required.

SHOCK

Shock is caused by a lack of oxygen to the tissues due to loss of blood or other body fluids or low blood pressure. Common causes include: burns, fractures, bleeding (internal or external), severe diarrhoea, vomiting, heat exhaustion, heart attack or pain.

The victim looks pale, may be sweating, feels thirsty, afraid and faint, or is unconscious. The pulse is feeble and rapid, and they may be breathing rapidly.

Place the victim on their back (or on their side if unconscious) and raise their legs to an angle of 30 degrees. Rehydrate with rehydration solution, and treat the cause of shock adequately. Give liberal doses of reassurance.

Medical Problems

TAKING A HISTORY

If one of your party falls sick and the cause is not obvious, take a detailed history of the complaint including any previous occurrence of the symptoms. Ask about the duration of the complaint, its severity and location, and the factors which help or make things worse. Continue your analysis by asking about cough and chest pains, palpitations, headaches, numbness, tingling, abdominal pain, urinary or bowel symptoms and whether the victim is taking, or is allergic to, any drugs. Take the temperature, and pulse and respiration rate, feel the abdomen, and record the urine output and colour.

At altitude (above 3000m) always suspect acute mountain sickness (read the appropriate section following). When examining the person, a well-lit, quiet place is ideal. Remember also that a confident, reassuring approach works wonders when a patient is injured or sick. See the Medication Chart for doses of drugs mentioned in this section.

DIARRHOEA

Diarrhoea is a common and often debilitating complaint with a folklore all of its own. The infecting agents include viruses, bacteria, and protozoa (amoeba or giardia). Your gut teems with billions of normal bacteria which are essential to health. Disease-causing organisms enter your gut and displace the normal bacteria, causing the bowel wall to secrete fluid and dissolved electrolyte salts. This flushes the invading organism from the bowel. On occasions mucus, blood or both will be excreted. The gut wall also produces antibodies against certain viruses and bacteria, which accounts for the immunity to diarrhoea acquired by locals or long-term travellers.

The diarrhoea-causing organisms are ingested by consuming food or drink contaminated with infected stools, or merely by touching contaminated objects such as door knobs and then touching one's mouth. This is called faeco-oral contamination, and is very common in areas which have not developed high standards of sanitation and food preparation.

Prevention

Here are some basic points to remember: wash your hands with soap and water frequently, especially after defaecating and before meals. Sterilise drinking water and prepare food as explained at the beginning of this chapter. Drink tea or bottled drinks.

General Assessment & Treatment

Rehydration is the key to treatment, and applies to all the varieties of diarrhoea detailed below. Encourage fluid consumption so there is a minimum of 500 ml of urine every 24 hours, preferably more. The aim is to have plenty of pale-coloured urine. Use a rehydration salt solution, such as Gastrolyte* or Jeevan Jal*, or make one up from half a teaspoon of salt, four heaped teaspoons of sugar, plus a squeeze of lemon (if available), in one litre of water. The addition of two tablespoons of ground dry rice makes the mixture even more effective. Imodium* and Lomotil* only treat the symptoms. They should only be used if stool frequency is excessive or distressing, or if a long bus journey is to be undertaken. The aim should be to slow the diarrhoea but to avoid constipation. Do not use Imodium* or Lomotil* if blood appears in the stool. Stay on a diet of bland foods (rice, porridge, biscuits and black tea) and avoid fatty food, dairy products and alcohol.

Diarrhoea can be classified as mild and self-limiting or severe and needing antibiotic treatment. The antibiotic to choose will depend on the cause of the diarrhoea. The following descriptions are designed to help you choose appropriately. Unfortunately it may not be possible to clearly differentiate every case from symptoms alone.

Bacillary Dysentery

This is caused by salmonella, shigella or other pathogenic bacteria. It is more severe than other forms of diarrhoea, with an abrupt onset of profuse watery stools, fever and malaise. Occasionally mucus and, less frequently, blood will appear in the stools. Use an antibiotic such as Bactrim DS* for two or three days.

Giardia

Giardia is caused by a protozoa with a whip-like tail. The incubation period is at least one week. Symptoms may be slow to appear and consist of abdominal pain and discomfort after eating, with rotten egg burps and farts. Stools are explosive. If untreated, weight loss is common. The antibiotic to use is tinidazole (Tinibar*) or metronidazole (Flagyl*). Treatment failures may occur and a repeat course of the antibiotics may be needed.

Amoebic Dysentery

Like giardia, amoebic dysentery is slower in onset than bacillary dysentery, with two to three stools of a porridge consistency, sometimes with mucus or blood. There is marked pain on moving the bowels. If untreated, weight loss and lassitude become marked. Treatment is as for giardia for three days.

Food Poisoning

This is caused by eating food contaminated by bacterial toxin. It starts suddenly with acute abdominal pains, nausea, vomiting which can be severe, and diarrhoea. The victim may be pale and sweating. After 12 to 24 hours recovery is usually underway. No antibiotic is required. Rest and rehydrate. Control the vomiting with Maxolon* or Stemetil* suppositories if prolonged.

Non-specific Severe Diarrhoea

If you cannot decide which antibiotic to choose, try Bactrim DS*. Change to tinidazole or metronidazole if there is no improvement after 48 hours.

RESPIRATORY PROBLEMS

Respiratory problems are common at altitude and are often associated with a cough.

Sore Throat

Stop smoking (if a smoker), gargle warm salt water and use steam inhalations and antiseptic lozenges. If the problem is severe or persistent, use an appropriate antibiotic.

Sinusitis

An infection of the sinus cavities around the nose, sinusitis has symptoms of facial pain (with either a sudden or slow onset), fever and nasal discharge of pus. The treatment is the same as for a sore throat, plus nasal washouts with warm salt water (an eighth of a teaspoon of salt in two thirds of a glass of water), and the use of an antibiotic and a nasal decongestant such as Drixine*.

Bronchitis

This infection of the respiratory tubes is marked by a productive cough, especially early in the morning when large amounts of phlegm may be expectorated. It can become a chronic condition. The early morning chorus of coughs that greets one in the Himalaya is mostly chronic bronchitis. Treatment is with steam inhalations and antibiotics.

Pneumonia

An infection which has invaded the lung tissue, pneumonia is indicated by shortness of breath, fever, headaches, and often chest pain. Treatment is as for bronchitis, plus descent and evacuation.

For many years acute mountain sickness was mistaken for pneumonia but AMS is far more likely to be the cause of respiratory distress at altitude than pneumonia. See the AMS section later in this chapter.

CLIMATIC PROBLEMS
Hypothermia

Cold, wet and windy conditions can cool people's core temperature down enough to kill them. This can occur in the mountains on cold, wet and windy days over a period of hours or days (chronic hypothermia) or after immersion in cold water (acute hypothermia). Anyone falling into a Himalayan river will suffer from some degree of hypothermia.

As the core temperature starts to fall, shivering begins, only to disappear as heat

MEDICATION CHART

Generic or Trade* Names	Uses	Dosage	Remarks & Side Effects
Pain killers			
Aspirin*, Tasprin*	inflamed joints, aches, pains, flu, headache, fever	300-600 mg, 6-hourly	may cause indigestion, stomach bleeding, retinal bleeding at high altitude; take with food
Paracetamol (Panadol*)	fever, flu, headache, aches and pains	250-500 mg, 6-hourly (max 4000 mg per day)	safest pain killer at altitude
Codeine phosphate	moderate to severe pain, burns	10-60 mg, 8-hourly	strong pain killer, may cause respiratory depression (beware at altitude), and constipation; avoid alcohol
Pentazocine (Fortral* tablets)	severe pain, fractures, burns etc	25-100 mg, 3 to 4-hourly, 600 mg max daily	may cause respiratory depression (beware at altitude), hallucinations, avoid alcohol, avoid if under 12 years
Antibiotics			
Ciprofloxacin (Cipro*, Cifran*)	first-line treatment for severe infections eg bacillary dysentery with fever and blood or mucus in stool (does not treat giardia and amoebic dysentery); also as a second-line treatment for respiratory, skin, urinary tract and other infections	500 mg, 12-hourly for 5 to 10 days	take on empty stomach, keep patient hydrated; may cause reaction in penicillin-sensitive persons, avoid alcohol. Avoid if aged under 16 years. Use only if not improving on other antibiotics
Co-trimoxazole (Bactrim DS*, Septrin Forte*)	respiratory, skin, kidney, pelvic and urinary infection	one 12-hourly for 5 to 10 days	avoid in sulpha-allergy, avoid alcohol, stop immediately if rash appears
Erythromycin (Erythrocin*, ERC*)	respiratory (throat), ear, skin, urinary tract and other infections	250 mg 6-hourly for 5 to 10 days	a non penicillin and non-sulpha alternative, avoid alcohol
Amoxycillin (Amoxil*)	respiratory, skin, ear, wounds, kidney and urinary infection	500 mg, 8-hourly for 5 to 10 days	avoid in penicillin allergy, avoid alcohol
Metronidazole (Flagyl*)	specific antibiotic for giardia	400 mg, twice a day for six days	metallic taste, can cause depression, heartburn, avoid alcohol
Tinidazole (Tinibar*, Fasigyn*, Simplotan*)	amoebic dysentery, giardia	2 gm daily in 1 dose for 3 days	take one hour before meals; can cause depression, heartburn; avoid alcohol
Eye & ear infection			
eye & ear drops (eg Soframycin *)		2-3 drops, 2 to 8-hourly	can cause allergy
Fungicidal			
(Cotrimazole*, Canestan*)	fungal infection, athlete's foot, vaginal thrush	apply 8 to 12-hourly	skin infection requires 10 to 14 days treatment

Generic or Trade* Names	Uses	Dosage	Remarks & Side Effects
Anti-motility (anti-diarrhoea)			
Loperamide (Imodium*) or diphenoxylate (Lomotil*)	slows the diarrhoea	eg for loperamide, 2 caps then 1 after each loose motion (max 8 per day)	can cause constipation, avoid if diarrhoea is bloody. Note: these drugs do not kill the infection.
Rehydration salts			
(Gastrolyte*, Jeevan Jal*)	makes up solution to treat or prevent dehydration	dosage per instructions	no side effects, give enough to produce plenty of clear urine
Anti-emetics			
Metoclopramide (Maxolon* or Stemetil*)	control nausea and vomiting	max: one dose 8-hourly	may depress respiration, avoid at altitude, avoid alcohol. Note: vomiting at altitude may be a sign of AMS – if in doubt, descend rather than just treat symptoms.
Antacids (indigestion)			
Antacid tablets	indigestion	chew 2 to 8 tablets a day	have frequent light meals, no alcohol, tobacco, coffee, tea or fat
Laxatives			
Durolax*	for relief of constipation	one or two tablets at night	increase fibre and fluid intake
Haemorrhoids			
Rectinol*, Haemorex*, Anusol* cream or suppository	for the treatment of internal and external piles	apply cream or insert suppository into the rectum daily and after each motion	do not take orally
Acute Mountain Sickness (AMS)			
Acetozolamide (Diamox*)	prevention and treatment of mild AMS	125 mg tablet morning and night	can cause tingling of lips and fingers, may aggravate deyhdration; useful for mild to moderate AMS symptoms. Descent is the best treatment for AMS. Prophylactic treatment may be useful.
Nasal congestion			
Drixine* or Dristan*	nasal decongestant	2 or 3 drops, 6 to 8-hourly	instilled with head upside down or on one side, only use for 5 days at a time
Allergies & itchy bites			
antihistamine cream (eg Anthisan*)	local application to bites and rashes	apply 2 to 3 times daily	helps control itching
Allergies, itchy bites, hayfever or swelling from acute allergic reaction			
Diphenydramine HCl (eg Benadryl*)	antihistamine tablet	25 to 50 mg, 6 to 8-hourly	mild tranquilliser, can cause drowsiness and drug rashes; caution at high altitude or if driving. Avoid alcohol.
Anti-inflammatory			
Hydrocortisone cream (eg Hydrocort*)	skin rashes, mild sunburn	apply 2 to 3 times daily	not to be used on infection, for external use only

continues to be lost. The brain starts to malfunction, behaviour becomes erratic and the patient uncooperative. The person starts to lose coordination, speech may become slurred, and fatigue is intense. Finally unconsciousness occurs, followed by death.

Hypothermia can be prevented by wearing sufficient wind and waterproof clothing, eating high-energy food and taking warm drinks. Seek shelter if conditions are severe, and make onward trek judgments according to the abilities of the weakest person of the group. If the victim is unconscious, treat with the utmost gentleness or the heart may stop. Shelter the person from the elements, remove wet clothing and place the person in a well-insulated sleeping bag. Add heat from stoves or other peoples' bodies. Warm the armpits, neck and groin with suitably insulated bottles of hot water. Hypothermia is a serious condition and the victim will take days or weeks to recover fully.

Frostbite

This is a freezing of body tissues. Initially the affected part is white, numb and frozen solid. Later it will turn black and blister. Rewarm it in water at 45°C (hot but bearable to your hand) and protect from injury with plenty of dressings. Do not walk on frostbitten feet after rewarming. Do not massage or rub snow on frostbitten parts. Evacuate.

Snow Blindness

This very painful condition is caused by UV light reflected from snow or ice. To prevent it use good sunglasses with protection underneath and at the sides. Symptoms include red, watery eyes and blindness. It lasts for two or three days, and is treated with cold compresses and pain killers.

Sunburn

UV light is much stronger at altitude. Use a hat with a brim, a good sun block and lipseal. Apply burn cream to the affected areas.

Prickly Heat

This is an itchy rash caused by excessive perspiration trapped under the skin. Keeping cool, bathing often and using talcum powder or prickly heat powders should relieve the symptoms.

Heat Exhaustion

Prolonged exercise in a hot environment can result in electrolyte and circulatory disturance. This may cause a fall in blood pressure and fainting. Keep the patient in the shade and rehydrate them with plenty of rehydration solution.

Heat Stroke

This is a more serious condition and must be treated as an emergency. Prolonged exercise in a hot environment and failure of the sweating mechanism can cause the person to collapse, become unconscious and possibly to start having fits. The skin feels dry and hot, and the temperature is elevated. Put them in cool water (not cold), or strip them and moisten the skin and cover with wet towels and fan to lower the body temperature. Rehydrate them with rehydration solution when able to swallow.

SKIN PROBLEMS
Blisters

Prevention is best: dry, clean and powder your feet, and wear clean socks and properly fitting boots. Any part which is rubbing should be protected with adhesive plaster or dressing, a ring of adhesive felt or moleskin.

All blisters should be cleaned with an antiseptic, the fluid aspirated with a sterile syringe and needle, and covered with a Band-Aid or adhesive dressing. Ulcer dressings such as Duoderm* can be very effective. Use a ring of adhesive felt or moleskin to protect the area from further rubbing.

Chafing

This is sometimes a problem in the groin, armpits, elbow or on the backside. Wear well-washed, well-rinsed soft cotton boxer shorts and wash, dry and powder the skin with talcum powder or apply vaseline.

Boils & Abscesses

Both boils and abscesses appear as red, pus-filled pimples, but can be larger. Do not squeeze them. Keep the area clean and cover. Use hot compresses frequently until they discharge themselves. If they are growing, spreading, very painful, or located on the head, give the patient an appropriate antibiotic and seek medical assistance for incision and drainage.

Fungal Infections

Fungal infections, such as tinea, are most likely to occur between the toes (athlete's foot) or in the groin (jock itch or crotch rot) or vagina (see Women's Health). To prevent fungal infections, wear loose and comfortable clothes, wash frequently and dry yourself carefully – antifungal powders are useful. If you get an infection, wash the area daily and dry well. Apply an antifungal preparation such as Canestan* cream. Try to expose the infected area to air and sunlight, and wash all towels and underwear regularly.

BITES & STINGS

Snakebite

Calm and lie the victim down. Compress the bitten limb with a firm elastic bandage from the region of the bite to the top of the arm or leg and back down to the tip. The bandage must be firm but make sure the circulation hasn't been cut. Check the circulation every 20 minutes. Evacuate.

Leeches & Ticks

Leeches may be present in damp rainforest conditions, and attach themselves to your skin to suck your blood. Trekkers often get them on their legs or in their boots. Guard against infection of the bite after removing the leech with a pinch of salt or a lighted match. Apply pressure to stop the bleeding and then cover with a Band-Aid. Do not scratch the bite or an infection will occur.

Ticks are found in scrub. You should always check your body thoroughly if you have been walking through a tick-infested area, as these creatures can spread typhus. Remove them using a loop of thread around their neck and pulling sideways. Spray your boots and legs with insect repellent to deter ticks and leeches.

Insect Bites

Do not scratch insect bites; use an antihistamine cream. Keep the bites clean and dry. Fleas and bed bugs can be discouraged by airing sleeping bags in the sun. Pyrethrin insecticide powder may be needed as a deterrent in heavily infested bedrooms.

OTHER PROBLEMS

Fever

Confirm whether there is a fever by using a thermometer and continue to check the patient's temperature regularly. Fever implies infection and it can be tricky to identify the cause.

Some of the possible causes include respiratory problems, kidney infection, and diseases such as malaria, typhoid and dengue fevers or hepatitis. Read the section on infectious diseases for more details. If the cause of a high fever cannot be identified and the patient is ill, it is permissible to use an antibiotic blind (such as ciprofloxacin 500 mg 12 hourly for five to 10 days).

Heart Attack

This may happen without warning. Usually there is central chest pain of a crushing nature, which may travel into the neck or arm(s). Shock usually occurs, and the victim may have difficulty breathing and may suffer from nausea and vomiting. The pulse may be hard to feel and irregular. Treat the shock, and give strong pain killers and one asprin tablet daily. Give CPR if the heart stops. Evacuate.

Eye & Ear Infections

Infection of the eye will cause pain and redness, and a discharge that will stick the lids together overnight. Only one eye may be affected to begin with.

Insert antibiotic eye drops (Soframycin*), but stop if the symptoms get worse, as allergy to the drops can occur. Don't confuse eye infection and snow blindness (see Climatic Problems).

Superficial foreign bodies in the eye should be removed with a cotton wool bud or the blunt end of a sterilised needle. Cover the eye and use an antibiotic eye drop if infection occurs.

If the foreign body has penetrated the eye, leave it alone. Put a cover dressing on both eyes and evacuate the patient as soon as possible. Avoid or prevent coughing, straining or vomiting.

Infection of the ear can cause pain, discharge of pus, or both. If there is a discharge, use antibiotic ear drops. If the ear is very painful with no discharge, use an appropriate antibiotic by mouth.

Painful Belly

Common causes of non-serious belly pain are diarrhoea, dysentery and food poisoning (read the appropriate sections). For menstrual and mid-cycle pains read the Women's Health section. For indigestion or peptic ulcer (sharp upper abdominal pain) chew or swallow antacid tablets. With belly pain, the main concern is to decide if the victim should be evacuated. Severe abdominal pain lasting for more than six hours is usually serious. The following conditions require evacuation and urgent medical treatment:

Appendicitis The symptoms are central abdominal pain, low fever, vomiting and loss of appetite. Pain moves to the right lower abdominal quadrant with marked tenderness. Treatment is with a combination of high doses of amoxycillin and metronidazole. Food should be withheld but keep the patient hydrated.

Perforated Peptic Ulcer Symptoms are a long history of indigestion and the sudden onset of severe pain, collapse and shock. Urgent evacuation will be needed. Treat as for shock and give nothing by mouth.

Kidney Stone The symptoms are severe colicky pains from the back through to the pubis or genitalia. There may be blood in the urine. Maximise fluid intake and give strong pain killers.

Other Causes These include incarcerated hernia, acute gall bladder disease, or pancreatitis. In all cases, evacuation and urgent medical treatment is essential.

Vomiting

Prolonged vomiting can cause dehydration and exhaustion. Common causes are food poisoning, meningitis, hepatitis, or acute mountain sickness. Frequent sips of water or rehydration solution (see the section on the treatment of diarrhoea) between bouts of vomiting will help, as a little fluid is absorbed each time. Stemetil* or Maxolon* tablets or, more effectively, suppositories may be used.

Aches & Pains

General aches and pains may be the onset of flu, or stiffness caused by unaccustomed exercise. Administer aspirin or Panadol*, massage the area and/or apply liniment.

Trekker's Knee

The knee joint may become painfully inflamed while walking, especially while descending. Stop walking as soon as possible and apply cold compresses, elevate the leg and apply a compression bandage. Give aspirin, two every four hours, until the pain settles down in a day or two.

ACUTE MOUNTAIN SICKNESS

If someone is seriously ill at altitude, and you are not completely sure of the cause, call it acute mountain sickness (AMS) and descend.

Description

AMS, also called altitude sickness, is a common and potentially fatal disease. It is caused by the failure to acclimatise to the low levels of oxygen at high altitude.

Acclimatisation to altitudes over 3000m takes time. The body undergoes a number of physiological changes. Some are immediate, such as increased pulse and respiratory rate, while others, such as the increase in red blood cells or changes in the acid-base balance, take days or weeks.

These changes, plus the effects of intense sunlight, hard walking and dehydration, may cause any of the following mild acclimatisation symptoms (mild AMS):

- loss of appetite
- fatigue
- headache
- nausea
- dizziness
- sleeplessness
- mild shortness of breath on exercising
- interrupted breathing while asleep, followed by gasping (Cheyne-Stokes breathing)

Severe AMS is the accumulation of fluid (oedema) in the lungs and/or the brain. Fluid in the lungs is called high-altitude pulmonary oedema (HAPE). Fluid in the brain tissue is called high-altitude cerebral oedema (HACE). These may occur together or separately, rapidly or gradually over a period of days.

Night time is a particularly dangerous period for people suffering AMS. Sleeping naturally lowers the respiratory rate and Cheyne-Stokes periodic breathing can exacerbate the lowering of the oxygen level in the blood. Partners and attendants are tired or asleep themselves and a sudden worsening of the patient's condition may be missed. A typical pattern is for someone to go to bed with symptoms of mild AMS and to develop severe symptoms while asleep. Many people, including doctors, have woken to find their partners dead. Vigilance especially at night time and the preparedness to take drastic action are essential to avoid death. An early warning sign of impending AMS is a resting pulse of over 110 beats per minute (check in the morning and at night in bed).

Symptoms of Severe AMS
To examine a person for AMS, take a good history and ask about the symptoms mentioned above of mild AMS and more specifically about the symptoms of severe AMS, as follows:

HAPE Symptoms include any of those described for mild AMS, and also:

- shortness of breath which persists at rest (more than 12 to 14 breaths per minute)
- coughing, often with a frothy, blood-stained sputum
- severe fatigue
- drowsiness
- pains in the chest or upper body
- wet sounds in the lungs on deep inspiration: place your ear on the bare skin of the patient's back below the shoulder blades and compare with a healthy person

HACE Symptoms include any of the symptoms described for mild AMS, and also:

- severe headache which does not respond to mild pain killers; it is often aggravated by lying down
- nausea and vomiting which may become pronounced and prolonged
- loss of coordination, inability to do the 'heel to toe walking test'
- loss of mental abilities (eg memory, arithmetic)
- double, blurred or failing vision
- drowsiness
- severe fatigue

Treatment
The best treatment is prevention. Avoid rapid ascent (that is, more than 300m a day). Take acclimatisation symptoms seriously, using adequate rest days. If you suspect someone of having early symptoms of AMS, keep them at that altitude, or descend until the symptoms clear. If the symptoms are severe or worsening, or if the patient is very ill, descend immediately. Descend as far as possible and as quickly as possible. This is the best treatment, and if necessary must be carried out whatever the weather or time of day. Avoid alcohol.

Pressure Bags Portable pressure chambers such as Gamow*, Certec* and PAC* have revolutionised the management of AMS. More and more trekking groups and mountaineering parties carry one.

The victim is placed in the bag which is continuously pressurised by a foot pump. It appears that sessions in the bag reverse the symptoms of mild AMS while severe AMS victims can be resuscitated prior to evacuation.

A major limitation in their use is claustrophobia, while damage to ear drums is a possibility. Their major application is in plateau situations.

Drug Therapy Drug therapy is no substitute for descent, and should only be used to buy time while descending with the patient, for example if the weather is extreme or if you are on a plateau and it will take some time to lose altitude. Diamox* (acetazolamide) may be given morning and night for acclimatisation symptoms. It appears to prevent AMS in some people. It will not mask the onset of AMS. If the person is getting worse, descend. Side effects are numbness or tingling of digits and lips. These are not serious.

Nifedipine for HAPE and dexamethasone for HACE should be administered. Give 10 mg of nifedipine every eight hours, starting with a 20 mg dose. Give four mg dexamethasone 12 hourly, starting with an eight mg dose.

Oxygen If available, oxygen should be given at the rate of two to six litres per minute, depending on the patient's condition. Once again, the only guaranteed treatment is early and adequate descent.

Infectious Diseases

Hepatitis A or Infective Hepatitis

This is a viral disease passed by the faecal-oral route. It starts with flu-like symptoms, loss of appetite, vomiting and tiredness. It may be mild or severe, with the virus attacking the liver after 10 to 40 days of incubation. After a week or so jaundice may occur, causing yellow urine, skin and eyes, and chalky stools. A person is usually non infective 10 days after the onset of jaundice. The disease takes three to six weeks to clear up, and up to six months for the liver to recover fully.

Rest, and a diet of carbohydrates and proteins, with no fats, constitute the basic treatment. Prevention is by gamma globulin injections every four months or immunisa-

tion. Do not share eating utensils with an infectious person.

Typhoid Fever

Typhoid is caused by salmonella bacteria and spread by the faecal-oral route. Incubation takes 10 days, then a flu-like illness develops with headache, sore throat, and a fever which increases daily up to 40°C (104°F). The pulse rate does not increase, and in the second week a fine pink rash may appear on the trunk. If there are no complications, the illness usually clears by the third or fourth week. Vomiting and diarrhoea may occur. Treatment is a 10 day course of ciprofloxacin 500 mg eight hourly, plus rest and rehydration.

Tetanus

Tetanus is a serious disease. It occurs when a wound becomes infected by tetanus bacteria. Tetanus is also known as lockjaw, and the first symptoms may be difficulty on swallowing, and a stiffening of the jaw and neck, followed by painful convulsions of the whole body. It is most important to clean all wounds thoroughly. Keep your tetanus vaccination up to date.

Rabies

Rabies is spread by bites from infected dogs, bats or monkeys. Avoid startling dogs or approaching dogs that are fighting. Rabid animals attack without warning, and often bite several people. Clean the wounds thoroughly by flushing with Dettol* for at least 10 minutes: this is important. Return to the nearest centre of population for anti-rabies treatment. All bites should be treated seriously, as they can also become infected or result in tetanus.

Meningitis

This is an infection of the brain's lining, which can occur in epidemics and is often fatal. Vaccination gives protection against some forms of the disease (Meningitis A and C). Symptoms are fever, a severe headache which is made worse if the knees are bent up to the chest, neck stiffness, nausea, vomiting and loss of consciousness. Treatment is ciprofloxacin 500 mg eight hourly plus amoxycillin 500 mg six hourly.

Tuberculosis

TB is prevalent throughout the Himalaya and is spread by droplet infection. It usually affects the lungs, producing a cough, often with blood-stained sputum, low fever and weight loss. It is a chronic disease – that is, it develops slowly and can last a long time. A healthy person is less likely to contract it than someone who is run-down and debilitated. It is exceedingly unlikely that a trekker will contract TB, but it is not uncommon to come across villagers suffering from it. TB needs hospital diagnosis and long-term treatment.

Malaria

This mosquito-borne disease is prevalent below 1000m (3280 ft) through most of the Himalaya. The victim starts to feel unwell with muscle aches and headache, develops a high fever which produces shivering fits, and then drops to near normal before rising again. The patient may feel quite well between bouts of fever. Treatment is normally given after hospital diagnosis. Prevention is by avoiding mosquito bites using repellent, long-sleeved shirts, nets, screens and mosquito coils.

The malarial prophylactics are described in the Preparations for a Trek section at the beginning of this chapter. These should be taken for two weeks before entering, and four weeks after leaving, the malarial area. They may cause nausea which appears worse at altitude.

If you suspect a case of malaria, consult a doctor. If you are in a remote area use the following regimen of chloroquine (250 mg tablets): four tablets, followed by two tablets six hours later, followed by two tablets 24 hours later, followed by two more tablets 48 hours later. You must have a check-up on return to civilisation.

Dengue Fever

This mosquito-borne disease endemic in northern India has an incubation period of five to 10 days. Symptoms start with an abrupt onset of high fever, headache and muscle ache. The aches and pains are prominent and the illness is also called 'break bone fever' as a result. There is often a faint rash.

There is no treatment for the disease, which lasts for a week followed by several weeks of debility.

Sexually & Blood Transmitted Diseases

STDs have become a real problem for travellers. Partners may include other travellers, villagers or prostitutes. The minor STDs such as herpes and chlamydia pale into insignificance when compared to AIDS and syphilis. Practise safe sex including the use of condoms or practise abstinence.

Sharing needles, having injections from non-disposable needles or having blood transfusions may result in AIDS and Hepatitis B or C, all of which have chronic health effects. Many travellers opt to carry their own sterile syringes and needles in case they are needed for the treatment of illness.

Women's Health

Urinary Tract Infection

This is much more common in women than in men. Infection of the lower urinary tract is called cystitis. The symptoms are the onset of frequency, urgency and burning pain when passing urine, and cloudy, strong-smelling urine. Upper urinary tract (kidney) infections have symptoms of back pain, fever, and cloudy, strong-smelling urine. The patient may be very ill. Treatment is the same for both problems. An antibiotic such as Bactrim DS* or amoxycillin is recommended – four days for cystitis, 10 days for upper tract infections.

In any urinary problem, increase the fluid intake until there is a frequent passing of clear urine.

Pelvic Infection

This is recognised by lower abdominal pain and fever. Give Bactrim DS* for 10 days.

Vaginal Fungal Infection (Thrush)

Poor diet, lowered resistance due to the use of antibiotics, and contraceptive pills can lead to vaginal infections when travelling in hot climates. Keeping the genital area clean, and wearing skirts or loose-fitting trousers and cotton underwear will help to prevent infections.

Thrush produces a thick, white, relatively odourless discharge accompanied by itching and soreness. Apply or insert cotrimazole (Canestan*) twice daily.

If the discharge persists and develops an odour, other causes of infection must be considered. If a medical opinion is not immediately available, the drug of first choice would be metronidazole 400 mg eight hourly for seven days.

Pelvic Pains

Mid-cycle pains can be recognised by sharp, one sided, lower abdominal pain halfway between periods. The pain can be quite severe and can mimic appendicitis. Repeated examinations will be necessary. Pain can be relieved with paracetamol or codeine. Pains occurring during menstrual periods sometimes require rest and paracetamol.

Avoid coffee. If pain is severe and the woman is ill, a tubal pregnancy could be the cause. In this case urgent evacuation will be required.

Pregnancy

Trekking and pregnancy are not completely incompatible. However, the decision to trek should not be taken lightly. High altitude, remoteness and infectious diseases all pose extra risks to mother and baby. Miscarriage is not uncommon in even a normal pregnancy and may need urgent surgery and blood transfusion.

It is best to avoid drugs in pregnancy, especially in the first three months when it is most likely to cause foetal abnormalities or miscarriage. Certain drugs such as Mefloquin* and oxytetracycline will cause foetal damage.

The effects of altitude during pregnancy are not known, therefore a rule of thumb is to avoid ascending above 3500m. Consult a doctor before the trip for advice.

Children's Health

More and more children are going trekking in the Himalaya. While this is a wonderful experience for all concerned, children can become ill alarmingly quickly. They are more susceptible to hypothermia and AMS. They have a lower ability to cope with respiratory infections, dehydration and blood loss than adults.

A general rule for children for dosage of medications is: from three to six years old give a quarter of the adult dosage; for seven to 12 years old give half the adult dosage (unless the directions say otherwise). Avoid giving children ciprofloxacin, oxytetracycline and pentazocine (Fortral*).

Rescue & Evacuation

Organising the evacuation of an injured person requires that you first ascertain the severity of the injury and how the patient is to be evacuated.

If the victim is not in dire straits it is best to organise for a riding horse or porters to carry the victim as quickly as possible to the nearest trailhead.

This may not be as daunting as it seems, as on many extended treks a shortcut to the trailhead can often be completed in a matter of a day or two. Send someone reliable ahead to organise onward transport and make the necessary medical arrangements.

If the evacuation requires a helicopter you will need to contact the nearest police or army post which will pass on your message by radio.

Ensure that comprehensive details are conveyed, including the patient's medical condition together with the full name, nationality, passport number, age, and sex.

Indicate the degree of urgency (for instance, most immediate, victim in danger of dying). Give a detailed description of the location of the victim, draw a map or send a marked map, indicate the altitude. If you intend to move, clearly indicate your evacuation route.

In most cases the Indian army will not send a helicopter unless they are sure of payment. The victim's embassy will need to be contacted. Many embassies will not authorise an immediate evacuation irrespective of the circumstances until they are satisfied that the victim is insured or that the next of kin is prepared guarantee to foot the bill. This process can take many hours, even days.

Helicopter evacuation is expensive, ranging from US$3000 upwards.

Insurance to cover emergency evacuation is available with most companies prepared to include trekking under the normal range of tourist activities and must be purchased before arriving in India.

Death

If someone dies in the mountains, take the details and the passport to the nearest police post. Do not attempt to cremate or dispose of the body until the police arrive. This is essential, even if the nearest police post is many days away. The police will help with arranging evacuation or burial, and advise you of the necessary procedures.

Treating Local People

This is a difficult and vexing problem. A rule of thumb is that if there is a direct emergency or trauma (and there is no hospital or village health post) then assistance should be administered. On the other hand,

for illnesses and most injuries the course of action is to direct the victim to the nearest village health post. Some examples may help to clarify the situation.

A few seasons ago a shepherd came to our camp site with a huge gash in his right arm caused by a bear attack. Overnight he had inserted birch bark to arrest the bleeding and the following day there was a dire problem with infection. He was many days walk away from the nearest hospital. In this instance we cleaned and dressed the wound and gave clear instructions regarding the course of antibiotics to take and the importance of completing the course.

However, if the shepherd had come to our camp with a bad cold and symptoms of TB then it would not have been advisable to treat him. In preference, he should be directed to the nearest doctor or health post.

In normal circumstances there are many cases which fall between these examples. Administering first aid to a horseman with snow blindness after crossing a snow-capped pass is fine; giving out tablets to every villager who complains of a headache is not. Generally, if you have hired porters or horsemen it is usual to deal with their acute problems as they arise. Chronic problems are best dealt with by writing a referral letter to the nearest village health post.

However, a problem arises when, for instance, a villager brings in a young child with a burn or cut. You can be assured that if you treat the child initially then there is little chance that the mother will go to the nearest paramedic for follow-up treatment, even if you stress the importance.

Over the last few decades across the Himalaya, systems of paramedics have gradually been set up in the remote mountain regions. These systems will not be respected if we undermine the status of the paramedics with short-term administration of medical help.

It is important you are aware of these issues. It is natural, of course, to want to help, but the long-term result may be detrimental to the establishment of local health and first aid facilities in mountain areas.

After Your Journey

Some illnesses picked up while travelling have a long incubation period, or can become chronic. These include worms and parasites, TB, malaria, giardia and amoebic dysentery.

If you are not feeling well after your return home, or are having symptoms of indigestion, weight loss, diarrhoea, fever, or general fatigue and malaise, consult your local doctor and, if necessary, ask for a specialist consultation.

Getting There & Away

Delhi is the gateway to India for the treks in Ladakh, Kashmir, Himachal Pradesh and Uttar Pradesh. For treks out of Sikkim and Darjeeling, trekkers have the option of either flying to Delhi and then flying on or travelling by train or road to Darjeeling or Gangtok. Trekkers from Australia and New Zealand will probably find it cheaper and more convenient to fly to Calcutta before either flying or going by train or road to Darjeeling or Gangtok.

AIR
The USA
There is a wide variety of excursion fares from the USA. The cheapest return fares from the west coast of the USA to India are around US$1350, while a six month excursion fare from New York to Delhi costs US$2410. Check the Sunday travel sections of the *New York Times* and the *San Francisco Chronicle/Examiner* for cheap fares. Consider flying to Hong Kong and buying a ticket to India from there.

Canada
The excursion fares from Canada are similar to the fares from the USA. From Toronto it is cheaper to fly to India via London, while from Vancouver the fare is around C$2340 via Tokyo. The travel sections in the *Toronto Globe & Mail* and the Vancouver *Sun* advertise the best deals available.

The UK
With many airline carriers flying to India, fares are very competitive. From London to Delhi, fares ranges from around UK£300/ 342 one way/return in the low season or UK£409/493 in the high season – cheaper short-term fares are also available. Check out bucket shops in London, and the travel pages in the *Times* or *Business Traveller*. Typical fares quoted in these magazines range from UK£295 return. Two reliable London bucket shops are Trailfinders (☎ (0171) 938-3366), 42/50 Earls C3ourt Rd, London W8; and STA Travel (☎ (0171) 937-9962), 74 Old Brompton Rd, London SW7 or 117 Euston Rd, London NW1.

Most British travel agents are registered with the Association of British Travel Agents (ABTA). If you have paid an ABTA-registered agent for your flight and they go out of business, ABTA will guarantee a refund or alternative. Unregistered bucket shops are riskier, but sometimes cheaper.

Australia & New Zealand
From Sydney or Melbourne, a 35 day return excursion fare to either Delhi or Calcutta costs A$1390 in the low season and A$1780 in the high season, which is from the third week of November till the end of January. For the best deals check with the travel sections in the *Sydney Morning Herald* or the Melbourne *Age*.

From Perth there is a 35 day excursion fare of A$1220 low season and A$1505 high season.

Advance-purchase return fares from the east coast of Australia to India range from A$1250 to A$1500 depending on the season and the destination in India. Fares are slightly cheaper to Madras and Calcutta than to Mumbai (Bombay) and Delhi. Fares are slightly cheaper from Darwin and Perth than from the east coast.

Tickets from Australia to London or other European capitals with an Indian stopover range from A$1200 to A$1350 one way and A$2000 to A$2500 return, again depending on the season.

Return advance-purchase fares from New Zealand to India range from NZ$1799 to NZ$1889 depending on the season.

STA Travel and Flight Centres International are major dealers in cheap air fares in both Australia and New Zealand. Check the travel agents' ads in the *Yellow Pages*, local newspapers and travel magazines, and ring around.

Continental Europe

Fares from continental Europe tend to be more expensive than from London.

From Amsterdam to Delhi a 60 day return excursion fare is about DFL 2440 while from Frankfurt to Delhi a 90 day return excursion fare is around DM1722

From Paris to Delhi, a 90 day return excursion fare costs around FF10,595. The magazine *Aventure du Bout du Monde* (116 Rue de Javel, 75015 Paris) details many of the best deals.

Nepal

Royal Nepal Airlines Corporation (RNAC) and Indian Airlines share the routes between India and Kathmandu. Both airlines give a 25% discount to those under 30 years of age on flights between Kathmandu and Delhi; no student card is needed.

From New Delhi there are daily flights to Nepal. The flight costs US$142. Other cities with direct air connections with Kathmandu are Calcutta (US$96) and Varanasi (US$71) – a convenient gateway after completing a

---

Arriving by Air in India

Most of the flights to India arrive in the middle of the night, which can make your first experience in India a tiring one. After clearing immigration and customs it is advisable to change money at the State Bank of India counter just outside the Customs Hall. While inside the airport you may also purchase a bus ticket or prepaid taxi ticket that will take you direct to your hotel. The bus tickets from both Calcutta and Delhi cost Rs 50 while the taxi rates vary from Rs 150 to Rs 200 depending on whether day or night rates are applicable.

Once outside the airport do not become separated from your baggage en route to the correct taxi/bus stand. On leaving the airport you will be asked to give your name and the name of hotel you are booked at. This is just a check to ensure that you get to your hotel without being waylaid and taken to an alternative hotel favoured by the taxi driver or overcharged. ■

---

trek in Uttar Pradesh. Travel agents may also be able to offer a fare to combine visits to India and Nepal that discounts the standard Delhi/Kathmandu add-on fare.

Pakistan

Pakistan International Airlines (PIA) and Air India operate flights from Karachi to Delhi for US$75 and Lahore to Delhi for about US$140. Flights are also available between Karachi and Mumbai on Indian Airlines.

Thailand

Bangkok is a popular departure point from South-East Asia into India with cheap flights from there to Calcutta and Delhi on Thai International. Expect to pay around US$250 Bangkok to Calcutta one way and US$300 Bangkok to Delhi.

From India

Cheap flights are available from many of the smaller travel agencies around Connaught Place in New Delhi. However, one-way onward tickets are expensive for those travelling overland and then flying to Australia or the UK. One-way fares to Australia vary from around Rs 25,000 from Delhi to Sydney. Fares from Delhi to London are about Rs 20,000 and from Delhi to New York Rs 35,000. These are the quoted fares through the airline offices but there is plenty of scope for bargaining. Expect around a 20% discount through one of the smaller travel agencies which have their offices in Connaught Place in New Delhi.

OVERLAND
Europe

The classic way of getting to India from Europe has always been the overland route, though political problems in the Middle East have considerably reduced the numbers travelling this way. Afghanistan is still off limits but the route though Turkey, Iran and Pakistan is straightforward.

Nepal

There are regular direct bus services between Delhi and Kathmandu, although often travellers find it cheaper and more satisfactory to organise this trip themselves. The most popular routes are from Raxaul (near Muzaffarpur) or from Sunauli (near Gorakhpur). If travelling from Darjeeling or Gangtok, the border at Kakarbhitta (near Siliguri) provides a direct route to Kathmandu and is considerably less expensive than going via Calcutta. From Darjeeling it takes half a day to drive to the border, where there are a number of buses that drive overnight to Kathmandu.

South-East Asia
In contrast to the difficulties of travelling overland through Central Asia, the South East Asian overland trip is still wide open and as popular as ever. While the most popular route includes a flight from Australia to Bali before heading north through Indonesia to Malaysia or Singapore, there is no direct overland route from Thailand to India. Crossing by land from Myanmar to India is forbidden by the Myanmar government – see Lonely Planet's *South-East Asia on a shoestring* for the complete picture.

LEAVING INDIA
It is important that you reconfirm your international booking out of India as soon as you are sure of your return date. Reconfirmation must generally be done in Delhi or Calcutta. You could confirm your flight by telex or fax but there is no guarantee that your message will not be garbled.

The flights from Delhi to Kathmandu are often overbooked and it is advisable to arrive early for checking in for your flight, particularly during the busy October and November period.

Departure Tax
Departure tax from India is Rs 300 if flying out of the Indian subcontinent, and Rs 150 if flying within the subcontinent, for example, to Nepal, Pakistan, Bangladesh or Sri Lanka. Generally you have to pay it before you check in, so look out for an airport tax counter as you enter the check-in area.

ORGANISED TREKS
There are many adventure travel companies which organise Himalayan treks. Packages offered usually consist of the trekking arrangement together with the various flights to and from Delhi or Calcutta to meet up with the group. Most of the agencies also cater for individual groups and can arrange custom-made itineraries. The benefits of travelling this way are outlined in the Facts for the Trekker chapter.

It is important to note that the agencies can also assist with flight arrangements and normally have a ticket quota during high-season periods when it is difficult to get a confirmed booking on a particular date.

Trekking Companies
The following companies have operated established Himalayan programmes for at least five to seven years, while some have been in the business well over 20 years. Many of them include comprehensive programmes in the Indian Himalaya.

Australia
> Peregrine Adventures, 258 Lonsdale St, Melbourne, Vic 3000 (☎ (03) 9663-8611; fax 9663-8618)
> World Expeditions, 3rd Floor, 441 Kent St, Sydney, NSW 2000 (☎ (02) 9264 3366; fax 9261-1974)

France
> Explorator, 16 Place de la Madeleine, 75008 Paris (fax 01-42-66-53-89)

UK
> Exodus, 9 Weir Rd, London, SW12 OLT (☎ (0181) 673-0859; fax 673-0779)
> Explore, 1 Frederick St, Aldershot, Hants, GU11 1LQ (☎ (0252) 319448; fax 343170)
> High Places, Globe Works, Penistone Rd, Sheffield, S6 3AE (☎ (0742) 822333; fax 820016)
> Himalayan Kingdoms, 20 The Mall, Clifton, Bristol, B58 4DR (☎ (0117) 923-7163; fax 974-4993)
> KE Adventure, 32 Lake Rd, Keswick, Cumbria CA12 5DQ (☎ (0176) 877-3966; fax 877-4693)
> Sherpa Expeditions, 131A Heston Rd, Hounslow, Middlesex, TW3 ORD (☎ (0181) 577-2717; fax 572-9788)
> World Expeditions, 4 Northfields Prospect, Putney Bridge Rd, London SW1 SIPE (☎ (0181) 870-2600; fax 870-2615)

Worldwide Journeys, 8 Comeragh Rd, London, W14 9HP (☎ (0171) 381-8636; fax 381-0836)

USA

Mountain Travel, 6420 Fairmount Ave, El Cerrito, CA 94530 (☎ (510) 527-8100)

Wilderness Adventures, 801 Allston Way, Berkeley, CA 94710 (☎ (510) 548-0420)

Inner Asia, 2627 Lombard St, San Francisco, CA 94123 (☎ (415) 922-0448)

WARNING

The information in this chapter is particularly vulnerable to change: prices for international travel are volatile, routes are introduced and cancelled, schedules change, special deals come and go, and rules and visa requirements are amended. Airlines and governments seem to take a perverse pleasure in making price structures and regulations as complicated as possible.

You should check directly with the airline or a travel agent to make sure you understand how a fare (and the ticket you may buy) works. In addition, the travel industry is highly competitive and there are many lurks and perks.

The upshot of this is that you should get opinions, quotes and advice from as many airlines and travel agents as possible before you part with your hard-earned cash. The details given in this chapter should be regarded as pointers and are not a substitute for your own careful, up-to-date research.

Getting Around

AIR
Indian Airlines, the government-run airline, flies to many of the destinations in the Indian Himalaya. In the last few years several private carriers have provided the government airline with some competition. These include Modiluft Airlines, Jagson Airlines, Archana Airlines, UP Air and Jet Airways.

Booking Flights
Indian Airlines has computerised bookings at all but its smallest offices, so getting flight information and reservations is quite straightforward. However, most of the flights are heavily booked so you need to book as far in advance as possible. The alternative is to get a chance number, that is, be put on the waiting list and hope that it clears. Even if you have an impossible waiting list number it is still worthwhile going to the airport. The chances are that seats will become available and you will be able to get away on time.

The alternative is to book your Indian Airline flights at the time that you purchase your international ticket and hope that the flight will clear by the time you require it.

Tickets
Indian Airlines tickets must be paid for in foreign currency, either in cash, travellers' cheques or by credit cards. Some outlying offices will not accept credit cards, so cash in the form of US dollars is essential. There are few discounts or standby fares, except for the youth fare for people between 12 and 30 years old which allows a 25% discount. There are no penalties for cancellations or no-shows, but if you bought the ticket abroad you can only get a refund from the place of purchase.

Unlike almost every airline in the world, Indian Airlines accepts no responsibility if you lose your tickets. They will not replace them, so treat them like cash, not travellers' cheques.

Check In
The check-in time depends on the type of aircraft. With airbuses it is 75 minutes; for all other flights it is one hour. With all flights to and from Srinagar, an extra half an hour is required.

On some internal routes you are required to identify your checked-in baggage on the tarmac immediately prior to boarding. This is an excellent security arrangement. For security reasons again, at some airports, such as at Leh and Srinagar, you may not be allowed any hand baggage. This includes camera gear and valuables which may have to be stored in the hold.

Excess baggage (carrying a multitude of trekking gear) can be a problem at check in. Actually excess baggage charges are quite small, being calculated at 1% of the 1st class fare. Therefore, expect to pay around US$1 per kg if flying between Delhi and Leh.

Indian Airlines Offices
The Indian Airlines offices listed below include the distance from the office to the airport. For the full list of offices consult Lonely Planet's *India – travel survival kit*.

Bagdogra (14 km)
    Hotel Sinclairs, Mallaguri, Siliguri (☎ 20-692)
Calcutta (16 km)
    Airlines House, 39 Chittranjan Ave (☎ 26-3135, 26-3390, 26-2548)
Chandigarh (11 km)
    SCO186-187-188 Sector 17C (☎ 40-539)
Delhi (16 km)
    Malhotra Bldg, Connaught Place (☎ 331-0517)
    Barakhamba Rd (☎ 331-3732)
    Domestic Terminal (24 hours) (☎ 144-141)
Leh (8 km)
    Ibex Guest Hotel (☎ 276)
Srinagar (13 km)
    Tourist Reception Centre (☎ 73-231)

Other Airline Offices
Offices (all in Delhi) of other airlines include:

Archana
41 Friends Colony East, Mathura Rd (☎ 684-2001)
Jagson
12E Vandana Bldg, 11 Tolstoy Marg (☎ 371-1069)
Jet Airways
3E Hansalaya Bldg, Barakhamba Rd (☎ 372-4727)
Modiluft
S1 Vandana Bldg, Tolstoy Marg (☎ 371-2222)
B-82 Defence Colony (☎ 464-2122)

Fares & Services

Delhi Indian Airlines operates daily flights from Delhi to Leh (US$86), Srinagar (US$92) and Jammu (US$84). Modiluft flights are a little more expensive: from Delhi to Srinagar (US$101), to Jammu (US$89), and a recently introduced service to Leh (US$105).

From Delhi to Bhuntar (in the Kullu Valley) there are daily flights with Jagson and with Archana. The fare is $US123. Note: Bhuntar airport is a 1½ hour drive by taxi from Manali. To Shimla, Archana operates three flights a week which cost $US96, while Jagson Airlines runs three flights a week to Gaggar (for Dharamsala) at a cost of $US100.

From Delhi, Indian Airlines flies three times a week to Bagdogra (US$156) while Jet Airways flies daily (US$156). From Bagdogra it is a further three to four hours by bus to Darjeeling.

Calcutta Indian Airlines flies five times a week from Calcutta to Bagdogra (US$65).

BUS

Most of the bus services heading north from Delhi to the hill stations and trekking-off points depart from the interstate bus terminal at Kashmir Gate. Services are operated by both the state governments and a multitude of bus companies, many of which have offices in Connaught Place. The buses are generally comfortable, not overbooked and provide a genuine alternative to trains for long-distance travel.

Express buses only stop every few hours, which makes you feel you are really getting somewhere. Both private and state buses operate throughout the day, and many have reclining seats, videos and air-conditioning

– your only problems are the Indian roads and drivers.

Delhi-Jammu

The deluxe bus takes around 12 to 14 hours and costs Rs 220.

Delhi-Dharamsala

The deluxe overnight service takes around 12 hours and costs Rs 300.

Delhi-Manali

There are many bus services, mostly overnight, taking around 15 hours. Fares range from Rs 300 to Rs 400 for a deluxe bus.

Delhi-Shimla

There are regular services which take around eight hours and cost Rs 225.

Delhi-Haridwar

Buses leave every hour and take five to six hours. Fares range from Rs 83 to Rs 175. From Haridwar change buses for Joshimath and Uttarkashi.

Delhi-Mussoorie

There are regular buses throughout the day which take between six to eight hours. The fares range from Rs 135 to Rs 250.

Delhi-Naini Tal

Regular services leave throughout the day and take around 10 hours. Fares range from Rs 155 to Rs 275.

Delhi-Almora

There are several buses running directly to Almora each day. The drive takes between 10 and 12 hours. The fares range between Rs 170 and Rs 300.

TRAIN

Indian Railways has a tourist quota on most express trains – a proportion of seats are reserved for foreign tourists until 48 hours before the train is scheduled to depart. There is little likelihood that you will get a reservation any other way, particularly out of Delhi going north in the summer time. Many of the normal berths on express trains are booked out for three to four weeks in advance. Now that Indian Railways is computerised, reserving a seat on the tourist quota is a comparatively straightforward process. In Delhi go to the New Delhi railway station at Paharganj, where there is a special booking office for foreign tourists. Bookings must be paid for in foreign currency.

Delhi-Jammu

There are four trains a day. The *Shalimar Express* departs at 4.30 am from New Delhi station while the *Jammu Super Fast* departs at 5.20 am. In the evenings the *Jammu Mail* departs at 9 pm and the *Jammu Express* leaves at 9.30 pm. These trains depart from Old Delhi station. The fares are Rs 530 (1st class) and Rs 170 (2nd class).

Delhi-Pathankot

Catch the Jammu train which arrives in Pathankot approximately three hours rail time before Jammu. The 1st-class fare is Rs 471, and the 2nd-class fare is Rs 147 for the daytime trains, and Rs 121 for the overnight trains.

Delhi-Chandigarh

There are two morning trains from New Delhi station. The *Himalayan Queen* depart at 6 am and the *Shatabdi Express* at 5.55 am. In the evening the *Shatabdi Express* departs at 5.15 pm. The fares are Rs 181 (1st class), Rs 270 (air-con chair car) and Rs 72 (2nd class).

Delhi-Shimla

The *Kalka Mail* departs from New Delhi station at 11 pm, arriving at Kalka at 5.30 am to connect with the local train to Shimla. If travelling during the day, catch the *Himayalan Queen* which departs at 6 am. It operates from New Delhi station and goes via Chandigarh. The cost is Rs 201 (1st class), Rs 290 (air-con chair car) and Rs 92 (2nd-class). From Kalka there are regular buses and taxis to Shimla. This journey takes three to four hours.

Delhi-Haridwar & Dehra Dun

The *Shatabdi Express* departs at 5.55 am and the *Dehra Dun Express* at noon from New Delhi station, while the *Mussoorie Express* departs at 11.25 pm from Old Delhi station. The cost to Haridwar is Rs 307 (1st class), Rs 295 (air-con chair car) and Rs 98 (2nd class), and to Dehra Dun it is Rs 327 (1st class), Rs 315 (air-con chair car) and Rs 118 (2nd class).

Delhi-Kathgodam

The *Ranikhet Express* departs from Old Delhi station at 11.00 pm and arrives the following morning at Kathgodam at 6.05 am. The cost is Rs 305 (1st class) and Rs 97 (2nd class). From Kathogodam there are many connecting buses to Naini Tal (Rs 20) and to Almora (Rs 70).

Calcutta-New Jalpaiguri & Darjeeling

There are at present three trains per day to Bagdogra. The *Brahmaputra* departs at 8.45 am and the *Ayadh Assam* at 8.50 am, while the *NE Express* departs at 4.25 pm. The cost is Rs 1042 (1st class) and Rs 288 (2nd class). From New Jalpaiguri station the *Toy Train* winds uphill the spectacular route to Darjeeling. However track upgrading can cause disruption to the service, so as an alternative consider the much faster bus service.

DELAYS

As a general rule always allow at least one day per week for non-scheduled delays. This is particularly important when planning a trek in July, August or early September when much of Himachal Pradesh and Uttar Pradesh are subject to monsoon rains. During a normal season, the roads will on average be washed away or blocked due to landslides for at least one or two days each season.

However, sometimes its gets worse, far worse. I can recall spending three days in August 1985 in Mandi in Himachal Pradesh waiting for rain to stop and for the road up the Larji Gorge to be cleared. More recently, anyone who was preparing to go trekking in early September 1995 would have experienced some of the heaviest rainfalls in living memory. All the main roads linking the mountain areas were washed away including the Kullu-Manali road, Manali-Leh road and the road from Chamba to Brahmaur in the Ravi Valley. At this time the roads were not repaired for the best part of a month, playing havoc with trekking plans. For those already trekking, the heavy snowfall caused groups to be stranded at Padum in the Zanskar region for many days until the road to Kargil was cleared. When this happens there is little you can do but wait and be patient. Consider all the alternatives and modify or even change your trekking plans completely. Above all, ensure before you leave home, that you are not on too tight an itinerary.

Ladakh

HISTORY

Ladakh is a land of high passes on the borderland of India and Tibet. It is an integral part of the Jammu & Kashmir (J&K) state and consists of three main populated regions. The first is Leh and the upper Indus Valley. This is the cultural heartland of Ladakh where many monasteries and palaces reflect the deep Buddhist heritage of the region. The Zanskar Valley is the second region. It is a comparatively isolated valley to the south of the Indus Valley and its high culture is also Buddhist. The third main region of Ladakh includes Kargil and the Suru Valley. This region, west of Leh down the Indus Valley, was an integral part of Baltistan until 1947. It supports an Islamic culture that can be traced back to the 15th century, when the region was converted to Islam.

The Khampa, the nomadic shepherds who roamed the Tibetan plateau, were the first inhabitants of Ladakh. Their horizons were restricted to the high, windswept grazing areas, and it was not until the coming of the Mons, Buddhist missionaries from India, that settlements were established in the valleys. Later, the Dards from Gilgit wandered up the Indus Valley and introduced irrigation to the upper reaches of the Indus.

In the 7th century the migration of the Tibetans from western Tibet, or Guge, slowly began to displace the Dards. These early rulers provided Ladakh with its first authentic history. Forts and palaces, such as that of Shey, were constructed, and the power of Ladakh, for the first time, stretched beyond the Indus Valley.

By now the Buddhist scriptures had been fully translated and carried across the Himalaya. Much of this can be attributed to the Tantric sage Padmasambhava. During his travels in the 7th century he did much to popularise the fundamental Buddhist precepts, while at the same time undermining the animistic Bon Po religion that had been central to the beliefs of the Tibetans. By the

Highlights – Ladakh
Trans Himalaya region. A rugged land of high passes that cross the Great Himalaya and the Zanskar ranges. In the depths of the valleys, tiny settlements thrive – oases in an otherwise arid landscape. Also known as Little Tibet because of cultural and geographic similarities with Tibet.

Strenuous treks, at altitude, out of Leh in the Indus Valley and Padum in the Zanskar Valley.

11th century, the wandering Buddhist scholar Ringchen Brangpo is said to have established 108 Buddhist monasteries throughout western Tibet and Ladakh. Many of the ancient sites, such as at Lamayuru and Alchi, were founded during this period together with Sani, close to Padum in the Zanskar Valley.

The Grand Route up the Indus Valley followed many of these ancient sites. Travellers would come up the valley as far as Khalsi, and from there follow the trail to Temisgam,

Likir and over the Rongdu La, to Basgo, Nimmu, and finally to Shey.

The highways to the east were also accessible. In the late 14th century, the famous Tibetan pilgrim Tsong Khapa visited Ladakh, and popularised a new Buddhist order. The order was essentially a reformist sect which, under the first Dalai Lama, sought to qualify many of the elaborate rituals and practices that had entered Buddhist teaching. The Gelukpa order, as it was known, gained popularity in Ladakh, and the monasteries at Thikse, Likir and Spitok were founded in the early 15th century together with Karsha, Lingshet and Mune in the Zanskar Valley.

By this time Kashmir had been converted to Islam, and by the early 15th century so had Baltistan. This left Ladakh vulnerable to attacks from the combined Balti-Kashmiri armies. It was an unenviable position for Ladakh, particularly since the kingdom was at the time divided. The lower kingdom was ruled from Basgo, while the upper kingdom was ruled from Shey. It was the famous Ladakhi ruler Tashi Namgyal who was able to unite these two divisions of Ladakh. The Basgo line of rulers established themselves at Leh, and built the upper fort, known as the Peak of Victory, to commemorate Ladakh's successful defence against invaders.

Ladakh was not to escape outside occupation completely. Tashi Namgyal was killed by a raiding army from Kashgar. In the early 16th century the kingdom was subject to the rule of Ali Mir, the ruler of Baltistan who forced the Ladakhi king Jamyang Namgyal to marry one of his daughters.

During the reign of Singge Namgyal (1570-1642), the son of Jamyang Namgyal and the Balti princess, Ladakh's fortunes improved. The palace at Leh was constructed, and the royal family assisted monks from the Drukpa order to establish the monasteries at Hemis and Stakna, and Bardan and Zangla in the Zanskar Valley.

Ladakh's territories expanded to include Guge, Zanskar and Spiti, as well as the Indus Valley. But this situation changed as Ladakh was drawn into a war with the powerful Tibetan-Mongol army under the fifth Dalai Lama. An appeal was sent to the Moghul governor of Kashmir, who sent forces to assist.

It was too late, however, as the Ladakh empire was reduced to the confines of the Indus Valley, while the mosque at the far end of the Leh bazaar was commissioned as a symbol of Ladakh's token affiliation with the vast Moghul empire.

In spite of this setback, Ladakh soon regained some of its former territories, and re-entered a trading pact with Tibet. This situation continued until the 1830s, when the Ladakhi king was exiled to Stok by the armies of Zorawar Singh, the famous general of Gulab Singh who was destined to become the first maharajah of Kashmir.

Despite the changing fortunes of the Dogra army in Tibet, Ladakh became part of the maharajah's state in 1846, and remained so until independence in 1947.

Since then, with the Chinese occupation of Tibet in the 1950s, Ladakh's connections with Tibet have been severed, while India's war with China in 1962 further exacerbated the problem of Ladakh's sensitive borders. For this reason, Ladakh remained closed to outsiders until 1974.

Today the situation shows signs of improvement. There have been continued discussions between the Indian and Chinese governments to reconcile many of the border disputes that arose in 1962. As the political tensions have relaxed so some of the more sensitive border regions have been opened to tourists.

This development has been enhanced by the fact that the Indian government is also keen to attract tourists to the region in view of the situation in Kashmir.

The region of Rupshu and Tso Morari, together with the Nubra Valley and the Pangong Lake district on the China-India border, is now open.

It is a matter of conjecture whether the land border between Ladakh and Tibet will open, affording the opportunity to drive from Leh to the base of Mt Kailas in a couple of days.

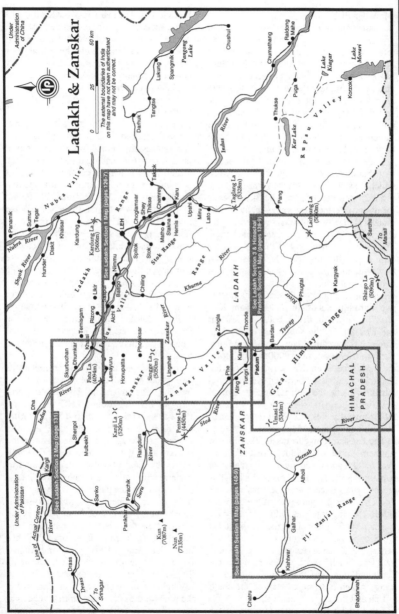

Ladakh & Zanskar

The external boundaries of India
on this map have not been authenticated
and may not be correct.

0   25   50 km

GEOGRAPHY

Ladakh is one of the most rugged regions of the entire Himalayan Range. It is often referred to as a Trans Himalaya zone because of its position between the Great Himalaya Range and the vast Tibetan plateau. It is also one of the highest regions in India, with altitudes, even in the depths of the valleys, rarely falling below 3000m. It is worth noting that the lowest villages in the Indus Valley are at a higher elevation than the highest settlements in Kashmir.

Ladakh is drained by the Indus River and its tributaries, including the Zanskar River, which flows into the Indus at Nimmu village some 25 km west of Leh. The Shyok River forms an intermediary valley between the Ladakh Range (the mountain range immediately north of Leh) and the eastern Karakoram. The third main tributary of the Indus is the Suru River (flowing from the Pentse La). It flows into the Drass River just below Kargil before flowing into the Indus.

The Great Himalaya Range, including the two highest peaks of Nun (7135m) and Kun (7087m), forms the divide between Kashmir and Ladakh. To the south-east of the Nun Kun massif, the Great Himalaya Range consists of many peaks over 6000m which form the divide between Ladakh and Himachal Pradesh. The passes between Kashmir and Ladakh include the Zoji La and the Boktol Pass, while the Umasi La, the Kang La and the Shingo La link the Zanskar region of Ladakh with Himachal Pradesh.

The Zanskar Range forms the backbone of southern Ladakh. It includes several peaks over 6000m and is separated from the Great Himalaya Range by the Zanskar Valley. It is breached only once, where the Zanskar River flows north creating a series of huge gorges before flowing into the Indus. Passes over the Zanskar Range include the Kanji La and the Singge La. The Rubrang La also traverses the Zanskar Range to the Markha Valley, a small fertile valley between the Zanskar Range and the snow-capped Stok Range which lies immediately to the south of Leh and the upper Indus Valley.

The Ladakh Range extends north of the Indus Valley. The main pass, the Kardung La (5606m), is the highest motorable road in the world. North of the Ladakh Range is the eastern Karakoram, with the Karakoram Pass providing the historic trading route between Leh and the markets of Khotan and Kashgar in Central Asia.

CLIMATE

Ladakh is one of the driest regions in northern India. Indeed Leh, the capital of Ladakh, experiences an average of only 110 mm of rainfall per year, making it one of the driest places in the Indian subcontinent. Ladakh's position to the north-east of the main Himalayan Range isolates it from the Indian monsoon. However, areas to the south of the Indus Valley and closer to the Himalayan Range experience a higher rainfall. Padum, in the Zanskar Valley, is subject to the occasional heavy storm that breaks over the Himalayan Range in July and August, while in winter the heavy snowfall blocks off the passes to the rest of Ladakh. Leh, on the other hand, is on the lee side of both the Himalaya and the Zanskar Range, and even in the middle of winter does not experience the heavy snowfalls common in the Zanskar and Suru valleys.

In the winter, the daytime temperatures throughout Ladakh do not rise much above freezing. The maximum daytime temperatures in Leh are around -3°C in January, while at night they can fall to -15°C. In spring the temperatures begin to rise, and the farmers shovel earth onto the snow in the fields to assist the snow melt. Few of the high passes are clear of snow until July, and in some remote valleys it is considered inauspicious to cross the passes until the snow has fully melted. Nonetheless, most passes can be crossed by the end of June, which is the earliest time to undertake an extended trek through Ladakh, Zanskar or out of Panikhar in the Suru Valley. During July and August the daytime temperatures rise to the mid-20°Cs. For trekkers, the heat and the intense UV light require special caution. This is also the time for the occasional storm, which can result in snow falling at higher elevations.

When planning a trek, you must therefore consider that the temperature may vary by over 20°C in a day.

While most treks are undertaken in July and August, autumn (from early September to mid-October) is also ideal for trekking. The maximum daytime temperatures fall on average to between 10°C and 15°C, while any instability caused by the Indian monsoon gives way to settled conditions.

Towards the end of October there is usually one significant pre-winter storm lasting two or three days, with the first of the prolonged winter snows falling by December.

MAPS & BOOKS
Maps
For treks out of Leh and the Zanskar Valley, refer to the Leomann series *Sheet 3 (Leh, Zanskar and Nubra Valley)* and *Sheet 5 (Kullu Valley, Parbatti Valley and Central Lahaul)*, while for treks out of Kargil refer to the Leomann series *Sheet 2 (Kargil, Zanskar and Nun Kun area)*.

With the U502 series, refer to the *Leh section ref 43-8* and *Martselang section ref 43-12* for the treks south of Padum. The *Palampur section 43-16* includes treks from Padum to Darcha. For treks out of Kargil, refer to the *Kargil section ref 43-7* until Rangdum, and from there refer to the *Leh section ref 43-8*.

Books
For background on the cultural history of Ladakh, consult *The Cultural History of Ladakh* Volume 1 by Snellgrove & Skorupski, *A History of Ladakh* by AH Francke and *Himalayan Art* by Madanjeet Singh.

For 19th-century accounts, read *Travels in Kashmir, Ladak, Iskardo etc* by GT Vigne and *Travels in the Himalayan Provinces of Hindustan and the Panjab* by Moorcroft & Trebeck, which includes a journal of a trek made in the Markha Valley in the 1820s. *A Journey into Ladakh* by Andrew Harvey provides relevant spiritual reflections while on the trail, while *Hiking in Zanskar and Ladakh* includes details on some other treks out of the Indus and Zanskar valleys.

For background on the cultural history of Zanskar, consult *The Cultural History of Ladakh* Volume 2 by Snellgrove & Skorupski, *Ladakh* by Heinrich Harrer and *Himalayan Art* by Madanjeet Singh.

For 19th-century accounts, read *Western Himalaya and Tibet* by Thomas Thomson, which includes a description of the trek over the Umasi La. *Zanskar* by Michel Piessel covers details of the trek over the Shingo La. *First Across the Roof of the World* by Graeme Dingle & Peter Hillary includes details of a trek across Zanskar, while *Across the Top* by Sorrel Wilby includes a similar foray from Lamayuru to Darcha.

GETTING THERE & AWAY
Air
From Delhi there are daily Indian Airline flights into Leh throughout the summer season from June till September. At other times the schedule is cut to three or four times per week. The flights cost US$86. From Srinagar there is a once-a-week service which is heavily booked. The cost is US$43. There is also a twice-weekly service from Jammu that costs US$50.

Modiluft also operates services to Leh six times a week. The flight from Delhi via Jammu costs US$105, while the Jammu to Leh sector costs US$55.

Road
Srinagar The road journey from Srinagar to Leh is one of the most demanding in the Himalaya. The 450 km drive is generally covered in two long days. The first stage (240 km) is from the Kashmir Valley over the Zoji La to Kargil. The second stage (210 km) proceeds from Kargil over the Fatu La to the Indus Valley and Leh.

From Srinagar, the road follows the Sindh Valley to the alpine pastures of Sonamarg. Beyond Sonamarg, the road steadily ascends towards the Zoji La (3530m), the spectacular road pass over the main Himalaya Range. The first of the Ladakh villages are at Matayan and Drass, where there is a police checkpost. From Drass, the road follows the course of the Drass River to its confluence with the Suru River. Here it is just a few km up the Suru Valley to the town of Kargil.

From Kargil, the road ascends a plateau to the Wakka Valley and to the first Buddhist settlement at Mulbekh. At the side of the road a famous Buddhist carving dates back to the 1st century AD, a time when Buddhist monks trekked from Kashmir to Leh, and on to Tibet. From Mulbekh, the road crosses the Namika La (3720m) before descending to the Bodkarbu Valley, populated by Shia Muslims. The drive continues past Heniskot to the Fatu La (4094m), the highest pass on the road over an outer rim of the Zanskar Range. From here you can appreciate the location of the Indus Gorge and the impressive Ladakh Range to the north.

If you have the time, it is worthwhile leaving the road at the Fatu La and walking down the old pilgrim trail for two to three km to Lamayuru. The trail leads past the ancient chortens and mani walls which date from the 10th century, when the monastery was founded. Lamayuru was later declared a holy site and here even criminals could seek sanctuary. For that reason it is known to Ladakhi as the Tharpa Ling, or the Place of Freedom.

The road from Lamayuru drops nearly 1000m in less than 20 km to reach the Indus River – a record for road construction in the Himalaya.

Beyond the village of Khalsi, the road has followed the former Royal Highway to the village of Nurla. The Royal Highway then branched up the valley to Temisgam and crossed the higher ridges to Likir and Basgo. These days, the road follows the banks of the Indus, and is actually hewn out of the mountainside as far as Saspul. The bridge over the Indus just below Saspul marks the turning-off point for Alchi, which can be reached either on foot or by jeep.

From Saspul to Nimmu even the Indus Gorge is too steep for modern road builders, so the road climbs up over the Rongdu La to Basgo. As you approach Basgo, it is not hard to see why it was of such strategic importance to Ladakh. It was here that the Ladakhi armies were able to repel the invading Balti forces for years at a time.

Nimmu is about 10 km further on, just below the confluence of the Zanskar and Indus rivers. From here it is 40 km to Leh. On this final stage, the Indus Valley is bounded on the south by the Stok Range and to the north by the Ladakh Range. Tucked into one of the sheltered side valleys is Leh.

The Srinagar-Leh highway is open for just four months of the year, from the middle of June until the middle of October. During the winter and early spring the section between Leh and Kargil remains open for local traffic.

There is a daily bus service from the J&K Tourist Office in Srinagar. The deluxe bus costs Rs 333 one way, and the A-class is Rs 222. Trucks are a viable alternative, particularly later in the season. Prices are about the same as the bus, while taxis cost around Rs 5500.

Manali The military road from Leh to Manali was opened to foreigners in 1988. Since then, it has become a popular means of reaching Leh, particularly for those wanting to avoid the Kashmir Valley. The bus drive takes two days. There are two classes of bus to choose from. The deluxe bus costs Rs 700 plus Rs 300 for the overnight halt at the camp at Sarchu, where there is tented accommodation. The local bus includes a very long first day down to Keylong in Lahaul, and an easier second day over the Rhotang Pass to the Kullu Valley. The cost of the local bus is about Rs 350 one way. The alternative is to hire a jeep, which is expensive – up to Rs 12,000 one way. See the Kullu Valley section in the Himachal Pradesh chapter for further details.

Travel Tax

As a result of the formation of the Ladakh Autonomous Hill Council, a tourist entry tax of US$10 per foreign tourist has been introduced. This will be collected at the various entry points into Ladakh (eg at Upshi on the road from Manali). It will also be collected at the airport for tourists arriving by air. Also, an additional $20 will be levied on tourists visiting the newly opened areas of the Nubra Valley, Pangong Lake, Tso Morari and the Dha-Hanu region.

Leh & the Indus Valley

LEH

Leh, the capital of Ladakh, is in a small, fertile valley north of the Indus River. The town is at the base of the trail leading to the Kardung La, the first of the high passes formerly crossed by trading caravans as they made their way to the Karakoram Pass and the markets of Kashgar. Even though these trading routes have been closed since 1947, the Leh bazaar retains much of its character and the Victory Fort and the king's palace reflect Ladakh's rich cultural history.

Treks

Spitok to Hemis via the Markha Valley
(moderate to strenuous; 7 stages)
Lamayuru to Chiling via the Dung Dung La
(moderate to strenuous; 5 stages)

History

The history of trekking through the Indus Valley dates back to the time when pilgrimages were made through Ladakh en route to Mt Kailas after the Buddhist Congress in Kashmir in the 3rd century BC. Leh and the upper Indus Valley were also crossroads for trading routes that linked India with Central Asia.

To the south of the Indus Valley, the trails through the Markha Valley would have been followed by villagers and monks for many centuries. In 1821-2, the eminent travellers William Moorcroft and George Trebeck wandered these valleys while awaiting permission to cross the Karakoram Pass. A record of their travels is included in Volume 1 of their book *Travels in the Himalayan Provinces of Hindustan and the Panjab, etc*.

When to Trek

The treks out of the Markha Valley can be undertaken from the end of June when the snows melt on the higher passes. The Kongmaru La (over to Hemis) and the Dung Dung La (to Lamayuru) remain open until the middle of October. However, a trek up the Markha Valley could be undertaken throughout most of the year by avoiding the high passes and following the trail along the Zanskar River before heading up the valley.

Accommodation in Leh

Ladakh was officially opened to tourism in 1974, and nowadays there are well over a 100 guesthouses and hotels. Most are run by friendly Ladakhi families and are often an extension of their own home. These places are generally clean, simply appointed and of solid construction in traditional two-storey, whitewashed style.

Leh is not a big place, and you can walk around and check out a few hotels in an hour or so. You should be able to bargain for considerably less than the government rates outside the main season between late June and the end of September.

Rooms vary in price, depending on their size and location. In the old town, where accommodation is designed primarily to hold warmth in winter, the rooms are simply furnished and you'll get a bucket of water to wash with. Mid-range rooms will often have a view – usually of the snow-capped Stok Range – and have an attached bathroom with running water. The up-market rooms are simply furnished, although they will have blankets and a doona on the bed, and an attached bath (with running water, most of the time).

The current rate for full board in the A-class hotels is Rs 1200 for a single and Rs 1500 for a double. In B-class hotels it's Rs 900 a single and Rs 1200 a double. These prices can be discounted by up to 40% out of the main season. Guesthouses are a comfortable alternative, charging anything from Rs 100 to Rs 300 per room.

Accommodation on the Trail

Over the last decade many tea stalls-cum-hotels have been established on the trek to the Markha Valley. There are tea stalls at Jingchan, Rumbak, Stok, Markha, Hankar and at Chogdo. There are also three or four houses at Shingo village where you can stay overnight. The only problem is at Nimaling, so you will need to take a tent just for that stage. An alternative is to stay overnight at Tahungtse, a camp run by villagers from Hankar, which is midway between Hankar village and Nimaling. However, this will necessitate a long stage over the Kongmaru La the following day. On the trek between Lamayuru and Chiling a tent is necessary as there are no tea stalls-cum-hotels beyond the first stage at Wanlah.

Trekking Agents

There has been a huge expansion in the number of trekking agencies in the 1990s. Now nearly 100 agencies vie for business. It is difficult to suggest a particular agency. Mountain Journeys on Fort Rd and Himalayan Adventures Extraordinaire opposite the taxi stand in Fort Road are two agencies run by friends of mine, while Yak Travel and Asia Adventures on Fort Rd and Yundung Tours opposite the taxi stand have also been recommended. Most provide a full trekking package including horses, guide and cook, tents and cooking equipment. Budget for around Rs 1000 each per day for a group of five or six people, Rs 1200 for two and Rs 1500 for one person.

Trekking Advice

Acclimatisation is the most important consideration on these treks. The Ganda La, en route to the Markha Valley, is at an altitude of 4920m, the Kongmaru La above Hemis is at 5030m, while the Konze La en route from Lamayuru is at 4950m. Some time, therefore, should be spent in Leh, and the initial stages of the treks should be taken very slowly. Remember that Leh, at 3500m, is only 300m lower than Tengboche monastery in Nepal, the acclimatisation camp en route to Everest Base Camp.

Also, it is worth considering very early starts every day, particularly in July and August, and completing each trek stage by midday. Dehydration is a problem in this intensely arid area, and fluid levels must be maintained. River crossings constitute a problem, although they are not as hazardous as on the more remote treks in the Zanskar region.

After heavy rainfall, trails can collapse in

the gullies and gorges. The sections from the Kongmaru La to Hemis on the Markha Valley trek, from the Dung Dung La to Chiling on the trek from Lamayuru, and from the Prinkiti La or the upper Shilakong Valley en route to Wanlah are particularly vulnerable.

Provisions

During the trekking season there is no shortage of fresh vegetables and fruit in the Leh bazaar. The produce is either locally grown or brought by trucks from Manali or Srinagar. Tinned foods are also available, together with basics including rice, flour, sugar and cooking oil. Stock up on supplies for the complete trek as there is little available beyond biscuits and basics once you leave the trailhead.

Horsemen & Porters

One of the biggest obstacles to getting started on a trek out of Leh is finding horsemen. During the summer months most are engaged in their fields. For those who are prepared to come, expect a delay of a day or two while they locate their horses, which are often grazing on the higher pastures well away from the villages. Using a local agent is therefore sometimes the only option. Expect to pay around Rs 200 per day for a horse (for three horses budget around Rs 500 per day) and Rs 150 for a donkey.

You could, of course, bypass the system and buy a mule. This was in vogue about a decade ago and I can recall a rather intrepid Frenchman, intent on trekking to Zanskar, pushing and cursing his newly acquired mule about one stage above Hemis. He had taken four days to reach the spot where I met him. The story going the rounds afterwards was that he finally gave up when the mule bolted back to its village just below Hemis. Needless to say, the sell-back price to the former Ladakhi owner was but a fraction of the original price paid by the Frenchman!

Access

Local buses (always crowded but never boring) leave from the bus station next to the polo ground, at irregular intervals, for most of the outlying villages and monasteries. These include daily services to Khalsi, Nimmu and Saspul, and also one service a day to Hemis, which stops at all places en route. There are two services a day to Stok and Spitok. If you are carrying all your trekking supplies, arrive early, as space on the roof is as limited as space inside the bus. Timetables are altered frequently, so it is best to enquire at the bus station the day before to find what is going when. The cost of the bus to Hemis is Rs 25, to Stok Rs 10 and to Spitok it is Rs 5. If trekking out from Lamayuru, take the Kargil bus at Rs 150. Trucks are an alternative, although they prefer full-paying passengers going all the way to Kargil or Srinagar.

Jeeps or taxis are a convenient alternative. If you band together with others, the fare works out to be reasonable. It costs about Rs 530 one way and Rs 680 return to Hemis, Rs 230 one way and Rs 330 return to Stok and Rs 1500 one way and Rs 2000 return to Lamayuru. There are fixed rates for such outings and you will have to bargain very hard to get any discount. A jeep to the airport will cost about Rs 70.

SPITOK TO HEMIS VIA THE MARKHA VALLEY
Map: Ladakh Section 1 (pages 126-7)
Ladakh – Spitok to Hemis via the Markha Valley

There are two approaches to the trek up the Markha Valley. The first is via Spitok, Jingchan and Rumbak villages to the base of the Ganda La; the second approach is via Stok village and over the Namlung La (4570m) to join the first route at Rumbak village. For those who are fit and well acclimatised, the Stok approach provides breathtaking views of the Indus Valley as you ascend to the Namlung La. Normally, one night is spent camping in the gorges above Stok, crossing the pass the following day before descending to Rumbak village. If you are not well acclimatised, the first route via Spitok and Jingchan is the better alternative.

Stage 1: Spitok to Rumbak
(Average walking time 6 to 7 hours)
It is a short drive from Leh to Spitok, below the airport. **Spitok monastery** is one of the oldest in the upper Indus Valley, founded at the same time as Thikse and Likir. The monastery, like that at Thikse, is on top of a small hill with a commanding view up the valley. The positioning of this monastery indicates a historic change in the location of monasteries in the Indus Valley which, up to the 15th century, were typically built in sheltered valleys, as at Alchi and Temisgam. Although the monasteries at Thikse and Spitok were not founded for strategic reasons, their location would have been a considerable asset during later periods of political turbulence.

From the monastery, cross the bridge over the Indus and, on the true left bank, follow the trail that stretches across the barren and exposed flats. It is advisable to set off early. This stage is not particularly interesting, and it can become quite warm by midday. After six or seven km, the Indus enters a tight gorge at its confluence with the Jingchan River. Follow the trail up the Jingchan Valley, which is lined with trees providing sufficient shade for rest stops. The main village at

Jingchan (3600m) consists of a few settlements with some camping stops in the vicinity. Either camp here, or continue for a few more km to the village of **Rumbak** (3750m).

Stage 2: Rumbak to Yurutse & Camp

(Average walking time 4 to 5 hours)
Beyond Rumbak there is a steady ascent up the valley that leads south to the village of **Yurutse** (4150m). Here, the large whitewashed house is owned by a very hospitable family whose supply of the local barley beer has curtailed many a day's trekking. For the less indulgent, there is a small camp site two to three km further up, which is complete with a small spring and views back to the Stok Range, including Stok Kangri (6121m).

Stage 3: Camp to Ganda La, Markha Valley & Skiu

(Average walking time 6 to 7 hours)
From camp, it is a steady climb for an hour or so to the **Ganda La** (4920m). The pass has the usual array of prayer flags and cairns with views south to the Zanskar Range. From the pass, the village of **Shingo** (4150m) can be seen a few km down the valley. The trail is well marked and there is a good camping area above the village. Below Shingo the trail enters a narrow gorge, lined with willows and wild rose bushes. After five to six km there are some small stupas which mark the confluence with the Markha Valley. Turn up the valley for one km or so, to the village of **Skiu** (3700m), where there is a rather marshy camp site immediately below the main house.

If time is not at a premium, then a rest day, with a walk down valley to the Zanskar River, is recommended. The route leads through the settlement of **Kaya** (3650m) complete with apricot orchards and a tiny village monastery. Kaya is soon to be thrust into the 21st century as the road from Nimmu is to extend up and alongside the Zanskar River. It is planned that the road will eventually link all the villages in the Markha Valley. While you are resting at the confluence of the Zanskar and Markha rivers, it is worth con-

sidering that there are plans eventually to continue the road up the Zanskar gorges to the Zanskar Valley. This will be easier said than done. These gorges are some of the steepest anywhere in the Himalaya, as anyone who has rafted the river will appreciate.

Stage 4: Skiu to Markha

(Average walking time 7 to 8 hours)
This stage of about 17 km can be covered in one day's walk. The terrain along the valley is not demanding, although the trail crosses the Markha River several times.

The river crossings in the valley were a problem in the past, but nowadays, with the construction of bridges, the stage is more or less straightforward. There are a few ancient chortens along the trail, and some wolf pits used to trap wolves descending to the valley during the winter months. There is no shortage of camping spots should you decide to appreciate the valley at a more leisurely pace.

Markha (3850m) is a substantial village, complete with a derelict fort on the hillside. Camp sites are normally selected from the ample grazing flats just beyond the village, and a small charge of a few rupees is sometimes collected. The villagers are inquisitive and friendly, and there is a small village monastery just above the village – worth a visit if you can find the caretaker who holds the key.

Stage 5: Markha to Nimaling

(Average walking time 7 to 8 hours)
This is another long stage which can be split with an intermediary camp at the grazing meadow of Tahungtse, three km beyond the village of Hankar. Beyond Markha, the trail remains on the true right of the valley, and after two to three km passes a narrow gorge which marks the route over the Rubrang La and Cha Cha La to Zangla and the Zanskar Valley. A few km beyond this point is the settlement of Umlung (3900m), after which the valley broadens and the imposing peak of Kangyaze (6400m) can be appreciated.

The village of **Hankar** (4000m) is the

highest village in the Markha Valley and from there the trail ascends the valley to the Nimaling Plains. The trail crosses the Nimaling stream just after Hankar, and from this point it is a steady climb to Tahungtse and the edge of the high grazing pastures. The trail splits on several occasions and it is necessary to follow the route leading up the valley rather than those leading towards the base of Kangyaze.

The encampment at **Nimaling** (4650m) consists of several stone shelters where the villagers from Hankar and Markha graze their yaks and goats during the summer months. It should be borne in mind that inclement weather can build up quickly in this area, and a tent and warm clothing are necessary even during midsummer.

There are many side trips which can be undertaken from the camp at Nimaling. Kangyaze peak is not technically difficult to climb but, as elsewhere in the Indian Himalaya, regulations stipulate that peaks over 6000m cannot be undertaken without a permit and an accompanying liaison officer. Fines have been imposed for illegal attempts on this and Stok Kangri (6121m), the prominent snow-capped peak to the south of Stok village.

Stage 6: Nimaling to Kongmaru La & Chogdo
(Average walking time 6 hours)
From Nimaling, cross to the true right side of the stream and start climbing up the well-defined trail to the Kongmaru La (5030m). The climb should take two hours at the most. If it has been snowing, get the shepherds to point out the general direction to you. The pass is at the top of the ridge and what you see is what you climb; there are no false ridges or further climbs, which are the hallmark of so many Himalayan passes. From the pass, there are uninterrupted views to Kangyaze, while to the north-east lie the Indus Valley and the Ladakh Range.

The initial descent is steep, down a series of zigzags to a meagre camp site which is often used by parties trekking up from Hemis. From here, the trail enters a gorge

and drops nearly 1000m to the highest village. The track may not always be in the best of condition, as flash floods wash away the hillside every few seasons. The resultant trail erosion illustrates clearly the delicate nature of the mountain terrain in Ladakh. Irrespective of the weather there are several river crossings on this stage before reaching **Chogdo** (4050m), the highest village. Here it is possible to camp in the stone enclosure opposite the houses.

Stage 7: Chogdo to Hemis
(Average walking time 4 to 5 hours)
The final stage of this trek follows the valley floor for four or five km to the village of **Sumdo** (3850m). From here, the trail improves as it approaches the Leh-Manali road. Turn left (westwards) by the large chorten above Martselang village, and follow the rather dusty trail to **Hemis** (3505m). There is a camping ground just above the village, complete with a restaurant, and perhaps a beer. There is a camping charge of about Rs 20 per night.

Getting Away
The bus from Hemis to Leh departs around midday, takes about two hours and costs Rs 25. The bus stops on the way at Thikse monastery and Shey palace, where there are small hotels for overnight accommodation. Details of the main palaces and monasteries follow.

Hemis
The monastery at Hemis is one of the most important in Ladakh. It is the principal monastery of the Drukpa order, and the head monk administers all the associated monasteries in the Ladakh and Zanskar regions. It was established in the 17th century under the patronage of Singge Namgyal, and since then has enjoyed the financial support of successive royal families. The monastery provides caretaker monks for the monasteries at Leh, Basgo and Shey.

The former head monk of Hemis was detained in Tibet when it was taken over by the Chinese. He has recently been able to return to visit the monastery after a period of 20 years. In the meantime, a monk from Dharamsala was appointed, and he has assumed jurisdiction over the monastery.

Each year the Hemis festival attracts more than its share of local visitors and tourists. It is held during the full moon in June, and is attended by monks and their families who have travelled from throughout Ladakh and the Zanskar Valley. The highlight of the festival is a series of masked dances commemorating the deeds of the Buddhist figurehead Padmasambhava, the sage who introduced Tantric Buddhism to the Himalaya. Once every 11 years a huge *tanka* (painting), one of the largest in the Tibetan world, is displayed on the walls of the Hemis courtyard. The next showing will be in 2002.

To fully appreciate the position of the monastery, and also gain some insight into the meditative practices pursued by the monks, a visit to the monks' hermitage, about an hour's climb behind the monastery, is recommended.

Thikse

The site of Thikse in the Indus Valley makes it one of the area's most impressive monasteries. It was founded in the early 15th century, along with Likir and Spitok, as the monks from Tibet spread the word of the reformist Gelukpa order, which is now associated with the Dalai Lama. The assembly hall is on top of the hill, with the monks' quarters below. The library at Thikse is supposedly one of the best in the West Himalaya, and a multi-denominational chapel has recently been constructed – proof indeed of the continuing vitality of Buddhism in Ladakh.

Shey

Shey was the former palace of the upper kingdom of Ladakh. Its foundation can be traced to the earliest history of Ladakh, while the inscriptions on the rocks below the palace date from the time when Buddhism was first introduced to the western Himalaya. The palace was occupied by members of the Ladakhi royal family until 1834, when

they were exiled to Stok. Since then, many of the buildings have fallen into disrepair, and the lake at the base of the hill is now marshland.

In the last decade there has been some restoration of the Buddhist artefacts, including the two-storeyed Sakyamuni Buddha originally commissioned by Singge Namgyal.

Stok

To complete the upper Indus cultural circuit, the imposing palace of Stok is an hour's drive south across the Indus Valley from Leh. It was built during the 1840s to house the Ladakhi royal family after they had been exiled by the Dogra army. The Rani (queen) of Stok has assumed responsibility for the maintenance and reconstruction of the Ladakhi palaces in Stok, Leh and Shey. The exhibits at the Stok museum include many of the important royal tankas, while the collection of headdresses is the most impressive in Ladakh. It is planned that the museum pieces will eventually be moved to the Leh palace, when sufficient funds are available.

LAMAYURU TO CHILING VIA THE DUNG DUNG LA
Map: Ladakh Section 1 (pages 126-7)
Lamayuru

The old caravan route to Lamayuru diverges from the Kargil-Leh road at the Fatu La. As you descend from the pass, you can appreciate the impressive line of mani walls and chortens which lead down to the village.

Legend has it that the upper reaches of this valley were once filled by a vast lake. This was miraculously breached by the sage Naropa. The site of the breach was revered, and became the location of the monastery which was built in the 10th century. Whatever the truth of the legend, Lamayuru is one of the oldest monastic sites in Ladakh. One of the original temples is just beyond the main assembly hall and has been renovated. The monastery subscribes to one of the older Tibetan schools, the Kargyupa order, which was followed by the noted sages Marpa (1012-97) and Milarepa (1040-1123). For many of the outlying monasteries in the region the doctrinal distinctions are merely technical – for example the monasteries at Wanlah, Phanjila and Khalsi, although affiliated with Lamayuru, also have close cultural links with the main Drukpa monastery at Hemis.

Stage 1: Lamayuru to Wanlah

(Average walking time 3½ to 4 hours)
From **Lamayuru** village (3420m) follow the trail leading down the valley for two km before diverting up the ridge to the east which leads to the Prinkiti La (see the Ladakh Section 1 map). The ascent is gradual and it should not take much more than an hour to reach the pass from Lamayuru village. From the **Prinkiti La** (3750m) the trail enters a narrow gorge which is at most times hot and dusty, although after a few days of rain the character of the gorge changes remarkably. After several km the gorge meets the Shilakong Valley and it is a further two to three km to the village and monastery of Wanlah. There is an established camp site just north of the bridge over the Wanlah River and some small hotels for overnight.

Wanlah monastery was established at the same time as the Lamayuru monastery and is nowadays serviced by the monks from Lamayuru. The monastery has a commanding position looking up the Shilakong Valley and the main assembly hall is open most of the day. One of the novice monks will have the key. The monastery has not attracted the same degree of restoration as Lamayuru and a nominal contribution of Rs 20 is expected.

Wanlah village has been connected by road with Khalsi in the Indus Valley. The road was completed in 1993, but there are still many places where it is subject to landslides. The bus is scheduled to reach Wanlah each day and return to Leh the next. Eventually the road will extend to Phanjila and then to Honupatta.

Stage 2: Wanlah to Hinju

(Average walking time 4 to 5 hours)
From **Wanlah** (3250m) cross the main bridge and follow the true right bank of the valley. The trek to Phanjila follows the road construction up the valley and takes around 1½ hours.

The village of **Phanjila** (3410m) is at the entrance to the Hinju Valley. It boasts a school and some apricot orchards. The fields extend two to three km up towards Hinju. Follow the trail on the true right of the valley until it enters a narrow gorge. Here it switches for a short distance to the opposite bank before re-crossing the valley to the true right side. There are small bridges to assist with the crossings.

Hinju village (3720m) consists of three main settlements: lower Hinju, the main village, and upper Hinju about three k.n further up the valley towards the Konze La. The main village consists of about 15 houses, some with solar heating. There is a choice of camp sites about two km above the village – an ideal base for the Konze La.

Stage 3: Hinju via Konze La to Camp

(Average walking time 6 to 7 hours)
From the camp above Hinju there is a steady climb past the settlement of upper Hinju and some goat enclosures. Beyond the settlement the trail gradually winds down to the valley floor and past a lone yak herder's encampment. This is the base of the pass.

From the yak herder's encampment, continue up the valley floor for two km before commencing the ascent which leads to the high ridge below the pass. There are impressive views back down the valley to Hinju village and on across to the outer rim of the Zanskar Range and the distant Karakoram Range. Looking back, it is easy to imagine the snow leopard ascending the windswept side ridges in search of prey. In fact there have been some snow leopard sightings around here.

The climb to the pass from Hinju village takes around three to 3½ hours – the time varying considerably at the margins of the seasons when fresh snow still covers the approach to the pass. From the **Konze La** (4950m) there are views to the Ladakh Range and the Karakoram, while to the east the Stok Range and the main ridges of the Zanskar Range can be appreciated.

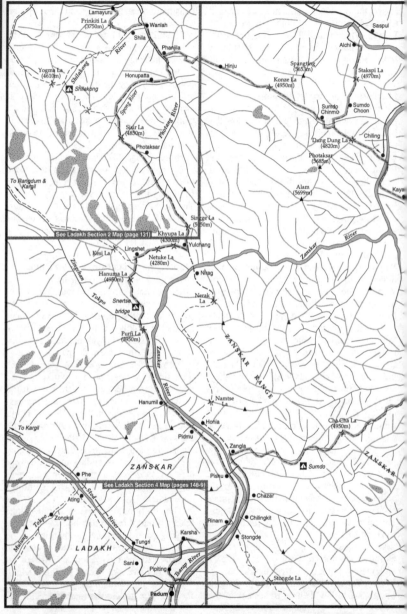

Lamayuru
Prinkiti La
(3750m)
Shila
Wanlah
Saspul
Phanjila
Alchi
Hinju
Yogma La
(4610m)
Spangting
(5663m)
Stakspi La
(4970m)
Shilakong
Honupatta
Konze La
(4950m)
Spong River
Sumdo
Chinmo
Sumdo
Choon
Chiling
Photang River
Sisir La
(4850m)
Dung Dung La
(4820m)
Photaksar
Photaksar
(5685m)
To Rangdum &
Kargil
Alam
(5699m)
Kaya
Singge La
(5050m)
Khyupa La
(4300m)
See Ladakh Section 2 Map (page 131)
Yulchang
Kesi La
Lingshet
Netuke La
(4280m)
Zanskar River
Nitag
Hanuma La
(4950m)
Zangchan
Tokpo
Snertse
bridge
Nerak
La
Purfi La
(3950m)
Zanskar
River
ZANSKAR
RANGE
Namtse
La
Cha Cha La
(4950m)
Hanumil
Honia
To Kargil
Pidmu
Zangla
Sumdo
ZANSKAR
ZANSKAR
Phe
Pishu
See Ladakh Section 4 Map (pages 148-9)
Chazar
Ating
Chilingkit
Stod
River
Malung
Tokpo
Zongkul
Rinam
Stongde
Tungri
Karsha
LADAKH
Sani
Pipiting
Tsarap River
Stongde La
Padum

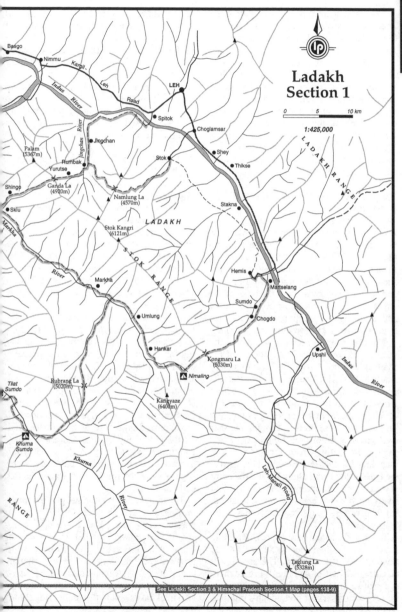

Ladakh
Section 1

0   5   10 km

1:425,000

See Ladakh Section 3 & Himachal Pradesh Section 1 Map (pages 138-9)

The descent from the pass is quite steep, over loose moraine with an ill-defined trail leading to the true left of the main valley. Once down to the valley floor it is a short distance to the first camp (convenient if walking in the opposite direction). The trail remains on the true left side of the valley, crossing some small side ridges before descending to an established yak herders' encampment at the confluence of a valley leading off to the south of the Konze La. These yak herders' huts (4500m) are occupied during the summer months by villagers from Sumdo Chinmu village.

Stage 4: Sumdo Chinmu to Base of Dung Dung La

(Average walking time 3 to 4 hours)
From camp, cross the main river and follow the trail on the true right of the valley. For a time the trail ascends a side ridge above the main valley which has some potential camp sites. It then winds down to the valley floor and another river crossing is the order of the day before re-ascending the opposite valley and following the irrigation channel on down to the village of **Sumdo Chinmu** (4300m).

There is a small monastery close to the village and some large stone statues of the Maitreya Buddha (the Buddha to come) nearby. The trail remains on the true left side of the valley for a further two km before winding down to the valley floor (4250m) which is covered in a thick canopy of willow trees and wild rose bushes. There is a further river crossing before reaching a small side stream emanating from the high peaks, including Photaksar (5685m). This is also the base of the Dung Dung La and the point at which the trails diverge. The trail to Alchi heads on down the valley for several km before diverting up a side valley towards the Stakspi La.

To reach the actual base of the Dung Dung La, a short, if rather steep, ascent over a side ridge (4430m) is required. The ascent will take the best part of an hour. En route there is a profusion of eldelweiss and other wild-flowers which survive on Ladakh's minimal rainfall. From the ridge there are views back

to the Konze La while there is a delightful meadow for camping at this upper base of the Dung Dung La.

The meadow (4400m) is used for grazing by yak herders from Chiling village who stay there throughout most of the summer months, arriving in early July and remaining till the end of September. The camp has also been an attraction for thoughtless trekking groups who have discarded numerous bottles and tin cans in the nearby bushes.

Option: Sumdo Chinmu Village to Alchi via the Stakspi La

(This option takes two to three stages to complete.)
From Sumdo Chinmu follow the trail down the valley past the base of the Dung Dung La. This entails following a rough trail which crosses the river several times before it diverts to a side ridge to the north of the valley. The trail then leads up and over to the village of Sumdo Choon (note: Sumdo Choon, 'little village', and Sumdo Chinmu, 'big village').

At Sumdo Choon there is a small monastery affiliated with Alchi, and the assembly hall displays a similar variety of wall paintings and carvings. It also has an impressive statue of the Maitreya Buddha in the adjoining temple. Above the village there is a trail leading to the base of the Stakspi La. On the second stage there is a short, steep ascent to the **Stakspi La** (4970m) and grand views of the Ladakh Range. (I recall being benighted on the pass many seasons ago after a long and tiring ascent from Alchi – not your average first day's trek – but there were superb views of the Ladakh Range in the early morning.)

The trail descends quite steeply to a small grazing area and shepherds' shelter and a possible camp site. (This is a useful camp spot if you're doing the trek in reverse out from Alchi.) It is a further three hours down to **Alchi** (3200m), where there is a regular camp site-cum-restaurant close to the monastery. A further three to four km along the jeep track takes you to the Alchi bridge, and the main highway to Leh.

Alchi The monastery complex at Alchi was founded in the 11th century when the noted teacher, Ringchen Brangpo, was sent by a local Tibetan king to lay the foundations for Buddhist monasteries throughout Ladakh and the Zanskar. Due to its sheltered location, Alchi has remained intact to the present day.

The major point of interest in the monastery at Alchi stems from the fact that the Tibetans, being newly converted to Buddhism, did not have the artistic skills necessary to decorate the temples. Artists from the Kashmir Valley (whose Buddhist temples have long been destroyed) were therefore commissioned to complete the walls and entrances.

For a complete survey of the Alchi temples, and a detailed history of the other monasteries in Ladakh, refer to Volume 1 of Snellgrove & Skorupski's *The Cultural History of Ladakh*.

Stage 5: Dung Dung La to Chiling

(Average walking time 6 hours)

It is not a particularly steep ascent from camp to the **Dung Dung La** (4820m). The trail winds past yak herders' camps before zigzagging across scree slopes to the pass. En route there are splendid views towards the Konze La and the Ladakh Range. From the pass there are unrivalled views – north to the Ladakh Range, east across the Stok Range and south to the Zanskar Range – while the depths of the Zanskar Valley appear way down below.

The route from the pass follows the contours around a high ridge for about two km before commencing a long and gradual descent towards Chiling village. The trail leads to the south, and in the immediate foreground there are views of the confluence of the Markha and Zanskar rivers. It is possible to pick out the lie of the land leading up the Markha Valley towards the Kongmaru La. About halfway down, the trail leads through a small settlement (4270m) where a lone woman from Chiling works the fields. From the settlement there is a short, steep descent towards the floor of a subsidiary valley just above Chiling. The trail is ill

defined after heavy rainfall and the horses and their charges are in for a good two hours work before reaching Chiling.

Chiling village (3550m) provides much of the copperwork entering the Leh market. The main village is up a ridge above the established camp site and is well worth the visit. The village is now connected to Nimmu on the Kargil-Leh road by a jeep road extending alongside the Zanskar River. Plans are afoot to continue the road up the Zanskar gorges towards the Zanskar Valley, while at the same time extending east up the Markha Valley.

Getting Away

The road was completed to Chiling in October 1995, however, there is no bus service yet. The alternatives are to arrange for a jeep to come from Leh to pick you up, or to trek down the valley for a further stage to Nimmu and the Indus Valley.

A further option is to trek up the road to the pulley bridge over the Zanskar River. Cross the river (Rs 80 per pulley ride) and then continue on the opposite, true right side of the river to the confluence with the Markha Valley. The trek up the valley to the confluence should take no more than two to three hours and from there it is a further two hours to the village of Skiu. For a description of the stages on to Markha village, the Kongmaru La and Hemis monastery, refer to the Spitok to Hemis via the Markha Valley trek description.

Kargil & the Suru Valley

For most people Kargil is just an overnight stop on the road between Srinagar and Leh or Padum. Yet before 1947 its position at the confluence of the Suru and Drass rivers made it an important trading town, linking Kashmir and Ladakh with Gilgit and Baltistan.

Trek
Panikhar to Heniskot via the Kanji La
(strenuous; 7 stages)

History

When Arthur Neve wrote his book *Trekking in Kashmir, Ladakh and Baltistan* in 1911, he devoted one section to Kashmir, one to Ladakh and one to Baltistan. Since the 1947 partition of India and Pakistan, Baltistan has been split between the two countries, and any notion of trekking the mountain trails from Kargil to Gilgit is nowadays out of the question.

The treks out of the Suru Valley, however, have been followed by villagers and Buddhist monks for many generations – the Suru Valley carrying much of the trade between the Zanskar Valley and the Indus. Indeed, even in the early 1970s the road up the Suru Valley did not extend past the village of Sanko, 20 km south-west of Kargil, and the yak and mule trains would continue right into the Kargil bazaar.

When to Trek

For most people, the trek from Panikhar to Heniskot or Lamayuru is an extension of the trek from Pahalgam in Kashmir. The trek could be completed from the end of June when the snow begins to melt on the highest pass, the Kanji La (5290m). It remains open until the middle of October when the first of the winter snows hasten the end of the season.

As a matter of note, the Pentse La (4450m), the motorable pass linking Kargil and the Zanskar Valley, is normally open to vehicles by the beginning of July. However, well-equipped trekkers can follow in the footsteps of the villagers who normally cross the pass from May onwards, making their way from the highest village of Abran to Rangdum monastery in one day.

Accommodation in Kargil

The Kargil bazaar is not exactly the best place to get a comfortable night's sleep. In spite of the downturn in business since 1990, there is still no shortage of rooms in the main bazaar from Rs 50 to Rs 300 per night.

The A-class hotels catering to the tourist groups charge Rs 1500/2000 a single/double on a full-board basis. The B-class hotels cost Rs 700/900. Rooms at the *J&K Tourist Bungalow*, above the bazaar, start at Rs 300 per night and at present are the best option, although travellers have reported that the complex has been temporarily closed due to lack of demand.

Accommodation on the Trail

The J&K Tourist Department has *Tourist Bungalows* at Sanko, Panikhar and Rangdum with rooms for Rs 80 per night. There are also tea-house lodges in Panikhar and at Juldo village before Rangdum monastery. If trekking over the Kanji La you must bring a tent. If travelling to the Zanskar Valley at the margins of the seasons it is possible to trek over the Pentse La and find shelter in the villages en route to Padum, although you must bring your own food supplies.

Trekking Advice

Before undertaking the trek over the Kanji La, it is important that you are well acclimatised. Plan on spending a few additional nights at Rangdum before crossing the pass.

The river crossings between Rangdum and the base of the pass are a problem in late June and July when the spring snow melt causes the rivers to flood.

Provisions

Most fruit and vegetables can be purchased in the Kargil bazaar, together with rice, flour, biscuits and other basics. Tinned foods and luxury items should be brought from Srinagar or Leh. You should also double check the availability of kerosene, which may be difficult to obtain, particularly at the beginning of the season. (Money should be exchanged before reaching Kargil.) Alternatively, biscuits and basics can be purchased at Panikhar, Juldo or Rangdum along the trek.

Horsemen & Porters

Most arrangements for horsemen can be made at one of the lodges at Panikhar. The horsemen, while not as fast as their Kashmiri

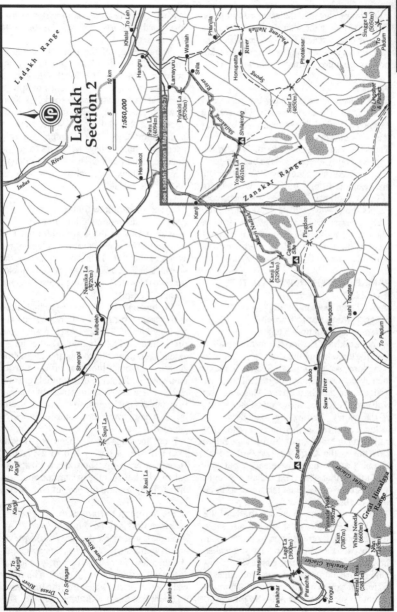

Ladakh
Section 2

1:550,000

0   5   10 km

To Leh

Khatsi

Hangru

Ladakh Range

Indus River

Fatu La
(4094m)

Heniskot

Namika La
(3720m)

Mulbekh

Shergol

Sept La

Rasi La

To Kargil

To Kargil

To Kargil

Drass River

Suru River

To Srinagar

Sanko

Panikhar

Namsuru

Lagti La
(3940m)

Parachik

Tongul

Parachik Glacier

Kun
(7087m)

White Needle
(6600m)

Pinnacle Peak
(6952m)

Nun
(7135m)

Barmal Peak
(5813m)

Great Himalaya Range

Shafat Glacier

Shafat

Suru River

To Padum

Juldo

Rangdum

Tashi Toqtse

Kanji La
(5290m)

Camp Site

Kanji Nullah

Pingdon La

Kanji

See Ladakh Section 1 Map (pages 126-7)

Lamayuru

Prijikiti La
(3750m)

Shila

Wanla

Phanjila

Yapola River

Shilakong

Shilakong River

Yogma La
(4610m)

Zanskar Range

Spong

Honupatta

Photang Nullah

Sisir La
(4850m)

Photaksar

To Lingshet & Padum

Singge La
(5050m)

To Padum

counterparts, are nonetheless good company. Expect to pay in the vicinity of Rs 100 to Rs 150 per day, which will include provision for their return journey. As elsewhere in Ladakh, porters are generally not available.

Access

From Kargil, there is a daily bus service to Panikhar which costs Rs 40. The service extends to Padum three times a week during the season. This fare is Rs 250 one way. Trucks are a convenient alternative and the cost is roughly the same as the bus. The cost is more if you sit in the driver's cabin. Jeeps are available from Kargil and cost about Rs 1200 to Panikhar. To Padum the jeeps cost Rs 6000 one way, and Rs 8000 return. The J&K Tourist Office or the bus station manager can give you an up-to-date assessment of the condition of the road, which is normally open to Padum by early July.

PANIKHAR TO HENISKOT VIA THE KANJI LA

Map: Ladakh Section 2 Map (Page 131)
Stage 1: Panikhar to Parachik
(Average walking time 5 hours)
From **Panikhar** (3350m) follow the metalled road for three km up the valley as if going to Rangdum (see the Ladakh Section 2 map), then divert through the villages and cross the bridge over the Suru River. This links up with a road under construction on the far side of the valley. Follow the road down the valley for a km or so, then turn off on the foot trail going uphill towards the dip in the ridge. This dip is the **Lago La** (3900m), which means 'pass of no consequence', but you won't think that when you're halfway up it. It is a deceptive pass that takes two to three hours to climb.

The springline is about two thirds of the way up the hillside, although it is advisable to take boiled water with you from Panikhar. As you reach the crest of the ridge you realise the climb has been worthwhile. The complete Nun Kun massif appears immediately in front of you. This magnificent panorama cannot be seen from the road. So it helps to give trekkers some sense of dignity the fol-

lowing day, when they are overtaken by a lorry load of tourists unaware of the views they have missed.

From the top of the pass, the camping areas can be seen. These are rich, green grazing areas for the local villagers at Parachik, and are fed by a series of spring-lines that are distant from the road. It is 300m down to the camp, and takes about 30 minutes. Although it's quite steep, there are many short cuts. At the camp you may encounter some garbage left by less discriminate trekking parties. This is unfortunately a sign of things to come as you progress further into Ladakh.

Stage 2: Parachik to Shafat
(Average walking time 6 hours)
This stage follows the jeep road for much of the way. The compensation is again the views of the main Himalaya, including the spectacular Parachik Glacier, which tumbles down to the water's edge just above Parachik village (3550m).

The trek initially involves a gradual climb to the open grazing areas often referred to as the Lingti plains. This takes on average about three hours. The Bakharval shepherds extend their migration to this area during the summer, although the local villagers from Panikhar and Parachik dispute their grazing rights. There have been instances of stealing from tents in this region, so it is worth ensuring that your overnight camp is properly guarded.

From the edge of the plains to **Shafat** (3850m) takes a further two to 2½ hours. Here there are some camp sites opposite the valley which marks the expedition route up the Shafat Glacier to the base of Kun peak.

Stage 3: Shafat to Rangdum
(Average walking time 5 hours)
After the comparative drudgery of the previous day, this stage always seems a delight. Within a few hours of setting off you arrive at the village of **Juldo** (3900m). The mani walls and chortens which line the trail leave no doubt that this is a Buddhist village. The monastery at Rangdum can be seen on top of

the sugarloaf mountain at the head of the valley.

From Juldo there is a variety of short cuts on to **Rangdum** (3980m) – that is, if you have a sense of adventure and don't mind traversing the occasional bog. Compensations include the many wildflowers that bloom until the middle of September, such as edelweiss, delphinium, tansy and genfianella.

Although there are many camp sites in the vicinity of the monastery, one alternative is to continue to the village of **Tashi Tongtse**, on the far side of Rangdum. The village is seldom visited by trekkers, and I have enjoyed many nights sharing the barley beer and joining the local women's dancing troupe! The villagers both here and at Juldo regard themselves as part of Zanskar, in spite of their location to the north of the Pentse La. Marriages between these villagers and those of the Stod Valley in Zanskar are common.

Many of the monks at Rangdum come from Tashi Tongtse and Juldo. The monastery was founded quite recently – only about 200 years ago – and is affiliated with the Gelukpa order, the Dalai Lama's sect. The entrance fee to the monastery is Rs 10.

Stage 4: Rangdum to Kanji La Base Camp
(Average walking time five to 6 hours)
The trail to Kanji follows the valley behind Rangdum monastery. Which route you follow up the valley depends on the water level in the river. In the early part of the season it is easier to follow the trail on the true left side of the valley. Later in the season, when the water crossings are less of a hazard, it does not matter which side of the valley you follow. After ascending the valley for a few km, there is a shepherd's hut on the true left bank. From the hut there is a series of rather tiring ups and downs for several km, before reaching the base of the Kanji La (4250m).

The camp site is at the junction of the main valley and the one leading down from the Kanji La. It is a small, rocky plateau about

50m above the water's edge, just beyond the narrow gorge leading to the Kanji La. To reach it necessitates crossing the main river (a stream later in the season), which may require the use of ropes if the river is in flood. Supplies will have to be off-loaded from the horses as the trail is not suitable for laden animals. There is scarcely space for tents, and the horse handlers rarely spend a good night here, as they have to watch the horses in case they take off back down to the greener pastures of Rangdum.

Stage 5: Kanji La Base Camp to Camp
(Average walking time 7 hours)
An early start is imperative. The climb in the shade should leave you sufficient reserves to reach the pass by mid-morning. From the camp, the trail leads up through a narrow gorge, so there is a possibility of wet boots early on. As you climb higher, the valley opens out, and you can appreciate the huge, jagged ridges of the Zanskar Range. There are no side streams en route to the pass, so water must be carried with you. The average time taken to the top of the **Kanji La** (5290m) is about three to four hours.

From the pass, there are clear views back to the main Himalaya, while ahead lie the peaks of the Karakoram. Even better views are gained by climbing either of the side ridges.

Care is needed on the initial descent from the pass. The trail down a steep gully is difficult under snow in the early part of the season. It then winds down the true left of the valley and across a series of boulder fields, until reaching a broad scree plateau. Cross the plateau and continue for several km, until the trail drops steeply to the main valley floor. The time taken from the pass is about two to three hours.

There is a camp site after this last steep descent, which is often used by trekkers coming from Kanji village. For fitter groups, the trail down through the gorge crosses the valley stream several times, until it reaches an open grazing area. The meadow is often frequented by yak herders from Kanji village, and there are several camp sites in the vicinity.

Stage 6: Camp to Kanji Village
(Average walking time 2 to 3 hours)
If trekking from the lower camp, this stage can be completed in a few hours. Remain on the true right side of the valley, which winds and turns for several km. En route you will probably meet villagers from Kanji, either with their flocks or tending the outlying barley fields. There is no need to cross the main river until you reach the gorge immediately above the village. Either camp here, or check out the option of camping in one of the enclosures in the vicinity of **Kanji** (3875m). A fee of around Rs 20 is payable, and it is essential that the horses do not stray into the barley fields, or you will face a stiff fine.

Kanji village is quite a prosperous settlement by Ladakhi standards, consisting of 20 or so families who farm the immediate area. The village is also the trail junction. For parties going straight to the trailhead at Heniskot, continue directly down through the gorge. The route to the Yogma La, and on to Lamayuru, follows the trail up the valley to the east of the village. See the Kanji to Lamayuru trek option outlined below.

Stage 7: Kanji Village to Heniskot
(Average walking time 2 to 3 hours)
The trail down through the Kanji gorges has been considerably upgraded in the past few seasons. No longer are there the numerous river crossings lower down the gorges, so this is now a comparatively easy stage. Indeed, unless the Kanji River is in flood there is little need to consider the alternative route over the Timti La to Bodkarbu which was often followed in the seasons before the trail was upgraded.

The village of **Heniskot** (3550m) is on the far side of the Kargil-Leh road, and is approached through a small gorge down the valley from where the Kanji trail meets the road. The village is worth a visit if your schedule includes camping at the trailhead overnight.

Option: Kanji to Lamayuru via Yogma La
This option takes three to four stages to complete. From Kanji village (see stage 7) follow the trail up the valley coming in from the east to camp below the Yogma La. This trek up the valley takes a couple of hours through the outlying fields and small settlements which are occupied by the villagers during the summer months. The climb on the next stage to the Yogma La is deceptively easy and affords good views of the immediate gorge country. The descent to the meadow below the pass takes a further 1½ hours. Camp here, or continue down to the Shilakong Gorge, a further three to four hours, with steep descents in places.

On the third stage you descend through spectacular gorges where huge cliff faces block out the sun for all but a few hours each day. Along the valley floor there are plenty of river crossings, which can prove hazardous after a summer storm. The time taken to reach Shila village, at the foot of the gorges, can therefore vary greatly. On average it takes five to six hours, leaving time the same day to visit the Wanlah monastery.

On the final stage, the trail leads up to the Prinkiti La. This is a hot stage once the sun hits the narrow gully. From the pass it is a further hour down to the monastery at Lamayuru.

Getting Away
If travelling from Heniskot to Leh, remember that most vehicles leave Kargil in the early morning, so you should be at the trailhead by 9 am to ensure you get to Leh that evening. Expect to pay Rs 100 for the seven hour drive. Getting to Kargil is more relaxed, as most vehicles don't reach Heniskot till 3 pm. Expect to pay around Rs 60 for the three to four hour drive. Alternatively, if going onto Lamayuru, the drive from Heniskot over the Fatu La (4094m) takes about one hour.

If thinking of extending your trek out of Lamayuru, you will have to backtrack over the Prinkiti La; you could then continue to Alchi or to the Markha Valley to Leh. See the Leh & the Indus Valley section. Alternatively, head to the Zanskar Valley and Padum via the Singge La before returning by road to Panikhar and Kargil. Details of this trek are covered in the Padum & the Zanskar Valley section following.

Padum & the Zanskar Valley

The Zanskar region is a small and isolated Buddhist kingdom wedged between the main Himalaya and the Zanskar Range (see the Ladakh Section 1 and Ladakh Section 3 & Himachal Pradesh Section 1 maps). It comprises two narrow valleys – the Stod Valley in the north-west and the Tsarap Valley in the south-east – which converge at Padum, the administrative centre of the region. Here the valley widens to support the several outlying villages and monasteries which form the nucleus of the kingdom. It extends to the north of Padum for nearly 50 km, where the Zanskar River enters the impressive gorges of the Zanskar Range as it flows down to the Indus Valley.

Treks

Padum to Lamayuru via Singge La
   (strenuous; 10 stages; see Ladakh Section 1 map)
Padum to Leh via Cha Cha La, Rubrang La & Markha Valley
   (strenuous; 10 stages; see Ladakh Section 1 map)
Padum to Darcha via Shingo La
   (strenuous; 7 stages; see Ladakh Section 3 & Himachal Pradesh Section 1 map)
Padum to Darcha via Phitse La & Baralacha La
   (strenuous; 8 stages; see Ladakh Section 3 & Himachal Pradesh Section 1 map)
Padum to Manali via Umasi La
   (strenuous; 9 stages; see Ladakh Section 4 map)

Other Treks

The trek from Udaipur to Padum via the Kang La (see Ladakh Section 3 & Himachal Pradesh Section 1 map) is described in the Lahaul & Spiti trek section of the Himachal Pradesh chapter.

History

The Khampa, the nomadic shepherds who originally roamed the grazing pastures of the Tibetan plateau, would have been familiar with the high passes into Zanskar many centuries before the villages of the Zanskar or the Indus Valley were established.

In the 11th century, the eminent scholar Ringchen Brangpo wandered the Zanskar Valley selecting sites for the 108 monasteries that were to be founded throughout the West Himalaya. At the same time, legend has it that the sage Naropa meditated at the site of Sani monastery.

The famous Hungarian explorer Coso de Koros was one of the first European travellers to visit the region. He spent nearly a year, in 1826-7, at the monastery at Phugtal translating Buddhist texts from Ladakhi into English. An inscription of his name can still be found in the monastery.

A few years later, the Dogra general Zorawar Singh led his army over the Umasi La during his conquest of Ladakh and the Zanskar. In 1834 he reduced the powers of the royal families in both Padum and Zangla to a nominal status and established the fort at the village of Pipiting just north of Padum. He is also said to have paid a small fortune to hire a local guide to lead his army directly across the passes of the Zanskar Range to the Indus Valley in order to mount a surprise attack on the king of Ladakh.

The Dogra conquest was recorded by Thomas Thomson, a member of the East India Company's Boundary Commission crossing the Umasi La in June 1848 en route through the Zanskar and Indus valleys to the Karakoram Pass.

When to Trek

For most people, the timing of a trek out of Padum is determined by the opening of the motorable road from Kargil over the Pentse La. The pass is normally cleared of snow by the beginning of July, and generally remains open until the end of October.

The alternative is to trek from Panikhar or Rangdum over the Pentse La. This can be completed in May, although it is advisable not to cross the high passes leading out of Zanskar until the end of June. By this time the villagers begin to cross the Singge La (en route to Lamayuru), the Umasi La (en route to Manali-Kishtwar) and the Shingo La and Phitse La (en route to Darcha and the Kullu Valley). These times should also be noted if you are planning to trek into the Zanskar Valley from Lamayuru, Leh or Darcha. The passes remain open until the middle of October, although freak storms in September have occasionally required treks to be re-routed.

River crossings also need to be considered when planning a trek. In particular, the route from Padum to the Markha Valley follows gorges where the late-spring snow melt makes the rivers difficult to cross until August.

For the intrepid, there are winter trails linking the Zanskar Valley with the Indus. From late January through February, the villagers and monks follow the route over the snow bridges that form in the depths of the gorges. When the ice begins to thaw, they follow a route over the Cha Cha La to the Khurna Valley and then trek down to its confluence with the Zanskar River. Here there are some places to ford the Zanskar River to reach Nimmu and Leh. This route is favoured by the locals in the springtime, until the deep snows on the Pentse La begin to thaw in May.

Accommodation in Padum

The majority of trekkers choose to camp on arrival at Padum. There is a camp site on the banks of the Tsarap River below the bridge. As always, check with the villagers in the fields to find out where camping is permissible. Fees seem to rise after you have pitched your tent, so make a deal at the outset. I sympathise with those who make deals and then find they are dealing with the wrong family, and later encounter yet another disgruntled landlord. Apart from this, there is a rather dirty camp site with a reasonable supply of water on the plateau close to the road.

Alternatively, you can stay in one of the many small tea houses-cum-hotels which are open during the season. The *Hotel Chorala*, the *Snow View* and the *Ibex* charge between Rs 80 and Rs 200 per room. For eating, there are also some tea stalls preparing noodles and other Ladakhi-cum-Tibetan dishes.

Accommodation on the Trail

Although tea-house trekking in the Zanskar is still in its infancy compared with the situation in Nepal, tea houses and lodges have been established on the two most popular treks – from Padum to Lamayuru and from Padum to Darcha. However, on some stages there are no villages or overnight accommodation spots. This is the case on the stages both before the Singge La on the Lamayuru trek and before and after the Shingo La on the trek to Darcha. You must therefore bring a tent with you.

On the trek over the Phitse La, you will also need a tent, as there are no villages beyond the Tsarap Valley until you arrive at Darcha.

The trek over the Cha Cha La to the Rubrang La leads through a wilderness area for nearly a week. Similarly, there are no villages for several stages before and after the crossing of the Umasi La; it is therefore necessary to be completely self-sufficient on both these treks.

Trekking Advice

On arrival in Padum you are required to register with the J&K Tourist Office. It is also advisable to detail the trek you intend to do. In the event of an accident this will help to get the administrative wheels moving, particularly if an evacuation is required.

Altitude is of primary concern when undertaking a trek out of Padum. Passes include the Shingo La (5090m), the Phitse La (5250m), the Cha Cha La (4950m), the Rubrang La (5020m), the Singge La (5050m) and the Umasi La (5340m). All of the treks included in this section are planned to give optimum time for acclimatisation. However, it is nonetheless recommended that you spend a few extra days in Padum, Karsha and Zangla. If undertaking any of the treks in the reverse direction (that is, from

Lamayuru over the Singge La to Padum, from Darcha over the Shingo La, or over the Phitse La to Padum), then extra stages must be included before crossing the main pass. It should also be noted that the trails over the Shingo La and the Phitse La cross small glaciers and you should equip yourself accordingly.

River crossing, particularly on the trek from Padum to the Markha Valley, can also be a problem.

Provisions

The development of the road from Kargil has made the region more accessible. Supplies can be purchased at Padum at a premium price. Kerosene, biscuits, rice, flour and a supply of fresh fruit and vegetables are available as soon as the road from Kargil is open. The occasional bottle of rum also finds its way into the stores. However, luxury supplies should be brought from Leh.

Horsemen & Porters

Prices for horses vary greatly throughout the season. You must budget on paying at least Rs 150 to Rs 200 per horse per day for a relatively easy trek from July through to the middle of August. During the harvest season, from the middle of August and throughout September, the reduced availability of horses may entail a wait of many days and a price of between Rs 200 and Rs 300 per horse per day. Porters are sometimes an alternative, but again, expensive in comparison to other regions of the Himalaya. If you're crossing the Umasi La you have no choice. Porters are asking up to Rs 2000 for the crossing over the Umasi La as far as the highest village on the Kishtwar side, while a similar amount is paid if crossing the Kang La to the Miyar Nullah in Lahaul.

Access

From Kargil this road journey takes two days with an overnight stop, normally at Rangdum. There is a regular three-times-a-week bus service that runs from July till the end of the season. The price is about Rs 250 one way. The buses are normally heavily booked,

and getting a truck from the Kargil bazaar is an alternative.

Truck prices are about the same as the bus. If you get a seat in the cabin it is likely to be a little more comfortable than sitting in the back. Whatever the choice, look forward to two very dusty days. The prospect of getting off and walking down the road from the Pentse La is properly contemplated by most travellers who would like to appreciate the fine Himalayan views in a modicum of comfort.

Jeeps can also be hired from Kargil, but they are expensive. Expect to pay Rs 6000 one way to Leh, or Rs 8000 if you're returning to Kargil within a few days.

PADUM TO LAMAYURU VIA SINGGE LA
Map: Ladakh Section 1 (pages 126-7)
Stage 1: Padum to Karsha
(Average walking time 2 hours)

Note that if you're coming from Kargil, it is possible to drive straight to Karsha and avoid this first stage. This very short stage allows you time to visit the monastery at Karsha, which is one of the most important in the Zanskar region. The route can be clearly seen from Padum and can, if you choose, lead through some villages away from the road (see the Ladakh Section 1 map). Follow the trail from Padum towards Pipiting village, and from there, cut across the fields to the bridge over the Stod River just above the confluence with the Zanskar River. There is a camp site just beyond the bridge, or alternatively, walk up to the village at Karsha, where there are some lodges where you can spend the night.

Karsha Karsha monastery is the largest in the Zanskar region. It is on a hillside with commanding views of the entire valley and the main Himalaya to the south. The monastery attracts monks from many of the surrounding villages, and at any one time up to 100 monks may be in attendance. The monastic site was probably founded in the 10th century, while the main prayer hall and monks' quarters would have been built in the early 15th

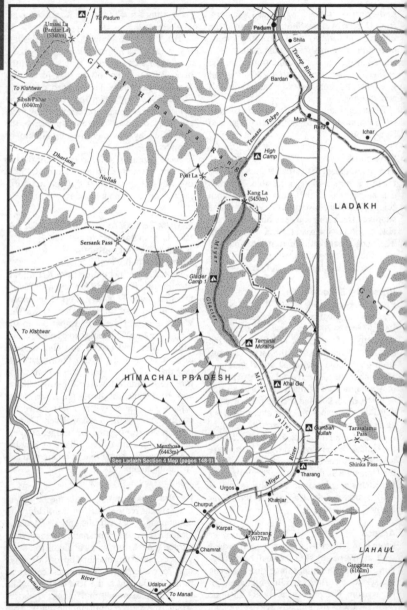

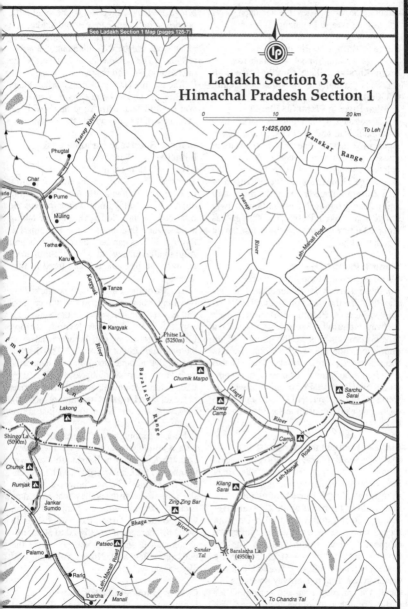

See Ladakh Section 1 Map (pages 126-7)

Ladakh Section 3 &
Himachal Pradesh Section 1

0   10   20 km

1:425,000

Zanskar Range

To Leh

Tsarap River

Phugtal

Char

Purne

rle

Muling

Tetha

Karu

Tsarap River

Kargyak

Tanze

Kargyak

Phitse La
(5250m)

Leh-Manali Road

River

Baralacha Range

Chumik Marpo

Lingti

Himalaya Range

Lakong

Lower Camp

River

Sarchu Sarai

Shingo La
(5090m)

Chumik

Rumjak

Jankar Sumdo

Zing Zing Bar

Kilang Sarai

Camp

Leh-Manali Road

Bhaga River

Patseo

Palamo

Sundar Tal

Baralacha La
(4950m)

Rario

Darcha

To Manali

To Chandra Tal

century, the time when the Gelukpa order was popularised in Ladakh.

Stage 2: Karsha to Pishu

(Average walking time 4 to 5 hours)
From **Karsha** village (3600m), the trail descends gradually to the village of **Rinam** (3550m) and then follows the banks of the Zanskar River to **Pishu** (3470m).

The entrance to the village is marked by a long mani wall and chortens, as are all villages in Zanskar. There is a convenient grassy camp site, complete with a spring, below the village and close to the river. This easy stage allows time in the afternoon to visit **Zangla** village and visit the monastery and palace grounds. Note: the famous twig bridge that linked Pishu and Zangla was replaced a few seasons ago by a substantial wooden bridge.

Stage 3: Pishu to Hanumil

(Average walking time 4 to 5 hours)
Another relatively level stage, the trail frequently skirts the banks of the Zanskar River. The village of **Pidmu** (3420m) is about halfway. **Hanumil** (3380m) comprises just a few houses, and is at the mouth of an impressive side gorge. The camp site is a short distance past the village. There is also a tea house-cum-hotel for overnight accommodation. Hanumil, Pishu and Pidmu on the west side of the river, and Chazar and Honia on the other side, constitute the tiny kingdom of Zangla.

Stage 4: Hanumil to Snertse

(Average walking time 5 hours)
This is a difficult stage for horses, which may have to be unloaded as the trail winds steadily up towards the **Purfi La** (3950m). The route follows the banks of the Zanskar River before a steep climb on a trail hewn from rocks to the pass high above the confluence of the Zingchan Tokpo and the Zanskar River. There follows a steep 500 metre descent down the juniper-covered hillside to the Zingchan Tokpo. Halfway down the hill there is a camping area and springline for parties coming in the opposite direction. The

bridge over the Zingchan Tokpo marks the boundary between Zanskar and Ladakh. It also marks the start of a steady 400m climb to the small shepherds' settlement of **Snertse** (3850m). The settlement is just below the dusty camp site and is not always occupied. Before leaving Hanumil check with trekkers coming in the opposite direction whether you need to take extra food as there is no guarantee of supplies on this stage to Snertse.

Stage 5: Snertse to Hanuma La & Lingshet

(Average walking time 5 to 6 hours)
The trail from Snertse ascends a narrow rocky gorge for about 500m before opening out to a level valley floor. It then follows the river bed for three to four km before taking a side valley that leads to the Hanuma La. River crossings can be a hazard in July and August after heavy rains. The climb from camp to the pass should take three to four hours.

The **Hanuma La** (4950m) is marked by two large chortens topped by prayer flags and has spectacular views to the Singge La and the main Zanskar Range. Below, Lingshet monastery can be appreciated on the opposite side of the valley. The descent to Lingshet is quite steep by any standards, with very sharp switchbacks to the valley floor before continuing around the outskirts of the valley to **Lingshet monastery** (4000m). The camp site and tea stalls are just above the monastery.

Lingshet monastery is set on the hillside with a commanding view over the valley. Like the monastery at Karsha, this one was founded by the Gelukpa order, with its teachings from Tibet. There is, however, an older site further down the valley that may date back to the same time as Sani and Alchi, when Buddhism was first established in Ladakh. There are normally 20 to 30 monks in attendance, and the monastery serves the outlying villages of Nirag, Yulchang and Skyumpata.

Option: Lingshet to Rangdum

From Lingshet, there is a rather ill-defined

trail leading to Rangdum. The route crosses the Kesi La to the north of the Hanuma La, and then the Pingdon La, before passing the base of the Kanji La to Rangdum. In places the trail is hard for horses. Three stages should be reserved to complete the trek.

Stage 6: Lingshet to Base of Singge La

(Average walking time 5 to 6 hours)
Although monks trek to Photaksar in one stage, this is not recommended for lesser trekking mortals. A midway camp is necessary, and the one below the Singge La, although not the most comfortable in Ladakh, is convenient for the climb to the pass the following day.

The trail from Lingshet gradually ascends to the first of the intermediary passes, the **Netuke La** (4280m), before continuing above the settlement of Skyumpata. Here a trail diverts past the lone yak herder's camp at Yulchang, and continues down to the Zanskar River and the settlement at Nirag. From here on there is a rough trail, unsuitable for horses, that returns to Zangla.

From Skyumpata the trail descends to the valley then there's a tiring 400m climb to the **Khyupa La** (4300m). It then gradually ascends to the base of the Singge La (4550m) where there is an adequate, albeit rocky, camp site beside the springline which eventually cascades down to the Zanskar River 1500m below. There is no tea house-cum-hotel here.

Stage 7: Singge La to Photaksar

(Average walking time 5 to 6 hours)
The climb up the rather steep scree slope takes about 1½ to two hours. Frozen waterfalls from the limestone cliffs form an impressive sight above the trail. The **Singge La** (5050m), literally the Lion Pass, is the highest pass on the route to Lamayuru. Heavy snowfalls on this pass preclude crossings in the winter and late spring, and the route is not normally open to trekkers until the middle of June. At the top of the pass, you can appreciate the lie of the land across to the Sisir La beyond Photaksar.

From the pass, there is a short descent to

a rather marshy grazing area, before the trail winds past mani walls to the Photang Valley and the village of **Photaksar** (4200m). The camp site is above the village, and the time taken from the Singge La to camp is about three to four hours. Photaksar supports two small monasteries which are serviced by monks from Lamayuru.

Stage 8: Photaksar to Sisir La & Honupatta

(Average walking time 6 hours)
From Photaksar, the trail ascends gradually up the valley before a series of steeper switchbacks lead to the **Sisir La** (4850m). The views back to the Singge La and the main Zanskar Range are particularly impressive. From the pass, other trek routes can be distinguished. The small pass at the head of the opposite valley marks the route to the Shilakong Valley, the Yogma La and Kanji village. Immediately below, the trail down to Honupatta cuts across the barren ridge to the Spong Valley, before a long and gradual descent to the village. The time from the pass to Honupatta is about two to three hours.

Three chortens mark the entrance to **Honupatta** (3760m), while the huge, ancient cedar tree in the village is flanked with Buddhist prayer flags. There are some tea houses, and the camp sites are just above the village.

In late autumn, when the river levels are lower, it is possible to descend directly from the village of Photaksar, through the gorges of the Photang Valley, straight to Phanjila village. This short cut bypasses the climb to the pass and Honupatta village, but must not be undertaken before consulting the villagers at Photaksar.

Stage 9: Honupatta to Wanlah

(Average walking time 5 hours)
From Honupatta, the trail descends gradually for three to four km to the confluence with the Photang River. Here it enters a gorge where the trail construction has been considerably upgraded in the last few seasons. Shortly after entering the gorge, a large chorten marks the confluence of the Photang River. Do not cross the bridge here, but

continue on the true left bank. At the end of the gorge the valley widens and the trail crosses to the true right bank to reach the apricot orchards of Phanjila (3410m). It is a further five to six km along the true right hand side of the valley to the village and monastery at **Wanlah** (3250m). Note the huge rock conglomerates brought down by a landslide about 25 years ago.

Wanlah boasts some tea houses-cum-hotels. There is also a camp site down by the main bridge opposite the monastery. The village is connected by road to the Kargil-Leh road just before it enters the Indus Valley. Plans are under way to extend the road towards Phanjila village and Honupatta. When this happens, the route from Photaksar to the Shilakong Valley and Lamayuru will be a better trekking alternative.

Stage 10: Wanlah to Lamayuru
(Average walking time 3 to 4 hours)
From camp, follow the Shilakong Valley upstream for three km to Shila village and the turn-off to the Prinkiti La. The entrance is marked by prayer flags and small chortens. The gully leading to the pass is devoid of water and vegetation. It is an apology of a pass but it takes its toll in the heat of the morning. At 3750m it is 500m below Wanlah, and the walk takes two to 2½ hours.

The descent to Lamayuru from the pass takes a further hour. The Kargil-Leh road is visible just below the pass, and shortly afterwards you gain the first impressive views of **Lamayuru monastery** (3420m). There are some local hotels in the vicinity of the monastery, and there is also a camping area in the fields immediately below the village.

Getting Away
The following morning it is advisable to be at the trailhead by 7 am to meet the first of the truck and bus convoys going to Leh. Expect to pay Rs 100 for the six to seven hour drive. If you are going to Kargil, you can enjoy a sleep-in, as the vehicles do not normally arrive at Lamayuru until early afternoon, to arrive in Kargil that evening. Expect to pay Rs 70 for a lift on a truck or the local Leh-Kargil bus.

PADUM TO LEH VIA CHA CHA LA, RUBRANG LA & MARKHA VALLEY
Map: Ladakh Section 1 (pages 126-7)
Stage 1: Padum to Zangla
(Average walking time 7 hours)
There is a choice of routes to Zangla. The first is to go via Karsha monastery, and then continue down the true left side of the Zanskar Valley to Pishu village, where you cross the bridge to Zangla. The alternative route is to cross the bridge over the Tsarap River at Padum, and then continue down the true right side of the Zanskar Valley via the village of Stongde. A description of the route via Karsha and Pishu is covered in the Padum to Lamayuru trek section above.

From Padum, the trail to Zangla crosses the main bridge over the Tsarap River and follows the well-graded track to **Stongde** (3500m), where there is an impressive monastery, affiliated with the orders at Karsha. The trail continues past the villages of Chilingkit and Chazar en route to **Zangla** (3370m). A jeep road now covers much of this route.

Ladakh and Zanskar are famed for dogs, big and small, but nowhere are there as many per family as in Zangla. They include some corgi lookalikes that appear on the roof of one of the largest houses in the village. This is the house of the king of Zangla. The old king, who was such a delightful host to trekking parties, died in 1989. Although for a century the king had held only a nominal title, his lineage can be traced back to when the royal lineage in Zanskar was split. One side of the family ruled from Padum, and the other from Zangla. During the invasion of Zorawar Singh in 1834, the king of Padum was killed. On hearing of this the king of Zangla was able to reach an accord which allowed him to retain a nominal rule over the nearby villages of Honia and Chazar, and the villages of Hanumil, Pidmu and Pishu on the far side of the valley. The head monk at Spitok is related to this family, and also administers the Zangla monastery, which is on the cliff just beyond the village.

Stage 2: Zangla to Cha Cha La Base
(Average walking time 3 hours)
Follow the trail beyond the chortens, up past the former fort high above the village. From here, the trail follows the Zulung Valley upstream with many river crossings. There is a camp site (3800m) after about eight km which marks the junction of the main valley and a small valley coming from the north. There is a wooded grazing area with sufficient shade in which to spend a restful afternoon before crossing the Cha Cha La the following day.

Stage 3: Cha Cha La Base to Camp
(Average walking time 6 hours)
The trail diverts from the main valley along a rough scree path for several km, then enters a large waterless side valley which marks the entrance to the pass. From here on, the trail ascends a series of glacial steps to the base of the pass. The final 200m to the pass is hard going, but the fine views back to the main Himalaya beyond Padum are well worth the effort.

From the top of the **Cha Cha La** (4950m), the trail drops steadily. The time down to the first camp (approximately 4000m) is about two hours.

Stage 4: Camp to Tilat Sumdo
(Average walking time 6 hours)
Care must be taken when making the numerous river crossings on this stage. Six hours is the average autumn walking time to camp. In summer, when the water levels are higher, you may be forced to do this in two stages, walking only in the morning when the water levels are lower. There is no shortage of camp sites, which are identified by thousands of sheep pellets. These are a legacy of the large flocks of sheep brought from the Rupshu region each autumn to trade for grain in the Zanskar Valley.

About five km before Tilat Sumdo, there is a small cave set in a limestone cliff just above the trail. In the cave there is reported to be a rock statue or lingam representing Lord Shiva, for barren Ladakhi women to touch in order to become fertile.

Tilat Sumdo (3750m) at the junction with the Khurna Valley is a delightful sandy camp site. It is also a convenient base to explore some of the remote gorge country nearby, which is famed for its wildlife.

Warning In some maps and guidebooks there is a trail marked down the Khurna River from Tilat Sumdo to the Zanskar River and on to the confluence with the Markha Valley. This track is probably a late winter or early spring track which the locals follow after some sections of the ice on the Zanskar River begin to melt. There is no summer trail along the Zanskar River between the Khurna and Markha rivers.

Stage 5: Tilat Sumdo to Base of Rubrang La
(Average walking time 5 to 6 hours)
The trail climbs alongside the Khurna River for two to three km, to the confluence with a side river coming from the north. Here the track leaves the main valley, and climbs a series of rocky cliffs where the horses may need to be unloaded. The trail to the **Rubrang La** continues up the valley for a further seven to eight km, to a grassy camp at the base of the pass (4350m).

On these sections of the trek you may encounter Khampa nomads, who come from the eastern region of Ladakh. The Khampa follow a nomadic lifestyle, very similar to that of the original inhabitants of Ladakh. They live in tents made of yak hair and rely on the produce of their yaks, goats and sheep. To supplement their income, they tend horses owned by the wealthier families from the Rupshu region. It is not uncommon to see them herding many hundreds of horses across these high grazing areas throughout the summer months.

Stage 6: Rubrang La Base to Markha
(Average walking time 6 hours)
The climb to the Rubrang La (5020m) takes about two hours. The trail ascends through a

gully which opens out just below the pass. To the north are uninterrupted views of the Stok Range. There is a small springline three km below the pass, and a camping area which is convenient for parties coming from the Markha Valley. The trail descends into a large gorge that leads down to the confluence with the Markha River. **Markha** village (3850m) is two km below the confluence on the far side of the valley.

Stages 7 to 10: Markha to Leh

From Markha village, the trek to Leh can be completed in three or four stages. The options are either: continue down the Markha Valley, and then cross the Ganda La to the Indus Valley and Leh; or go up the valley to Nimaling, and cross the Kongmaru La to Hemis in the Indus Valley. Details of these stages are outlined in the Spitok to Hemis via Markha Valley trek in the Leh & the Indus Valley section.

PADUM TO DARCHA VIA SHINGO LA
Map: Ladakh Section 3 & Himachal Pradesh Section 1 (pages 138-9)
Stage 1: Padum to Mune
(Average walking time 6 hours)
This stage is quite long if you're coming straight from Kargil. The first 10 km to **Bardan** is along a rather dusty jeep road. Bardan monastery (3620m) is one of the most important in the valley. It is attached to the Drukpa order and has close ties with Hemis. The main assembly hall was extensively renovated in the 1980s, while the huge prayer wheel is famed as one of the largest in Ladakh.

From Bardan, the trail continues alongside the Tsarap River for four or five km, crossing the Temasa Tokpo (stream) and the turn-off to the Kang La, before ascending to a plateau and the village and monastery of **Mune** (3900m).

Stage 2: Mune to Purne
(Average walking time 8 hours)
This is another long stage, which could be shortened by visiting and camping at the village of Ichar en route. The main trail cuts across the Mune plateau, bypassing Reru village. However, for trekkers coming direct from Purne, or having camped overnight at Bardan, there are some excellent camp sites on the outskirts of **Reru** (3850m).

After crossing the main tributary beyond Reru, there is a short climb before a gradual descent to the main valley. The trail reaches the river bank close to the village of **Ichar** (3650m) and from there it climbs and falls as it crosses some small side rivers. En route, the only village of note is that of **Surle** (3670m), where there is a limited camping area. From Surle, it is a further three to four km to the confluence of the Tsarap and Kargyak rivers, and the village of **Purne** (3700m).

Cross the bridge over the Kargyak River, and ascend the opposite bank to the main house, near which there is a camping area. Unfortunately the camp is a mess as the delicate Ladakhi environment has not been able to accommodate the plastic bags, tin cans and the associated rubbish left behind by careless groups.

Stage 3: Purne to Phugtal & Tetha
(Average walking time 4 hours return to Phugtal then 2 hours on to Tetha)
From Purne, the trail to Phugtal follows the true left bank for several km before it reaches a makeshift bridge over the Tsarap River. From the bridge it is two to three km on to **Phugtal monastery** (3850m).

The sight of the monastery on the limestone cliffside never fails to impress. The main assembly hall is carved out of a huge cave, with the monks' quarters scattered down the hillside. Inside the monastery there is an inscription to Coso de Koros, one of the first Europeans to visit the Zanskar region and the first to translate the Buddhist texts from Ladakhi into English.

After returning to Purne, there is ample time to continue four to five km on to the village of **Tetha** (3950m). The trail remains in the gorge for several km before ascending to a large fertile plateau which supports some prosperous whitewashed villages. Tetha is the first village you come to, with a delightful camp site off the main trail, close to the village. The camping fee is Rs 20 per tent.

Stage 4: Tetha to Kargyak
(Average walking time 7 hours)
From Tetha the trail is marked by a series of well-maintained chortens to the village of **Karu** (3990m). The track is lined by substantial stone walls to protect the barley fields from straying pack animals. This is a definite problem during the season, and can cause disputes between the villagers and the horse handlers of trekking parties.

After Karu, the trail descends back to the river bank, then crosses a bridge to the village of **Tanze** (3850m) on the far true right side of the valley. It is a further four to five km to the village of **Kargyak** (4050m), the highest permanent settlement in the Zanskar region. There is no shortage of camp sites, and for those without a tent, there are some houses in the village which will provide shelter and food for the night.

If time is not at a premium, an extra day can be spent wandering the valley opposite the village. The valley extends into the main Himalaya Range, and there are some smaller settlements which make this an interesting day's option.

Stage 5: Kargyak to Lakong
(Average walking time 6 to 7 hours)
Remain on the same side of the valley as you continue up towards the impressive rock monolith known as Gumburanjan. After passing the rock face, there are plenty of places to ford the upper reaches of the Kargyak River, then the trail heads across to the yak grazing pastures and shepherds' encampments which are known locally as Lakong (4470m).

There is a series of camp sites to choose from, the most convenient being those on the highest pastures closest to the pass. For those without a tent, there are some small stone encampments that will shield you from the worst of the elements.

Stage 6: Lakong to Rumjak
(Average walking time 6 to 7 hours)
The climb to the Shingo La is not hard by Himalayan standards, and can be completed in a couple of hours. It may take longer early in the season when the approach is completely under snow. The route follows the true left side of the valley across a couple of side rivers before ascending a large snowfield. The gradient of the ascent to the pass is not demanding and the trail across the scree and snow is defined. A series of prayer flags marks the **Shingo La** (5090m). It is set beneath an impressive backdrop of 6000 metre snow-capped peaks defining both the main Himalaya and the Baralacha Range.

The descent should not present any real difficulties. The path is well trodden, and the trail down the small glacier avoids the obvious crevassed areas. Once off the glacier, head across the scree slopes to the true right side of the valley. Then descend past the shepherd huts at **Chumik** (4640m) and continue down to the grassy camp site at **Rumjak** (4290m). Overnight shelter is limited here to a stone encampment, and food must be carried on this stage.

Stage 7: Rumjak to Darcha
(Average walking time 6 to 7 hours)
The descent is quite gradual until the last section where the trail meets the main valley floor at Jankar Sumdo (3860m). Until a few seasons ago it was essential to time your crossing of the river here with care. Nowadays there are no problems about getting your boots wet as a pulley bridge is manned by the villagers from Rarig and Darcha till quite late in the season. They also maintain some tea houses-cum-hotels. The cost of using the pulley bridge is Rs 20 per crossing. Once on the far bank, the trail crosses some side streams and boulder fields before recrossing the river over a permanent stone bridge at **Palamo** (3600m). From there it is a few km down the valley, past the village of **Rarig** (3430m), to **Darcha** (3350m) and the confluence with the Bhaga Valley.

Getting Away
At Darcha there are tea stalls, and an adequate camp site. The local bus to Manali departs early in the morning and costs Rs 45.

If heading north, there are also regular truck convoys which could provide a lift to the Indus Valley and Leh.

Trekking from Darcha to Padum
Many trekkers follow the above trek from Padum to Darcha in the opposite direction. If you follow this route it is essential that you spend at least a few extra days acclimatising before crossing the Shingo La. On the first stage, plan to trek from Darcha to Jankar Sumdo. This should take around seven to eight hours. Here you can spend a rest day before making it up to the stone shelter huts at Chumik (4640m) below the Shingo La on the following stage.

The next stage over the Shingo La to Lakong in the upper Zanskar Valley takes six to seven hours. The pass crossing is not so arduous when compared with other passes over the main Himalaya Range. From camp, there is a gradual ascent for the first 2½ hours to reach the terminal moraine at the base of the pass. The trail then steepens, crossing a rocky slope to the true right of the glacier before rounding a large crevasse to a chorten in the centre of the valley. This is not the top of the pass. However, most of the climb is over, and a gradual ascent to the pass (5090m) follows. The pass is marked by a series of cairns and mani walls draped in prayer flags.

The initial descent from the pass is quite steep, and care must be exercised when crossing the snowfield as it is often very icy just beneath the surface. The route heads to the true left of the valley across scree slopes before the final descent to the valley floor. After crossing a large side stream there is a choice of camp sites on the meadows known locally as Lakong (4470m). There are no tea stalls, but there are shepherds' huts where you can shelter overnight.

From Lakong, it is a further six to seven hours trek to Kargyak. From there on to Padum, allow four stages. The first takes you to Tetha village and the second to Purne and Phugtal monastery. The third stage should see you at Reru and the fourth stage at Padum, with time that day to organise onward transport to Kargil.

PADUM TO DARCHA VIA PHITSE LA & BARALACHA LA
Map: Ladakh Section 3 & Himachal Pradesh Section 1 (pages 138-9)
Stages 1 to 3: Padum to Tetha Village
Follow stages 1 to 3 of the previous trek.

Stage 4: Tetha Village to Tanze
As for stage 4 of the previous trek, but stop near Tanze for the night.

Stage 5: Tanze to Phitse La Base
(Average walking time 7 hours)
Shortly after Tanze, the trail to the Phitse La heads up a side gorge which ascends steeply out of the Kargyak Valley. The climb is steep for nearly 500m until it opens out at the head of the gorge. A short walk back across the plateau will provide a bird's-eye view down the Kargyak Valley to Purne. There is a good camp site a few km up the valley – in fact the best between Tanze and the pass. However, in order to make an early start over the Phitse La the following morning it is necessary to continue on up valley to a more restricted camp site at the base of the pass (approximately 4800m).

Stage 6: Phitse La Base to Camp
(Average walking time 7 hours)
The climb to the pass is short and steep, with the final ascent up a scree slope to the well-defined **Phitse La** (5250m). From the pass there are views across to the main Himalaya, while the climb up the small ridge to the north side of the pass will afford panoramic views across to the Zanskar Range.

The descent from the pass crosses a series of scree slopes, and is steep in places down to **Chumik Marpo** (4880m). This is an ideal camp if you're coming from the opposite direction. The area is grazed by yak herders from the village of Kargyak during the summer months. It is the only settlement on this route between Tanze and Darcha. From the herders' camp, the trail follows a series of ridges before dropping into a narrow gorge to the main Lingti Valley. Continue down the valley to the first main tributary of the Lingti River, and camp for the night (approximately 4400m).

Stage 7: Camp to Kilang Sarai
(Average walking time 6 to 7 hours)
Cross the main tributary early in the morning. The high water level during the summer could present difficulties, but from September onwards, this and the other side rivers are easier to negotiate. The trail winds across ridges covered with juniper and past dilapidated mani walls before reaching the confluence of the Tsarap and Lingti valleys. The route then heads up the Tsarap valley across extensive pastures which form the upper grazing limits of the Gaddi shepherds from Himachal Pradesh. A few km on, the military road from Leh crosses the valley at a point below the **Kilang Sarai** (4600m) where there is an adequate camp site. There is an army camp nearby, but the soldiers are friendly and glad of a diversion from their duties.

Stage 8: Kilang Sarai to Baralacha La
(Average walking time 3 hours)
From the camp, the trail joins the Leh-Manali road to the **Baralacha La** (4950m). The steady climb is rewarded by impressive views of the peaks, many of which are over 6000m. Between the switchbacks on the road you can take shortcuts until you reach the pass. The Baralacha La is one of the most historically famous passes in the Himalaya. It is a double pass, at the convergence of the Tsarap Valley in the north, the Chandra Valley to the south, and the Bhaga Valley to the west. There is no shortage of camp sites on the pass, complete with wildflowers and an impressive mountain backdrop.

Getting Away
From the pass, it is a double stage down the Bhaga Valley via the camp sites of Zing Zing Bar and Patseo to Darcha. If the thought of trekking on the road does not appeal, it should be easy to hitch a ride by truck to Darcha or the Kullu Valley.

A pleasant alternative is to continue trekking down the Chandra Valley to the lake Chandra Tal. This can be completed in two to three stages until you reach the Kullu-Spiti road below the Kun Zum La. Details of this trek are covered in the Lahaul trek section in the Himachal Pradesh chapter.

PADUM TO MANALI VIA UMASI LA
Map: Ladakh Section 4 (pages 148-9)
Stage 1: Padum to Zongkul Monastery
(Average walking time 6 to 7 hours)
From Padum follow the road past the monastery at Sani to the Tungri bridge. Do not cross the bridge, but instead follow the trail on the true right bank of the Stod River to the village of **Ating** (3600m) and the entrance to the Zongkul Valley. **Zongkul monastery** is three to four km up the valley, high above the valley floor. According to legend, the monastery was founded by the sage Naropa in the 11th century. Nowadays it is serviced by half a dozen monks from Sani monastery. There is a choice of camp sites (around 3750m) below the monastery.

Stage 2: Zongkul Monastery to Base of Umasi La
(Average walking time 6 to 7 hours)
If you drove to Padum it is advisable to either include a rest day before trekking higher or complete this stage over two days.

From Zongkul monastery the trail leads up the true left side of the Mulung Tokpo to a natural rock bridge. Cross the river here and ascend the grassy meadows (ideal for an intermediary camp site) before the route diverts up a steep ridge to enter a side valley, on the true right of the main valley. There follows a tiring stage through an extensive boulder field to a wide glacial valley where a cluster of stone shelters and a small grassy meadow mark the overnight camp (4400m).

Stage 3: Umasi La Base to High Camp
(Average walking time 7 hours)
From the camp commence the ascent up the glacial valley. The glacier is not heavily crevassed and the distance to the base of the pass can be covered in 1½ hours. The route

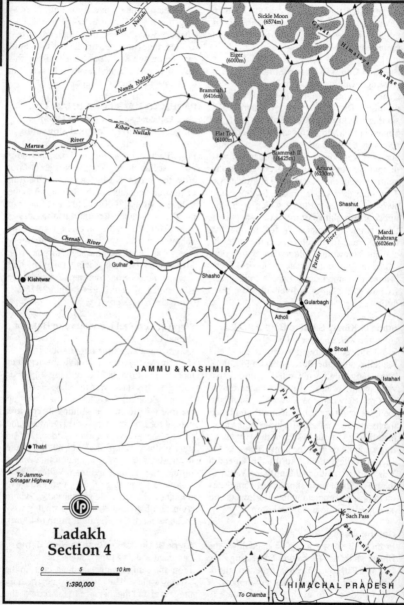

Ladakh
Section 4

0   5   10 km

1:390,000

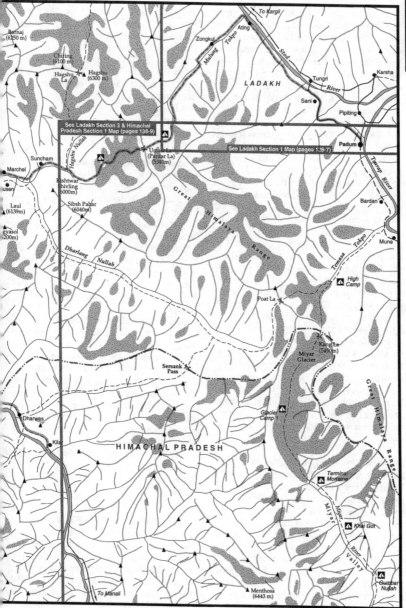

to the **Umasi La** (5340m) then diverts up the moraine-strewn trail to the true left of the glacier. The route, marked by a series of rock cairns, becomes progressively steeper. Just below the pass there is a very steep section up an ice gully (if coming in the opposite direction a top rope would be handy).

The pass is just a small gap in the cliff wall, marked by the usual array of prayer flags offered by the monks from the Bardan and Sani monasteries who regularly cross the pass.

Thomas Thomson was the first European to cross the pass in late June 1848. He travelled via Chamba and the Pardar Valley, en route to reach the Karakoram Pass later that year. From his account, he was denied the views, reaching the pass during a heavy snowstorm. Yet he did not neglect his duties and set about boiling a pan of water. The water finally came to the boil at 180.3°F (82.2°C), from which he was able to calculate the height of the pass to be at least 18,000 ft (5490m) – about 150m higher than the present-day calculation.

From the pass there is a steady descent to a large snowfield (crevassed in places) that flows into a larger glacier flowing in from the south. Before reaching the confluence of these two glaciers, the trail turns north (along the true right of the valley) and opens out with impressive views of the Kishtwar Himalaya. There is a flat, if somewhat rocky, camp site (4890m) beneath a huge rock overhang where most porters elect to spend the night.

Stage 4: High Camp to Suncham
(Average walking time 8 hours)
From the overhang camp there is a steep 300 to 400m descent beside the hanging glacier to the main glacial valley floor. On reaching the glacier the walking is easier. Follow the glacier down the valley for about three km before heading to the lateral moraine on the true right of the valley. The route is again marked by rock cairns through the moraine.

The trail through the moraine descends to a small sandy camp site before a further steep descent down a grassy slope to a broad alpine

valley. The trail remains on the true right of the valley to the confluence of the Hagshu Nullah and some Bakharval shepherd encampments in a birch grove (3500m). To the south, the peak of Kishtwar Shivling (6000m) rears above the valley. It was first climbed by the British climbers Stephen Venables and Dick Renshaw in autumn 1983.

A few km down the valley the trail crosses a large boulder field before reaching the settlement of **Suncham** (3250m).

Stage 5: Suncham to Marchel
(Average walking time 3 hours)
This comparatively short stage allows time to explore the Buddhist villages in the upper Pardar Valley and also to organise porters or horsemen, as the porters from Sani rarely go further down the valley.

From Suncham the trail descends on the true right side of the valley to the confluence of the Dharlang Nullah (and a possible route to the Poat La – a pass to the south-east of the Umasi La leading back to the Zanskar Valley).

While descending to Marchel the trail leads past several small villages founded when Ladakhi farmers migrated to the region about six generations ago. **Marchel** (2790m) and the nearby village of **Lusen** support simple Buddhist monasteries, which are periodically serviced by the monks from Bardan and Sani monasteries in Zanskar. Other ties with Zanskar are also maintained and marriages are arranged on both sides of the Himalaya.

There is a police checkpost at Marchel, but it is mainly to steer foreigners away from the Pardar sapphire mine on the far side of the mountain.

Stage 6: Marchel to Atholi/Gularbagh
(Average walking time 8 hours)
From Marchel the trail leads down the true right of the valley affording grand views down to the Chenab Valley and across to the Pir Panjal Range beyond Atholi. The well-defined trail descends to the village of **Shashut** (2600m). There is a Forest Rest

House just above the village, while there is a simple Hindu temple in the village.

Below Shashut the route crosses a substantial wooden bridge to the true left side of the valley. The trail then passes a series of excellent camp sites amid deodar and conifer trees. Logging operations are also evident further down the valley. The trail re-crosses the Pardar River further down the valley before reaching a series of settlements set amidst chestnut, oak and deodar forest.

The small bazaar at **Gularbagh** is just above the confluence of the Pardar and Chenab rivers. It is populated by people of Ladakhi origin, traders who originally settled in the upper Pardar Valley. The town of **Atholi** (2250m) lies on the opposite, south side of the valley. It is the district headquarters, and there are both primary and middle schools as well as a police station.

Until the 1830s, the Pardar district was an integral part of Chamba. In fact, during the period from 1820 to 1825, the locals supported the Chamba forces in their invasion of the Zanskar region. Allegiances changed a decade later. After invading Ladakh and Zanskar, Zorawar Singh led his Dogra forces back over the Umasi La en route to Jammu. The Pardar people were suspicious of the Dogras, particularly when a small party of Dogra troops was left behind to 'facilitate communications' with Ladakh. The Pardar people killed the contingent of Dogras, and on hearing of this, Zorawar Singh returned the following year (1836) and annexed the region to Jammu.

The road from Kishtwar to Atholi was completed in 1992. It is envisaged that it will eventually link up with the road being built down the Chenab Valley from Lahaul and Manali. The project was commenced by the J&K and Himachal governments in the 1970s to provide an inner Himalayan road that would service the villages of the Chenab Valley while at the same time providing a more direct transport route between the Kullu Valley, Kishtwar and the Kashmir Valley.

Until recently most trekkers would take the bus from Atholi to Kishtwar (three times

a day, Rs 10) and the following day catch the bus to Jammu or Srinagar and the Kashmir Valley. However, this option is not recommended for the time being. The current political situation in Kishtwar is worse than in the Kashmir Valley with many of the J&K separatist groups active in the region.

The alternative is to continue trekking up the Chenab Valley for three stages to the village of Kilar and onward transport to Manali and the Kullu Valley.

Stage 7: Atholi/Gularbagh to Shoal
(Average walking time 2½ to 3 hours)
This short stage is made even shorter if you elect to follow the road construction up the Chenab Valley. The trekking trail is more demanding, ascending high above the Chenab River before a long and gradual descent to the village at **Shoal** (2400m). There is a convenient camp site next to a side river about a km beyond the village.

Stage 8: Shoal to Istahari
(Average walking time 6 to 7 hours)
From Shoal, the trail heads over to the next side valley before commencing a steep 500 metre climb that leads high above the Chenab River. The ascent passes a potential camp site just above a beautiful waterfall. It is also an ideal place for a rest stop before the trail finally climbs to the ridge top. From here, there are bird's-eye views down the valley, while the forested ridges on the far side of Kishtwar can be seen in the distance.

From the ridge the trail drops gently, skirting the village of **Thari** to a potential camp site. It is a further two hours to Istahari. Note: the main horse trail does not go down to the village at Thari.

Istahari (2800m) is the last main village in J&K state, and from the Forest Rest House you can distinguish the ridge line of the Shopu Dhar, which marks the border with Himachal Pradesh.

Stage 9: Istahari to Kilar
(Average walking time 6 to 7 hours)
Leaving Istahari it is a long haul down to the Chenab River. The descent takes a couple of

hours to the Shophu Nullah. The bridge over the Shophu Nullah is reconstructed each year, making the trail from Atholi to Kilar suitable for horses from mid-May onwards.

The trail continues, gradually ascending for a few km to a small cairn on the side of the trail that marks the border between J&K and Himachal states. It is a further two hours to **Dharwas**, where the village (2520m) is about 100 metres above the main trail. The climb to the village is worthwhile to appreciate the small Hindu temple in the main square. On the trail below there is also a well-maintained Forest Rest House. Here there is a signpost dating back to the British administration, which sets out the trek's stages up the Chenab Valley to Lahaul – a delightful trek until the construction of the road.

Beyond Dharwas it is a further two hour trek to the village of **Kilar** (2750m), the headquarters of the Pangi district and the present roadhead.

Getting Away

The jeep road to Kilar has only just been completed and it may take a season or two for the road to be upgraded for a regular bus service to Lahaul and Manali. In the meantime, trucks will be an alternative. Allow at least two days to reach Manali.

Kashmir

HISTORY

According to legend, the Kashmir Valley was once a vast lake populated by Nagas, or half-human, half-serpent beings, who, when the waters of the lake subsided, escaped to the higher lakes in the mountains. Belief in the Nagas remained an integral part of Kashmir's history. As the Aryans migrated up the Indus Valley to Kashmir, Aryan and Naga priests were able to develop an accord. Even the introduction of Buddhism, during the time of Ashoka in the 3rd century BC, did not undermine this relationship. The Buddhist *viharas* (monasteries) were soon reconstructed as temples to commemorate Shiva or Vishnu, while every lake, spring and stream was sanctified by the Naga priests.

The culture of Kashmir was preserved for many centuries and reached a high point during the time of the great Utpala and Karokta dynasties, when the power and influence of Kashmir stretched far beyond the confines of the valley. During the 8th and 9th centuries huge temples, such as those at Avantipura, Parihasipura and Patan, were built to commemorate the kings. But a series of weak rulers hastened a period of cultural and political decline.

It was against this backdrop that Kashmir was converted to Islam in the early part of the 14th century. It was a peaceful conversion, with many of the followers of Shah Hamadan, the noted Persian leader, seeking refuge in the valley. Among the enlightened Islamic rulers was Zain-ul-Ab-ul-Din who, after returning in his youth from the Moghul courts of Samarkand, introduced many of the handicrafts for which Kashmir is now famous, including carpet weaving and papier-mâché.

In 1585 Kashmir came under the Moghul empire. The emperor Akbar upgraded the administration of Kashmir and instituted more equitable systems of land distribution. During Akbar's time the lower ramparts of the walls of the city of Srinagar were built at the base of the Hari Parbat Hill, while

Highlights – Kashmir
The alpine hill stations were, until recently, popular retreats for trekkers. There are traditional Muslim villages and Gujar shepherd encampments, alpine lakes, pine forests, flowered meadows and the Great Himalaya Range.

Introductory to strenuous treks out of the hill station of Pahalgam, including the famous Amarnath pilgrimage.

Akbar's son Jehangir and grandson Shah Jehan were responsible for establishing the famous gardens, including those at Nishat and Shalimar, on the banks of Dal Lake.

With the gradual decline of Moghul rule, the local administration again fell into decline. The valley was invaded in the 1750s by the despotic Durranni rulers from Afghanistan, and later by the Sikhs, who constructed the impressive fort on the top of Hari Parbat above the old city.

Following the Treaty of Amritsar in 1846, Kashmir and the adjoining regions of Jammu, Baltistan and Ladakh became part of the maharajah's state of Jammu & Kashmir (J&K). Four Dogra maharajahs – Gulab Singh, Ranbir Singh, Pratap Singh and Hari Singh – were to rule Kashmir. In May each year they moved from Jammu to Srinagar to conduct their summer administration. The Dogras shared a peculiar relationship with the British. The British assumed control over the state's external affairs, while the maharajahs were able to determine their own domestic policy. Indeed the British were unable to own land in the valley, hence the development of the houseboats along the banks of the Jhelum River. The Residency (now the Government Arts Emporium) was built nearby, while the shops in Polo View, together with Nedou's Hotel, reflected the commercial interests of the day.

The British presence in the later part of the 19th century also revitalised an interest in Kashmir's history among scholars such as Auriel Stein, who translated the *Rajatarangini*. This huge volume, originally completed in the 12th century, was the definitive guide to Kashmir's early history. At the same time, one of Kashmir's most noted administrators, Land Reform Commissioner WR Lawrence detailed the land policies that had been adopted in the Kashmir Valley since the time of the Moghuls.

During the 1930s a Quit Kashmir movement evolved against the maharajah. This campaign was similar to that of the Quit India movement that the British faced in other parts of India. It drew considerable support from the Kashmiri people, the majority of whom were Muslim and had very little in common with the Hindu maharajah.

The partition of India in 1947 brought the Kashmir situation to a head. Maharajah Hari Singh wanted an independent Kashmir, yet Kashmir was predominantly Muslim and culturally closer to Pakistan. Economically its strength was tied up with India. To break the deadlock, a Pathan force from Pakistan was sent to liberate Kashmir. The manoeuvre failed. Hari Singh called in the Indian forces

to protect him and retreated to Jammu. A full-scale war between India and Pakistan resulted, lasting until a UN ceasefire came into effect on 1 January 1949.

In 1954 J&K formally ratified its accession to India, a development strongly contested by Pakistan. India and Pakistan were at war over the issue in 1965, when Pakistani forces infiltrated very close to Srinagar. During the conflict over Bangladesh in 1971, it was India that took the offensive, and Pakistan was pushed back to a position not far from the original ceasefire line.

Following this conflict, Indira Gandhi and Ali Bhutto, the prime ministers of India and Pakistan, reached an understanding, which was expressed in the Shimla Agreement, signed in 1972. In 1975, the ever popular Kashmiri leader Sheikh Abdullah was released from one of his many periods of imprisonment and returned as Kashmir's chief minister. From then until his death in 1982, the National Conference party in Kashmir had convivial relations with the Congress party in Delhi.

Following Sheikh Abdullah's death, his son Farooq Abdullah became chief minister. It was not an easy transition. Rivalries within the National Conference party and demands from the ruling Congress party in Delhi characterised the years until 1987.

In 1987 Farooq Abdullah made an accord with the Indian prime minister Rajiv Gandhi, and for the first time the National Conference and Congress parties shared a political platform during the J&K state elections. For many Kashmiri people such a situation was unacceptable. The National Conference party had until then always tried to maintain its independence from Delhi. A political vacuum was created and there emerged growing support for a number of separatist parties, including the Jammu & Kashmir Liberation Front (JKLF). The JKLF demanded autonomy for Kashmir, while another group, the Hizb ul Mujahideen, maintained that Kashmir should become part of Pakistan.

By January 1990 there was mass support for the separatist groups. Farooq Abdullah,

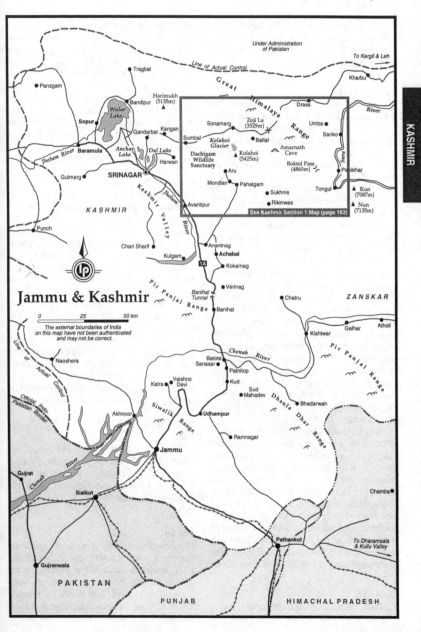

Jammu & Kashmir

0   25   50 km

The external boundaries of India
on this map have not been authenticated
and may not be correct.

KASHMIR

realising the impossibility of the situation, resigned, and the Indian government imposed President's Rule over the state – a situation which remains in force.

GEOGRAPHY

During the 19th century, British geologists were able to confirm that until quite recent geological times the Kashmir Valley was a vast inland lake. It was created when a combination of silt and rock landslides caused the Jhelum River to become blocked just below the present site of the town of Baramula. The valley filled with water, and a lake formed with its surface around 200m to 300m above the present valley floor. The pressure of water during a flood cleared the blockage, the lake drained, and the valley became one of the most fertile regions of northern India.

The Pir Panjal Range encloses the valley to the west and south, rising on average to elevations of around 5000m. To the north, the North Sonamarg Range provides an equally impressive backdrop, including the sacred peak of Harimukh (5135m). To the east, the Amarnath and Kolahoi ranges rising above Sonamarg and Pahalgam and extending south to the Pir Panjal Range include peaks such as Kolahoi (5425m). The ramparts of the Kashmir Valley are breached only once, to the north of the valley, where the Jhelum River flows through a narrow gorge en route to the Indus River.

Most trekking possibilities are to the east of the valley, where the Amarnath and Kolahoi ranges merge with the main Himalaya Range. In this region a series of alpine valleys including the Sindh and the Lidder provide the major routes into the main Himalaya.

The Great Himalaya Range is the main mountain divide between the region of Kashmir and Ladakh. In Kashmir, it extends south-east from the vicinity of the Zoji La. It includes Nun (7135m) and Kun (7087m), two of the highest peaks in the West Himalaya.

CLIMATE

Kashmir has a modified monsoonal climate, with the Pir Panjal Range to the south and south-east of the valley providing the main barrier to the passage of the monsoon rains.

The Kashmir Valley has long and cold winters which extend from mid-December through to the beginning of March. At this time heavy snow falls in the mountain regions. During the springtime there is a rainy period that can last for several weeks before the temperatures begin to rise in early May. From then on, until the end of June, the snow melts rapidly, although the occasional storm can produce late snowfalls.

While most of the West Himalaya is subject to the monsoon rains from early July till mid-September, the Kashmir Valley remains hot and humid. In contrast, the temperatures in Pahalgam rise to the low 20°Cs, making this an ideal time to undertake a trek.

By mid-September, the daytime temperatures begin to fall. It becomes less humid in the valley, while the mountain regions experience prolonged periods of settled conditions that continue till the end of October. There is, however, usually an autumn storm that can occur at any time in October or even in late September, which blocks the higher mountain passes and puts paid to extended treks over the main Himalaya Range. Treks can still be completed up the alpine valleys until November before the daytime temperatures begin to drop and the first of the winter snows fall on the lower mountain ranges.

MAPS & BOOKS
Maps

Most of the treks out of Pahalgam are covered on the Leomann series *Sheet 1 Jammu and Kashmir*, which includes Srinagar, Kolahoi and Kishtwar. With the U502 series, refer to the *NI 43-07 Kargil* sheet.

Books

Beautiful Valleys of Kashmir and Ladakh by Samsar Chand Kaul (Utpal Publications, 1971) includes descriptions of treks made out of Pahalgam in the 1930s, as does *Kashmir in Sunlight and Shade* by Tyndale Biscoe (Sagar Publications, reprint 1971). *The Tourist's Guide to Kashmir, Ladakh &*

Skardo edited by Arthur Neve provides an interesting comparison between trekking descriptions and styles in the interwar years and today. Also refer to *Kashmir* by Francis Younghusband (reprint 1970) for descriptions of the wildlife in the valleys close to Srinagar at the turn of the century. The *Climbing and Trekking Guide to Sonamarg* by John Jackson (J&K Tourist Department, 1976) includes descriptions of treks and climbs that can be undertaken from both Pahalgam and Sonamarg.

If trekking between Kashmir and Ladakh, *Thirty Years in Kashmir* by Arthur Neve (1984) includes a section on the exploration of passes near the Nun Kun massif.

SRINAGAR

Most travellers arrive in Srinagar, the capital of Kashmir, before heading off to commence a trek. It is in the centre of the Kashmir Valley, affording fine views of the mountain ranges encircling the valley.

Srinagar was the place to organise supplies and arrangements if considering a fully organised trek. Until 1990 there were over 100 travel agents and trekking offices, all of which claimed to be able to organise treks. Combine the attraction of staying on the houseboats with the rich cultural history in the vicinity of Srinagar, and you would be hard put not to spend at least a few days here, either before or after a trek.

Information

With the current political situation, there is much conflicting information about what can and can't be done in J&K state. Reliable, up-to-date information is invaluable, and here the J&K Department of Tourism offices fail miserably. Even after a group of foreign trekkers were taken hostage in June 1995, the J&K Tourism office in Delhi was still insisting that all was under control in Kashmir and that there was no problem. As the boxed aside clearly shows, this was not the case at all.

The J&K Tourism office in Srinagar is no better. If you have a morning to spend you can wander through the musty corridors

The Political Situation

Kashmir has never been closed to tourists. In July 1990 certain areas of Kashmir were given a 'disturbed area' status that is, the Indian military and reserve police forces were given extraordinary powers of arrest and so on. However tourists were still permitted to go to Kashmir. There are no restrictions on movement except the ones already in force, such as the ban on travel to areas close to the India-Pakistan ceasefire line, or to areas under curfew.

Until recently there have been very few incidents that have involved tourists. Neither the state government nor the Kashmir separatist forces had any objection to foreigners visiting the region, and between 1992 and 1994 the number of tourists visiting the valley steadily improved. While the numbers were still only one tenth of those visiting the valley in 1989, there were still nearly 5000 foreigners visiting Kashmir each year.

As far as trekking is concerned there were no problems until June 1994 when two British trekkers were abducted between Aru and Lidderwat, about 20 km from Pahalgam. The men were released without being harmed a week later.

However, the following year, in July 1995 four trekkers (two American, two British) were abducted by a fundamentalist group again in the Aru area. The consequences were far more serious. One of the American trekkers was able to escape and in retaliation two more trekkers (Norwegian and German) were captured. In August, shortly after the annual Amarnath pilgrimage, the Norwegian trekker was beheaded, while the four remaining trekkers were held captive. This led to protests by other separatist groups concerned that an innocent tourist had been killed.

As of December 1996, the four remaining hostages had still not been released, although there were fears that they had been shot in December 1995 or might have died of cold or sickness. In spite of pleas made by other separatist groups, there seems little hope that the situation will be resolved in the near future.

What this amounts to is that, although the Indian authorities have not closed Kashmir to foreigners, it would be extremely foolhardy to even consider a visit to Srinagar, let alone go trekking. Even if the situation was to improve it would not be advisable to contemplate trekking or visiting Kashmir until there was a categorical statement made on behalf of all the separatist groups that tourists would not be harmed or involved in political disturbances: an impossible dream at present. ∎

KASHMIR

where there are no fewer than five assistant directors and three deputy directors, most of whom have little or nothing to do except shuffle dusty files from one end of the desk to the other. The only person who has a clue what is going on is the Director of Tourism, who was formerly the Trekking & Mountaineering Officer. Appointments can be made between 2 and 4 pm each day – worth following up should there be any improvement in the current political situation.

Trekking Agents

Nowadays most of the local trekking agencies in Kashmir have either closed down or relocated to Delhi. Those that remain have their offices in Polo View or on The Bund, although most are open in name only.

As an alternative, travellers who have previously visited Kashmir may be able to recommend a particular houseboat family to set up your arrangements. Some families are more professional than others, and it is not recommended that you use any houseboat-based trekking service unless it has been previously tried and tested, particularly if undertaking extended treks. If you're uncertain of your plans, arrangements of a less comprehensive nature can always be made at Pahalgam.

Accommodation in Srinagar

Even in the current political situation most of the houseboats are still open for business. Indeed, there are few alternatives available in Srinagar, as most hotels are now occupied by the Reserve Police Force or the Indian army.

The houseboats are comfortable floating homes, normally 30 to 50 metres long, consisting of a lounge, dining room, sundeck and two or three bedrooms, linked by a corridor. Constructed of pine and lined with cedar, the boats are furnished in what could only be described as 1930s chintz. When staying on a houseboat you rent a room on a full-board basis and share the lounge and dining room with other visitors. Houseboats are divided into various classes, ranging from deluxe to the local *dunga* (traditional

barge) style. Most boats are moored on Dal Lake near the Boulevard, the main thoroughfare of Srinagar. For those intent on getting away from it all, Nagin Lake, eight km out of town, is a good alternative.

Houseboats provide an ideal opportunity for gaining an insight into Kashmiri life. Each boat is owned by a family who will cook and maintain the boat for you. Friendships can be made, and you can become part of the family in no time.

To find a houseboat to suit your taste and budget, wander down to Dal Lake, hire a *shikara* (gondola) and row over to the 'To Let' signs. The current government rate per night for a double room with full board is Rs 800 for a deluxe boat, Rs 600 for A class, Rs 400 for B class, Rs 210 for C class, and for the local-style dunga boats around Rs 50 without food. However, these rates are the maximum rates and bargaining should result in a considerable saving.

Getting There & Away

Delhi to Srinagar Indian and Moduluft airlines operate daily flights from Delhi to Srinagar that cost US$84/89.

Since partition in 1947, the Kashmir land borders between India and Pakistan have been closed. Until the late 1950s the land route over the Banihal Pass to the south of the valley took three days; the first from Delhi to Pathankot, the second by road to Banihal, and the third to Srinagar. The opening of the tunnel under the Banihal Pass in 1958 reduced the travelling time between Jammu and Srinagar to eight to 10 hours, and made Kashmir accessible throughout the year.

Nowadays, it takes 24 hours by train and bus from Delhi to Srinagar. The trains from Delhi to Jammu leave from both the New and Old Delhi stations in the evening and arrive in Jammu the following morning. The buses leave Jammu after the trains arrive and reach Srinagar late that evening. The train from Delhi to Jammu costs Rs 530 in 1st class and Rs in 170 2nd class. The express bus from Jammu to Srinagar costs Rs 210, the deluxe bus Rs 133, the A class Rs 94, and the B class Rs 72. Taxis from Jammu cost Rs 2200 and can be hired on a per seat basis.

Srinagar to Leh Indian Airlines operates a weekly service from Srinagar to Leh that costs US$43.

There are daily bus services to Leh operated by the J&K government from the tourist office in Srinagar. The services operate from the time the road over the Zoji La is clear of snow, normally around the first week of June. The pass remains open from then until the first week of October. The drive takes two full days with an overnight stop at Kargil.

Expect lengthy delays on the first day while driving over the Zoji La as the Indian army has been widening the road over the last decade. The deluxe bus costs Rs 333, A class Rs 222 and a taxi Rs 5500 one way. For trekkers going to the Zanskar Valley the cost of the deluxe bus to Kargil is Rs 167, the A class bus Rs 111 and a taxi Rs 3300.

Srinagar to Kishtwar There is a daily bus service to Kishtwar. It is operated by a private bus company opposite the main (KMD) bus stand in Lal Chowk. The cost is Rs 60 and the trip takes 10 to 12 hours.

Getting Around

At present there are no bus services operating from the tourist office in Kashmir to places within the Kashmir Valley. A local bus service, run by the KMD Bus Drivers Association, operates from Lal Chowk in the city. The bus to Pahalgam costs Rs 19 while the one to Sonamarg costs Rs 18. Both services operate three times a day. Taxis are also available, but are expensive compared to the bus. Expect to pay, for example, about Rs 900 one way to Pahalgam or Sonamarg.

PAHALGAM

At the confluence of the east and west Lidder rivers, Pahalgam (2140m) still attracted a steady flow of trekkers until a group of foreign trekkers were taken hostage in June

1995. Since then the Indian army has temporarily closed off the region to trekkers, with the notable exception of the annual Amarnath pilgrimage that is still undertaken by many thousands of Hindu pilgrims during the July-August full moon. This section is therefore included for reference, and in the hope that the current situation will improve before the next edition of this book.

Treks

Pahalgam to Kolahoi Glacier & Tar Sar
(introductory; 5 stages)
Pahalgam to Sumbal via Sonamous Pass
(moderate; 5 stages)
Pahalgam to Amarnath Cave via Mahagunas Pass
(moderate; 6 stages)
Pahalgam to Suru Valley (Ladakh) via Boktol Pass
(moderate to strenuous; 8 stages)

History

The local shepherds have been following the trekking trails out of Pahalgam for many generations. The grazing routes lead to the rich alpine pastures above the Lidder and the Sindh valleys where they graze throughout most of the summer months (see the boxed aside The Shepherds of Kashmir, later in this chapter). As for the Bakharval (goat herders) from Jammu, it is believed that one of the early Dogra maharajahs invited them to come to Kashmir as a means of raising revenue while also keeping stock of the valuable wool which is made into the finest Kashmir shawls. It is therefore probable that they have followed the mountain routes for most of the last century.

The discovery, probably by shepherds, of the Amarnath Cave led to one of the most important pilgrimages in northern India. Details of the history of the pilgrimage to the cave are included in the boxed text with the Amarnath Cave trek description on page 167.

The route from Pahalgam over the Boktol Pass has been followed by traders and armies for centuries. In 1834 the pass gained prominence when it was crossed by the Dogra general Zorawar Singh as he made his first foray into Ladakh. At the time the Sikhs held Kashmir, so the army made its way from Kishtwar up the Warvan Valley to complete an ambitious traverse into Ladakh. It also marked their first attempt to expand their Himalayan territory. Indeed, after a series of battles with the king of Ladakh, the Dogra horizons expanded further, and by the early 1840s they had taken Baltistan. In 1842 they attempted unsuccessfully to overrun western Tibet, and Zorawar Singh was killed.

When to Trek

You can undertake a trek out of Pahalgam to Lidderwat from early May onwards, although avalanche debris on the trail will make it hard for pack ponies to proceed past Aru. By early June the first trekkers reach the base of the Kolahoi Glacier, although most of the route is still under snow until early July.

The trek over the Sonamous Pass can be undertaken in June, although at this time only with porters or by backpacking (laden horses can't make it over safely until July). The descent from the pass to the camp at Sonamous is particularly steep, and only experienced horsemen will consider undertaking this route before the beginning of July. The same applies to trekking over the Gul Gali, the pass linking Pahalgam to the upper Warvan Valley en route to Ladakh. Although it is possible to backpack over the pass in June, horsemen will again be reluctant to undertake this trek until early July. The Boktol Pass (the pass over the main Himalaya Range which needs to be crossed to reach Ladakh) is also under deep snow until the end of June.

The trekking season out of Pahalgam is not interrupted by the monsoon. Treks can be undertaken from July until early October. After this time the first of the winter snows block the highest passes on the main Himalaya, including the Boktol Pass. However, the lower passes linking Pahalgam to the Sindh Valley remain open longer and it is possible to complete the trek over the Sonamous Pass, or trek to the Amarnath Cave, until mid-October. Treks up the Lidder Valley can still be completed through November and even in early December if you are equipped for the long, cold nights.

Accommodation in Pahalgam

Until 1990 Pahalgam was a thriving hill station with many hotels and trekking lodges, and there were more in the nearby pine forest above the West Lidder River. Nowadays nearly all these places have closed and the main bazaar remains deserted for most of the season. Hotels that have remained open include the *Hotel Grandview* at Rs 100 a double. Some of the smaller lodges also open from time to time, so there is a choice of accommodation if you decide to stay in Pahalgam for a night or two before undertaking a trek.

Accommodation on the Trail

On the trek to the Kolahoi Glacier there are lodges at Aru. The *Friends Guest House*, *Paradise Guest House* and *Royal Guest House* have rooms from Rs 40 to Rs 80. There is also a *Paradise Guest House* at Lidderwat for Rs 40. The owner lives in Aru and will trek up to Lidderwat when there is sufficient demand. The chowkidar who runs the *Forest Rest House* at Lidderwat also lives in Aru and will come up to Lidderwat when necessary. Rooms are Rs 40. Beyond Lidderwat there are only Gujar huts, so a tent must be carried.

The Amarnath trek is well serviced with tented accommodation during the time of the main pilgrimage. At other times there are *Forest Rest Houses* at Chandanwadi, Sheshnag and Panchtarni with rooms for about Rs 50. It is necessary, however, to check whether they are open with the J&K Tourism office in Pahalgam as the chowkidars are not always in attendance, particularly at the beginning and the end of the season. If trekking to Ladakh, there are no tea houses or rest houses beyond Sheshnag so you must be self-sufficient on these stages.

Trekking Advice

While the treks out of the Pahalgam are some of the most accessible in Kashmir, good preparation is still essential. Rivers, especially in late June and early July, must be crossed with care. I can recall some very sad accounts of accidents that could have been

KASHMIR

The Shepherds of Kashmir

Beyond the village of Aru, the trekking region between Pahalgam and Sonamarg is essentially a wilderness area for over six months of the year. During the short summer grazing season, from June to mid-September, the Kashmiri shepherds, the Gujar buffalo herders and the Bakharval goat herders drive their animals up the Lidder and Sindh valleys. This annual migration has followed a traditional grazing pattern for many generations.

The actual locals are the Kashmiri shepherds, who confine their grazing to the lower altitudes, settling in the pastures within a few km of Pahalgam or Sonamarg. The Kashmiri shepherd is easily distinguished by his *ferun*, the woollen smock he wears and under which he carries his *kangri* or traditional clay firepot.

The Gujar, with their herds of water buffalo, migrate higher up the valleys. They subsist by selling buffalo milk in the local villages, and usually have a small flock of sheep to supplement their income. These shepherds originally migrated many centuries ago from Gujarat to the Himalayan foothills. As the pressure of land usage built up on the plains, the Gujar continued to migrate higher to the hills, crossing the Pir Panjal Range each summer in search of new grazing areas. These days the J&K state government has adopted a policy of resettlement for the Gujar, and many now spend the winter months close to the villages below the summer grazing pastures. The Gujar who graze their animals at Satalanjan in the Lidder Valley, for instance, now settle in the villages just below Pahalgam during the winter. Similarly, the shepherds from Sonamous take their buffalo down to the villages in the lower Sindh Valley. The Gujar are easily identified by their turbans and the brightly coloured blankets that cover their shoulders. They are still considered to be outsiders and rarely intermarry with the Kashmiri people.

The third group of shepherds are the Bakharval, the goat herders who move their huge flocks to the highest pastures during summer. The Bakharval are the 'cousin brothers' of the Gujar, and have a lucrative business. Goat wool is sold at a high price as it is made into the famous Kashmir shawls. The Bakharval still lead a seminomadic existence, sometimes driving their flocks over the passes into Ladakh. As the winter approaches they return over the Pir Panjal passes back to the Reasi district of Jammu. It is these shepherds who make it easier for us to trek in Kashmir. They assume responsibility for reconstructing the bridges over the high-flowing streams, and clear rock scree from the trails, so that we can follow in their footsteps. ■

---

avoided if trekkers had used a little common sense.

The snow bridges are actually less hazardous than is generally thought. Wide cracks appear well before they collapse, and they are abandoned by the shepherds long before they become dangerous. If the shepherds are still using them you can consider them safe.

If undertaking a trek to Ladakh, bear in mind that the route to the Boktol Pass is glaciated and particular care needs to be taken while trekking just below the pass. Here the crevasses are concealed early in the season or after a snowfall.

Provisions

Basic supplies such as tea, sugar, vegetables, dhal and cooking oil can be purchased in the Pahalgam bazaar. They may also be purchased at Aru and at Chandanwadi around the time of the Amarnath pilgrimage. All other provisions, including kerosene, should be brought from Srinagar.

Horsemen & Porters

While porters are available for most of the treks out of Pahalgam, most trekking is undertaken with horsemen and packhorses. There is a Ponymen's Union in Pahalgam at the top of the bazaar which displays the fixed rates set by the J&K Department of Tourism. These are around Rs 70 per day per horse. However, these are minimum rates and you should budget on Rs 100 per horse, plus a 50% return payment if your trek does not return to Pahalgam. Once hired, the horsemen are generally reliable, willing to help, and worth what you pay above the official rate.

Access

From Pahalgam it is possible to drive to Aru or Chandanwadi although the roads are rough and subject to landslides. In fact, the road to Aru was blocked in early 1995 by a large landslide just out of Pahalgam, so there was no choice but to trek. Even when the choice exists it is advisable to trek the first stage. It is possible to avoid walking on the road, and the mountain scenery fully compensates for any intrusion of traffic.

PAHALGAM TO KOLAHOI GLACIER & TAR SAR
Map: Kashmir Section 1 (page 163)
Stage 1: Pahalgam to Aru
(Average walking time 3 hours)
Although the first stage of this trek follows a jeep road, it is a convenient opportunity to get accustomed to your boots and attuned to the fine alpine scenery. After the village of **Mondlan** there are a number of places where you can shortcut the jeep road that winds gradually up the West Lidder Valley. After five to six km there are some impressive views back down the valley towards Pahalgam and across to the snow-capped mountains which form the divide between the Lidder and Warvan valleys.

The village of **Aru** (2410m) is at the confluence of the Nafran and Lidder rivers, amid a large open meadow. The village boasts a number of lodges and tea houses where food is available. Unfortunately, the meadow in the immediate vicinity of Aru has been subject to a number of shanty developments that seem to be the hallmark of progress in the valley. It is recommended, therefore, that you camp a few km further up the valley, well away from the jeep track.

Stage 2: Aru to Lidderwat
(Average walking time 3 hours)
This is another short stage. From Aru the trail ascends the bridle track behind the village. The climb is quite steep in places until the trail reaches a small meadow. From here the track levels out through pine forest for two to three km, before reaching an alpine meadow that forms one of the most picturesque settings in Kashmir. The meadow is populated by Gujar and Kashmiri shepherds who are fully acquainted with trekkers. The

well-marked trail gradually ascends the meadow before dropping down to the side of the Lidder River a few km before Lidderwat. Continue past the confluence of the Lidder River and the river coming from Tar Sar, then cross the bridge that leads to **Lidderwat** (3050m).

In spite of the shanty lodges, the meadow retains much of its charm and beauty. For those going it alone and without a tent, the lodges provide convenient shelter and food. The set-up is similar to the tea-house lodges in Nepal. In addition, there is a *Forest Rest House* on the far side of the meadow.

Note that although Lidderwat can be used as a base for treks to the Kolahoi Glacier and Tar Sar, both stages are quite long, and it is recommended that you camp higher – at Satalanjan for the Kolahoi Glacier trek, or at Seikwas for the Tar Sar trek. If this is not possible, then an early start is imperative if you are to reach Kolahoi or Tar Sar and return to Lidderwat before nightfall.

Stage 3: Lidderwat to Kolahoi Glacier & Return
(Average walking time 8 to 9 hours return)
The trail from Lidderwat continues along the true right bank of the Lidder. Do not re-cross the bridge. From Lidderwat it is about two or three hours to Satalanjan. In the early part of the season the trail could be under snow, so ensure you have strong walking boots and find a reliable stick to assist your balance. The trail is quite level by Himalayan standards, with few ups and downs, until you reach the birch forests just below Satalanjan. The rock outcrops above are a perfect habitat for brown bears, which have been sighted wandering down to the water's edge at first light. *Meconopsis laitifolia*, one of the famous blue poppy species of the Himalaya, has also been found near here.

The Gujar village at **Satalanjan** (3150m) is the most substantial in the Lidder Valley. The shepherds are familiar with the arrival of trekkers, and the children lose little time in approaching for hand-outs. If you're camping at Satalanjan, there is an ideal spot on the meadow below the huts. From here

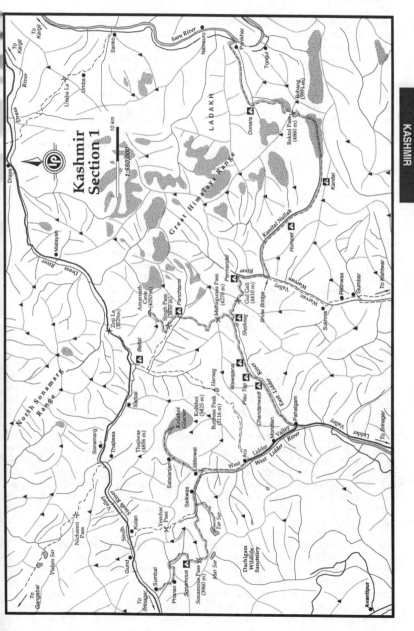

you can explore the surrounding ridges later in the day, and continue to the snout of the Kolahoi Glacier early the following morning.

From Satalanjan it is a further three hours to the base of the glacier. The trail continues across the meadow to the bend in the main valley. From there you will appreciate the profile of the upper Lidder Valley. Essentially the trail ascends gradually across a series of small meadows set among moraine which extends to the snout of the glacier. The peak of Kolahoi (5425m) is high above the opposite valley. It is known locally as Gashibrar (the Goddess of Light) and was first climbed in 1912 via the east ridge.

Note that the best views of the peak are from the last meadow before you reach the terminal moraine. However, to appreciate the character and size of the glacier, it is necessary to continue for a further two or three km over the terminal moraine to the snout of the glacier (3400m). Watch closely for the rock cairns that mark the way through the boulders or you will waste energy on trail-finding when you can least afford it.

Return to Lidderwat by the same route.

Stage 4: Lidderwat to Seikwas, Tar Sar & Return

(Average walking time 8 to 9 hours return)
From Lidderwat the trail ascends the steep hillside to the west of the meadow and continues up to the tree line. From here on the track becomes easier, and after a few km opens out to a series of meadows that lead to **Seikwas** (3430m). After four to five km the trail crosses two gullies before winding below a rocky outcrop that can prove difficult for packhorses early in the season. It is a further two km to the confluence of the Lidder River and the river coming from Tar Sar. This whole area is known as Seikwas.

In the early part of the season you may be able to cross the river by snowbridge, even lower down the valley, in which case the day's trek is considerably reduced. But by early summer (late June onwards) the chances are that you will have to ascend for a few more km to a safe crossing point before continuing to Tar Sar. This can be time con-

suming, but there is no alternative. From the river confluence it is a further two to three hours walk to **Tar Sar** (3900m), which can be hard going if the terrain is still under snow. It is important to head for the middle ridge beside the Tar Sar stream, and from here ascend the series of grassy ridges that lead to the lake. This part of the trek can be tiring, but the views back down to Lidderwat and across to Kolahoi peak compensate. Tar Sar is a glacial lake about three km long and, at its maximum, one km wide. It is enclosed on three sides by snow ridges up to 1000 metres above the water's edge – a perfect camp site as soon as the snows melt.

If camping back down at Lidderwat it is advisable to return without undue delay, especially in the early part of the season. The river levels rise significantly by the afternoon. To avoid the worst of this, you should aim to return to Seikwas by lunchtime. For the rest of the afternoon you can admire the profusion of wildflowers that appear after the spring snow melts.

Options If you started at Seikwas you could return by climbing the first ridge on the true left of the lake. This affords excellent views of the lake, and leads to the valley en route to the Sonamous Pass. The descent from this ridge is quite steep and is under snow during the early part of the season. From the valley floor, it is a couple of km back down to the upper Seikwas camp site to complete the circuit.

A further option is to trek around the lake to the ridge at the far end of the valley. This route leads to the upper Dachigam Sanctuary, and from the ridge you can appreciate Mar Sar, whose waters eventually flow into the Kashmir Valley at Harwan, not far from Dal Lake.

Stage 5: Lidderwat to Pahalgam

(Average walking time 5 hours)
Starting from Lidderwat you should be able to return to Pahalgam by lunchtime. The trail is generally downhill, and it is always possible to jump on the back of a truck if you want to save time on the stage below Aru.

Getting Away

There are three buses a day from Pahalgam to Srinagar, The first leaves at 7 am and the last around 3 pm. If you should miss the last bus, catch the bus to Anantnag and change buses here to Srinagar. It is therefore possible to trek from Lidderwat and return to Srinagar in one day.

PAHALGAM TO SUMBAL VIA SONAMOUS PASS
Map: Kashmir Section 1 (page 163)
Stages 1 to 3: Pahalgam to Seikwas
Refer to the Pahalgam to Kolahoi Glacier & Tar Sar trek in previous section.

Stage 4: Seikwas to Sonamous Camp
(Average walking time 5 hours)
From Seikwas there is a choice of three passes leading to the Sindh Valley. The right-hand (east) valley leads to the **Yemhar Pass** (4350m) – a moderate climb with a short, steep descent to a camp at the meadow at Khem Sar. The following day it is a further three to four hour descent to the roadhead at either Kulan or Gund. This trail is seldom used nowadays by horsemen as the track immediately after the pass is exposed and dangerous for laden ponies.

The unnamed pass directly above the Seikwas camp involves another steady ascent to the pass (4200m), and from there it is a further 1½ hour descent to where this valley joins the valley coming from the Sonamous Pass. This pass is not recommended for the inexperienced, and is unsuitable for horses.

The valley to the west of Seikwas leads to the **Sonamous Pass** (3960m). The trek to the top of the pass takes, on average, about three hours. The trail involves a steady climb for the first two km until it crosses the main stream to the true left of the valley. The trail levels out, passing a small lake, before crossing a rather marshy trail that leads back across the valley. In late spring the trail is normally under snow, and an early start from camp is essential for both packhorses and trekkers. There is little to show that you have reached the pass. It is, in fact, just a short incline as you near the head of the valley. From here there is a steep descent to a grassy plateau, from where there is a bird's-eye view of the camp at **Sonamous** (3340m).

The final section is steep and difficult, particularly early in the season when the slopes are under snow. The mules are sometimes unloaded at this point, and the baggage rolled down the slopes. Early in the season it is essential for trekkers to have good boots, and a sturdy stick or an ice axe is also useful. It also helps if you feel confident in crossing relatively steep snow slopes. If you do not, then plan to cross the pass after mid-July. By then the snow will have melted and a trail will have been cleared across the boulder fields down to the camp at Sonamous.

Stage 5: Sonamous to Sumbal
(Average walking time 3 to 4 hours)
The final stage of this trek descends steeply to the Sindh Valley. It is not the easiest trail to follow, particularly through the forest, so some care should be taken to avoid any bush-bashing or backtracking.

Cross the Sonamous stream beside the shepherd encampment, and follow the trail through the forest for one km until you cross a large side stream. Here the trail descends below a small Gujar settlement, and then continues above the main river through the forest until after four or five km it descends steeply to a side river flowing from the east. Cross the log bridge and continue down the trail, which is now just above the main river.

After a km or so the trail crosses to the true left of the Sonamous River via a substantial bridge. The trail passes through the Gujar village of Pharao and follows the river bank until it recrosses the river a couple of km down the valley. The trail widens here as it continues to the outskirts of **Sumbal** (2120m). Here the pony trail skirts the village fields, while the trekking trail cuts through the rice and cornfields to the roadhead.

Getting Away
At Sumbal there are a number of tea stalls where you can rest before catching the local bus. There are regular services till 4 pm

KASHMIR

taking two to three hours to return to Srinagar (cost Rs 13). The last bus to Sonamarg leaves Sumbal around 3 pm. The journey takes about two hours and costs around Rs 7. From here there are a number of alternatives, including boarding a truck or bus onward to Ladakh and completing a trek there or spending a day in Sonamarg and continuing your trek onto Vishen Sar and Gangabal before returning to Srinagar.

PAHALGAM TO AMARNATH CAVE VIA MAHAGUNAS PASS
Map: Kashmir Section 1 (page 163)
Stage 1: Pahalgam to Chandanwadi
(Average walking time 4 hours)
The trail leaves Pahalgam on a bitumen road, past the Shankar temple and along the East Lidder Valley. The trail is easy to follow, indeed it is suitable for jeeps as far as **Chandanwadi** (2900m). There are many obvious short cuts on the route, and a number of tea stalls as this first stage always seems to be quite hot. The camp site is in a pleasant glade just before the main line of tea stalls.

Stage 2: Chandanwadi to Sheshnag
(Average walking time 5 to 6 hours)
From Chandanwadi the trail winds steeply for 500m to the summit of a ridge known as **Pisu Top** (3390m). From here, there are commanding views back down the valley to the mountains beyond Pahalgam. During the main pilgrimage, the tea-stall owners do a thriving business which keeps the pilgrims going on the long incline to the next main resting area at **Wawajana** (3550m). From here it is two to three km further to **Sheshnag** (3720m). The glacial lake is set in remarkable surroundings, its waters reflecting the snow-capped peaks of Vishnu, Shiva and Brahma. Rumour among pilgrims has it that the lake is inhabited by a serpent of Loch Ness monster proportions, so it's advisable not to camp too close to the water's edge.

Stage 3: Sheshnag to Panchtarni
(Average walking time 6 hours)
The trail gradually ascends from Sheshnag with magnificent views of the mountains

immediately above. The ascent towards the **Mahagunas Pass** winds up to a grassy plateau, and from there on to the pass it is a further hour's climb. Written signs of encouragement amuse the weary: ' Just a hop and you're on the top'. The sign at the top of the pass states the height as 4270m. It is not a dramatic pass, but it is still no mean achievement for the pilgrims, many of whom have never been beyond the Indian plains before. The descent to **Panchtarni** (3450m) is quite long and tiring, but there are frequent flowered meadows to rest in and admire. The camp site can be seen from afar; and behind, on a further ridge, the bare, treeless mountainscape resembles the terrain on the far side of the Himalaya. There are more spacious camp sites upstream from the main camping area, and these are also a little cleaner.

Stage 4: Panchtarni to Amarnath Cave & Return
(Average walking time 5 hours return)
The actual time to the cave will depend on whether your trek coincides with the main pilgrimage. During the pilgrimage an early start is essential, with many of the pilgrims leaving well before first light. The pilgrims move more steadily and slowly than on the rest of the trek, as if in awe of their surroundings. The climb to the **Singh Pass** (3850m) is gradual before the trail enters the Amarnath Valley. It descends to a permanently blackened snow bridge which fords the Amarvati stream before ascending the true right bank to the base of the mountain. From here the final ascent is up a series of concrete steps to the entrance to the **Amarnath Cave** (4050m).

It is not hard to imagine why the pilgrims believe this to be one of the most sacred places in the Himalaya. The cave is approximately 150m high and wide, and contains a huge natural ice stalagmite, the symbol of Shiva. The ice is formed by water trickling through the limestone roof, and the lingam is said to reach its maximum size during the full moon. Occasionally the ice does not form at all, and this is considered extremely inauspicious for the pilgrims. If you intend

The Amarnath Trek

The trek to the Amarnath Cave is the most important pilgrimage in Kashmir. Each year on the Shavan (July-August) full moon about 20,000 Hindu pilgrims trek to the cave to view the ice statue which symbolises the presence of Shiva, the Hindu god of destruction.

There are many legends regarding the discovery of the cave, but little historical fact. In all probability it was discovered as shepherds wandered the valley in search of fresh grazing areas. Not only is the cave an ideal refuge for meditation, but it is at the head of one of the important tributaries of the Indus River. According to the legend, Lord Shiva related his theory of reincarnation to his consort Parvati in the cave on a full-moon night. As if to validate the legend, a huge ice statue formed in the cave. It is said to wax and wane with the moon. The ice statue represents the lingam, a symbol of Shiva, the source of creation, while the huge size of the cave is a symbol of Parvati and the vast womb of the universe.

For the wandering *sadhus* (holy men), the pilgrimage starts in Srinagar. It takes a week to reach Pahalgam, with rest stops at the temples at Bijbihara and Martand en route. At Pahalgam they join the main body of pilgrims who have driven directly from Srinagar and are now preparing for the trek.

For some, walking with 20,000 Hindu pilgrims isn't exactly the ideal way to trek, as moving with such a large mass of people rather undermines any notion of isolation. On top of this you have to contend with the obvious associated hygiene problems. One alternative is to visit the cave before the August full moon: the trail is open by early July and remains open until October. However, most people who have walked to the cave during the main *yatra* (pilgrimage) have not regretted it, although most would not want to do it again. It is very much a once-in-a-lifetime experience.

For those making their own arrangements, food can be purchased from the numerous tea stalls en route, and limited tent accommodation is available at the camp cities that form each night to accommodate the pilgrims. It is necessary to stress the fact that drinking water from all the streams should be avoided, and a careful watch needs to be kept on all your baggage. Ponies are available for the trek, and it is also possible to be carried to the cave on a *dandy* (wooden platform) supported by four bearers who charge around Rs 3000 for the round trip.

In the last few years the Indian government has made elaborate plans to ensure the safety and wellbeing of the pilgrims. During the yatra, stages of the walk are carefully controlled by the authorities. The first stage of the trek is to Chandanwadi, the second to Sheshnag and the third over the Mahagunas Pass to Panchtarni. Many pilgrims visit the cave from Panchtarni and return to Sheshnag the same day, walking back to Pahalgam on the fifth day. ■

KASHMIR

to enter the cave during the pilgrimage, be prepared for a long wait. The J&K police manning the entrance to the cave only permit a limited number of pilgrims inside at any one time.

Stage 5: Panchtarni to Chandanwadi
(Average walking time 8 hours)
Many pilgrims return from Panchtarni to Chandanwadi in one day. After completing their pilgrimage to the cave most are happy to trek as far as they can the following stage.

Stage 6: Chandanwadi to Pahalgam
(Average walking time 4 hours)
On the final stage most pilgrims arrive back in the Pahalgam bazaar with enough time to complete the drive to Srinagar or Jammu the same day.

Option: Amarnath to Baltal & Sonamarg
From the Amarnath Cave return along the pilgrim trail as far as the junction of the Panchtarni and Amarvati rivers. Here the trails divert, with the track to Baltal heading down the true right of the valley. The trail is often in poor condition, particularly after heavy rainfall, and the J&K police may often close this route for safety reasons. The trail is prone to rock avalanches where it traverses large scree slopes, and you should be wary of descending without first checking its condition. If there are no problems, the trek to **Baltal** (3100m) can be completed in about four hours.

Getting Away From Baltal there is a regular bus service during the pilgrimage period, getting back to Srinagar that night. At other times, camp at Baltal and continue to

Sonamarg at a more leisurely pace the following morning. From Sonamarg there are three buses a day to Srinagar. The drive takes around five hours and costs Rs 19.

PAHALGAM TO SURU VALLEY (LADAKH) VIA BOKTOL PASS
Map: Kashmir Section 1 (page 163)
Stages 1 & 2: Pahalgam to Sheshnag
Refer to the first two stages of the Amarnath Cave trek in the previous section.

Stage 3: Sheshnag to Permandal over the Gul Gali
(Average walking time 5 to 6 hours)
From Sheshnag, ascend the rocky gully immediately beyond the lake. It takes about three hours to complete the 700 metre climb to the **Gul Gali** (4410m), which can be quite tiring under soft snow in the early part of the season until mid-July. On reaching the pass, the main Himalaya Range can be appreciated for the first time. From the pass there is an initially steep descent before the trail leads down the gully to the Sain Nullah and the upper Warvan Valley. Before reaching the valley floor, keep to the trail on the true left of the gully that leads to the Bakharval encampment at **Permandal** (3610m).

Stage 4: Permandal to Humpet
(Average walking time 5 to 6 hours)
The trail from the Permandal camp winds high above the valley floor across a series of shepherd encampments. The walk is shaded by birch groves, and affords good views up the Kanital Valley and the mountains beyond Humpet. From the viewpoint opposite Humpet, the trail begins to descend, zig-zagging steeply down to the valley floor and a snow bridge over the river. Once across the snow bridge, the trail proceeds up the valley on the far bank. At the confluence of the upper Warvan and Kanital rivers, divert up the Kanital Valley through birch groves and past waterfalls until two short, steep climbs bring you out onto an open plateau and the summer grazing areas of the Bakharval shepherds. The camp site at **Humpet** (3400m) is

beyond the shepherd encampment on the main valley floor.

Note that some maps indicate an alternative route to Panikhar that crosses the Kanital River and ascends the valley opposite Humpet. This is not correct. However, if a rest day is warranted, then it is still worthwhile wandering up the Kanital Valley. Consult the shepherds beforehand about the best crossing point, and watch the level of the river or you may be forced to swim across on the way back. It is very cold and rather puts a damper on the day, as I will testify.

If you take a rest day here you will find that the shepherds are keen to check you out and are willing to offer goat's milk, curd and corn chapattis in return for the odd Swiss Army knife or two. Give them ample warning if you decide to visit their encampments, as the dogs are particularly fierce and will need to be chained.

Stage 6: Humpet to Kanital
(Average walking time 3 hours)
Leaving Humpet, the trail follows the true left bank of the river and continues along the valley floor around to the camp site at **Kanital** (3680m). The track crosses meadows which are covered in wildflowers during the summer months, while the glacial bed is rich in fossils. There is one side-stream crossing en route, where the valley turns to the east. From here, the Boktol Glacier and the main Himalaya come into view, including the peak of Bobang (5971m) to the immediate east of the pass.

There are a number of camp sites to choose from, including one beside a waterfall on the last large open meadow before the moraine. Alternatively, you can trek further towards the glacier for about two to three km, and camp beside one of the smaller shepherd settlements. This will save time on the pass crossing the following morning.

Stage 7: Kanital to Boktol Pass & Donara
(Average walking time 8 to 9 hours)
The **Boktol Pass** (4860m), sometimes referred to as the Lonvilad Gali, has been the

most popular back-door route for pilgrims and armies crossing into Ladakh. Indeed the famous Dogra general, Zorawar Singh, led his army over this pass in 1834 on his quest to invade Ladakh.

From the camp, continue along the trail until you reach the last shepherd's hut, and then make for the right hand side of the terminal moraine. Check the rock cairns as you commence your ascent through the boulders. There is, believe it or not, a trail for the horses to follow up the moraine, and it should not take you more than an hour before the track descends from the boulders onto the centre of the glacial valley floor.

From here there is a gradual climb up the centre of the glacier. As you ascend the glacier, avoid the obvious crevassed areas and move towards the true left of the glacier. In the early part of the season the crevasses on this side of the valley may even be covered in snow, so a local guide is advisable. The ascent is not particularly tiring for a high Himalayan pass and within three hours of leaving camp you should be opposite a small defile that marks the top of the pass. From this point, cross the glacier to the foot of the pass. There follows a short ascent to a grassy plateau, with views up the icefall leading to the Nun Kun massif. It is a further 150 metre climb to the pass, and then you are in Ladakh.

From the pass there is an initial steep descent to the main glacier. Trek on down the glacier to where it meets a boulder trail on the true left side of the valley. Here the track crosses the lateral moraine before winding down to the high pastures and the first possible camp site. The trail then cuts across the pastures to the shepherd camp at **Donara**

(3780m), where there are camp sites on either side of the river.

Stage 8: Donara to Panikhar
(Average walking time 2 to 3 hours)
From Donara, follow the trail on the true left side of the valley. The trail is well defined, and en route you may pass some of the local village women collecting juniper for winter fuel. Midway down the valley the peak of Nun is visible, and not long after the trail widens to a jeep track. From here it is a short distance to the road bridge and the road from Kargil. Cross the bridge to the village of **Panikhar** (3350m).

As with most camp sites in Ladakh, a small fee of about Rs 20 is payable. The best site is in the shady grove beside the river. Trekkers are warned to pitch their tents with care, as small children from the village delight in opening up irrigation canals and swamping the unwary. Ponies can be hired in Panikhar, which is fortunate as the Kashmiris are seldom enthusiastic about continuing on with their horses further into Ladakh.

Getting Away
From Panikhar there are local buses to Kargil. The drive takes about four hours and costs Rs 25. Alternatively, you may wish to continue to trek. Options are to continue via Parachik to Rangdum and then over the Kanji La to Heniskot or Lamayuru (see the Kargil & the Suru Valley section in the Ladakh chapter), or to catch a truck to Padum and commence a trek in the Zanskar region (see the Padum & the Zanskar Valley section in the Ladakh chapter).

Himachal Pradesh

HISTORY

Himachal Pradesh (HP) is one of the youngest states in India. It is a composite of many hill kingdoms including Kullu, Lahaul, Spiti, Chamba and Kangra, all of which had maintained a long history of independence until the mid-19th century. Following the Treaty of Amritsar in 1846 these kingdoms were formally annexed to British India and administered as part of the Punjab. It was a situation that continued until 1966, when the Punjab was partitioned into the states of Punjab, Haryana and Himachal Pradesh. Himachal Pradesh was given formal recognition as a state within the Indian Union in 1971.

Many of the hill kingdoms, including Kullu, Lahaul, Spiti, Chamba and Kangra, trace their history back to the 10th century. It was around this time that the Kullu kingdom was established with its capital at Jagatsukh. The local rajah ruled the upper part of the valley between Sultanpur (Kullu) and the Rohtang Pass. It was not until the 15th century that the boundaries of the kingdom extended south to Mandi.

To the north of the Kullu Valley, most of Lahaul's early history depended on the fortunes of the rajahs of Kullu and the kings of Ladakh. In the 11th century, Lahaul was ruled by the king of Ladakh and, with nearby Spiti, became part of the vast West Tibetan kingdom known as Guge. In later centuries both the Kullu rajahs and the Ladakhi kings laid claim to Lahaul. The claim was not resolved until the 17th century when Ladakh's power was curtailed after its defeat by the combined armies of Mongolia and Tibet. A new balance of power evolved, with Lahaul split into two regions. Upper Lahaul paid tribute both to Ladakh and the Kullu rajahs, while lower Lahaul became part of the newly expanded kingdom of Chamba. Trade agreements evolved between Kullu and Ladakh. Lahaul was considered a neutral territory where trade was conducted on the vast Lingti plains beyond the Baralacha La throughout

Highlights – Himachal Pradesh
The mountains of Kangra, Chambra, Kullu, Lahaul, Spiti and Kinnaur; forested hillsides; alpine pastures beneath the Dhaula Dhar, Pir Panjal and the Great Himalaya ranges. The dominant Hindu culture contrasts with Buddhist Lahaul & Spiti bordering Tibet.

Introductory and strenuous treks starting from Dharamsala, Manali, Brahmaur and Kinnaur.

the summer months. In contrast, Spiti was more geographically isolated than Lahaul and continued to pay tribute to Ladakh until well into the 19th century.

The history of the Kangra Valley is reflected in the strategic position of the Kangra Fort at the base of the Himalayan foothills. Much of the valley's trading wealth was deposited in the famous temple of Bajreshwari Devi, and the Mahmud of Ghanzi reputedly gained a fortune in gold, silver and jewels when he raided the temple in 1009.

The kingdom of Chamba, between the Kangra Valley and the high Himalaya, also derived its wealth from using its strategic position to the best commercial advantage. In particular, the rajahs controlled trade in the region of Pangi in the Chandra Valley, which was one of the main routes through the inner Himalaya linking Kashmir, Lahaul and Kullu. Many of Chamba's temples date back to the 10th century, including the Lakshmi temples close to the Rang Mahal in the centre of town.

During the Moghul period, Chamba, Kangra and Kullu paid tribute to the emperor's court. For Kangra it was a period of uncertainty, with many artists seeking refuge in the hills. The Kangra school of painting derived from these artists and their technique of depicting, in miniature, many of the local rajahs and the Hindu gods including Vishnu and Shiva. Their inspiration and design, while Moghul in origin, were patronised by the hill courts and remained a notable art form and historical record until the 19th century.

With the decline of the Moghuls, Kangra's famous ruler, Sanser Chand, expanded his kingdom, attacking the nearby kingdoms of Chamba and Kullu. He met opposition from the emerging Gurkha army from Nepal. With the assistance of deposed Chamba and Kullu armies, the Gurkhas forced the Kangra leader to retreat to his fort.

The region of Kinnaur, bounded to the west by Spiti and to the north by Tibet, retained its independence from both West Tibet and Ladakh throughout most of its history. It was only during the time of the Gurkha invasion in the late 18th century that it was subject to outside rule. Following the Gurkha wars, Kinnaur was required to make a nominal tribute to the British Superintendent of the Shimla hill states.

The emergence of the Sikhs changed the balance of power in the West Himalaya. Both Kullu and Lahaul were invaded by the Sikh armies in 1840-1, and the position was not resolved until after the Sikh wars with the British and the Treaty of Amritsar in 1846. After the signing of the treaty, most of the hill states came directly under British administration, although for a time there were exceptions. The initial ruling of the treaty specified that the first maharajah of Jammu and Kashmir be granted the terrain between the Ravi and the Indus, including Chamba. A deputation, however, was sent to Calcutta and it was agreed that the Chamba state (including the nearby region of Pangi in the Chandra Valley) would come under the British administration.

The British established their administration at Dharamsala. They proposed to establish a sanatorium in the nearby Dhaula Dhar that might even rival Shimla. A site near Chamba was chosen and named after the viceroy, Lord Dalhousie. However, Dalhousie did not share the advantages of Shimla and was never considered a viable alternative to the summer capital.

In the later half of the 19th century many of the roads and forest trails were upgraded in the Chamba, Kullu, Lahaul and Kinnaur districts. Forest areas were explored, and the Public Works Department (PWD) and Forest Department moved into the mountain regions. In Lahaul there were accounts of how huge logs were hauled over the Rohtang Pass by over 200 porters, under the system of *beggar* (forced labour) which enabled the contractors to improve the roads and living conditions in the remoter villages.

In the Kullu Valley, the British appointed a district officer, which in turn attracted some British families from Shimla to settle in the valley. They followed trails over the Jalori Pass. If coming directly from the plains their route was via Kangra and the Dulchi Pass to the south-west of the Kullu Valley. The first motorable road into the valley up the Larji Gorge was completed in 1927. For many of the British settlers this was the beginning of the end of their tranquil life in the valley, and many of the established families were on their way home well before 1947.

GEOGRAPHY

Three main mountain ranges extend across Himachal Pradesh. The first is the Dhaula Dhar Range, which rises to an average elevation of

HIMACHAL PRADESH

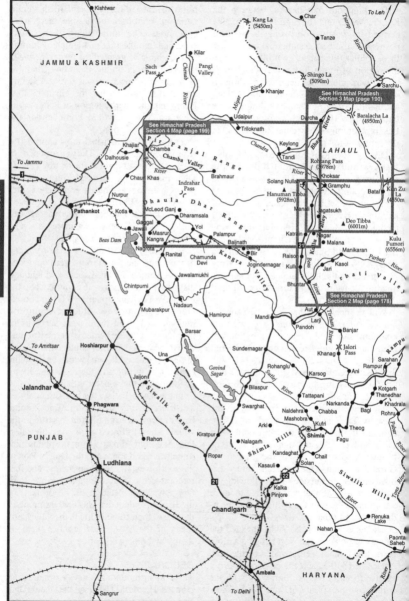

JAMMU &
KASHMIR

Kye

Spiti River

Kaza

Spiti Valley

SPITI

Dankar Tabo Sumdo

Sangam

Pin River

Nako

Leo Pargial
(6791m)

CHINA
(TIBET)

Mud

Pin Valley

KINNAUR

Sutlej River

Puh

Rekong
Peo

Kalpa

Morang

Sutlej

alley

ichar Tapri

Wangtu

Kinnaur Kailas
(6050m)

Sangla River

Sangla

Valley

See Himachal Pradesh
Section 5 & Uttarakhand
Section 1 Map (page 203)

UTTAR
PRADESH

Himachal Pradesh

To
Dehra Dun

0   30   60 km

The external boundaries of India
on this map have not been authenticated
and may not be correct.

Rajaji Wildlife
Sanctuary

HIMACHAL PRADESH

between 4500m and 5000m. It is the range north of Dharamsala which divides the Beas River and the Kangra Valley from the Ravi River and the Chamba Valley.

To the north of the Dhaula Dhar is the Pir Panjal Range. Its snow-capped peaks and ridges rise to an average of 5000m and it extends from the head of the Kullu Valley north-west to Kishtwar and the Kashmir Valley. This range is to the north of Chamba and Brahmaur and divides the Chamba Valley from the Chenab Valley.

To the north of the Pir Panjal is the Great Himalaya Range – the backbone of the West Himalaya – which separates Himachal Pradesh and Ladakh. Many of its peaks rise to over 6000m, while the glaciated passes, including the Kang La and the Shingo La, are over 5000m.

While these mountain ranges are clearly defined in the regions of Kangra, Chamba, and the Kullu Valley, they are harder to identify in Lahaul and east towards Spiti and Kinnaur.

Beyond the Shingo La, the main Himalayan range tilts on a south-east axis across Lahaul to merge with the Pir Panjal in the vicinity of the Bara Shigri Glacier. The main Himalaya Range then extends south-east, providing the divide between the Kullu Valley and the region of Spiti. It continues to the north of the Pin Parbati Valley to Kinnaur, before forming the Kinnaur Kailas Range on the far side of the Sutlej River.

To the north, the Zanskar Range runs parallel to the main Himalaya Range and forms the mountain divide between the Spiti Valley and the Tibetan plateau. To the east, beyond Spiti, it forms an impressive range between Himachal Pradesh and Tibet. Like the main Himalaya Range, it is also breached by the Sutlej River a short distance from the current border with Tibet.

Between the Zanskar and the main Himalaya Range are other mountain ranges, including the Baralacha Range. This mountain range, in the vicinity of the Baralacha La, is a link between the main Himalaya and the Zanskar Range. It is the range crossed at the Phitse La while trekking to the Zanskar Valley.

To complete the picture, the Siwalik Hills extend across the south of the state. They are crossed by road when driving from Chandigarh to Manali, and extend across to the Shimla Hills, with views north to the Great Himalaya and south to the Indian Plains.

CLIMATE

The region of the Chamba, Kangra and Kullu valleys comes under the influence of the Indian monsoon. The pre-monsoon clouds build up in mid-June and the first heavy rainfall is normally experienced by the first week of July. The heaviest rainfalls are in August, and continue through to the first week of September. Daytime temperatures vary considerably, rising to over 20°C, even at higher altitudes, and dropping to below freezing during some of the worst storms, which deposit snow on the higher elevations.

The region of Lahaul experiences a modified monsoon climate, with much of the rain falling on the lee side of the Pir Panjal Range. The occasional storm does, however, break over the Pir Panjal into Lahaul and can cause heavy rainfall for a day or two in July or August.

Spiti lies outside the influence of the monsoon and is not subject to the heavy rainfalls experienced in other parts of the state. The same holds for that part of the Kinnaur region north of the main Himalaya Range, although southern Kinnaur is subject to much of the monsoon rain in July and August.

The post-monsoon season in Himachal is normally settled and lasts from mid-September through to October. Daytime temperatures at this time of the year begin to fall to between 15°C and 20°C. Towards the end of October, the first of the permanent winter snows fall on the passes. Temperatures drop rapidly, although November and December are pleasant times to undertake shorter treks and tour the many hill stations of Himachal Pradesh.

By the end of March, the temperatures begin to rise and the winter snows begin to thaw. However, with the exception of the mountain passes to the south of Manali, there are few that are not snowbound until at least the beginning of June, and some even remain blocked until the first monsoon rains in early July.

MAPS & BOOKS
Maps

The Leomann series *Sheet 5 Himachal Pradesh*, which includes the Kullu Valley, Parbati Valley and central Lahaul, covers treks out of the Kullu Valley and also the Chandra Tal trek in Lahaul. Consult *Sheet 6 Himachal Pradesh* (Kalpa, Kinnaur, Spiti and Shimla) for the trek from Manikaran to Spiti and for the trek around Kinnaur Kailas. *Sheet 4 Himachal Pradesh* (Chamba, Dhaula Dhar Range, Pangi Valley & western Lahaul) covers the trek from Udaipur to the Kang La and the treks out of Dharamsala and Brahmaur.

Books

Manali & the Kullu Valley For historical background refer to *History and Culture of the Himalayan States Vol 2* by Sukhdev Charak (1979). For 19th-century accounts, try and get a copy of *The Himalayan Districts of Kooloo, Lahaul and Spiti* by AFP Harcourt (1982). The standard reference written in the 1960s on the temples and alpine treks out of Kullu is *Kulu: the End of the Habitable World* by Penelope Chetwode (1980). Also refer to *Himalayan Circuit* by GD Kholsa (1989) for details of the trek from Manali to Lahaul in the 1950s. For contemporary recollections of trekking out of the Kullu Valley, *At Home in the Himalayas* by Christina Noble (1991) is a mine of information. For details of climbing expeditions in the region, refer to *Exploring the Hidden Himalaya* by Soli Mehta & Harish Kapadia (1990).

Lahaul For historical background, refer to *History and Culture of the Himalayan States Vol 2* by Sukhdev Charak and *The Himalayan Districts of Kooloo, Lahaul and Spiti* by AFP Harcourt. For cultural background, refer to the chapter on Lahaul & Spiti in *Himalayan Art* by Madanjeet Singh (1968) and *Lahaul & Spiti* by SC Bajpai (1991). Somesh Goyal, a former police officer in Keylong, has recently compiled *Trekking beyond the Habitable World* (Arya Publishing, Delhi, 1991). For climbs and treks in Spiti read *Himalayan Odyssey* by Trevor Braham (1974) and the relevant section in *High Himalaya, Unknown Valleys* by Harish Kapadia (Indus Publishing, Delhi, 1993).

Dharamsala & the Kangra Valley For historical background, refer to *History and Culture of the Himalayan States Vol 1* by Sukhdev Charak. For recent background on the migration of the Gaddi shepherds, refer to *Over the High Passes* by Christina Noble (1987). Also worth referring to is *Travels in the Western Himalayas* by MS Randhawa (Thomson Press, Delhi, 1974).

Brahmaur & the Ravi Valley For historical background, refer to *History and Culture of the Himalayan States Vol 2* by Sukhdev Charak. For a description of the trek around Mani Mahesh Kailas, refer to *High Himalaya, Unknown Valleys* by Harish Kapadia. *Over the High Passes* by Christina Noble is also worth referring to.

Kinnaur & the Sangla Valley For historical background, refer to *Kinnaur* by SC Bajpai (Indus Publishing, Delhi, 1991). For a description of other trekking possibilities in Kinnaur, refer to *High Himalaya, Unknown Valleys* by Harish Kapadia.

GETTING THERE & AWAY
Delhi to Manali & the Kullu Valley
Jagson and Archana airlines operate daily flights to Bhuntar airport in the Kullu Valley for US$123. From Bhuntar, the taxi fare to Manali is Rs 500 and the trip takes about two hours. There are daily bus services from Delhi to Manali – deluxe, super deluxe, and super deluxe with video. The services operate overnight and normally take 18 hours (about the length of four to five Hindi movies). The fare is between Rs 300 to Rs 400 depending on the facilities, the bus company and the season. Alternatively, if you are not an Indian movie fan, there are fast trains from New Delhi station to Chandigarh. The *Himalayan Queen* departs at 6 am and arrives in Chandigarh four hours later, with enough time to catch a taxi to Manali and arrive that evening. The train costs Rs 270 for air-con chair, Rs 72 for 2nd class. The taxi costs Rs 2500 to Rs 3000 and can take up to five passengers.

Manali to Leh
The 473 km road from Manali to Leh was constructed in the 1960s after India's war with China over the Aksi Chin region, and was upgraded after India's wars with Pakistan in 1966 and 1971. Most travellers take two days to complete the drive. The tourist bus takes 10 to 12 hours to reach Sarchu on the first day, and a similar time to reach Leh the following day. The local bus goes to Keylong on the first day, before a very long second day to reach Leh. Jeeps are an alternative, and often drive to Keylong on the first day, the camp at Pang beyond Sarchu on the second, and Leh on the third.

The cost of the tourist bus is Rs 700 plus Rs 300 for the tented accommodation at Sarchu; and the local bus Rs 350, with an overnight at Keylong. Jeeps are approximately Rs 10,000 to Rs 12,000 one way for two days and three nights and a maximum of four passengers.

From Manali the road ascends the upper Kullu Valley to Murhi and the tea stalls just below the Rohtang Pass (3978m). The approach to the pass is under snow till at least the end of June. From the pass, there is a steep descent to Khoksar and the Chenab Valley, where there is a police checkpost. The road then passes through the villages of Sissu and Gondhla to Tandi at the confluence of the Chandra and the Bhaga rivers. It diverts up the Bhaga Valley (118 km from Manali, 3350m) to Keylong, the headquarters of the Lahaul region.

From Keylong, it is a further 27 km and 1½ hours to Darcha (145 km) the starting-off point for treks into the Zanskar Valley. The road continues up the Bhaga Valley via the shepherds' camps of Patseo and Zing Zing Bar to the Baralacha La (189 km). Just below the pass is the lake of Sundar Tal, which can be appreciated as soon as the snow melts by mid-July.

The Baralacha La (4950m) was once an important trading pass between Ladakh and the Kullu Valley, but nowadays is the habitat of the Gaddi shepherds who graze their flocks throughout the summer. The road then winds down to Keylong Sarai and across the Lingti plains to Sarchu (222 km, 4500m). Here, there are some fixed camps which provide a camp bed and meals. Dinner/bed and breakfast is Rs 300 per person. Sarchu, on the banks of the Tsarap River, marks the border between Himachal Pradesh and the state of Jammu & Kashmir. The road continues across the Lingti plains for about 30 km before climbing steeply to a plateau at 4500m to cross the Lachalung La (5030m) over the Zanskar Range. The next stop is at Pang (229 km) where there are tea houses and tented accommodation. The drive from Sarchu to Pang takes about four hours.

From Pang, the road ascends to the Chanspa plains, which mark a western extremity of the vast Tibetan plateau. Nomads, with their yaks and yurts, complete the setting. From the plains, the road follows a series of switchbacks to the Taglung La (5360m), the second highest motorable road in the world. There is a small multi-denominational temple at the top of the pass. From the pass there is a gradual descent to the Indus Valley and the first village at Upshi. From Pang to Upshi takes about five hours. Here the road enters the Indus Valley for the final 49 km to Leh.

Delhi to Dharamsala (McLeod Ganj) & the Kangra Valley

Jagson Airlines operates a flight to Gaggal, 15 km from Dharamsala. The cost is US$100. From Gaggal the taxi to McLeod Ganj is Rs 250. There are direct buses from Delhi to Dharamsala which take around 12 hours and cost Rs 330. If travelling by train, you have

a choice of the *Shalimar Express*, which departs at 4.30 am from New Delhi station, or the *Jammu Super Fast*, which departs at 5.20 am. Both trains should arrive at Pathankot with time to catch the last bus to Dharamsala. The train costs Rs 471 for 1st class and Rs 147 for 2nd class, while the onward bus costs Rs 75. Alternatively, catch the train to Pathankot and then the bus to Dharamsala. The *Jammu Mail* departs at 9 pm and the *Jammu Express* at 9.30 pm. Both trains arrive at Pathankot the following morning before a three to four hour bus drive to Dharamsala. The cost of the train is Rs 471 for 1st class and Rs 147 for 2nd class to Pathankot, while the bus costs Rs 39. Taxis are an alternative and cost Rs 700 from Pathankot and Dharamsala.

Delhi to Brahmaur & the Chamba Valley

Most travellers to Chamba catch the overnight train from Old Delhi station. The *Jammu Mail* departs at 9 pm and the *Jammu Express* at 9.30 pm. Both trains arrive at Pathankot the following morning with plenty of time to catch the bus to Chamba. The cost of the train is Rs 471 for 1st class and Rs 147 for 2nd class to Pathankot, while the bus to Chamba costs Rs 85. Note: if you catch one of the morning trains from Delhi (see the above section) you have to overnight in Pathankot and catch the bus to Chamba the following day. From Chamba there are three buses a day to Brahmaur. The drive takes around four hours and costs Rs 28. Jeeps are an alternative and cost Rs 700 one way.

Delhi to Kinnaur & the Sangla Valley

There are many buses from Delhi to Shimla which cost around Rs 225. Alternatively, catch the *Kalka Mail*, departing from New Delhi station at 11 pm, and arriving at Kalka at 5.30 am to connect with the local train to Shimla.

From Shimla there is an early morning bus to Sangla the following day which takes 14 hours and costs Rs 80.

Manali & the Kullu Valley

Manali is the most popular base for trekking in Himachal Pradesh. It is to the north of the Kullu Valley, and was once the last staging post before commencing the journey to Lahaul and Ladakh. Nowadays it provides both a starting point for trekking and a convenient stop en route before commencing a trek to the Zanskar Valley or continuing by road to Ladakh.

Treks

Manali to Chandra Valley via Hampta Pass
(moderate; 5 stages)
Jagatsukh to Base of Deo Tibba
(introductory; 4 stages)
Nagar to Parbati Valley via Chandrakani Pass
(moderate; 4 stages)
Manikaran to Spiti Valley via Pin Parbati Pass
(moderate; 9 stages)

History

The treks out of Manali follow trade and grazing routes which have been followed for many generations. This is the case with the trek over the Hampta Pass, while the rich grazing pastures beneath Deo Tibba would have been attractive for both the villagers from Jagatsukh with their flocks and the Gaddi shepherds from Kangra. The trek over the Chandrakani Pass would have been followed by villagers from Malana since the time they settled there prior to the Moghul period. According to Hindu legend, the trek up the Parbati Valley was the route the Pandava brothers followed as they made their escape from India through Spiti to Tibet. More recently, this trek would have been followed by villagers from Spiti carrying goods for trade to the lower Kullu Valley before the development of roads in the region.

When to Trek

From late May to early June onwards, well-equipped parties can cross the snowbound Hampta Pass to Lahaul, or the Chandrakani Pass to the Parbati Valley. Porters can be engaged to cross these passes in June, while packhorses usually wait until the end of the month before crossing. This applies on the trek to the base of Deo Tibba and for the treks to Spiti or Barabhangal. In July and August there is periodic monsoonal rainfall. It is, however, the best time for appreciating the rich array of wildflowers, and trekkers can spend many rewarding days wandering the alpine pastures of the Jagatsukh or Parbati valleys.

The post-monsoon period, which lasts from mid-September to mid-October, is an ideal time for trekking. The passes are free of snow and the days are mostly clear and settled. The first of the winter snows falls by mid-October, generally marking the end of the trekking season.

Trekking Agents

The Mountaineering Institute in Manali is a helpful intermediary, as is the Himachal Pradesh Department of Tourism office in the main bazaar, which holds a list of all recognised agents. Just to the north of the main bazaar is Himalayan Journeys, run by local skier and mountaineer Iqbal Sharma, who schedules regular departures over the Hampta Pass during the summer season. Paddy's Treks, run by another colourful local character, Paddy Singh, is at present across the Beas in Vashisht village. Other local agencies, including Himalayan Adventures opposite the tourist office in the main bazaar, have also been recommended. To find any of these, ask at the main bazaar, as office locations seem to change by the season.

An alternative, particularly if trying to share costs, is to check out the notice boards in the local restaurants such as the Mayur, the Chopstick and Mt View.

Accommodation in Manali

At the time of writing, the situation in Kashmir has resulted in a huge increase in the number of hotels in Manali, particularly those catering to Indian domestic tourists and honeymoon couples. Ideally, avoid these and head for one of the small guesthouses

HIMACHAL PRADESH

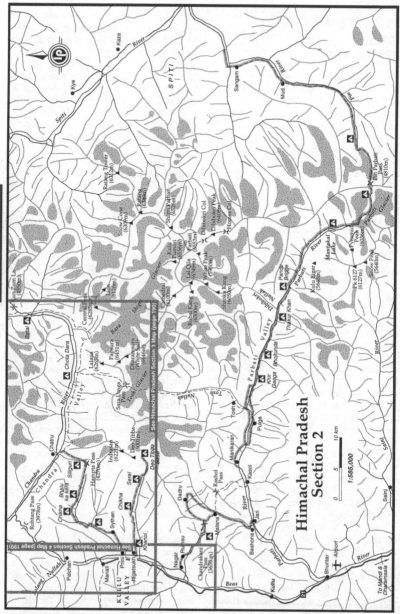

Himachal Pradesh
Section 2

1:585,000

0   5   10 km

which still provide a modicum of tranquillity.

The HP Tourism office recommends the government-run hotels. However, there are many card wallahs in Manali, both outside the tourist office and at the bus stand, to help expand the selection. Manali is not a large place, and a short walk around town should turn up something to suit your taste and budget.

Rooms are more expensive from April to mid-June, and from September to mid-October, particularly during the Dussehra festival.

Up-market hotels and guesthouses are about Rs 900 per double for full board, but can be bargained down. In the mid-range, rooms are about Rs 400 a double, room only. There is a large choice of budget hotels from Rs 100 per room upwards. As in Leh, many hotels are family-run and it is difficult to recommend a specific place. They all have their attractions, and are convenient for a rest before undertaking a trek.

Accommodation on the Trail

On the trek over the Hampta Pass there are no Forest Rest Houses or PWD huts and the only tea stall is below the village of Sythen above the Kullu Valley. The same situation applies for the trek to the base of Deo Tibba and the trek to Malana over the Chandrakani Pass. For the trek to Spiti, there are hotels-cum-tea stalls at the village of Pulga. There are also tea stalls at Khir Ganga for meals and overnight accommodation, but this is about it until you reach the village of Sangam in Spiti.

Trekking Advice

A few rest days for acclimatising should be included before crossing the Hampta Pass (4270m). Before you leave Manali, it is imperative to check on the condition of the log bridge over the Indrasan River which the Gaddi shepherds rebuild each season. Sometimes the logs are washed away during floods. If there is any doubt about the condition of the bridge, take a length of rope with you. While the trek to Malana village is relatively straightforward, there is a real need for boots when descending the steep trail from the Chandrakani Pass to the village. It is also worthwhile allowing an additional stage before crossing the pass at the margins of the season, as snow conditions can make progress difficult.

The trek to Spiti involves a few stages where rock scrambles are the order of the day. The approach to the pass is hard going over rock scree, while the snowfields on either side of the pass are crevassed. A rope, harness and karabiners should be taken, and all members of the party should know how to use them safely. This gear will also prove useful for the wire bridge river crossing at Sangam. A road bridge is under construction, but until it is completed, the single-wire bridge without a pulley is the only way to cross the river.

Provisions

All food supplies and kerosene can be purchased in Manali. During the season there is a wide variety of fruit and vegetables plus a large stock of tinned food. If trekking out of Nagar, Jagatsukh or Manikaran it is advisable to carry supplies by road from Manali.

Horsemen & Porters

Packhorses cost in the vicinity of Rs 150 per day. They are in short supply during the apple harvest in September. Porters are an alternative, and there has been an influx of Nepalese porters in the last few seasons. They are generally reliable, hard-working and well worth considering. It is advisable to contact one of the local agencies in Manali for help. Allow Rs 150 per porter per day and budget for the return days and transportation. Note that packhorses are unsuitable for the trek to Malana village and also for the trek over the Pin Parbati Pass.

Access

From Manali there are regular local bus services to the various trekking-off points. The bus fare is Rs 12 from Manali to Nagar and the trip takes about two hours. From Manali to Prini village takes 30 minutes and costs

Rs 3, while it takes a further 30 minutes to Jagatsukh and costs Rs 5. There are two direct bus services each day to Manikaran which take four to five hours and cost Rs 45. Taxis are a convenient alternative, particularly if you are sharing costs, and can considerably cut travelling time. The taxi fare is about Rs 200 one way to Nagar, Rs 400 to Jagatsukh, and Rs 1100 to Manikaran.

MANALI TO CHANDRA VALLEY VIA HAMPTA PASS
Map: Himachal Pradesh Section 2 (page 178)
Stage 1: Prini to Sythen & Camp
(Average walking time 3 to 4 hours)
From Manali it is a short walk or drive to Prini village. Climb the trail to the small temple above the village before commencing a steep climb up an eroded ridge to the sparse pine forest below Sythen village. Just before reaching the village there is a tea stall and a welcome rest stop. **Sythen** (2710m) was settled by villagers from Spiti several generations ago. From here the trail levels out before entering a narrow pine-forested valley. The camp is a small clearing near a springline with an adequate water supply throughout the season.

Stage 2: Camp to Chikha
(Average walking time 3 to 4 hours)
From camp the trail crosses meadows where Gujar shepherds herd their buffalo and graze their sheep from the end of May till September. Immediately after the Gujar camp site, cross the bridge over a side river before descending to the Hampta River. In the early part of the season, until mid-July, there should be a snow bridge over the river. If the shepherds are crossing the snow bridge you can follow suit; if not, continue on the true left bank for about two km until the river widens and it is safe to cross. The exact place should not be difficult to locate. There may even be an improvised bridge to save you getting your feet wet! After crossing the river, the trail passes through a series of meadows before a short ascent to the grazing meadows at **Chikha** (3270m).The camping ground is set beneath waterfalls and is

covered in wildflowers as soon as the snow melts in late June. It is also about the upper limit of the trees, except for a few birches scattered on the nearby ridges.

Stage 3: Chikha to Bhalu ka kera
(Average walking time 3 hours)
This comparatively short stage is included in order to allow you to acclimatise before crossing the Hampta Pass. From camp the trail winds high above the valley floor on the true right of the valley. There are some side streams to cross before descending back to the main valley floor. This area is popular with the Gaddi shepherds in the early part of the season, grazing their flocks before continuing their migration to Lahaul.

The camp at the base of the Hampta Pass is named **Bhalu ka kera** (3700m); brown bears are said to hibernate in the nearby rock caves during the winter.

Stage 4: Bhalu ka kera over Hampta Pass to Siliguri
(Average walking time 7 hours)
From camp there is a short, steep climb over scree slopes before reaching a plateau where you can gain views back down the Hampta Valley and across to the peaks on the far side of the Kullu Valley, including Hanuman Tibba (5928m). The last 200m to 300m to the pass are steep, with views of rock spires and hanging glaciers completing the panorama. The **Hampta Pass** (4270m), is on the true right side of the valley. However, there is an excellent vantage point for viewing the Lahaul Range, which can be reached by diverting from the main trail through the moraine towards the centre of the valley. From here, the peaks of Deo Tibba (6001m) and Indrasan (6221m) can also be appreciated.

The history of climbing these peaks dates back to 1912 when CG Bruce led a British team on the first ascent of Hanuman Tibba. The next ascent, however, was not until 1966. In between, the first ascent of Deo Tibba was made in 1952 after many attempts, while Indrasan was first climbed in 1962.

From the pass there is a very steep descent down switchbacks to the valley floor. In

June, when the trail is under snow, an ice axe is necessary. On reaching the valley floor, there is a choice of camp sites at around 3750m. Those which are normally selected are on the true left of the Indrasan River. This area is referred to as **Siliguri**.

Stage 5: Siliguri to Chatru

(Average walking time 3 hours)
An early morning river crossing is the order of the day before following the valley down on the true right through the boulder field to your first views of the Chandra Valley. It soon becomes apparent why you descend on this side of the river, as the cliffs on the opposite side do not lend themselves to easy trekking. In fact, unless you are exceptionally sure-footed, forget it. Some of the Gaddi shepherds follow this route, but they are more sure-footed than the average mountain goat.

Continuing down to the valley floor, there may be a problem recrossing the Indrasan River to reach the road bridge and Chatru. The Gaddi shepherds have been commissioned to complete a bridge over the river, but you cannot rely on this, particularly if the bridge is swept away during the monsoon storms. A carefully selected crossing spot and, preferably, the aid of a rope is necessary before continuing on for about one km to where the trail meets the road coming down from the Rohtang Pass.

Chatru (3360m) consists of some tea houses-cum-hotels and a Government Rest House a short distance up the road.

Getting Away

From Chatru you can catch the bus back to Manali. The bus coming from Spiti normally stops at Chatru around midday and will see you back in Manali later that afternoon. If continuing a trek to Chandra Tal and the Baralacha La, catch the Manali to Spiti bus for the 50 km drive to Batal. The trek from Batal to the Baralacha La is covered in the Lahaul & Spiti section later in this chapter.

Note that the trail marked (see the Himachal Pradesh Section 3 map) along the true left bank of the Chandra River is for trekkers

following the route over the Sara Umga Pass from the Tosh Nullah. The many side-river crossings do not make it a viable alternative trek route to Batal.

Alternatively, you could catch a truck from Chatru to Khoksar and from there continue by bus to Darcha. From here you could commence a trek over the Shingo La into the Zanskar region. This trek is covered in the Padum & the Zanskar Valley section in the Ladakh chapter.

JAGATSUKH TO BASE OF DEO TIBBA
Map: Himachal Pradesh Section 2 (page 178)
Stage 1: Jagatsukh to Khanol

(Average walking time 2 hours)
The town of **Jagatsukh** (1850m) was the capital of the Kullu Valley at a time when traders from Spiti and Lahaul still held influence over the region. The town's origins can be traced back to the 9th century, and the original foundations of the Sandya Devi temple date from this period. The temple was rebuilt in the 15th century, and some of the carvings from that period can still be seen.

From Jagatsukh, the trail ascends gradually through a series of small villages to the camp site at **Khanol** (2280m), a small clearing where cattle are grazed by the local villagers. If you started early from Jagatsukh it is recommended that you continue on to Chikha, although there are no intermediary camp sites en route.

Stage 2: Khanol to Chikha

(Average walking time 4 to 5 hours)
The trail remains on the true right of the valley – at first through thickets and then across a series of large scree slopes. From here the trail ascends the side of the heavily forested gorge. It is a steep ascent to be avoided, if possible, in the heat of the day as the air in the gorge is thick and oppressive. During the summer, a profusion of orchids and other wildflowers line the forest trail as it climbs for nearly 600m to the head of the gorge. The route then enters the glaciated upper valley, and continues for several km through some thickets and open pastures to the Gujar camp at **Chikha** (3100m).

HIMACHAL PRADESH

Stage 3: Chikha to Serai
(Average walking time 4 to 5 hours)
From Chikha the trail continues along the true right side of the valley ascending through pastures and birch groves, and past tumbling waterfalls. After four to five km the valley turns to the north, revealing a series of hanging glaciers at the base of Deo Tibba at the head of the valley. The trekking becomes progressively easier as the valley gradient levels out. **Serai** (3900m) is a particularly rich pasture where Gaddi shepherds graze their sheep from the end of June until September.

Stage 4: Serai to Deo Tibba Base & Return
(Average walking time 7 hours)
This stage may take considerably longer in the springtime before the snows have melted. Cross the Jagatsukh stream, and ascend the grassy ridge to the true left side of the waterfall. If you have any problem locating the trail, get one of the shepherds to point it out for you.

The climb up the ridge takes about two hours before leading around the clifftop above the waterfall. From this vantage point, you gain excellent views across to the high ridges beyond the Kullu Valley, while to the north is the impressive south-west face of Deo Tibba (6001m). The trek continues up the valley across the grassy slopes that lead to the terminal moraine (approximately 4800m).

Chandra Tal (not to be confused with the Chandra Tal in the nearby Chandra Valley) is a small glacial lake. Although marked prominently on some maps it is by no means easy to find; it is, in fact, on the high ridges opposite Deo Tibba. It has no significant outflow and virtually dries up later in the season.

Return to Serai by the same route.

Option: Serai to the Malana Valley
From Serai there is an alternative route into the Malana Valley. The trail follows the side valley to the south, opposite the camp at Serai, and ascends to a pass known locally as the **Goru Pass** (approximately 4800m). From the pass, there is a steep descent to the upper Malana Glacier, and from there it takes four to five hours to complete the trek to Malana village. There are, however, some intermediary camp sites once you are off the glacier, at places where the Gaddi shepherds graze their flocks during summer.

From Malana an interesting circuit can be made back to the Kullu Valley by crossing the Chandrakani Pass to Nagar. See the next trek section for details of the stages between Malana and Nagar.

Stage 5: Serai to Jagatsukh
(Average walking time 7 hours)
The return to Jagatsukh can be completed in a long morning. During the descent it is easy to appreciate the correlation between the altitude and various vegetation zones. The birch trees appear at about 3700m; the rhododendron bushes at 3600m; conifers at 3500m; and, further down, the holly bushes at 2150m.

Getting Away
There is a regular local bus service from Jagatsukh back to Manali which runs until about 5 pm each day.

NAGAR TO PARBATI VALLEY VIA CHANDRAKANI PASS
Map: Himachal Pradesh Section 2 (page 178)
Stage 1: Nagar to Rumsu & Camp
(Average walking time 2 to 3 hours)
This trek commences from the village of **Nagar** (1840m), about two hours by bus from Manali. Nagar castle is steeped in legend and commands an imposing position, looking across the Kullu Valley. Part of the castle has been converted into a comfortable hotel, and a day or two can be peacefully spent here. One of the main attractions is the Roerich Gallery, where samples of the work of the famous painter and philosopher Nicholas Roerich are displayed. His reputation as one of the avant-garde post-1917 Russian painters was enhanced during his stay in the Kullu Valley in the 1930s, when he made Nagar his home.

Where you camp on this first stage depends what time you set off from Nagar. The trail goes past Roerich's cottage and

Malana Village

Malana is not the most inviting village in the Himalaya even though the rules governing a visit are not as rigidly enforced as they were a decade ago. You are no longer required to take off your leather boots to walk through the village, but you must stick to the main trail and you must not touch the children, the walls or the Jumla temple. Failure to observe these rules can lead to a fine. Apparently the god Jumla is fond of money, but the purchase of a goat is the normal means of penance. You can take photographs and you can stay in the village dispensary; as well, there is a good camp site beyond the main settlement, about 100m from the second spring. The village itself consists of 50 or 60 houses and is fairly self-sufficient, although there are plans to connect it to the electricity grid. Until a few generations ago, the local people married only those from their own community. This has changed in recent times: the men still tend to stay in Malana, but the women sometimes marry into families in the Parbati Valley, or in Rumsu or Nagar. ■

HIMACHAL PRADESH

along a main bridle path for one km, before branching uphill to the village of **Rumsu** (2060m). There is a camp site in the village, although most people continue up through the coniferous forest. While ascending the trail it is essential that you check your bearings regularly and avoid the many side tracks. After about two hours there is an open meadow in which to camp, although a shortage of water later in the season may cause problems. Check with the villagers at Rumsu before proceeding.

Stage 2: Rumsu to Camp below Chandrakani Pass

(Average walking time 5 hours)
The trail leading to the pass frequently crosses other grazing trails so the services of a local guide are recommended. The ascent continues through coniferous forest and meadows, which afford a bird's eye view down to the Kullu Valley. As the trail gradually climbs above the birch trees, the location of the Chandrakani Pass can be appreciated. There is a choice of meadow camps at around 3000m which afford even more breathtaking views – from the snow-capped Dhaula Dhar Range in the south to Hanuman Tibba at the head of the Solang Valley and north to the Ghalpo peaks in Lahaul.

Stage 3: Across the Chandrakani Pass to Malana

(Average walking time 6 hours)
From the high camp, the trail gradually

crosses a series of pastures before a short, steep climb to the pass. This climb is harder at the margins of the season, in June and after mid-October, when the pass and upper meadows are under snow.

The **Chandrakani Pass** (3650m) is marked by prayer flags and cairns. The trail then continues along the ridge, with views of the upper Malana Valley and the high peaks in the upper Tosh Valley, including White Sail (6446m) and Papsura (6451m). After completing the traverse, the trail heads around a rocky gully that descends steeply to the village of **Malana** (2650m). The walk down to the village takes a couple of hours.

Malana is an isolated village community which has its own language, customs and laws; governed by a system of village elders. The village beliefs were determined, it is said, by the god Jumla, who was pre-Aryan and independent of the Hindu gods which ruled the Kullu Valley.

The existence of this village was apparently recorded in the *Moghul Annals*. Until recently the villagers resisted intrusion from the outside world.

Option: Chandrakani Pass to Upper Malana Valley

An alternative is to continue along the upper valley, across a series of ridges that leads to the summer grazing pastures of the Gaddi. The trail, rocky in places, proceeds through birch groves before descending through thicker forest to a series of alpine meadows referred to as *thaches* by the Gaddi shepherds. It has the added attraction of crossing some clearings that are frequented by brown bears. Our small party came face to face with a bear once in late October; it really took its time retreating up the hillside. This incident ensured that the porters didn't stay too far behind us for the rest of the day!

After camping in the alpine meadows, it is possible to continue up the valley and spend a few days camping near the Malana Glacier before returning down to Malana village – highly rewarding if you have sufficient time and supplies.

Option: Malana to Kasol

This option takes one or two stages to complete. From Malana there is a steep ascent through the forested hillside to the Rashol Pass (3260m). From the pass the trail leads down to Rashol village before descending to Kasol (1580m) eight km below Manikaran. The stage from Malana to Kasol and Manikaran can be completed in a full day, although it is possible to overnight at the *Forest Rest House* at Rashol village.

Stage 4: Malana to Jari

(Average walking time 4 to 5 hours)
From Malana it is a steep descent for 800m to the valley floor. This narrow, precipitous trail is unsuitable for horses. On the following fairly level walk through beautiful gorges, the track frequently crosses the river by either wooden or snow bridges. The first main village is at **Bashona** (1400m) where the Malana River joins the Parbati River. From here there is a steady climb for the last few km to the road at **Jari** (1520m).

Getting Away

There are two direct, daily bus services from Manikaran to Manali which pass through Jari. They depart from Manikaran at 7 am and 5 pm and cost Rs 45. Alternatively, there are frequent buses to Bhuntar and Kullu, where you will need to change buses to reach Manali the same day. Alternatively, you could catch the bus to Manikaran and undertake the trek over the Pin Parbati Pass to Spiti. See the following section for details.

MANIKARAN TO SPITI VALLEY VIA PIN PARBATI PASS

Map: Himachal Pradesh Section 2 (page 178)

Stage 1: Manikaran to Pulga

(Average walking time 4 to 5 hours)
From **Manikaran** (1700m) cross the main bridge and follow the true right bank of the Parbati River. The trail winds past some small villages with small temples patronised by pilgrims on their way to Khir Ganga. There are also some tea houses serving biscuits and basics to the variety of travellers en route to Pulga and Khir Ganga. Three to four km below Pulga, cross the bridge and ascend through the pine forest to the village (2100m).

Pulga is well served with tea stalls and simple hotels built in the apple orchards. It is a popular retreat for foreigners escaping from the pace of the Kullu Valley.

Stage 2: Pulga to Khir Ganga

(Average walking time 4 to 5 hours or 5 to 6 hours via the forest trail)
From Pulga, follow the trail up the valley before recrossing the bridge over the Parbati River. This is also the route for entering the Tosh Nullah. Follow the horse trail through the various villages before recrossing the river about 1½ hours below Khir Ganga. There is an alternative forest trail from Pulga which follows the true left of the valley. It leads through coniferous forests and past waterfalls.

It can be tiring, however, in sections where logs block the trail. Just before the trails converge, there is a particularly impressive waterfall which requires a steep ascent to a crossing high above the side gorge.

The camp at **Khir Ganga** (2850m) is in an open meadow, while the tea stalls and hot springs are a further 100m up the meadow. Note: if you are trekking only as far as Khir Ganga, ascending by the established trail and returning by the forest trail is recommended.

Stage 3: Khir Ganga to Bhojtunda
(Average walking time 5 hours)
From the camp there is a steady ascent out of the gorge. The valley then widens and the trail crosses several delightful pastures supporting a variety of wildflowers in the summer. On the opposite bank there are several Gaddi shepherd encampments, while on the true left bank there are some Gujar encampments where the buffalo are grazed throughout the season. **Bhojtunda** (3200m) marks the lower limit of the silver birch trees. There is a shelter hut at Bhojtunda and there are fine alpine views down the valley. The waterfalls tumbling down the cliffs on the opposite side of the valley are impressive.

Stage 4: Bhojtunda to Thakur Khan
(Average walking time 4 to 5 hours)
For the first few km you pass through birch groves on an ill-defined trail crossing rocks and dense vegetation. After a tiring few km, the trail descends to the river bank, where there is a pulley bridge used by workers engaged on the dam construction. Do not cross the bridge; remain on the true left of the valley.

The following section up the valley is difficult in places, as the trail frequently skirts rock faces which are difficult for laden porters. A climbing rope would be a useful asset for some of the steeper sections. Just before entering the cliff country leading to Thakur Khan there is the wreck of an Indian army helicopter which was assigned in autumn 1993 to rescue a trekker who had fallen on the rocks. The helicopter did not make it: after landing, it toppled over and defied recovery.

The camp at **Thakur Khan** (3400m) is above the cliff section of the valley opposite the Dibibokri Nullah. This is the site for the proposed dam, and teams of Nepalese workers camp there throughout the season. An alternative camp site, a few km up the valley from Thakur Khan, affords the first views of the snow-capped peaks in the vicinity of the Pin Parbati Pass.

While the dam construction continues, there is a debate about how to reconcile the demands for electricity of the villagers in the lower Kullu Valley with the need to preserve this beautiful valley. Indeed, even while the construction is progressing, the Himachal government is considering plans to designate the Parbati Valley and the catchment area to the north, including the Tosh Nullah, a national park.

Stage 5: Thakur Khan to Mantakal Lake
(Average walking time 6 to 7 hours)
Beyond Thakur Khan, the trail passes several Gaddi encampments before crossing a side river by a natural rock bridge, which leads back down to the Parbati River. Just above this crossing is the Pandu bridge, another natural rock bridge over the Parbati River. According to Hindu mythology, the bridge commemorates the retreat of the Pandava brothers to the region of Spiti and Tibet. The climb to the top of the huge boulder can be made without difficulty before descending a rock staircase to the opposite bank. The trail then ascends gradually through a series of flowered meadows interspersed with boulder fields brought down by the many side streams. To reach **Mantakal Lake**, complete the 200 metre ascent over the boulder fields to a broad plateau (4070m). For much of the season the lake is nothing more than a series of braided rivulets blocked by the terminal moraine which occasionally back-fills to form a lake. There is a choice of grassy camp sites just beyond here.

Stage 6: Mantakal Lake to High Camp
(Average walking time 7 hours)
From the camp, cross the outer streams on the true right of the valley to the terminal moraine. Locate the cairns that mark the route and follow what is a comparatively straightforward trail through the boulders. If the going gets tough, and you need to resort to clambering over boulders, then it is imperative that you find the cairns again rather than waste energy at this stage.

The Pin Parbati Pass is due east of the

Parbati Glacier. After passing the second side valley, on the true right of the glacier, commence a steep 300 metre climb out of the main valley floor. The climb affords a bird's-eye view of the Parbati Valley, and directly below, the Parbati River gushes out of the main glacier. The peaks on the far side of the valley also come into full view – including Pyramid Peak (6036m), Snow Peak (5640m) and the unnamed peak (6127m), the highest in the region.

After scrambling over boulders and scree out of the main valley, the trail crosses a series of meadows before a further steep climb of 150m to the side valley leading to the Pin Parbati Pass. Camp here, or continue to a higher camp at the base of the pass (which is under snow until mid-July).

To reach the high camp continue up the side valley and ascend the lateral moraine. There is no well-defined trail and it is a very tiring two hour ascent before reaching a flat sandy camp site (4550m) with a good water supply. There are magnificent views of the surrounding peaks including those on the far side of the Parbati Valley. Closer to this camp there are a number of accessible snowfields, and a rest day could be spent ascending these to the base of the peaks along the main ridge line.

Stage 7: High Camp to Pin Parbati Pass & Pin Valley Camp

(Average walking time 5 hours)
From the high camp, there is a steep 200m ascent over boulders to a large snowfield below the pass. The pass is a small col immediately to the south of the prominent rock monolith. The trek to the pass is straightforward, across the snowfield, but you should rope up, particularly early in the season when the crevasses are concealed. The **Pin Parbati Pass** (4810m) is marked by rock cairns and prayer flags. The alpine views to the snow-capped ranges towards the Kullu Valley contrast with the barren mountain ridges which stretch east towards Spiti.

The descent from the pass is gradual, over a snowfield. Maintain caution though: we

met one unfortunate Indian trekker coming in the opposite direction who had fallen into a small crevasse within minutes of stepping onto the snowfield. Luckily he had a porter to assist him. To reach the Pin Valley, follow the trail over scree to the true right of the valley. It becomes very steep in places. At the confluence with a valley coming in from the north, cross the side river and continue down the true left side of the main valley for two km to a grassy camp site (4550m).

Stage 8: Pin Valley Camp to Mud

(Average walking time 8 to 9 hours)
From camp, continue down the true left side of the valley. There is no trail for the first few km, and it is advisable to stick close to the valley floor. Whichever route is followed, there is a fair amount of walking on loose scree, which makes for a tiring start to the day. There are also some side streams to cross. After five to six km, the route leads to a small plateau above the valley floor. This marks the upper limit of the grazing pastures for the shepherds from Mud and the nearby villages. It is also the beginning of a trail which winds down to a grassy camp site (3850m) opposite a large valley coming in from the south to south-west, and a possible route to the Sutlej Valley.

This camp site is often used by groups trekking in the opposite direction, and marks the halfway point to Mud. The trail down the valley is well defined, although there is a large torrent after four to five km which needs to be forded with care. Just below this crossing, the village of Mud can be seen beneath a huge cliff face. The outlying barley fields are tended by the village children who have not yet latched onto the 'one pen' mantra chanted on the more popular trails in Ladakh. The camp site of **Mud** (3600m) is in a small enclosure before the main village.

Note that the catchment area of the Pin Valley, up to the main Himalaya Range separating the Pin and Parbati valleys, has been designated a national park. There have been reports of snow leopards roaming the upper stretches of the valleys, and of herds of bharal grazing the high pastures during the summer months.

Stage 9: Mud to Sangam

(Average walking time 4 to 5 hours)
An early start is imperative to ensure you arrive at Sangam village in time for the daily bus service to Kaza. The trail continues, on the true left side of the valley. There is no need to cross the bridge below Mud village; it services the villages on the opposite side of the valley. The trail is hard in sections, as it skirts the cliffs high above the valley floor a few km above the village of Sangam.

Sangam (3500m) lies at the confluence of the Pin and a subsidiary valley coming in from the west, referred to on some maps as the Khamengar River. Sangam is the largest village in the Pin Valley. After passing through the village, follow the trail above the river confluence. At present there is no bridge across the river, only a length of wire. Thus you have little choice but to off-load your gear, attach yourself to the wire and haul yourself across to the far bank. A karabiner and a harness would be very useful to secure yourself. If you have no means to cross the wire safely, then wait for the locals to assist. They all seem to carry some means of attaching themselves, be it a hollowed-out animal bone attached to a length of yak rope or whatever! There is a commemorative stone dated August 1993, marking the spot where a road bridge will be constructed. It will, however, take a few seasons to complete.

Getting Away

The trailhead is two km below the river crossing and there is a daily bus service to Kaza in the Spiti Valley. It departs around 1 pm each day. The drive takes two hours and costs Rs 8.

When in Kaza, an extra day at least should be reserved to visit the nearby Kye monastery. From Kaza there is a daily bus service back to Manali. The bus leaves at 4 am, takes a full day, and costs Rs 80.

Lahaul & Spiti

For most people Lahaul is a halfway point for trekking into the Zanskar Valley, while Spiti marks the conclusion of a trek over the Pin Parbati Pass from the Kullu Valley. It is therefore not surprising that neither Keylong (the headquarters of Lahaul) nor Kaza (in the Spiti Valley) is recognised as an established trekking centre. However, there are some excellent treks, starting from Lahaul in particular, which can be undertaken by well-organised parties.

Treks

Batal to Chandra Tal & Baralacha La
   (moderate; 4 stages)
Udaipur to Padum (Zanskar) via Kang La
   (strenuous; 8 stages)

History

Until the development of roads in Lahaul & Spiti in the 1960s, the routes over the Baralacha La and the Kun Zum La were important trading routes linking the Kullu Valley to Lahaul & Spiti. William Moorcroft and George Trebeck were the first Europeans to cross the Baralacha La during their epic journeys in the 1820s. Prior to this, the trek to the Baralacha La was the established trade route between the Kullu Valley and Ladakh. Huge camps were established on the Lingti Plains just beyond the pass, where the trading took place. More recently, the trekking routes through upper Lahaul have followed the migration of the Gaddi shepherds on their route from Kangra over the Hampta or Rohtang passes to the rich grazing pastures around the Baralacha La.

The route over the Kang La does not have such a rich and varied history. The yak herders from the Zanskar Valley would have been aware of the large crevasses and extensive glaciers leading to the pass, and preferred to take their herds over the Shingo La before diverting to the summer grazing pastures high in the Miyar Nullah. The villagers of the Miyar Nullah would have also been familiar with the pass over the main Himalaya Range, but would have normally opted for the easier route over the Shingo La to visit friends and relatives in the Zanskar Valley.

When to Trek

The treks out of Lahaul are generally in areas not affected by the full impact of the Indian monsoon. If trekking to Chandra Tal and the Baralacha La, the upper reaches of the valley will be under deep snow till at least mid-July. Thereafter, the trail remains open until mid- October. River crossing can, however, be problematic, particularly in July and August.

While it is possible to trek the lower stages of the Miyar Nullah from late June onwards, it is advisable to wait for a month until late July before crossing the Kang La. The pass remains open until the end of September when the first of the winter snows fall on the main Himalaya Range.

Accommodation in Lahaul & Spiti

Outside Keylong and Kaza, the respective headquarters of Lahaul and Spiti, most accommodation is limited to PWD huts, Forest Rest Houses or simple tea houses-cum-hotels. You can normally stay at the rest houses without prior reservation. The chowkidar often lives in the nearby village, and is quite amenable to visitors. The rooms are simply furnished and cost from Rs 50 for the room only. In some villages, such as Darcha, Udaipur and Khoksar in Lahaul, and Dankar and Tabo in Spiti, there are tea houses-cum-hotels which provide basic food and shelter for the night.

Keylong This village is used as a night halt for local buses going to and from Leh and Manali. Hotels include the *Tourist Bungalow*, which costs Rs 200 per room or Rs 50 in the dormitory – a dark, dusty and dilapidated building. Nearby, the *Hotel Gyespa* has rooms at Rs 120 with a pleasant outlook and atmosphere. Up the road is the well-located *Hotel Gangstang* with similar prices.

Kaza The *Government Rest House* has rather dreary rooms for Rs 250 for foreigners and Rs 100 for Indian tourists. The *Zambala*

Hotel across the road is more friendly, with rooms for about Rs 100. There are some newly constructed hotels closer to the bus station. These include *Sakya Abode*, with doubles for Rs 150, and the *Snowland*, next to the bus stop, which is very convenient and friendly. Its rooms cost Rs 100, complete with buckets of hot water and a cooperative manager willing to wake you at 4 am for the bus back to Manali.

Accommodation on the Trail

Beyond Udaipur there are no Forest Rest Houses or tea houses-cum-hotels except at the village of Urgos. You must therefore be self-sufficient until you reach the far side of the pass and the Zanskar Valley. A tent is the only option as well when trekking to Chandra Tal and the Baralacha La. There are tea stalls at Batal, but that's about it apart from the Gaddi shepherds' shelters, en route to the Baralacha La.

Trekking Advice

The trek to the Baralacha La involves some river crossings, and it is recommended you follow the advice of the Gaddi shepherds as to the most suitable crossing points. In the early part of the season, residual snow bridges are often in place, making the river crossings quite straightforward. From mid- July, care must be taken; a rope and harness, plus experience in their safe use, are necessary. As elsewhere in Lahaul, acclimatisation is imperative, and a few days should be spent slowly ascending between Batal and Chandra Tal before continuing to the Baralacha La.

The crossing over the Kang La is more serious. The Miyar Glacier is one of the longest in the western Himalaya – over 28 km from the snout of the terminal moraine to the top of the pass. The terrain is only for experienced parties who are well equipped with ice axes, ropes and karabiners.

Provisions

All food supplies, together with kerosene, should be brought from Manali. There are no villages from Batal to the Baralacha La, while in the Miyar Nullah, the village store only stocks biscuits and a few very basic essentials.

Horsemen & Porters

If undertaking a trek to Chandra Tal, it is advisable to organise horses from Manali. The horsemen can double-stage from the Kullu Valley and reach Batal the following day. Allow Rs 150 per packhorse per day, plus return stages with a 50% loading. On the Kang La to Padum trek, horses will carry as far as the terminal moraine. Thereafter, porters from Manali can carry up to 20 kg each. The charge is around Rs 150 per day, but you will also have to budget for their relocation: first, to get to the Miyar Valley, and then for their return via the Shingo La to Darcha and Udaipur. All up, budget for up to Rs 2000 per porter to complete the pass crossing.

Access

From Manali, there are daily bus services to Udaipur which cost Rs 57. For the Chandra Tal trek, catch the Spiti bus and alight at the small roadside hotel at Batal. The cost from Manali to Spiti is Rs 80 and for the trip to Batal around Rs 50. If planning a trek to the Zanskar Valley, there are daily buses to Darcha which cost Rs 45.

Manali to Spiti Nowadays there are no restrictions on foreigners travelling from the Kullu Valley to Spiti. However, the current regulations only permit groups of four persons or more to travel beyond Spiti to the Sutlej Valley, which leads to Kinnaur and Shimla. The cost of a jeep from Manali to Spiti and on to Shimla is between Rs 12000 and Rs 14000. Regulations are, of course, subject to change and it is imperative that you check with the HP Tourism office in Manali for the latest information.

There is a daily bus from Manali to Kaza costing Rs 80. The drive takes 12 hours and there are few concessions to comfort.

If continuing past Kaza, there are regular local bus services to the monastery at Dankar or further down the valley to the renovated monastery at Tabo. Tabo is at present as far as foreigners can go without an inner line permit.

Manali to Lahaul From Manali, there are regular buses from Manali to Keylong (Rs 40) and Darcha (Rs 45). If trekking to Chandra Tal, catch the daily bus to Spiti and get off at Batal. The fare is about Rs 50. For Udaipur, there is also a daily service which costs Rs 57.

The road developments further down the Chandra Valley are progressing rapidly. To date, jeeps can go as far as the village of Tandi, and it is envisaged that the road will reach Kilar, the headquarters of the Pangi region, in the next season or so. It will eventually be extended all the way down the Chandra Valley to Kishtwar.

BATAL TO CHANDRA TAL & BARALACHA LA
Map: Himachal Pradesh Section 3 (page190)
Stage 1: Batal to Chandra Tal
(Average walking time 6 to 7 hours)
From Manali catch the Spiti bus which goes via Chatru to Batal at the base of the Kun Zum La. This will take eight to nine hours so an overnight camp at **Batal** (3950m) is necessary.

Batal consists of a small, grassy camp site a short distance from the road. During the summer, it is often occupied by geology students studying the mountain formations. The area is particularly important geologically as the Pir Panjal Range, the main Himalaya and the Baralacha Range merge near the Kun Zum La.

From Batal, cross the road bridge over the Chandra River and head up the road leading to the Kun Zum La. After a few km, a jeep track diverts up the Chandra Valley. The trekking on this stage can be hot and dusty. Views back down the valley compensate. Mountains include Lalana (6265m), Papsura (6451m) and Dharamsura (6446m) above the Bara Shigri Glacier – one of the largest glaciers in the West Himalaya.

After several km, the Chandra River enters a gorge. The trail to Chandra Tal cuts away from the river valley and gradually

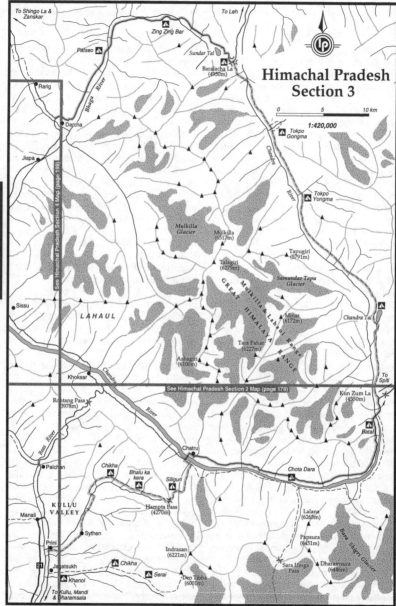

HIMACHAL PRADESH

Himachal Pradesh
Section 3

0   5   10 km

1:420,000

To Shingo La &
Zanskar

To Leh

Zing Zing Bar

Patseo

Sundar Tal

Baralacha La
(4950m)

Rarig

Bhaga River

Darcha

Tokpo
Gongma

Jispa

Chandra River

Tokpo
Yongma

See Himachal Pradesh Section 4 Map (page 199)

Mulkilla
Glacier

Mulkilla
(6517m)

Tapugiri
(5791m)

Talagiri
(6279m)

Samundar Tapu
Glacier

GREAT HIMALAYA RANGE

Mulkilla & Lahaul Range

Sissu

LAHAUL

Minar
(6172m)

Chandra Tal

Tara Pahar
(6227m)

Ashagiri
(6100m)

Khoksar

See Himachal Pradesh Section 2 Map (page 178)

To Spiti

Rohtang Pass
(3978m)

Chandra River

Kun Zum La
(4550m)

Beas River

Chatru

Batal

Palchan

Chikha

Bhalu ka
kera

Siliguri

Chota Dara

KULLU
VALLEY

Hampta Pass
(4270m)

Lalana
(6265m)

Manali

Sythen

Papsura
(6451m)

Bara Shigri Glacier

Prini

Indrasan
(6221m)

Sara Umga
Pass

Dharamsura
(6446m)

21

Jagatsukh

Chikha

Khanol

Serai

Deo Tibba
(6001m)

To Kullu, Mandi
& Dharamsala

ascends, through boulder fields at first, before meeting the stream coming from the lake. From here on, the trail becomes steeper, passing over grassy ridges towards a fertile plateau which acts as a divide between the main Chandra Valley and the side valley fed by the stream from Chandra Tal.

As you climb higher, the peaks of the Lahaul Range become visible, including Minar (6172m), Talagiri (6279m), Tara Pahar (6227m), and also Mulkilla (6517m), the highest peak at the head of the Samundar Tapu Glacier.

Chandra Tal appears as a welcome relief from what is quite a strenuous day's trek. Follow the Gaddi trails around to the side of the lake (4250m). The best camp site is at the head of the lake. You should spend at least one rest day here acclimatising and appreciating the spectacular scenery.

Stage 2: Chandra Tal to Tokpo Yongma
(Average walking time 6 hours)
From the lake, head up the valley across a series of trackless scree slopes, with constant, abrupt ascents and descents that take their toll on the leg muscles. The track then runs along a high bank above the Chandra River, with patches of wildflowers along the banks of the side streams, which provide welcome relief from the dun-coloured scenery. The camp beside the **Tokpo Yongma** ('lower river') at 4350m is the most suitable for the night, particularly in order to cross the river early the following morning.

Stage 3: Tokpo Yongma to Tokpo Gongma
(Average walking time 6 to 7 hours)
The time taken on this stage depends on the ease with which you cross the Tokpo Yongma. Until early July, the snow bridges should be in place, but from then to the end of August the river can be a problem. Seek the assistance of the local Gaddi to find the best crossing points. It is not advisable to attempt to cross on your own.

After the river crossing, the trail is well defined, with a steady ascent through boulder landscape which offers little relief.

After about five hours there is a raging side stream, and care is needed to select the best crossing place. Ropes are again essential. There is a small camp site just beyond this side stream; or you can continue to the confluence with the next large side river, the **Tokpo Gongma** ('upper river') at 4650m.

Stage 4: Tokpo Gongma to Baralacha La
(Average walking time 4 hours)
Cross the Tokpo Gongma with care. Again, seek the help of the Gaddi shepherds if the water level is still high. From the river bank, the trail climbs a steep scree slope before the country opens out. The trail is well defined by a series of rock cairns as it crosses the open meadows which lead gradually to the pass.

The **Baralacha La** (4950m) is a double pass. It marks the divide between the main Himalaya and the Lahaul Range, and also between the Himalaya and the Baralacha Range, which extends north to the Zanskar. The mountain ranges provide an impressive backdrop, and a night's camping will afford fine views.

Getting Away
From the Baralacha La you can return to Manali, catching a truck to Keylong and from there the daily bus service to Manali. Alternatively, you should have no problem getting a truck to Ladakh, which will probably stop overnight at Sarchu or Pang before reaching Leh. A trekking alternative is to continue across the Lingti plains and follow the route to the Phitse La and the Zanskar Valley. This itinerary is described in the Padum & Zanskar trek section of the Ladakh chapter.

UDAIPUR TO PADUM (ZANSKAR) VIA KANG LA
Map: Ladakh Section 3 & Himachal Pradesh Section 1 (page 138-9)
Stage 1: Udaipur to Chamrat
(Average walking time 4 to 5 hours)
The drive from Manali to Udaipur takes a full day. At **Udaipur** (2650m) there is a *PWD*

HIMACHAL PRADESH

Rest House on the outskirts of the village in which to stay. You can also camp in the enclosure. An excursion could be made to the nearby Triloknath temple on the far side of the Chenab Valley.

From Udaipur, follow the road which has been recently constructed through the narrow gorge marking the entrance to the Miyar Valley. While it is possible to drive this section, the rocky overhangs make walking it a safer proposition. To avoid the road works, cross the wooden bridge just below the village of Chamrat and continue on the true left of the valley.

The village of **Chamrat** (2950m), with its mani walls and prayer flags, is the first of the Buddhist villages in the Miyar Valley; the villagers settled here a few generations ago. There is a camp site in the forest just beyond the village.

Stage 2: Chamrat to Urgos
(Average walking time 4 to 5 hours)
The trail leads through flowered meadows and pea and millet fields before recrossing the Miyar River on a well-constructed bridge to the village of Churput. Here the trail is likely to meet up with the road which is being constructed up the valley and will eventually extend to Urgos, the main village in the valley.

Urgos (3250m) is at the confluence with the valley leading to Mt Menthosa (6443m). An optional day can be spent trekking up the side valley to the glacier beneath the Urgos Pass and the base of Menthosa. Urgos is also the place to hire a guide and additional porters for crossing the Kang La.

Stage 3: Urgos to Plateau Camp
(Average walking time 4 hours)
From Urgos the trail descends to the river floor, where a newly constructed bridge allows laden horses to continue right up to the base of the Miyar Glacier. After crossing the bridge, it is a further two km on the true left side of the valley, to the village of **Khanjar** (3450m). The trail then crosses a wide alluvial fan before a gradual ascent to the highest settlement at Tharang. This is the limit of the coniferous trees. From the settle-ment, it is a steep 200m climb to a beautiful camp (3700m) with views back down the valley to the snow-capped peaks of the Pir Panjal Range on the far side of the Chenab Valley.

Stage 4: Plateau Camp to Gumbah Nullah
(Average walking time 5 to 6 hours)
From camp, there is a gradual ascent over rich grazing pastures to a substantial Gaddi camp. Yak herders from Padum also graze their yaks here, coming from the Zanskar Valley via the Shingo La and the nearby Tarasalamu Pass. All the side streams on this stage are crossed by log bridges. The meadows are covered in wildflowers as soon as the snow melts in early July. The camp at **Gumbah Nullah** (3900m) is one of many that can be chosen in the upper Miyar Valley. From the camp you gain the first glimpses of some of the 6000m peaks of the main Himalaya, although the Kang La is well out of view.

Stage 5: Gumbah Nullah to Base Camp
(Average walking time 5 to 6 hours)
From the Gumbah Nullah it is two hours trek to the shepherds' camp locally known as **Khai Got** (approximately 4100m). It consists of a large rock shelter which shields shepherds during inclement weather. There is a silver-birch grove opposite the camp, marking the upper limit of the trees.

From Khai Got, the trail winds through open meadows crossing some side streams which may result in wet boots. Just before the terminal moraine (approximately 4200m) there is a Gaddi encampment. Do not approach the camp until the dogs have been well and truly chained up.

The huge boulders at the snout of the Miyar Glacier mark the limit for the pack-horses. There are some sheltered camp sites set amid small glacial lakes, providing for a comfortable base before heading to the Zanskar Valley.

Stage 6: Base Camp to Glacier Camp
(Average walking time 8 and 9 hours)
The Miyar Glacier is 28 km long, and to

GARRY WEARE

GARRY WEARE

GARRY WEARE

Top: Pack horses ascending the Hampta Valley, Himachal Pradesh
Middle: Kye Monastery near Kaza, Spiti, Himachal Pradesh
Bottom: Chandra Tal in Lahaul, Himachal Pradesh

GARRY WEARE

Camp site en route to Har ki Dun, Uttarakhand. This valley enjoys a relatively mild winter and an extended trekking season and offers the trekker spectacular scenery.

reach the base of the Kang La can take two stages. However, well-equipped groups start early and complete a long day up the glacier to an intermediary camp, then cross the pass late on the second day.

From camp at the snout of the glacier there is a choice of routes. You could trek across the terminal moraine to the true left side of the glacier. However, that route necessitates many tiring ups and downs along an increasingly ill-defined trail. With a full pack on a hot day this is a very hard stage – or perhaps I was just feeling the first symptoms of middle age. When all is considered, the route up the centre of the glacier, through the labyrinth of moraine and packed ice, is the best option. The terrain is demanding for the first six to seven km until the confluence with a glacier flowing from the east side (approximately 4600m), which is also the upper limit of the terminal moraine. From here on, the going is easier, with a gradual ascent over smooth, black ice. There is the occasional well-exposed crevasse to negotiate, but that is about it. Just above the confluence with the side glacier you have the option of camping, or climbing higher if you intend to cross the pass the following day.

Stage 7: Glacier Camp to Kang La & High Camp
(Average walking time 8 to 9 hours)
The route on the middle to upper sections of the glacier gradually ascends the ice and intermediary rock scree. There are magnificent views down the valley to Menthosa (6443m), while the appearance of unsurveyed (and unclimbed) 6000m peaks enclosing the upper valley is a sure indication that you are getting closer to the pass. At the head of the glacier, a large snowfield curves to the east around to the base of the pass. The actual 250m to 300m ascent from the snowfield to the pass is not hard by Himalayan standards, but all members of the party should be roped up as the area is crevassed.

The **Kang La** (5450m) is about 1.5 km long, enclosed by rock cliffs to the north and snow walls to the south. The route heads to the true left (east) side, avoiding the huge crevasses below the rock cliffs. There is also another possible route heading for a narrow trail around the rock cliffs above the pass. This route is fine, but requires a tricky descent onto the glacier at the far end of the pass.

Towards the Zanskar end of the pass, the route zigzags around crevasses as it descends to the snowfield and the terminal moraine. The descent over the moraine is steep in sections, till it reaches the valley coming from the Poat La. Here there is a small, grassy camp and a springline (approximately 4800m).

Stage 8: High Camp to Bardan Monastery & Padum
(Average walking time 10 hours)
From the high camp, follow the true right side of the valley, crossing the many side streams and grassy camp sites two to three km down the valley. (These are worth considering if you took an additional stage to cross the Kang La.) On reaching a rocky plateau, the trail descends steeply in places through meadows and boulder fields. It remains on the true right bank of the Temasa Tokpo as it descends to a grassy meadow and springline just above the Tsarap Valley and the established trail to Padum. Once on this trail, it is a further two to three hours to Bardan monastery, and from there, 1½ to two hours to Padum (3540m).

Getting Away
There are regular bus services from Padum to Kargil, stopping at Rangdum monastery overnight. Trucks are a viable alternative, leaving Padum very early and stopping overnight at Panikhar in the Suru Valley.

There are also some trekking options out of Padum. These include a trek over the Singge La to Lamayuru or a trek over the Cha Cha La and the Rubrang La to Hemis and Leh. Details of all these treks are covered in the Padum & the Zanskar Valley section of the Ladakh chapter.

HIMACHAL PRADESH

Dharamsala & the Kangra Valley

At the base of the Dhaula Dhar Range, Dharamsala (1280m) was the district headquarters of the British administration of Kangra, Kullu and Lahaul until 1947. Nowadays, it is the residence of the Tibetan Government in Exile, headed by the 14th Dalai Lama, who settled here in the early 1960s. Most of the Tibetan settlement is at McLeod Ganj (1860m), 10 km by road to the north of Dharamsala. From here, many treks into the Dhaula Dhar commence.

Treks

There are a dozen or more treks over the Dhaula Dhar, and you could spend a delightful season exploring them. Only one is outlined in this section. This is the most popular trek out of McLeod Ganj, and also the easiest to organise:

McLeod Ganj to Machetar via Indrahar Pass
(moderate; 5 stages)

History

The trekking routes over the Dhaula Dhar have been followed for generations by the Gaddi shepherds (see the boxed aside) who cross the Indrahar Pass in the late spring en route to the summer pastures in the Chamba Valley and Lahaul.

When to Trek

There are a number of short treks out of Dharamsala which do not cross the Dhaula Dhar and can be undertaken from April onwards. However, if you are trekking over the range, it is recommended that you only do so after at least some of the winter snows have melted (by mid-June). The region experiences a particularly heavy monsoon, which lasts from the beginning of July to early September and precludes trekking over the Dhaula Dhar until mid-September. From then until mid-October, the days are generally clear and fine, making this an ideal time to trek before the first of the winter snows settle on the high passes.

Trekking Agents

The Mountaineering Institute at McLeod Ganj is well worth a visit before you commence your trek. The institute is run by a keen and informative team who know the trails and passes of the Dhaula Dhar Range as well as the Gaddi shepherds do. There are some maps available for inspection, and a three-dimensional model of the range. Below the institute there is a local trekking agency, Yeti Trekking, the most established agency in Dharamsala, which can organise porters and guides for around Rs 150. Eagle Height Trekkers in the Mall opposite Hotel Bhagsu is run by two friendly brothers, Prem and Daya Shagar, who can also organise guides and porters. Their charges are higher – for instance, guides come at around Rs 250 per day – but the guides are well educated and trained at the local Mountaineering Institute – an important factor considering the nature of many of the Dhaula Dhar pass crossings. The two brothers can also organise an inclusive trek service for around Rs 800 per person. Dhaula Dhar Adventures near the Shiv Mandir is a recently established agency.

Accommodation in McLeod Ganj & Dharamsala

McLeod Ganj is where most people stay. It has a happy atmosphere, with the Tibetans engaged in shopping and trading in the main bazaar, and small shops selling Buddhist mementoes and pictures of the Dalai Lama. There is a wide variety of accommodation to choose from. Hotels near the bazaar are mostly owned by Tibetans and cost between Rs 50 and Rs 400 per room. The HP government-run *Hotel Bhagsu* costs from Rs 450 upwards, while the new, up-market hotels opposite cost from Rs 1000 per room per day.

In Dharamsala at the HP government hotel, the *Dhaula Dhar*, Prices range upwards from Rs 450 per double. Its main failing is its position beside the taxi stand – with all the associated mechanical sounds in the

The Gaddi Shepherds
The Kangra and Chamba districts are the home of the Gaddi – the colourful Hindu shepherds who tend their flocks on the Dhaula Dhar and Pir Panjal ranges throughout the summer months. Each spring they take their flocks from the Kangra foothills over the Dhaula Dhar to the Ravi Valley. From there they continue across the Pir Panjal to the pastures south of the main Himalaya, or to the grazing areas beyond the Baralacha La on the border between the states of Jammu & Kashmir and Himachal Pradesh.

The Gaddi can be distinguished by the *chola* – a warm, knee-length cloak of naturally coloured wool, spun and woven by hand – which they wear tightened at the waist by a black woollen cord. The Gaddi trace their origins back to when the first Rajput settlers made their way to the Himalayan foothills, although it was not until the late Moghul period that some of the families chose to settle in Brahmaur and Chamba. The annual Gaddi migration, like that of the Bakharval shepherds in Kashmir, means they reconstruct bridges and clear scree from the mountain trails every year. This ensures their own safe passage over the passes, and is well appreciated by anyone undertaking a trek early in the season. ■

early morning. There are also several very adequate Tibetan guesthouses at much cheaper prices.

Accommodation on the Trail
There is a *Forest Rest House* at Triund, and also at Machetar on the final stage of the trek. You will need to book the Triund Rest House at the Forest Office in Dharamsala. You can shelter for the night under the rock overhang at Lahesh before crossing the Indrahar Pass. However, you will still require a tent for camping on the far side of the pass.

Trekking Advice
While struggling for many hours over boulders en route to the Indrahar Pass, I reflected that the Dhaula Dhar Range does not lend itself to easy pass crossings. Indeed, you should ensure you are fit, as this is not an introductory trek. A few days should also be reserved at Triund or Laka Got for acclimatisation before crossing the pass at 4350m.

Provisions
All provisions, including vegetables, fruit and tinned food, can be purchased in McLeod Ganj, and there is generally no problem getting kerosene here too.

Porters
Porters can be hired from Yeti Trekking or Eagle Height Trekking. Budget for around Rs 150 plus return transportation to Dharamsala. Sometimes, however, they can be in short supply, especially in the post-monsoon season. If the local agency cannot assist, try the Mountaineering Institute, which has some contacts. Normally porters carry 15 kg each plus their food.

Access
From Dharamsala, there are regular bus services up to McLeod Ganj. The fare is Rs 4. Taxis are also available and cost Rs 70. Alternatively, if staying in Dharamsala, then the five to six km trek up to McLeod Ganj avoids most of the road and will help your fitness preparation! From McLeod Ganj you trek

straight out of the main bazaar when commencing the first stage of the trek to Triund.

MCLEOD GANJ TO MACHETAR VIA INDRAHAR PASS
Map: Himachal Pradesh Section 4 (page 199)

Stage 1: McLeod Ganj to Triund
(Average walking time 3 to 4 hours)
Turn left at the Mountaineering Institute and continue past the tea stall at **Dharamkot** to the ridge known as Galu Devi, where there is a small temple. From here on, the trail is well defined to Triund. An early start from McLeod Ganj is recommended, since the trail faces south and there is little in the way of shade. It tends to become very warm by mid-morning and there are few, if any, springs to quench the thirst. The final few km up to the meadow are quite steep, but it is worth the effort to savour the views to the south, across the Beas Dam to the Indian plains; and to the north, where the snowy ridges of the Dhaula Dhar provide an impressive backdrop.

There is a comfortable *Forest Rest House* at **Triund** (2975m), complete with an obliging caretaker. Rooms should be booked in advance from Dharamsala as this place is very popular with Indian trekkers. There are some good camping spots nearby – an ideal place to spend a day or two out from McLeod Ganj.

Stage 2: Triund to Lahesh Cave
(Average walking time 4 to 5 hours)
The time taken on this stage will depend largely on fitness. The trail follows the ridge behind the prayer flags above the Gaddi encampment. The trail ascends gently through oak and pine forests and across open meadows to the shepherd encampment at **Laka Got** (3350m). This is an ideal place to rest before beginning the ascent up through the scree to the right of the main gully which leads to the pass.

It is a tiring scramble for 200m to 300m to **Lahesh Cave** (approximately 3600m), a huge rock overhang which can serve as shelter for the night. Nearby are a few level,

grassy ridges on which to pitch a tent, while water is supplied from a small stream in the main gully. The cave is distinguished by brown and black markings, and is big enough to house a large party of porters, trekkers and shepherds. Advance bookings cannot be made from Dharamsala!

Stage 3: Lahesh Cave to Indrahar Pass & Chatru Parao
(Average walking time 6 to 7 hours)
The ridges of the Dhaula Dhar do not have easily defined passes. The pass is not immediately apparent from the camp, and a guide is essential if you are to conserve energy. In June the snow plod is very tiring, while in September and October the rock scramble to the pass will take from four to five hours. At times you'll feel like giving up: one series of boulders follows another, and at this point nobody would deny the porters their modest payment. Do not underestimate the climb. The search for gullies and footholds over boulders, while by no means technical, is not the easiest introduction to trekking.

On the climb, the route remains on the true right of the main gully, and it is only on the final km that you actually traverse the ridge to the **Indrahar Pass** (4350m). The view from the pass is very impressive. To the south, the Indian plains stretch as far as the eye can see, and to the north, the snow-capped ridges of the Pir Panjal Range provide an imposing backdrop. The peak of Mani Mahesh Kailas (5656m) can be seen to the east, while the depths of the Ravi Valley can be appreciated in the middle foreground.

The descent from the pass is initially very steep, down a gully strewn with loose boulders. The walking then levels out across a plateau marked with huge boulders which, when under a covering of snow, make the walking anything but easy. The trail down to the camp at **Chatru Parao** is often muddy and slippery, and very tiring at the end of what can be a long day. The camp (3700m), consists of a few shepherds' huts set in an open meadow.

Stage 4: Chatru Parao to Kuarsi
(Average walking time 5 to 6 hours)

The trail follows the true left side of the valley for the first few km. It is narrow, and no more than a goat track in places. Early in the season it would be worthwhile abandoning the trail altogether, and descending across the snow bridges on the main valley floor. After about two hours the track crosses the valley on a permanent snow bridge, and then ascends steeply on the opposite bank to an open meadow. There is a springline here, and the meadow is an ideal spot for a rest. Continue down the true right side of the valley, following a trail which is more suitable for goats than trekkers. The track peters out in places, and has plenty of ups and downs before you finally descend to the village of **Kuarsi** (2730m).

There is a camp site above the main springline in the village, or you could continue on for another 10 minutes to a secluded camp by the main river.

Stage 5: Kuarsi to Machetar
(Average walking time 6 hours)

Make an early start to tackle the climb out of the valley and over the ridge to the trailhead. After descending to the valley floor and crossing the bridge, the trek up the hillside, about 700m, can be very hot and sticky. The trail ascends through high grassland and forest to a springline about three-quarters of the way up the hill. Thereafter it becomes easier, and you traverse around to a well-defined pass marked with tridents and cairns.

The mountain views from the top of the ridge extend across the whole region. To the south, the Dhaula Dhar is seen from a new angle. To the north-west, is the Pir Panjal, while snow-capped ridges of the Mani Mahesh Range are to the east. From the pass, there is a long, steady descent for a couple of hours, through barley fields and forest, to the Ravi Valley. Just above the road, the *Forest Rest House* at **Machetar** (1800m) charges Rs 20 per room. It is recommended that you spend the night here before catching the bus to Chamba or Brahmaur the following day.

Getting Away
One word of advice about the bus. The first one in the morning slips by at about 7 am. To say it is normally crowded would be an understatement, even by Indian standards. Be prepared to run behind the bus and climb onto the roof at a moment's notice. This is no problem, except that in places the cliff overhangs the road with little or no room for baggage or passengers. It can be an eventful few hours until the village of Karamukh, where many alight to take the side road to Brahmaur. It is then a relatively pleasant two to three hour drive to Chamba.

This trek over the Dhaula Dhar can easily be combined with a trek out of Brahmaur over the Kugti Pass. If going to Brahmaur, there is no need to go to Chamba. Instead catch the same crowded bus to Karamukh, where the road diverts to Brahmaur. See the following Brahmaur & the Chamba Valley section for trek details.

Brahmaur & the Chamba Valley

Brahmaur, the ancient capital of the Chamba state, is 65 km from Chamba above the Budhil River, a tributary of the Ravi River. Apart from being an important market for the Gaddi shepherds, it is also the base for the pilgrimage to Mani Mahesh Lake and Mani Mahesh Kailas (the most sacred peak in this region of the Himalaya), and for treks over the Pir Panjal Range to the Chandra Valley in Lahaul.

Trek
Hardsar to the Chandra Valley via the Kugti Pass
  (moderate; 5 stages)

History
Pilgrims (mostly from Chamba, Kangra and the Punjab) have been trekking out of Brahmaur to Mani Mahesh Lake for many centuries. Although it does not attract the huge numbers who trek to Vaishnu Devi or

HIMACHAL PRADESH

Amarnath, it is still well attended, particularly on the 15th day of Janmashtami (Krishna's birthday), which falls between mid-August and early September.

By contrast, the routes over the Pir Panjal passes, including the Kalicho (4803m), the Chobia (4966m) and the Kugti (5040m), have been followed regularly by the Gaddi shepherds for many generations as they make their annual migration to the summer pastures of Lahaul.

When to Trek
Although north of the Dhaula Dhar, Brahmaur still experiences periodic heavy rainfall throughout July and August. The pre-monsoon period in June is the earliest for trekking to Mani Mahesh Lake; Gaddi shepherds do not normally cross the Kugti Pass until the end of June. The post-monsoon season, from mid-September till mid-October, is the best time to trek. At this time the passes are generally free of snow, and they remain so until the first of the winter snows fall towards the end of October.

Trekking Agents
The staff at the Mountaineering Institute in Brahmaur can provide reliable information and can also assist with the hiring of guides and porters. Budget on around Rs 100 to Rs 120 per day per porter.

Accommodation in Chamba & Brahmaur
In Chamba, the most popular and convenient hotel is the HP government-run *Iravati Hotel*, which charges Rs 350 per room per night.

In Brahmaur, there are some small hotels in the main bazaar, but most people stay at the *PWD Rest House*, where the rooms are Rs 250 per night. There is also dormitory accommodation at the *Mountaineering Institute*, with beds around Rs 15 per night.

Accommodation on the Trail
There is a *Forest Rest House* at Kugti village and some rock overhangs for shelter en route to the Kugti Pass. A tent is therefore advis-

able for this trek. If undertaking the option to Mani Mahesh Lake there are *pilgrim huts* at Dancho, nine km below the lake, which should be sufficient for one night before trekking to the lake and returning the same day to Brahmaur.

Trekking Advice
The Kugti Pass trek is followed regularly by Gaddi shepherds. However, the route in the immediate vicinity of the pass is sometimes hard to follow. Care should be taken when ascending the small glacier beneath the pass. By contrast, the trek to Mani Mahesh Lake is well defined and should present no difficulties during the main pilgrimage season.

Provisions
Fresh fruit and vegetables and most provisions can be purchased in Brahmaur; luxury items, including tinned cheese and dried fruit, should be bought in Chamba.

Porters
Porters can be hired from the Mountaineering Institute. By all accounts they are dependable and reliable. Budget on Rs 100 to Rs 120 per day plus their return stages to Brahmaur.

Access
The bus between Chamba and Brahmaur costs Rs 28 and the 70 km drive takes around four hours. Taxis cost in the vicinity of Rs 700. From Brahmaur there are local jeeps for the 13 km drive to Hardsar. The cost is around Rs 30 per seat or Rs 150 per jeep.

HARDSAR TO THE CHANDRA VALLEY VIA THE KUGTI PASS
Map: Himachal Pradesh Section 4 (page 199)
The trek over the Kugti Pass can ideally be combined with a trek to Mani Mahesh Lake. This information was compiled by Judy Parker.

Option: Hardsar to Mani Mahesh Lake
This option takes two or three stages to

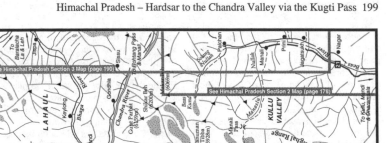

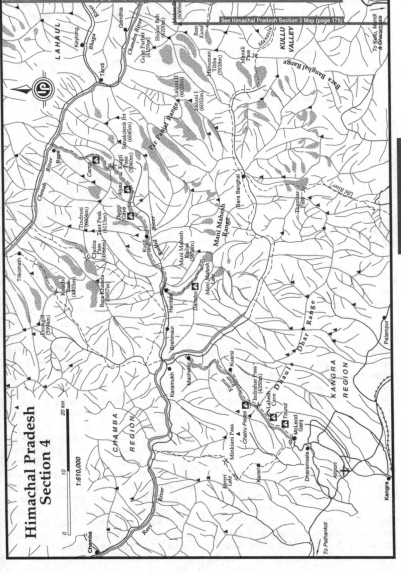

See Himachal Pradesh Section 3 Map (page 190)

See Himachal Pradesh Section 2 Map (page 178)

Himachal Pradesh
Section 4

1:610,000

0   10   20 km

HIMACHAL PRADESH

complete. From Hardsar (2280m) the pilgrim trail commences the steady climb towards Dancho. At times it crosses flowered meadows before entering a small valley to reach the camp site of Dancho (2550m), where most pilgrims spend the night. It takes three hours to walk this seven km stage.

From Dancho it takes a further three hours to climb alongside the Gauri stream to Mani Mahesh Lake. The trail is well defined, although the steep upper sections will be under snow at least until the end of June. Mani Mahesh Lake (3950m) is set beneath the peak of Mani Mahesh Kailas, the traditional seat of Lord Shiva. Most pilgrims trek from Dancho to the lake and return to Hardsar in one day.

Stage 1: Hardsar to Kugti Village
(Average walking time 5 hours)
From Hardsar the trail enters a narrow valley, where, in places, it winds high above the true left bank of the Budhil River. The trail leads through deciduous and coniferous forest, including deodar, spruce and silver birch, before crossing the Budhil River over a substantial wooden bridge about five km below Kugti village. The *Forest Rest House*, about 1.5 km before the village, is in a rather sad state of repair, and it might be better to camp closer to the village.

Kugti village (2640m) is 13 km from Hardsar. It comprises some ornately carved timber houses complete with a school and temple in the main courtyard. However, it has little of the cultural charm of Brahmaur or the thriving bustle of Hardsar, and is cut off for three to four months each winter by heavy snow.

Stage 2: Kugti Village to Duggi Cave
(Average walking time 4 to 5 hours)
From Kugti the trail winds up through the forest and fields to the **Kailang temple**. For the Gaddi shepherds this is one of the most important temples on their migration to Lahaul. The temple is dedicated to Kailang Nag, a benevolent serpent who is said to

ensure that the grazing animals remain healthy throughout their summer migration over the Pir Panjal passes. Animal sacrifices are made here in the springtime. From the temple the trail ascends steeply in places to a series of meadows, including one beside the Budhil River. There is a huge rock overhang in the vicinity known locally as the **Duggi Cave** (3200m). Although it is possible to extend this stage towards the pass, it is not advisable unless you are already fully acclimatised.

Stage 3: Duggi Cave to Alyas
(Average walking time 4 hours)
From camp, the climb over pastures and moraine to the base of the Kugti Pass is gradual. In the late spring the pastures are fully grazed by the Gaddi sheep and goats right up to the margins of the snow melt. This, as elsewhere in the West Himalaya, causes overgrazing and limits the growth of wildflowers at this time. However, during the monsoon in July and August the meadows support a wide variety of wildflowers. From the meadows there are dramatic views across to Mani Mahesh Kailas and the Dhaula Dhar Range.

The camp at **Alyas** (4000m) is set in a small meadow amid extensive boulder fields. There are some stone shelters here, although these will be occupied by the Gaddi during their spring and autumn migration.

Stage 4: Alyas to Kugti Pass & Camp
(Average walking time 6 hours)
From camp, there is a gradual climb over terminal moraine to the snout of the glacier beneath the pass. It is recommended you follow the Gaddi trail, as the glacier is crevassed and many of the crevasses are partially covered by snow, especially in the early part of the season. Above the glacier the trail enters a narrow gully. This involves a steep ascent for some 300m. Again, care is needed as the gully is subject to rock slides, particularly when animals dislodge the occasional boulder.

The **Kugti Pass** (5040m) is a small gap in the upper wall of the Pir Panjal Range. It is marked with tridents and prayer flags to placate the gods of the pass. From the pass there are distant views of the main Himalaya to the north, and, to the south, Mani Mahesh Kailas and the Dhaula Dhar Range.

Immediately below and to the west of the pass there is a long traverse across a crumbling rock face. The traverse is not technically demanding as a trail of sorts winds across the shale. However, it is exposed in sections, with the cliff dropping steeply to an extensive snowfield. An ice axe would be useful for this stage.

From the base of the moraine the trail continues more easily down to an impressive temple dedicated to Shiva. Animal sacrifices are made here by the Gaddi in gratitude for a safe pass crossing. There are camp spots nearby (3650m).

Stage 5: Camp to Rape

(Average walking time 4 hours)
From the temple the trail traverses the upper grazing meadows to a vantage point (or minor pass) with good views down the Chandra Valley. It is worth noting here that the Pir Panjal blocks a considerable amount of the monsoon rain, and the geographic contrast between the verdant forests of the Budhil Valley and the more arid landscape of Lahaul is immediately noticeable.

From the minor pass there is a steep descent down the grazing trails to the village of **Rape** (2600m) alongside the Chandra River.

Getting Away

From Rape, cross the Chandra River to the road linking Udaipur and Tandi. From here there is a daily bus service between Udaipur, Tandi and Manali. The drive over the Rohtang Pass takes eight to nine hours. Alternatively, continue along the road for 12 to 15 km to Tandi village, where there are frequent bus services from Darcha or Keylong back to Manali.

Kinnaur & the Sangla Valley

The Sangla Valley (sometimes known as the Baspa Valley) has been described as one of the most picturesque in the West Himalaya. It is in the eastern region of Kinnaur, to the south of the Kinnaur Kailas Range. The range includes the peaks of Phawarang (6349m), Jorkanden (6473m) and the sacred Kinnaur Kailas (6050m), all of which form an integral part of the main Himalaya Range.

Trek
Kinnaur Kailas Circuit
  (strenuous; 4 stages)

History
Pilgrimages have been made to the base of Kinnaur Kailas for many centuries. Treks to the Sangla (or Baspa) Valley were also made regularly by forest officers after the British government secured a lease on the state's forests in 1864. Many of the valleys and passes were explored, particularly those going south to the Har ki Dun Valley or east to Harsil and Gangotri.

When to Trek
The heavy snowfall on the Charang La (5260m) precludes trekking until mid-June. The season continues through July and August, as the monsoon rains are not as heavy here as they are in other regions in Himachal Pradesh. In autumn, the views of the mountains are clearer, and this pattern continues till mid-October and the onset of the winter snows on the ridges above the Sangla Valley.

Accommodation in the Sangla Valley
In Sangla there is *tented accommodation* run by the HP Department of Tourism for Rs 150 (tent only). At Chitkul and Sangla there are *PWD Rest Houses*. However, these need to be pre-booked by the office at Karcham, where the clerks spend the best part of an hour or more stamping forms in triplicate,

verifying your identification and checking availability. Rooms cost Rs 200 for foreigners and Rs 100 for Indians. Rather than waste time, it is best to camp or to do a deal with the local chowkidar.

Accommodation on the Trail

While there are *PWD Rest Houses* at Chitkul, Thangi and Charang, plus a simple stone pilgrim shelter at Lalanti, there is also a camp below the Charang La. It is still advisable to bring a tent with you to ensure some flexibility before crossing the pass.

Trekking Advice

The biggest concern on this trek is the height of the Charang La (5260m). If trekking out of the Sangla Valley, at least four or five days should be reserved before attempting to cross the pass. The approach to the pass from the Sangla Valley is also very steep and for this reason it is recommended that you complete the trek into, and not out of, the Sangla Valley.

Provisions

Most fruit and vegetables are available at Sangla and Karcham. However, other luxury items and tinned foods, as well as kerosene, should be brought from Shimla.

Horsemen & Porters

Porters are available from Sangla and also from Thangi village. Budget on around Rs 150 per porter, plus Rs 50 for transport back to Thangi at the end of the trek.

Access

From Shimla there is a daily bus service to Sangla. It costs Rs 80, departs early in the morning and takes a full day (14 to 15 hours) to reach Sangla. If trekking from Thangi village, change buses at Karcham. The local bus costs Rs 20.

KINNAUR KAILAS CIRCUIT

Map: Himachal Pradesh Section 5 & Uttarakhand Section 1 (page 203)

The following description has been compiled by Dr Jim Duff and Rejane Belanger,

who completed the circuit in 1992, the first season that inner line permits were not required to complete this trek.

Stage 1: Thangi to Lambar

(Average walking time 4 to 5 hours)

The large village of **Thangi** (2760m) has a medieval tower fortress, a small Buddhist monastery and a health post. It has only recently been reached by a jeep road, which will eventually extend up the valley to Lambar. However, the construction in progress will not undermine an appreciation of the magnificent granite gorge on the first stage of this trek.

The trail from Thangi gradually ascends for the first four or five km before a steep descent through coniferous forest to a large meadow and a potential camp site. Beyond here, the gorge begins to widen, although the granite walls still rise about 700m above the valley floor. It is a further two hours trek along the upper sections of the gorge to the small settlement of **Lambar** (2890m). Here there is only one primitive hotel-cum-tea house, although there are many camp sites in the vicinity.

Stage 2: Lambar to Charang

(Average walking time 5 to 6 hours)

From Lambar the trail continues up the true right side of the Tirung Valley. Several km above Lambar the trail enters a narrow gorge, where in places the path is scarcely above water level. The trail continues to twist and turn before emerging near some ancient cliff dwellings that are now deserted.

Cross the Tirung River to the true left side of the valley to an army post where the stream descends from Lalanti. While it may be tempting to make a short cut directly up this gorge, this is not possible. Instead, continue up the main valley to the village of **Charang** (3500m).

At Charang there is a post office, and some of the houses have solar-powered heating (introduced here in the late 1980s). One km above the village is a small Buddhist monastery set at the entrance to a scenic side valley. Access to the monastery must be arranged

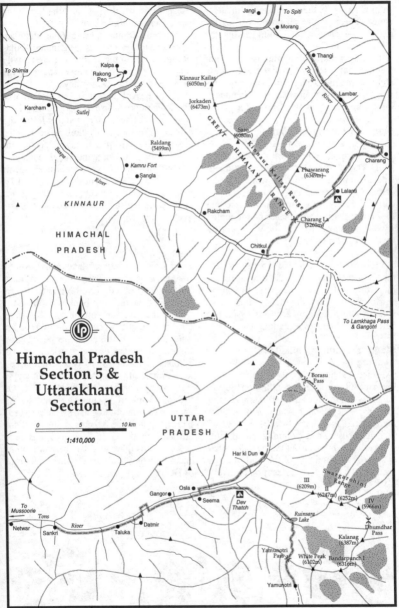

To Spiti

Jangi

Morang

Thangi

Kalpa

Rakong
Peo

To Shimla

Kinnaur Kailas
(6050m)

Tirung
River

Lambar

Jorkaden
(6473m)

Karcham

Sutlej

GREAT

Charang

Raldang
(5499m)

Saro
(6080m)

Phawarang
(6349m)

Beypa

Kamru Fort

River

Sangla

HIMALAYA

Lalanti

KINNAUR

Kinnaur Kailas Range

RANGE

Rakcham

Charang La
(5260m)

HIMACHAL

PRADESH

Chitkul

To Lamkhaga Pass
& Gangotri

**Himachal Pradesh
Section 5 &
Uttarakhand
Section 1**

0   5   10 km

1:410,000

Borasu
Pass

UTTAR

PRADESH

Har ki Dun

Swargarohini
Range

III
(6209m)

II
(6247m)

II
(6252m)

IV
(5966m)

Osla

Gangor

Seema

Dev
Thatch

Ruinsara
Lake

Kalanag
(6387m)

Dhumdhar
Pass

To
Mussoorie

Tons

River

Datmir

Netwar

Sankri

Taluka

Yamunotri
Pass

White Peak
(6102m)

Bandarpunch I
(6316m)

Yamunotri

from Charang as there is no monk in attendance. There is also an army post, as the region was subject to fighting during the 1962 war with China.

If time is not at a premium it is recommended that you stay two nights at Charang and visit the monastery during the day. This will also improve your chances of acclimatising before you cross the Charang La.

Stage 3: Charang to Lalanti
(Average walking time 4 hours)
From Charang, return down the trail to the *PWD Rest House* before striking up the hillside to your left. The trail winds up and across to a ridge top marked by a series of cairns. However, it is important to note that the trail forks in some places as the alpine grazing meadows are regularly crossed by local shepherds throughout the summer months.

From the cairns there is a steep descent to the Lalanti Valley. Ford the stream to the pilgrim shelter and the large shepherd encampment at **Lalanti** (4420m). It is advisable to camp here to acclimatise further before ascending to the Charang La.

Stage 4: Lalanti to Chitkul via the Charang La
(Average walking time 7 to 9 hours)
From the pilgrim shelter, continue on the true left side of the valley and walk alongside the impressive terminal moraine and boulder fields. After two hours there is a series of glacial lakes and a potential camp site. Above the lakes watch out for the rock cairns that mark the direction of the trail through the moraine. The trail becomes progressively

steeper towards the pass and the last 200m are a hands-and-knees job.

From the **Charang La** (5260m) there are spectacular views across the Kinnaur Kailas Range, while to the south there are equally impressive views of the range separating the Sangla and Har ki Dun valleys.

From the pass there is a steep descent over the scree slopes to an extensive boulder field and an ill-defined trail on the true left of the stream. The trail to Chitkul descents very steeply with no respite, bar a small camp site about halfway down to the Sangla Valley.

Chitkul (3450m) is the highest village in the Sangla Valley. It consists of around 20 houses and a police checkpost where you are required to register and produce your passport.

Getting Away
From Chitkul it is possible to walk down to Sangla in a long day. There is an intermittent bus service that will have been extended to Chitkul by the time this book is published.

Note that if you are continuing to Spiti, the current regulations require you to have an inner line permit. This can either be issued at Shimla, or at the district headquarters of Kinnaur at Rakong Peo. The permit stipulates a minimum group size of four, although it is no longer necessary to travel as part of a group organised by a recognised travel agency. To ensure the regulations are enforced, there are police checkpoints at Sumdo at the entrance to the Spiti Valley. Rules are, however, changing and it is best to double check with the HP Tourism offices in Shimla or Delhi.

Uttarakhand

HISTORY

The Himalayan north-west of Uttar Pradesh (UP) state, known as the Uttarakhand Himalaya, has been a source of spiritual inspiration and the scene of countless pilgrimages since the time of the early Aryan settlers. The various sources of the Ganges – Yamunotri, Gangotri, Kedarnath and Badrinath – are still visited by many thousands of Hindu devotees each year.

Gangotri is recognised as the source of the Ganges, though the actual point where the stream emerges from the snout of an impressive glacier is at nearby Gaumukh at the base of the Bhagirathi peaks. Yamunotri is the source of the Yamuna River, a main tributary of the Ganges. Kedarnath is recognised as one of the divine resting places of Lord Shiva, while Badrinath is assigned to Vishnu.

The geography of Uttarakhand, with its deep valleys, gorges, and mountains, was conducive to the establishment of small kingdoms separated by high mountain ridges. Many of these kingdoms maintained their independence by establishing a *garh* or fortress, a strategic position from which to protect themselves against their neighbours and against invading armies from the plains of north-west India. The terrain was gradually divided into two regions: Garhwal to the west, as far as the Tons River, and Kumaon to the east, extending to the Kali River and the present-day India-Nepal border.

In the early 16th century, the powerful Panwar dynasty united many of the independent hill kingdoms to form the Garhwal; in 1517 it established its capital at Srinagar. It was an impressive area, including much of the terrain as far west as the Yamuna River. At the same time, the Kumaon was united by the Chand Dynasty, leading to a period of stability in the region which lasted for nearly 300 years, until 1790.

During the time of the Moghuls, the various rajahs paid tribute to the Moghul court. It was a flexible arrangement, however, with

Highlights – Uttarakhand
Comprises the regions of Garhwal and Kumaon. Includes Nanda Devi (7816m), the Great Himalaya and Zanskar ranges. Deep gorges, luxuriant forests and flowered meadows, Hindu temples and pilgrimages to the source of the Ganges River.

Includes introductory and moderate treks to the Valley of Flowers, Har ki Dun, the sacred lake of Rup Kund, and the Milam and Pindari glaciers.

the Moghul emperors having little desire to establish absolute rule over the vast mountain region. The arrangement was mutually beneficial. It was recorded, for instance, that Rajah Bahadur Chand (1638-78) assisted Shah Jehan's forces in the foothills, then later called on the emperor's army to assist him in border disputes with the Tibetans, who were harassing Indian pilgrims on their way to Mt Kailas.

In 1790 both the Panwar and the Chand kingdoms were subjected to attack by the

Gurkhas. For the Gurkhas, it was part of an ambitious plan to form a Himalayan kingdom extending as far as the Sutlej River. Their ambitions attracted the attention of the British East India Company, which was wary of the Gurkhas and the Sikhs joining forces to form a vast Trans Himalaya empire. The British thought it essential to maintain a neutral Himalayan territory between the two powers in order to protect their own trade with Tibet. When the local rajahs asked the British to intervene, the East India army fought a number of wars with the Gurkhas, which resulted in the Treaty of Siliguri in 1817. This treaty brought Nepal's western borders back to the Kali River.

The British, anxious to exercise their authority over the region, established direct rule over the Kumaon, including the districts of Almora and Nainital. They also decided to rule Dehra Dun and the eastern districts of Garhwal. The western region of Garhwal was restored to the local rajah, Sadarshan Shah (1815-59), who established his capital at Tehri (known as Tehri Garhwal).

Hill stations were built to accommodate the British officials, notably at Dehra Dun, Mussoorie, Nainital and Ranikhet. To complete the picture, Shimla was established at the same time, becoming the summer capital of India in 1864.

The British districts in the Garhwal were initially administered by the Residency of Bengal before becoming part of the North-West Frontier Province, and finally part of the United Provinces. In 1947, after India's independence, the region became part of the state of Uttar Pradesh, and the ruler of the Tehri Garhwal, Maharajah Manvedra Shah, finally merged his kingdom with Uttar Pradesh on 1 May 1949.

In 1968 two separate divisions, Garhwal and Kumaon, were created. Chamoli, Dehra Dun, Pauri Garhwal, Tehri Garhwal and Uttarkashi were administered from Pauri, while Almora, Nainital and Pithoragarh were administered from Nainital. A line running north-east from the town of Gwaldam up the Pindar Valley and then east along the outer ridge of the Nanda Devi Sanctuary is the accepted division between the two regions.

GEOGRAPHY

Nanda Devi (7816m) is the highest mountain situated completely in India, and forms part of the main axis of the Great Himalaya Range. To the north of the Himalaya, the Zanskar Range forms a formidable divide between India and Tibet. To the south of the Himalaya Range the main tributaries of the Ganges and the Kali River form rugged gorge country before cutting through the Siwalik Range, where the peaks rarely exceed 3000m.

The Great Himalaya Range forms the backbone of the Garhwal and Kumaon regions. In western Garhwal, it includes the Swargarohini Range with Swargarohini I (6252m) at the head of the Tons River, and the Bandarpunch Range, including Bandarpunch (6316m), forming the main divide between the headwaters of the Yamuna and the Bhagirathi rivers.

The main Himalaya extends to the Gangotri region, where a huge concentration of peaks almost encloses the Gangotri Glacier. The peaks include Yogeshwar (6678m), Sri Kailas (6932m) and Mana Parbat (6794m) to the north; and Kedarnath (6490m), Kedar Dome (6831m) and Bhrigupanth I (6772m) to the south. Up at the head of the glacier, the Chaukhamba Range, including Chaukhamba I (7068m), provides an impressive divide between the headwaters of the Bhagirathi and Alaknanda rivers.

To the east of Badrinath, the peaks of Nilgiri Parbat (6474m), Ghori Parbat (6708m) and Hathi Parbat (6727m) are the highest of the Himalayan peaks, while to the north, Kamet (7756m), Mana Peak (7272m), Abl Gamin (7355m), and Mukut (7242m) are some of the 7000m peaks forming the main axis of the Zanskar Range.

The Nanda Devi Sanctuary provides another concentration of high peaks. The sanctuary is drained by the Rishi Ganga whose gorges defied the most intrepid mountaineers until the 1930s. Some of the well-known peaks forming the northern rim of the sanctuary include Dunagiri (7066m), Changabang (6864m) and Kalanka (6931m). To the south, the peaks of Nanda Ghunti (6309m), Trisul I (7120m), Devtoli (6788m) and Nanda Kot

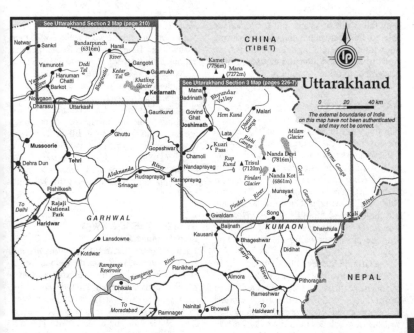

(6861m) are familiar to trekkers following the trails along the outer rim of the sanctuary.

To the east of the sanctuary, the recently opened route up the Gori Ganga to the Milam Glacier is ringed by many impressive peaks, including Hardeol (7151m), Tirsuli I (7074m) and Rishi Pahar (6992m). South-east of these peaks is the Panchchuli Range, including Panchchuli I (6904m), which forms the mountain divide between the Gauri Ganga and the Kali River – the border between India and Nepal.

Note: it is a matter of dispute whether the Swargarohini and Bandarpunch ranges are part of the main Himalaya or part of the Dhaula Dhar Range. Kenneth Mason in his *Abode of Snow* argues that these ranges are part of the lesser Himalaya and continue east to include the peaks to the south of Gangotri Glacier, including Kedarnath and Kedar Dome, before merging with the Great Himalaya Range at the head of the Gangotri Glacier.

CLIMATE

With the exception of the remote valleys to the north of the Great Himalaya Range, the Uttarakhand region is subject to the Indian monsoon.

The monsoon clouds begin to form by mid-June, with the first heavy rainfall generally occurring by the first week of July. Rain continues through August until the first week of September, then by mid-September settled conditions return.

The first of the winter snows falls in mid to late October. By then, the trails to Yamunotri, Gangotri, Kedarnath and Badrinath are subject to snow. Heavy snowfall on the main Himalaya Range precludes any thoughts of trekking during the winter months, and it is not until the beginning of May that the snow melts sufficiently to reopen the main trails into the mountains.

To the south of the Himalaya Range, some of the valleys, including the Har ki Dun, enjoy milder climates. At lower altitudes the snowfall is not so severe and the locals are able to trek between villages even during midwinter. The trekking season here is from April to June, and after the monsoon, from September to mid-November.

MAPS & BOOKS
Maps
The treks out of Mussoorie and Uttarkashi are covered in the Leomann series *Sheet 7 Uttar Pradesh (Garhwal)*, while the treks out of Joshimath and Nainital are covered in *Sheet 8 Uttar Pradesh (Kumaon)*. Also refer to the U502 series, section *NH-44-05 Dehra Dun*, which includes Gangotri, Kedarnath and the Garhwal foothills, while *NH 44-06 Nanda Devi* includes the East Garhwal plus the peaks enclosing the Nanda Devi Sanctuary.

The Ground Survey of India trekking map series is also available from UP Department of Tourism offices. The series includes three useful colour sections: *Gangotri-Yamunotri* includes treks out of Mussoorie and Uttarkashi; *Badri-Kedar* includes treks out of Joshimath; and *Kumaon Hills* includes the Nanda Devi Sanctuary and the Kumaon region.

Of particular note for the Nanda Devi region is the detailed aerial survey *Garhwal Himalaya Ost*, published by the Swiss Foundation for Alpine Research, based on the Survey of India maps and drawn by Ernst Huber at a scale of 1:150,000 and published in 1992.

Books
The Nanda Devi Affair by Bill Aitken provides a highly readable account of the author's exploits in the Nanda Devi area, while his *Mountain Delight* (English Book Shop, Dehra Dun, 1994) includes accounts of his travels in Uttarakhand over the last 30 years. *Beautiful Garhwal* by Ruskin Bond (Dev Dutt Pt Ltd, 1988) provides an overall appreciation of the Garhwal by one of the region's most prolific writers. *Garhwal Himalaya* by Gurmeet & Elizabeth Singh (Frank Bros, New Delhi, 1987) is a well-illustrated trekking guide to the Garhwal. Eric Shipton's

Nanda Devi is included in *Eric Shipton – The Six Mountain-Travel Books*, while *HW Tilman – The Seven Mountain-Travel Books* includes Tilman's *The Ascent of Nanda Devi*. Frank Smythe's *The Valley of Flowers* provides an account of his climbs in the region in 1937. *Exploring the Hidden Himalaya* by Soli Mehta & Harish Kapadia is the reference book for climbing in the Indian Himalaya, including the ascents in the Garhwal. Jill Neate's *High Asia – an Illustrated History of 7000 metre Peaks* (1989) includes a comprehensive section on the Uttarakhand peaks. Also refer to the classic *Abode of Snow* by Kenneth Mason.

GETTING THERE & AWAY
Delhi to Mussoorie
There are many tourist buses costing around Rs 250. Alternatively, take the train to Dehra Dun. Trains include the *Shatabdi Express*, which departs at 5.55 am, and the *Dehra Dun Express*, departing at 6.25 am, both from New Delhi station. The cost is Rs 327 1st class, Rs 315 air-con chair and Rs 118 2nd class. From Dehra Dun there are regular buses to Mussoorie for between Rs 9 (for the local bus) and Rs 22 (for the deluxe bus).

Delhi to Uttarkashi
Buses depart from Delhi every hour throughout the day and most of the night. The drive takes five to six hours and costs between Rs 83 for the local bus and Rs 175 for the tourist bus. From Haridwar there are three buses a day to Uttarkashi. The drive takes around eight hours and costs Rs 80. Alternatively, catch the *Shatabdi Express* to Haridwar then take the bus to Uttarkashi. The cost is Rs 307 in 1st class, Rs 295 in air-con chair, and Rs 98 in 2nd class. The train arrives in Haridwar by 11 am, which means that you will make the bus connection to reach Uttarkashi that night.

Delhi to Joshimath
Unless you want to spend a night in Haridwar, which is very hot and humid in May and June, it is recommended that you catch one

of the overnight trains from Old Delhi station and arrive in the early morning. This allows enough time to catch the morning bus to Joshimath. The *Mussoorie Express* departs from the Old Delhi station at 11.25 pm and costs Rs 307 in 1st class and Rs 98 in 2nd class. The bus to Joshimath costs Rs 97 and takes 10 to 12 hours. Note: the road to Joshimath, like other roads in the Garhwal, is subject to landslides during July and August, and can take up to three days to clear.

Delhi to Nainital/Almora

There are daily deluxe buses from Delhi to Nainital. They take 10 hours and cost between Rs 155 and Rs 275. There are also buses to Almora that take from 10 to 12 hours and cost between Rs 170 and Rs 300.

Mussoorie & the Har ki Dun Valley

The popular hill station of Mussoorie, at 1920m altitude and 35 km north of Dehra Dun, is in the Uttarkashi district of the Garhwal. It was founded in 1827 in a commanding position overlooking the Doon Valley; to the north, it affords spectacular views of the Garhwal Himalaya. It is a convenient transit point before undertaking a trek to the Har ki Dun Valley.

Treks
Sankri to Har ki Dun & Ruinsara Lake
(introductory; 6 stages)

There are many extensions to this trek, including the route over the Borasu Pass to the Sangla Valley. At present, foreign trekkers cannot undertake the trek to the Sangla Valley and Kinnaur in Himachal Pradesh, but these regulations are being reviewed.

History
The route to Har ki Dun follows the established village trail to the highest settlement at Osla. Thereafter, Gujar shepherds follow

tracks with their buffalo for grazing around both Har ki Dun and Ruinsara Lake. The trails over to Kinnaur have not been followed by the villagers from the Har ki Dun Valley for several generations, although it is acknowledged that there was a trade route over this and the adjoining passes in earlier centuries. The trek to Yamunotri, or over the Dhumdhar Pass to Harsil and Gangotri, has been followed by pilgrims since long before the roads into Garhwal connected Hanuman Chatti and Uttarkashi.

When to Trek
A trek into the Har ki Dun Valley can be undertaken from mid-April until mid-November. However the passes, if you are continuing on, are snowbound until early June, while the monsoon is prevalent in July and August. As in other regions in Garhwal, the post-monsoon season from mid-September till the end of October, is ideal for trekking. The first of the winter snows fall in the upper reaches of the Har ki Dun Valley in November, and in the lower sections of the valley from mid-December until the end of February. However, even during the heart of winter the villagers continue to trek up the valley as far as Osla.

Trekking Agents
Himalayan Trekkers at the head of the Sankri bazaar is helpful when hiring porters, guides and cooks. In Dehra Dun, Garhwal Treks & Tours is a long-established company organising treks to Har ki Dun and other regions of Garhwal.

Accommodation in Mussoorie
There is a wide range of accommodation in Mussoorie, which includes some hotels with a touch of faded Raj character. Most have been partially refurbished since 1947, and include the up-market *Savoy* and the *Hotel Padmini Niwas*, with rooms around Rs 1000. The more affordable *Hotel Broadway* in Kulri bazaar has been recommended, with rooms in the vicinity of Rs 100 per double. There are, however, many budget hotels in the mall and library area, where rooms are available

UTTARAKHAND

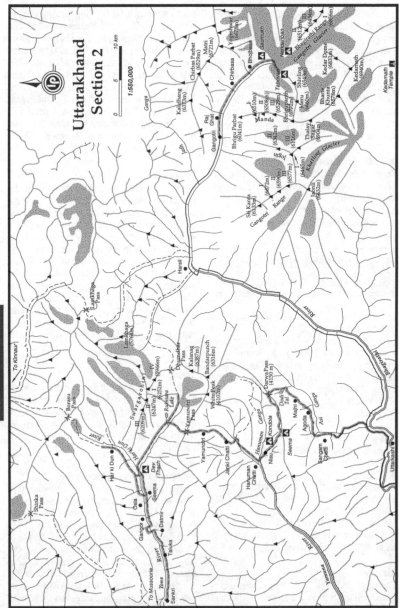

even during the height of the season in May and June.

Accommodation on the Trail

There are *Forest Rest Houses* in Sankri, Taluka and Osla, although most trekkers stay in the Garhwal Mandal Vikas Nigam hotels *(GMVN hotels)* which have also been constructed in these villages. There is a *Forest Rest House* up at Har ki Dun, while a *GMVN hotel* is also being completed there. Rooms cost around Rs 150 to Rs 200, with dormitory beds at Rs 50. If continuing to Ruinsara Lake, you will need a tent.

Trekking Advice

The trails to Har ki Dun and Ruinsara Lake are well defined and should not pose any problems for trekking. However, if going higher, there is a need for sound preparation and acclimatisation before crossing the passes to Harsil or Yamunotri.

Provisions

In contrast to other towns in the Garhwal, there is a complete lack of fresh fruit and vegetables in Sankri. Supplies should therefore be brought from Mussoorie or Dehra Dun. Biscuits and basics can be purchased in Sankri, and in the villages of Taluka and Osla. Kerosene must be brought from Mussoorie, together with any other luxury items, including chocolate, nuts and dried fruit.

Horsemen & Porters

Although packhorses can be hired at around Rs 160 per day for the trek to Har ki Dun, most trekking groups hire porters. They can be hired from Himalayan Trekkers in Sankri. Rates are around Rs 100 per day, while guides are Rs 200 and cooks Rs 150.

Access

There are regular bus services from Mussoorie and Dehra Dun to Sankri. The drive takes six hours and costs Rs 84. There are also buses to Sankri from Shimla (Rs 75) and from Uttarkashi (Rs 72). Beyond Sankri there is a jeep road to Taluka, and jeeps are available for Rs 300 one way.

SANKRI TO HAR KI DUN & RUINSARA LAKE

Map: Uttarakhand Section 2 (page 210)

Stage 1: Sankri to Taluka

(Average walking time 3 hours)

From **Sankri** (1450m), a jeep road has been completed all the way to Taluka. However, it is recommended that you walk this stage as the road is often blocked and the ride in a jeep or truck is far from comfortable. Besides, the walk through the forest on the first day gives time to wear in your boots and appreciate the wild roses and irises, chestnut, sycamore and deodar trees and bamboo which line the trail. There is a camp site about two km below Taluka, beside a beautiful stream, which might be useful if you were to leave Sankri late in the day.

The village of **Taluka** (1800m) is devoid of charm. It is centred around a concrete depression which will eventually be a fish breeding pond. The pond is complemented by the imposing concrete structure of the *GMVN hotel*. It is a pity that the UP government could not have drawn on the traditional building styles of the village houses in the Har ki Dun. To complete the tale of woe, the *dhabas* (tea stalls) are among some of the most fly-blown anywhere in northern India. It takes a lot for me to refuse a cup of tea, but it happened during a recent visit to this abysmal village.

Stage 2: Taluka to Seema

(Average walking time 5 to 6 hours)

This stage can be shortened by trekking past Taluka on the first stage to one of many forest camps.

From Taluka, the trail descends to the river valley and continues through the forest on the true left side of the valley. In spring, there are plenty of Gujars camping as they make their way to the higher pastures at the head of the valley. After two to three km, the trail winds below the village of **Datmir** (1950m). It is one of a number of villages which can be by-passed on the direct trail to Osla. A few km past the turn-off to Datmir, the main trail crosses the river by a substantial bridge before recrossing to the true left side about one km further up the valley. There is a camp site just above the second bridge.

Do not cross the bridge to the village of Gangor; the trail continues on the true left side of the valley, winding through barley and wheat fields and apple orchards for several km until the village of **Osla** (2560m) appears on the opposite side of the valley. The main trail does not divert to Osla. Instead it leads through a row of dhabas and a Forest Rest House known as **Seema** (2500m). There is also a newly constructed *GMVN hotel* managed by a lively and obliging chowkidar (until he found we weren't staying). As with the GMVN hotel at Taluka, the style of this hotel has made no concessions to the local environment.

There is a camp site a few km up the valley on the route to Har ki Dun. It is close to the upper bridge over the river, close to a small springline.

Stage 3: Seema to Har ki Dun
(Average walking time 4 to 5 hours)
From Seema, cross the main bridge directly above the village. The trail remains on the true right side of the valley all the way to Har ki Dun. There is a gradual ascent through the fields as the trail winds high above the valley floor. After two to three km there is a higher bridge (and route to Ruinsara Lake).

One km beyond the higher bridge, the trail splits. Take the upper trail and continue up a steep section which winds above wheat fields tended by the villagers living in the two highest houses in the valley. The trail then winds high above the confluence of the Har ki Dun and Ruinsara rivers to a vantage point where the peak of Har ki Dun can be seen at the head of the valley. It is a further three or four km to camp, following a trail that leads through pine forest and a series of meadows where the villagers from Osla graze their cattle in the summer months.

Har ki Dun (3510m) is beyond the confluence of two alpine valleys. Above the main meadow there is a *Forest Rest House* in need of restoration and a *GMVN hotel* in the process of construction.

Options: Trails beyond Har ki Dun
From Har ki Dun there are a number of trekking options. These include a three km trek to the base of the Har ki Dun peak, across a series of flowered meadows of gentians, anemones, and buttercups in spring. From here, there are excellent views back down the valley, while the route towards the Borasu Pass and the Sangla Valley and Kinnaur can also be appreciated.

A second option leads up the alpine valley to the north of Swargarohini Range including Swargarohini I (6252m). This peak is famous in Hindu legend, being 'the gateway to heaven' taken by the Pandava brothers. It's a day's trek to the snout of the Jamdar Glacier and return to the Har ki Dun camp.

Stage 4: Har ki Dun to Dev Thach
(Average walking time 3 hours)
It's a short stage back down the valley to the Gujar meadow above Seema. It is important not to take any short cuts on this stage. Although the local porters may indicate the presence of a log bridge built between two huge boulders just above the confluence of the the Har ki Dun River and the river flowing from Ruinsara Lake, this bridge crossing is dangerous. Instead, go back down the trail as if returning to Osla and Sankri. En route the large meadow on the opposite side of the valley – known as **Dev Thach** (3000m) – can be appreciated. Follow the trail to the higher of the two bridges above Seema. Cross here and ascend the three km to the meadow, where local Gujar shepherds graze their buffalo throughout the summer months.

Stage 5: Dev Thach to Ruinsara Lake & Return
(Average walking time 7 hours)
From Dev Thach, pass the Gujar huts, then take the trail which descends steeply to the bridge over the Ruinsara River. Cross the bridge to the true right side of the valley and commence a gradual ascent of the valley. The trail leads through mixed forest and meadows of forget-me-nots and buttercups. In the early part of the season there are residual snowfields covering the trail and

also several side-stream crossings, none of which pose any problem. The trail also passes under some impressive waterfalls before ascending above the pine and fir forest. About halfway to the lake, the valley widens and crosses a series of flowered meadows where shepherds from the nearby villages graze their flocks in the summer. There are also some delightful birch copses and juniper – a sure sign that you have ascended above 3000m.

Ruinsara Lake (3350m) is considered sacred by the villagers in the Har ki Dun Valley. It is above the main valley floor on the true right side, surrounded by alpine pastures and low rhododendrons beneath the impressive Swargarohini Range. From the lake, it is a two to three hour descent back to Dev Thach.

Options: Trails beyond Ruinsara Lake

From the lake, it takes a further stage to get to the base of the Yamunotri Pass. The route to the pass descends to the valley floor below Ruinsara Lake, where the braided river is easiest to cross. The trail then heads up the side valley to the terminal moraine at the base of the pass. The trek over the pass and steeply down to the temple at Yamunotri takes a further stage.

An alternative trek up the valley leads to the base of the Dhumdhar Pass. After crossing this pass, there are three stages down the alpine valley to the trailhead at Harsil village, 28 km below Gangotri.

Stage 6: Dev Thach or Seema to Sankri

(Average walking time 6 hours)
The return stage back to Sankri can be completed in a long morning. The trek from Seema to Taluka can be completed in three hours (add an additional hour from Dev Thach to Seema). From Taluka you may be fortunate enough to find a jeep or truck which can be hired on a per seat basis. If not, it's a further 2½ hour trek to Sankri.

Getting Away

From Sankri there are daily buses to Mussoorie, Dehra Dun and Uttarkashi. These leave from Sankri in the early morning between 5 and 5.30 am. An overnight stay in Sankri is therefore necessary.

Uttarkashi

On the banks of the Bhagirathi River is the pilgrim town of Uttarkashi (1160m). The town is famous for its Shiva temples, including the Vishwanath temple just to the north of the town. From the beginning of May till the end of October, it is an important place of pilgrimage for Hindu devotees before they continue on the drive 107 km further up the valley to Gangotri.

Uttarkashi is the headquarters of the Uttarkashi district of Garhwal, and the famous Nehru Mountaineering Institute is just above the town.

Treks

Uttarkashi to Hanuman Chatti via Dodi Tal
(moderate; 4 stages)
Gangotri to Gaumukh & Tabovan
(introductory; 2 stages)

History

The pilgrimage to Gaumukh (the recognised source of the Ganges) has been undertaken for many centuries. Until recent geological times the snout of the huge glacier extended as far as Gangotri, and this would have been the destination for most pilgrims. The first European survey of the area was undertaken in 1808. The Bengal Survey was led by Lieutenant Webb, who explored the upper Bhagirathi Valley and the source of the Ganges. The main aim of the survey was, however, to ascertain whether there was an easy passage from Gangotri into Tibet, particularly since the Gurkha forces had at this time occupied the nearby regions of Kumaon and Garhwal.

While mountaineers and explorers have paid frequent visits to the impressive number of peaks and glaciers in the region throughout most of the present century, the road to Gangotri was only completed in the early 1980s. Today, the overwhelming majority of the pilgrims go no further than Gangotri.

Only a fraction undertake the trek on to Gaumukh or higher, to Tabovan and the base of Shivling (6543m), leaving the high alpine pastures to the many mountaineering expeditions that visit the region each season.

The trek to Dodi Tal is taken by the Gujar shepherds, who herd their buffalo to the rich alpine pastures during the summer months. A handful of pilgrims and sadhus also trek from Hanuman Chatti to Uttarkashi before walking along the road to Gangotri. Indeed, some even bypass Dodi Tal and follow a higher trail to Harsil, a village 28 km below Gangotri.

When to Trek
The trek to Gaumukh officially opens on the day of Akshaya-Tritya, which occurs around the last week of April or first week of May. The season concludes during the Diwali festival towards mid or late October. The area is subject to the monsoon, which keeps all but the most devoted pilgrims away in July and August.

The trek to Dodi Tal and Hanuman Chatti can also be undertaken from May to the end of October, but avoid July and August.

Trekking Agents
Trekking agencies in Uttarkashi include Mount Support, Al Fresco, Highland Trek & Tours and Crystal Adventures, all of which have their offices on Bhatwari Rd. Most of the staff are enthusiastic about the treks in the area and can arrange porters (mainly Nepalese), guides and cooks. Guides can be hired for Rs 200 per day and cooks for Rs 150. They also require an equipment allowance. Trekking gear can be hired: tents go for Rs 40 per day, foam mats for Rs 3, sleeping bags for Rs 10 and rucksacks for Rs 15. A security deposit is required and can be as high as Rs 3000, depending on the condition of the gear.

Accommodation in Uttarkashi
The *GMVN Tourist Rest House* is well located in the centre of the town with prices from Rs 120 to Rs 425 a double. There are numerous other hotels and guesthouses, although most are heavily booked by pilgrim parties during the pre-monsoon period from May until the end of June.

Accommodation on the Trail
There are many dhabas, providing both food and shelter, on the trail between Gangotri and Gaumukh. At Tabovan there are shelter huts, but food must be carried from Gangotri. The *GMVN hotel* at Bhojbasa is very crowded and well worth avoiding, while the *dharamsala* (pilgrims' lodging) was destroyed by fire in 1994.

If trekking to Dodi Tal, there are dhabas in and just beyond the village of Agoda and also at Dodi Tal. Beyond Dodi Tal there is no accommodation, and a tent must be carried.

Trekking Advice
There are no problems in following the trail to Gaumukh. However, if going beyond Gaumukh to Tabovan and Nandanban then it is imperative that you acclimatise. The trail between Gaumukh and Tabovan winds across the terminal moraine of the Bhagirathi Glacier. The route is ill-defined and tiring and it is important to keep a good lookout for the rock cairns marking the way. The glacial traverse from Tabovan to Nandanban is more serious and a local guide is imperative.

By contrast, the trek to Dodi Tal is quite straightforward. Beyond Dodi Tal the shepherd trail over the Darwa Pass to Hanuman Chatti is less well defined. Till the beginning of June, some sections of the trail just beyond the pass are under snow, and an ice axe and/or ski pole are useful for traversing the steeper gully sections.

Provisions
Most fruit, vegetables and food supplies can be purchased in Uttarkashi. Kerosene should also be purchased here. Some fruit and vegetables can be purchased in Gangotri, together with biscuits and basics.

Horsemen & Porters
The trekking agencies in Uttarkashi can organise porters for both Gangotri and Dodi Tal. Allow Rs 80 to Rs 100 per day per porter. Porters can also be hired directly in Gangotri

for the official UP government rate of around Rs 70 per stage, for which they carry a maximum of 25 kg.

Access

From Uttarkashi there are regular buses to Gangotri which take four to five hours and cost Rs 50. Jeeps cost around Rs 1500 one way. The construction of Lanka Bridge completed the road to Gangotri in 1982. However, the road is subject to landslides during the monsoon, and can take several days to clear.

The trailhead to Dodi Tal is about 10 km up the Asi Ganga Valley from the road to Gangotri, and 15 km from Uttarkashi. There are three bus services per day. The bus costs Rs 7 while jeeps cost Rs 200. There are plans to extend the road to the village of Agoda.

UTTARKASHI TO HANUMAN CHATTI VIA DODI TAL

Map: Uttarakhand Section 2 (page 210)

Stage 1: Uttarkashi to Agoda

(Average walking time 2 to 3 hours)

From Uttarkashi, it is four km to the jeep track leading up the Asi Ganga Valley. From the turn-off, the road continues for about 10 km to **Sangam Chatti** (1350m). Buses and jeeps come this far from Uttarkashi (see Access above); however, the road is subject to landslides and this should be taken into account when planning this first stage.

Sangam Chatti consists of several dhabas beside a tributary of the Asi Ganga. Cross the bridge over the side stream and follow the trail on the true right side of the valley leading to Agoda. It is a steady ascent through deciduous to semitropical forest. As it approaches the village, the trail is lined with rose bushes and hedgerows. The spring wheat crop is harvested in May, allowing time for a second crop by autumn.

Agoda (2250m) consists of 20 to 30 houses, double-storeyed, slate-roofed and each with a stone courtyard. There is a *Tourist Rest House* at the far end of the village. Just beyond the village there are some other small hotels-cum-tea stalls run by the local villagers, where meals are also available.

Stage 2: Agoda to Dodi Tal

(Average walking time 6 hours)

From Agoda, the trail gradually ascends through the forest high above the Asi Ganga before entering a side valley leading to Dodi Tal. This trail is followed regularly by Gujar shepherds as they carry their buffalo milk and produce to the market at Uttarkashi. There is a substantial Gujar settlement at **Majhi** (3150m) about five km before Dodi Tal, on a ridge that affords a glimpse of Bandarpunch (6316m). The camp site here could be convenient if you have made an early start from Uttarkashi and do not want to spend half the day at Agoda.

From Majhi it is a pleasant trek through rhododendron, oak, pine and bamboo forest around the hillside to **Dodi Tal** (3310m). The lake is set in forest and is about half a km wide. There is a recently constructed temple at its southern end. There are a couple of dhabas and a *Forest Rest House* here. There are camping spots next to the rest house and at the far side of the lake.

Fishing is banned in the lake, but this does not deter the average trekker from trying. When questioned about this flagrant breaking of the rules, the fishing inspector assured me that it didn't matter, as he had never seen an amateur angler catch a fish.

Stage 3: Dodi Tal to Seema

(Average walking time 6 to 7 hours)

The trail to the Darwa Pass ascends the valley at the far end of the lake. It crosses the stream flowing into the lake several times before the valley widens. The trail then follows the true right valley which heads towards the pass. It's a pleasant climb through flowered meadows with the rows of rhododendrons remaining in bloom until mid-June. The final climb up the alpine meadows to the pass is short and steep.

The climb from Dodi Tal to the **Darwa Pass** (4150m) can be completed in two to three hours, so it could be undertaken as a day walk out of Dodi Tal. However, an early start is imperative if you are to appreciate the range of peaks stretching beyond Gangotri as far as Nanda Devi. To the north of the pass, the peak of Bandarpunch (6316m) dominates

UTTARAKHAND

the upper part of the valley, while further to the north-west the Swargarohini Range, including Swargarohini I (6252m), rises above the Har ki Dun Valley.

From the pass there is a further climb along the ridge to the south. This is under snow until mid-June. The narrow trail continues along the ridge line for three to four km, with commanding views of Bandarpunch and the main Himalayan Range. For the remainder of this stage the trail heads up and down across the alpine ridges just above the tree line. A number of idyllic camping spots can be seen from the high trail. These include the magnificent camp site at **Seema** (3450m) – a beautiful meadow where rhododendron bushes dot the pastures and frame Bandarpunch and the other snow-capped peaks at the head of the Hanuman Ganga.

Option: Darwa Pass to the Base of Bandarpunch

This option takes two to three stages to complete. Directly over Darwa Pass a steep descent leads through the meadows and forest to the Hanuman Ganga. Cross the river by a birch bridge (of sorts) and continue up the true right side of the valley. The trail follows the valley floor for one km before ascending a low ridge and leading through a series of meadows and rhododendron forests to the upper valley. The time from the pass to the alpine camp (approximately 3700m) is two to three hours. From the camp, a day walk can be made to the snout of the Bandarpunch Glacier.

There is also an interesting optional walk up the gully to the west of the valley. I thought this was the route leading to the Sonpara Pass – the pass marked on some maps as the way to Yamunotri. It took four hours of scrambling and effort to discover that the trail led to a pass that literally goes nowhere! The route over the Sonpara Pass is in fact from much lower down the valley, and the pass can be seen from near Seema when descending the ridge to Hanuman Chatti.

Stage 4: Seema to Hanuman Chatti
(Average walking time 4 hours)
The trail drops steeply – in fact, very steeply

in places – past a series of meadows to the settlement at **Kondola** (3050m), where goats and sheep from the lower villages graze during the summer. From here it is a short descent to the first village of **Nisu** (2700m). The trail is well maintained from here to Hanuman Chatti. One km or so before **Hanuman Chatti**, cross a bridge over a tributary of the Hanuman Ganga before joining the pilgrim trail into the main bazaar (2400m).

Option: Hanuman Chatti to Yamunotri

This is nominated as the first of the four main pilgrimages undertaken each season by many thousands of Hindu pilgrims. After completing the trek to Yamunotri the pilgrims drive to Uttarkashi and Gangotri for the trek to Gaumukh. The temple of Kedarnath also involves a trek, before the final drive to Joshimath and Badrinath.

From the main bazaar of **Hanuman Chatti**, the pilgrim trail crosses the bridge over the Hanuman Ganga to lead up the Yamunotri Valley. The first stage of the trek is normally to the village of **Janki Chatti** (2650m), where there are many hotels, dhabas and rest houses. There is also a camp site on the far side of the valley. As it takes about three to four hours (seven km) to reach the village, the rest of the day can be spent appreciating the complete spectrum of Indian society undertaking the pilgrimage. The rich families hire riding horses or are even carried on dandies (wooden platforms) supported by four or five porters, while the less affluent make their way slowly and surely with the aid of a walking stick and their travelling companions.

On the second stage of the trek, the pilgrims leave early to reach Yamunotri before returning to Hanuman Chatti the same day. From Janki Chatti, the trail begins to steepen and there are plenty of switchbacks as it enters a narrow gorge in the upper sections of the valley. It takes about two hours to complete the five km stage to Yamunotri (3185m). The temple is in the centre of the valley, enclosed by high, snow-capped ridges. The return to Hanuman Chatti is completed in three to four hours depending on the number of dandies and horses on the trail.

Getting Away
From Hanuman Chatti there are regular buses to Mussoorie and Dehra Dun, which cost Rs 70 and take six to seven hours. There are also three buses each day to Uttarkashi. They take around six hours and cost Rs 55, with the last bus leaving around 2 pm.

GANGOTRI TO GAUMUKH & TABOVAN
Map: Uttarakhand Section 2 (page 210)
Stage 1: Gangotri to Bhojbasa
(Average walking time 6 to 7 hours)
From **Gangotri** (3050m) the trail passes the Gangotri temple on the true right side of the valley. There is no need to cross the bridge over the river. Just beyond the temple there is a series of concrete steps leading up to the main trail. From here on, the trail is well defined with stone markers every km. After the first four km there are some dhabas at **Raj Ghat** (3250m), where a tributary flows into the valley. It should be noted that the former pilgrims' trail can be seen in places following the valley floor, and the present trail has only been upgraded in the last 20 to 30 years.

Beyond Raj Ghat the glacial valley begins to widen, and just before Chirbasa you gain the first views of the Bhagirathi peaks, including Bhagirathi I (6856m), at the head of the valley.

At **Chirbasa** (3600m), nine km from Gangotri, some dhabas line the trail. There is a sheltered camp site below the trail close to the river, which is recommended for acclimatising if planning to trek beyond Gaumukh. Just beyond Chirbasa, the trail passes the last of the silver birches, which frame the Bhagirathi Range and the upper section of Shivling (6543m). To the south, the peak of Bhrigu Parbat (6041m) looms high above the valley.

The trail gradually ascends the next five km to Bhojbasa, which is reached in around two to $2\frac{1}{2}$ hours. It is now above the tree line, although juniper bushes are scattered up the otherwise barren hillside. Just below Bhojbasa,

the trail leads through an extensive boulder field – a hot and dusty section on a warm day.

Bhojbasa (3790m) is a rather desolate camp. It consists of a crowded *GMVN hotel* and a dharamsala recently destroyed by fire. There are a small temple and some garbage-strewn camping spots down towards the river.

Stage 2: Bhojbasa to Gaumukh & Gangotri
(Average walking time 2 hours to Gaumukh & 6 hours return to Gangotri)
For most pilgrims, Bhojbasa is a convenient overnight camp before continuing to Gaumukh early the following day. At Gaumukh they conduct their *darshan* (prayer) at the river's source, before returning to Bhojbasa by mid-morning. Most pilgrims then plan to return to Gangotri the same day.

It is about a $1\frac{1}{2}$ hour walk from Bhojbasa to the dhabas below Gaumukh. This is as far as the porters and the horses go. It is a further two km to **Gaumukh** (3890m). The trail on these final km leads through moraine and the boulders deposited by many landslides. It is hard going, particularly for those pilgrims who until now have been on horseback. The last 500m to the source of the Ganges follows a trail along the river bank. The gush of the river emerging from the abrupt glacier wall is sure to impress even the less devout.

Option: Gaumukh to Tabovan & Return
(Average walking time 5 to 6 hours)
It is imperative that you include a rest day in your itinerary before continuing to Tabovan (4450m). The trek from Gaumukh to Tabovan is normally completed in three to four hours, plus two hours to return.

The trail to Tabovan diverts from the main pilgrim trail next to the last dhabas, just before the final 500m to Gaumukh. It ascends the terminal moraine of the Bhagirathi glacier for about one km.

Here it splits. The trail to the true right side of the valley leads to Nandanban, while that to the true left side (to the south side of the valley) leads to Tabovan. Even with the stone cairns marking the trail, the route is by no means easy to follow and a local guide is

UTTARAKHAND

The Gaumukh Trek

In the UP Government Rest House at Bhojbasa there is a large poster distributed by the Himalayan Adventure Trust setting out relevant points for preserving the Himalayan environment. However, the message has by no means been translated into action: the camp site in the immediate vicinity of Bhojbasa is one of the filthiest in the Himalaya.

The trek to Gaumukh should be a showpiece for many first-time pilgrims and trekkers, allowing them to admire and enjoy the mountainous landscape. Instead, the fragile environment reflects all the problems of overtrekking. If it were not for the religious sensibilities of the pilgrims, it would not be inopportune for the UP government to close the Bhagirathi Valley off for a decade or so.

Although the Himalayan Adventure Trust has commenced cleaning-up operations, constructed toilet blocks at Gangotri, Chirbas and Bhojbasa and installed an incinerator at Gangotri, there is still much to be done.

In particular, there is an obvious need to stop the deforestation of the Bhagirathi Valley, much of which is attributed to the demand for fuel of the 15 to 20 dhabas along the route between Gangotri and Gaumukh. Indeed, it would not be too difficult for the UP government to ban the use of wood fires for cooking in the valley. It could require each dhaba to purchase a kerosene stove, and supply them with kerosene at a subsidised rate. Any shortfall could be made up by charging pilgrims a fee of, say, Rs 20, and foreign trekkers, say, Rs 100 as they left Gangotri. Sadhus need not be charged. The system would not be hard to administer. As well, a concerted effort on the part of the forest officers could help to reforest the hillside before the effects of soil erosion make this impossible. ■

essential for all but the most experienced of trekkers.

The trail traverses the terminal moraine above Gaumukh before rising abruptly up a very steep track up the side ridge to Tabovan. Care must be taken on this section not to dislodge rocks and boulders onto the trekkers below. This should be especially noted by the groups of students completing this section as a day trek out of Gaumukh, who seem oblivious to the danger they put themselves and others in as they try to race each other down the ridge after visiting Tabovan.

After the climb, **Tabovan** (4450m) is a very pleasant surprise. It is a large meadow complete with bubbling streams and wildflowers and camp sites set beneath the imposing peak of Shivling (6543m). On the far side of the glacier the Bhagirathi peaks, including Bhagirathi I (6856m), Bhagirathi II (6512m) and Bhagirathi III (6454m), provide an equally impressive backdrop. It is little wonder that sadhus choose this spot for extended meditation during the long summer months.

From Tabovan there is an option of crossing the Gangotri Glacier to the camp at **Nandanban** (4340m). The route from Tabovan down and onto the glacier leads from the upper section of the meadow. It takes three to four hours to cross the Gangotri Glacier, plus an additional hour to climb up the scree to Nandanban.

From here it is a further two hours back down to the lateral moraine on the far side of the valley to Gaumukh. This option should not be undertaken without an experienced local guide, nor by groups with no previous experience of crossing glaciers. The route is icy and crevassed and is not a viable option for the novice trekker.

If returning to Gaumukh the same day, watch the weather conditions. They can change very rapidly, making the return trek to Gaumukh something of an epic.

Getting Away

From Gangotri there are local buses to Uttarkashi which take six to seven hours and cost Rs 50. The last bus from Uttarkashi to Haridwar leaves around 2 pm. Alternatively, the trek to Gaumukh can easily be combined with a trek out of Uttarkashi to Dodi Tal or Hanuman Chatti.

Joshimath

The town of Joshimath (1890m), in the Chamoli district of Garhwal, is above the confluence of the Dhauli Ganga and the Alaknanda River. A small temple and an ancient tree just above the town mark the place where the famous Hindu philosopher Shankara gained enlightenment. Many Hindu pilgrims pay homage here before proceeding to Badrinath.

Joshimath was once a thriving town for trekkers and expeditions requiring staff and porters before entering the Nanda Devi Sanctuary. But with the closing of the sanctuary in 1983, there has been a lull in activity. However, many alternative treks can still be organised out of Joshimath, and if time is not at a premium, a visit can also be made to Badrinath, 40 km up the Alaknanda Valley.

Treks
Valley of Flowers & Hem Kund
(introductory; 4 stages)
Joshimath to Ghat via the Kuari Pass
(introductory; 5 stages)
Ghat to Mundoli via Rup Kund
(moderate; 7 stages)

History
The passes and terrain north of Joshimath have been followed by pilgrims and traders since the 9th century, when Shankara travelled up the Alaknanda Valley and established a seat of learning or *matha* at Badrinath. Traders continued further north, exploring the Zanskar Range for accessible passes into Tibet. They would undoubtedly have discovered both the Niti and the Mana passes.

This information was first conveyed to European explorers in 1808 when the Bengal Survey led by Lieutenant Webb provided the first reliable geographical data on the region. Passed on to Calcutta, it would have been of interest to William Moorcroft who, nine years later, followed the Alaknanda Valley to its source before crossing the Niti Pass into Tibet.

The trek to Rup Kund, at the base of Trisul, would have been familiar to pilgrims and villagers from the Garhwal for many centuries. The lake is steeped in tradition, with pilgrims undertaking the Raj Jat, the important pilgrimage to pay homage to Nanda Devi, every 12 years.

It was on one of these earlier pilgrimages that over 300 pilgrims perished in a storm. Skeletons of the dead were preserved in the icebound lake. Recent analysis has dated the bones at around the 14th century.

The trek over the Kuari Pass was popularised by Lord Curzon when he was Viceroy of India. During his time as viceroy, he undertook several treks in the Garhwal, including one over the Kuari Pass to Joshimath. The party had been trekking for some weeks when they were attacked by a swarm of bees in a village just before the Kuari Pass. The trek was abandoned, but the Kuari Pass is often referred to as the Curzon Pass as a token of the respect the local people held for the viceroy.

In 1931, after the first ascent of Kamet, Frank Smythe, the noted British mountaineer and botanist, trekked the Bhyundar Valley and was so impressed by the wildflowers that he described it as the Valley of Flowers. He returned in 1937, crossed the Kuari Pass before reaching the Bhyundar Valley, climbed Nilgiri Parbat (6474m) and attempted Rataban (6166m) before meeting up with fellow climber Peter Oliver to climb Mana Peak (7272m). They then crossed the Zanskar Pass to Badrinath and attempted Nilkanth (6596m) before ascending the Ramani Gorge to attempt Dunagiri (7066m). They also had plans on the east summit of Nanda Devi – all in one three-month season. Smythe's book *The Valley of Flowers* includes an account of these expeditions.

The sacred lake of Hem Kund attracts many thousands of Sikh pilgrims each year. In the Sikh holy book, the *Granth Sahib*, the Sikh guru Govind Singh recounts how in a previous life he meditated on the shores of a lake surrounded by seven snow-capped mountains. Hem Kund, according to the Sikhs, fitted the description and was designated the holy lake. Nowadays, many thousands of Sikhs complete the trek to the shores of the lake to immerse themselves in the icy waters.

When to Trek
This region of the Garhwal attracts heavy snows during winter; indeed, Auli, just above Joshimath to the south, is one of the most popular ski resorts in northern India. The snows do not begin to melt on the upper elevations (over 3000m) until May, and the

Nanda Devi Sanctuary

Nanda Devi (7816m) is the highest peak situated completely within India. It is surrounded by a huge circle of mountain walls with only one outlet where the Rishi Ganga forges a route through deep, almost impenetrable gorges before flowing into the Alaknanda River. Given these natural defences, it was not until 1934 that the first mountaineers were finally able to reach the base of Nanda Devi.

In the 1830s GW Traill, the first commissioner of Kumaon, explored the glacial systems to the south and east of the sanctuary. He ascended the Pindari Glacier and crossed the Pindari Kanda (known also as Traills Pass) to the Gori Ganga. However, neither he nor the parties that also took this route in the following decades attempted to enter the sanctuary.

In 1883 WW Graham, a distinguished climber of his time, attempted a route following the course of the Rishi Ganga. The small expedition managed to make its way over the Dharansi Pass (4667m), a small ridge just to the north of the Rishi Ganga, before heading down the steep, slippery slopes to the junction of the Rishi Ganga and the Ramani River. Here they discovered that the Nanda Devi Sanctuary consisted of an inner and outer sanctuary. They had reached the outer sanctuary, with access to the north up the Ramani Glacier to Changabang and Dunagiri, while to the south a huge glacier flowed from the base of Trisul. However, the inner sanctuary and the base of Nanda Devi were further up the Rishi Ganga through a formidable gorge.

In 1905 the British mountaineer Dr GT Longstaff explored a possible route to the east of the sanctuary, climbing a pass (the Longstaff Col), south of Nanda Devi East (7434m). This route, however, proved to be unfeasible with a series of steep ice cliffs falling away into the inner sanctuary. Longstaff returned two seasons later in May 1907. This time he followed the route over the Dharansi Pass but was defeated by the spring snow that had not yet melted. Undeterred, the small party made its way north to the Bagini Glacier and over the Bagini Pass (6128m), a high pass between Dunagiri and Changabang. The party then descended the Ramani Glacier to the Rishi Ganga to the point reached by WW Graham's party in 1883. Faced with the same problems of finding a route up this section of the Rishi Gorge, the party directed its efforts to exploring the outer sanctuary with Longstaff making the first ascent of Trisul (7120m) later that season.

In 1932 Hugh Ruttledge explored the possibility of reaching the inner sanctuary via a pass at the head of the Sunderdhunga Glacier. The attempt was unsuccessful with reports of a huge 3000m icewall at the head of the glacier.

In 1934 HW Tilman and Eric Shipton together with their three Sherpas attempted the route up the Rishi Ganga. After reaching the confluence of the Ramani River and the Rishi Ganga, they forged a route through the Rishi Gorge to become the first party to enter the inner sanctuary and the base of Nanda Devi. Later that season they returned to recce a climbing route up Nanda Devi before heading south over the Sunderdhunga Col and Sunderdhunga Glacier, which drew unqualified applause from the climbing circles of the day.

Two seasons later, in 1936, while Shipton was engaged on Everest, Tilman and a group of American mountaineers made the first successful ascent of Nanda Devi, before exiting via the Longstaff Col to the Gori Ganga. Three seasons later, in June 1939, a Polish expedition made the first ascent of Nanda Devi East (7434m) climbing a route via the Longstaff Col.

However, it was not until the postwar years that increasing numbers of expeditions entered the sanctuary. In particular, the lifting of the inner line restrictions in 1974 resulted in a large number of climbing expeditions and trekkers making their way up the Rishi Ganga. Within a few seasons the large herds of bharal and musk deer were forced from their natural habitat, and there was wholesale destruction of the birch trees – either cut down for bridge construction or to provide fuel for camp fires when groups returned to base camp.

Mounting environmental pressure finally led the UP government to close the sanctuary in 1983. Since then the forest guards at Lata village, below the Dharansi Pass, have not permitted expeditions or local shepherds with their flocks inside the sanctuary. Whatever the future plans of the government, it is unlikely that the inner sanctuary will be reopened in the near future. Even if it were to reopen, trekking and climbing groups would be carefully controlled to ensure that there was minimum impact on the fragile environment. ■

villagers do not normally cross the Kuari Pass until the beginning of June. By contrast, the trails between the villages to the south of the Kuari Pass are normally passable for most of the year. The trek between Ghat and Loharjang can be completed from April onwards, although the excursion to Rup Kund is normally under snow until the end of June and sometimes well into July. To the north of Joshimath, the Valley of Flowers and the trek to Hem Kund can normally be done from May until the end of June.

The monsoon rains commence in early July and continue through August until the first week in September. The moist monsoon clouds push up the Alaknanda Valley before meeting the drier air currents from the Tibetan plateau. According to Frank Smythe's accounts, during the climbing season in 1937, 'there were the occasional clear spells through July to early August, but from then on there was hardly a clear day between then and the middle of September'. This, unfortunately, is the best time to appreciate the wildflowers in the Valley of Flowers and on the *bugyals* (high-altitude meadows) above Joshimath.

The post-monsoon period, from mid-September to the end of October, is a period of settled weather and the ideal time for trekking before the first of the winter snows fall in late October or early November.

Trekking Agents

Auli Mountain Treks near the GMVN hotel can supply Nepalese porters and staff. Nanda Devi Travels, otherwise known as Garhwal Mountain Services, has its office in the Nanda Devi hotel and provides a similar service.

Accommodation in Joshimath

The *GMVN hotel* in Joshimath, directly above the main bazaar, is run by friendly staff, although the rooms are dark, dank and in need of upkeep. The room tariff ranges from Rs 150 to Rs 200.

Accommodation on the Trail

There are many hotel-cum-lodges at Ghangaria on the trek to Hem Kund and the Valley of Flowers. On the trek over the Kuari Pass there is a *GMVN hotel* at Auli, mainly catering for the winter ski season. There are also *Forest Rest Houses* in most of the villages on the route to Ghat. However, there is no convenient shelter near the Kuari Pass, so a tent is necessary.

On the trek to Rup Kund there are lodges or *Forest Rest Houses* at Ramni, Sutol and Wan and *GMVN hotels* at Wan and Loharjang. The rest houses charge around Rs 50 per room and the GMVN hotels between Rs 180 and Rs 220 (room only). Above Wan, at Badni Bugyal, there is a basic hut maintained by the Forest Department. The official rate is Rs 15, but expect to pay at least Rs 50 if you want to get the surly chowkidar to take the lock off the door. There are also basic shelter huts at Bhugu Basa, immediately below Rup Kund. However, given the condition of the huts, it's advisable that you bring your own tent.

Trekking Advice

There are no particular problems with the trek over the Kuari Pass, for the trail up to the pass is well maintained by the local villagers throughout the season. The same applies to the trek to Rup Kund, although the higher stages of the trek, in the vicinity of the lake, are demanding and often remain under snow until mid-July. Even later in the season, the rock ridges are icy in the morning and sturdy boots are the order of the day. The climb above Rup Kund to the Jyuri Gali involves a bit of a rock scramble, but should not present a problem to the sure-footed. Acclimatisation is a concern if commencing the trek from Loharjang and a few additional days should be reserved before ascending to Rup Kund (4450m).

The trek to Hem Kund is undertaken by many thousands of pilgrims each year, so there is little chance of getting lost. The lake is, however, at an altitude of 4330m, and for that reason most pilgrims descend quite rapidly to Ghangaria and Govind Ghat after completing their darshan at the lake.

Provisions

While most food and supplies can be purchased at Joshimath, it is worthwhile double-checking at Haridwar or Srinagar regarding the supplies of kerosene. Items such as dried fruit, tinned cheese and jam should be brought from Haridwar or Delhi. Note: in spite of signs to the contrary, neither the banks nor the local agents in Joshimath can change foreign currency. It is best to change all necessary money before leaving Delhi.

Horsemen & Porters

Porters hired out of Joshimath are very reliable and the agencies charge around Rs 100 per porter per day plus return days and transportation. If commencing the trek from Ghat, porters are also available for around the same rates. For treks to the Valley of Flowers, packhorses are available at Govind Ghat and cost around Rs 150 per horse for the stage to Ghangaria.

Access

For the trek over the Kuari Pass, there is a daily bus from Joshimath to Auli leaving around 10 am. It takes two hours and costs Rs 7.

For the trek to Hem Kund there is a regular bus service to Govind Ghat that costs Rs 7, while the local jeeps cost about Rs 300 one way.

For the trek from Ghat to Rup Kund it is necessary to catch one of the buses from Joshimath going to Nandaprayag. Here there are local jeeps, which can be hired on a per seat basis for Rs 25 for the 20 km drive to the trailhead at Ghat.

VALLEY OF FLOWERS & HEM KUND
Map: Uttarakhand Section 3 (pages 226-7)
Stage 1: Govind Ghat to Ghangaria
(Average walking time 7 hours)
Govind Ghat (1830m), on the true right bank of the Alaknanda River, includes some local hotels, tea houses, pilgrim shelters and ritual bathing areas, together with vendors selling colourful bangles and combs.

Cross the suspension bridge over the Alaknanda River and commence the 14 km stage to Ghangaria. The well-defined trail follows an easy gradient for the first few km. It becomes progressively steeper (and more slippery after rainfall). After passing the village of **Pulana** (2100m), the trail continues through mixed forest of oak, chestnut and bamboo before winding down to the dhabas at Bhyundar and the bridge over the Hem Ganga. After crossing the bridge, the trail remains on the true left side of the valley, gradually ascending to Ghangaria.

Ghangaria (3050m), also known as Govind Dham, is a large pilgrim complex, including a *gurdwara* (Sikh temple) with free board and lodging, some small hotel-cum-tea houses and a *GMVN hotel*. At the camping ground about one km below Ghangaria the GMVN has also established some fixed camps to cope with the pilgrim overflow.

Stage 2: Ghangaria to Hem Kund & Return
(Average walking time 8 hours return)
Cross the bridge above Ghangaria which fords the Hem Ganga as it descends from Hem Kund. Here the trail splits, with the smaller trail to the north leading to the Bhyundar Valley. The trail to Hem Kund climbs steeply beyond the tree line high above the river on the true right side of the valley. This six km stage can be completed in around three hours and there are some dhabas approximately halfway up to the lake.

Hem Kund (4330m) is encircled by high cliffs, although you have to climb the high ridges above the lake to get clear views of the snow-capped peaks of the main Himalaya. A Sikh temple beside the lake provides shelter for the pilgrims during inclement weather. After the ritual bathing, the majority of the pilgrims return to Ghangaria the same day.

Stage 3: Ghangaria to the Valley of Flowers & Return
(Average walking time 5 to 6 hours)
From Ghangaria, recross the bridge over the Hem Ganga and commence the climb to the entrance of the Bhyundar Valley. A forest checkpost just above the crossing charges a daily entrance fee of Rs 100 for foreigners and Rs 20 for Indian trekkers. There is also a Rs 50 camera fee. Note: no overnight camping is permitted inside the park.

About two to three km after the checkpost, the trail crosses the stream flowing from the Bhyundar Valley, then continues on the true right side. The five km climb is more gradual than the stage to Hem Kund. On the ascent, the trail enters a narrow gorge before the valley widens. There is a permanent snow bridge over one of the larger side streams, which marks the entrance to the Bhyundar Valley.

The Bhyundar Valley is a glacial valley about 10 km long and two km wide, at an altitude of between 3650m and 3950m. It is characterised by alpine glades, silver birch trees and rhododendrons, and is enclosed by Nar Parbat (5855m), Nilgiri Parbat (6474m), Rataban (6166m) and Ghori Parbat (6708m).

Some well-marked trails lead to flowered meadows which support a profusion of primulas, anemones, saxifrages, asters, gentians, marigolds and delphiniums. A minimum of three days is recommended to appreciate the multitude of flowering species. Since 1983, grazing has been banned in the park and there has been debate about whether this has had a detrimental effect on the variety of wildflowers. Unfortunately, the best time to appreciate the wildflowers is when the monsoon rains are at their heaviest in August. This is also the time when the mountain roads to Govind Ghat are subject to landslides.

Stage 4: Ghangaria to Govind Ghat
(Average walking time 5 hours)
The return trek to Govind Ghat can be completed in a morning, allowing sufficient time to return to Joshimath.

Getting Away
From Govind Ghat there are regular buses back to Joshimath for the onward connection to Srinagar and Haridwar.

JOSHIMATH TO GHAT VIA THE KUARI PASS
Map: Uttarakhand Section 3 (pages 226-7)
Stage 1: Joshimath to Chitraganta Meadow
(Average walking time 6 to 7 hours)
From Joshimath hire a jeep or catch the local bus for the 12 km drive to Auli. Alternatively, the trek rising 900m through the forest can be undertaken in two to three hours. **Auli** (2750m) is a small settlement which recently has developed into a thriving ski resort. It also supports a sizeable army camp.

From Auli, the distinctive summit profile

of Nanda Devi can be appreciated at the head of the sanctuary.

The trail from Auli heads up the hillside beyond the ski lift, before reaching a small oak and holly forest. Through the forest it passes a small temple before emerging at the base of an extensive series of meadows known as **Gurson Bugyal**. The shepherd trails are at times hard to follow, but local shepherds should put you right if you stray off the main trail.

There are no end of vantage points to appreciate the classic route up the Rishi Ganga into the Nanda Devi Sanctuary, and the trail via Lata and Lata Kharak to the Durashi Pass (4260m) can be appreciated on the far side of the valley.

The trail beyond Gurson Bugyal is steep in places, before an ascent over and around a rocky outcrop to a small lake situated alongside a well-constructed trail coming from Tabovan village.

From the lake the trail continues through a mixed pine and oak forest for two to three km before a short descent to the meadow at **Chitraganta** (3310m).

From the meadow, the impressive snow-capped ridge, including Chaukhamba I (7138m), II (7068m), III (6974m) and IV (6854m) can be appreciated beyond Joshimath.

The shepherds living near here are mostly from Rishikesh or Haridwar and graze their flocks of sheep and goats throughout summer. There is a small springline for replenishing your water supplies at the head of the meadow.

Stage 2: Chitraganta to Dakwani via Kuari Pass
(Average walking time 4 to 5 hours)
The trail ascends the ridge above Chitraganta. Some cairns mark the track, which is at present being upgraded by the villagers from Tabovan. Just below the pass, the trail leads through a large meadow affording spectacular views of the Himalaya and Zanskar ranges. North of Joshimath are the Chaukhamba Range, Nilkanth (6596m) and Narayan Parbat (5965m); while the peaks of the Zanskar Range, including Mana Peak (7272m), Kamet (7756m) and Abi Gamin (7355m) extend to

UTTARAKHAND

the Tibet border. In the middle foreground, the main Himalayan chain in the vicinity of the Bhyundar Valley and Hem Kund includes Nilgiri Parbat (6474m), Rataban (6166m), Ghori Parbat (6708m) and Hathi Parbat (6727m). Dunagiri (7066m) dominates the peaks to the north of the Nanda Devi Sanctuary, which also include Changabang (6864m) and Kalanka (6931m).

There are many camp sites nearby, and a short stage from Chitraganta could be combined with a trek along the adjoining ridge that heads towards the Nanda Devi Sanctuary. Here there are possible vantage points to view Nanda Devi's distinctive profile including the twin peaks of the main summit (7816m) and the east summit (7434m).

The **Kuari Pass** (3640m) is by no means demanding – just a small col in a grassy ridge. Looking south from the pass, there are impressive views across the forest ridges, while the small clearing at Dakwani can also be appreciated. The initial, steep 200m descent is difficult at the best of times and even more so when wet and slippery during the monsoon. Later in the season, unladen horses can be coaxed down the gully. The route then heads on the true right side of the gorge past a small shepherd encampment to a clearing at **Dakwani** (3300m), marking the upper limit of the mixed oak and pine forest.

Stage 3: Dakwani to Ghangri
(Average walking time 7 hours)
The forest trail descends to a small wooden bridge over the river flowing from the Kuari Pass. After crossing the bridge, the ascent is steep to a small ridge, before a short descent to an impressive waterfall. It is then a long and gradual ascent to **Sutoli** meadow (3420m). If considering reaching Sutoli direct from the Kuari Pass, allow two to 2½ hours to complete this stage.

The shepherds from the nearby villages tend their buffalo here during the summer months. There are clear views back to Dakwani and the Kuari Pass, while the tips of the peaks beyond Joshimath peep above the ridge to the west of the valley. From the meadow, the trail rounds a wooded ridge with views of

Nanda Ghunti (6309m) on the western rim of the Nanda Devi Sanctuary.

On the gradual descent to **Pana** (2950m), a prosperous village, there are some intermediary camp sites. Beyond the village, the trail crosses a small tributary by a concrete bridge. One km beyond this point the trail splits – the upper route leading to Irani village, the district headquarters, while the lower trail goes direct to Ghangri. The descent to the Brithi Ganga is steep and steamy in places with bamboo, tropical undergrowth and the occasional troop of monkeys. Cross the large suspension bridge over the river before a 200m ascent to Ghangri.

Ghangri (2000m) is a small village at the entrance to the upper Brithi Ganga Valley. There is a well-maintained *rest house* immediately above the village. Alternatively, you may spend the night at the schoolhouse set in a well-maintained garden of marigolds. While wandering the village it makes a pleasant change not to hear calls of 'one pen' from the children.

The villagers at Ghangri take a full day to trek down valley to Chamoli; in winter they are cut off by snow between December and the end of February.

Stage 4: Ghangri to Ramni
(Average walking time 5 to 6 hours)
Climb for 450m up through the forest to a small clearing. Cross the clearing before a further ascent to a wooded ridge (2900m) marking the watershed between the Brithi Ganga and the Nandakini valleys. The time taken from Ghangri village to the pass is about four hours. On the pass there is a well-constructed cairn, while just below the ridge there is a camp site with views back across to Pana village.

From the pass, a gradual descent takes you through the pastures and forests where the villagers from Ramni graze their animals during the summer. After three to four km, the trail crosses an open meadow with views of Kunol village and the route to Wan and Rup Kund. To the north, the snow-capped ridges of the Chaukhamba Range are easily recognisable beyond Joshimath. There is also

GARRY WEARE

GARRY WEARE

Top: Atop Jyuri Gali above Rup Kund, Uttarakhand. The climb up here involves some rock scrambling.
Bottom: Scenic Har ki Dun camp, Uttarakhand, on the Sankri to Har ki Dun trek

GARRY WEARE

GARRY WEARE

GARRY WEARE

Top: The sacred peak of Padim (6691m) on the east ridge side of the Prek Valle
western Sikkim
Bottom Left: Forest trail above Yuksam, western Sikkim
Bottom Right: Bazaar below the former Tea Planters' Club, Darjeeling

a small springline for an ideal camp. **Ramni** village (2550m) includes a few shops serving the outlying villages, together with some tea shops. A *rest house* for overnight accommodation has been constructed just above the village.

Stage 5: Ramni to Ghat
(Average walking time 3 hours)
From Ramni, the trail to Ghat follows the wooded ridge before descending through coniferous and mixed forests. Remain on the true right side of the valley until the bridge over the Nandakini River takes you to the small village and dhabas at **Ghat** (1330m).

Getting Away
From Ghat local jeeps can be hired on a per seat basis, costing Rs 25 for the 20 km drive to Nandaprayag. From here, there are regular buses either up the valley and back to Joshimath or down to Srinagar and the connecting buses to Haridwar. Alternatively, you could continue from Ramni on the following trek to Rup Kund.

GHAT TO MUNDOLI VIA RUP KUND
Map: Uttarakhand Section 3 (pages 226-7)
Stage 1: Ghat to Ramni
(Average walking time 5 hours)
From Ghat (1330m) cross the bridge over the Nandakini River and commence the ascent to Ramni. The well-defined trail is steep in places before crossing a small ridge, the Bota Khal, over to the village of **Ramni** (2550m). There is a choice of staying in the village *rest house* or camping above the village to gain views of the Chaukhamba Range and the peaks beyond Joshimath.

Stage 2: Ramni to Sutol
(Average walking time 6 to 7 hours)
A well-defined trail leads high above the river along the true right side of the Nandakini Valley. **Ali** (2350m) is the first of a number of well-maintained and friendly villages. Some of the more prosperous houses have commissioned ornate woodcarvings

above their entrance doors, such as statues of Ganesh (the elephant-headed god). A tourist hut is being built. From Ali, the trail gradually ascends to the small village of **Pehri** (2500m), then descends to a tributary. From the bridge it is a further five km on to **Sutol** (2200m). The village is quite substantial, with some lodges and a store. Just beyond the village there is an excellent camp site beside the Nandakini River.

Stage 3: Sutol to Wan
(Average walking time 5 hours)
From Sutol the forest trail ascends to Kunol. Steep in places, the trail is lined with orchids and luxuriant ferns as it passes through one of the finest mixed forests in Garhwal. Barking deer have been seen in the forest clearing, while the heavy, spiked collars worn by the shepherd dogs indicate a need for protection from forest leopards.

The village at **Kunol** (2650m) is set in an idyllic location with views of the high peaks north of Joshimath. It has a *Forest Rest House*. Above the village, the rhododendron trees remain in full bloom from April till the beginning of June.

To reach Wan, there is a small ridge pass (2900m) to cross. The pass is not demanding to climb and the views of the main Himalaya to the north are complemented with impressive views south down the Badni Ganga towards the Indian plains. Immediately below the pass is the sizable village of **Wan** (2450m). If continuing on to Rup Kund there is no need to descend to the village. There is a *Forest Rest House* about 100m above Wan, together with a *GMVN hotel* run by a helpful chowkidar. The village temple is just above the Forest Rest House.

Option: Wan to Mundoli
From Wan, it is a four hour trek down the valley to the trailhead at Mundoli. For trekkers coming from Mundoli, this trek stage can easily be completed in a morning. From Wan, the trek to Rup Kund follows the same stages whether coming from Mundoli or Ghat.

UTTARAKHAND

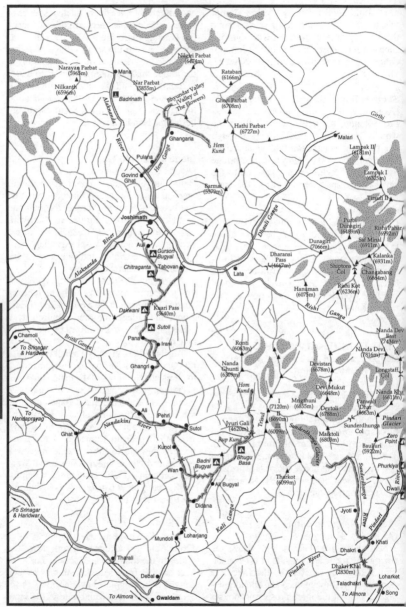

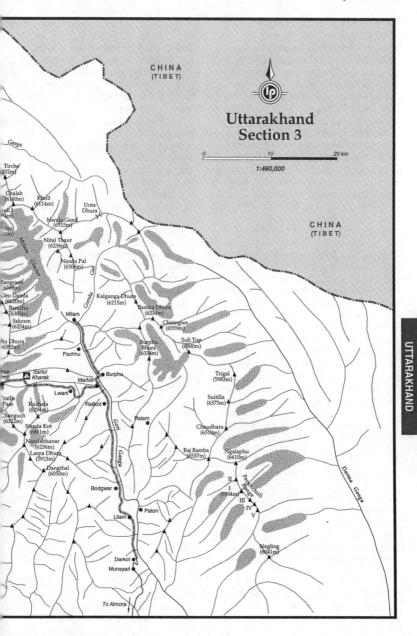

Stage 4: Wan to Badni Bugyal

(Average walking time 5 hours)

From the Forest Rest House follow the trail down the valley for one km. Here the trails diverge, with the upper one leading to Badni Bugyal. Ascend this trail for two km to an open meadow and a small temple with views of Trisul at the head of the valley. This is an excellent camp site with a good water supply.

From the meadow, there is a short descent to a small tributary, before commencing the long ascent to Badni Bugyal. The trail through the forest is steep in places. Here a welcome break on my trek was enlivened by watching jungle cats climbing the tallest oak trees. The oaks persist to around 3000m, and the pines and rhododendrons thin out at 3200m. This marks the upper limit of the forest, as there are no silver birch trees in this region of Garhwal. The 800m climb through the forest takes around three hours. It is a further three km across the meadows to Badni Bugyal.

The alpine camp at **Badni Bugyal** (3350m) rivals the best in the Himalaya. To the west and north-west, the views of the Himalaya stretch as far as the peaks in the vicinity of Gangotri, while the Chaukhamba Range and the peaks beyond Joshimath are also visible. To the north-east, the peaks of Trisul and Nanda Ghunti rise above the alpine ridges. The wildflowers in the meadows remain in bloom until mid-September and are, by all accounts, magnificent during the monsoon in July and August. Just above the meadow is a small temple where pilgrims make their offerings en route to Rup Kund. There are a few huts for shelter nearby.

Unfortunately there are also some ugly concrete pillars in the centre of the meadow to provide support for canvas shelters used by the pilgrims. It seems incredible that such a beautiful meadow should be so scarred when it would be a simple matter to bring mess tents up on packhorses a day or two before the pilgrims were due to arrive.

Stage 5: Badni Bugyal to Bhugu Basa

(Average walking time 4 to 5 hours)

From camp, there is a gradual climb up and along the north-east ridge towards Trisul. After one to 1½ hours, the trail reaches a cairn overlooking Badni Bugyal. To the north, uninterrupted views of Trisul and Nanda Ghunti can be appreciated. Here the trail splits. A route to the west leads eventually to Sutol, while the higher trail heads north towards Rup Kund.

The Rup Kund trail follows the contours for about three km before ascending steeply in places to a small temple on the ridge. This ridge is an extension of the one crossed between Sutol and Wan, and marks the divide between the catchments of the Badni Ganga and the Nandakini River. After making an offering at the entrance to the temple and ringing the temple bell, descend gradually to the camp at Bhugu Basa.

Compared with the beauty of Badni Bugyal, it is hard to imagine a more desolate, boulder-strewn camp site than that of **Bhugu Basa** (4100m). It is exposed to icy northern winds which whip around the stone shelter huts. If you choose to stay in the small, sheltered camp site about half a km beyond the huts, it is necessary to retrace your steps to the limited water supply.

Stage 6: Bhugu Basa to Rup Kund & return to Badni Bugyal

(Average walking time 7 to 8 hours)

After savouring the panoramic views of the main Himalaya, the 500m climb to the sacred waters of Rup Kund should take around two to three hours. The trail is often under snow until mid-July, making route-finding a problem. Even in the post-monsoon season there are some steep, rocky sections just before Rup Kund which may require a bit of scrambling.

Rup Kund (4450m) is 50m below the trail at the head of the valley. It has no outflow, and the human bones remaining beneath the surface are a reminder of the time when a party of pilgrims was trapped by bad weather in the 14th century.

An onward climb to the pass of **Jyuri Gali** (4620m) is steep and requires a few hand-holds in places. From the pass, there are superb views of Trisul and Nanda Ghunti.

The pass marks the divide between the headwaters of Rup Kund and Hom Kund, the main sources of the Nandakini River. **Hom Kund** (4060m) is on the far side of the opposite valley, and to reach the lake there takes a further three to four hours. An overnight camp would therefore be necessary before returning via Jyuri Gali the following day.

From Rup Kund it takes about 1½ hours to return to Bhugu Basa and a further 2½ to three hours back to Badni Bugyal.

Stage 7: Badni Bugyal to Mundoli

(Average walking time 6 to 7 hours)
Follow the trail to the south of Badni Bugyal and cross the alpine grazing meadows to Ali Bugyal. The views are again magnificent, both across to Joshimath and south to the Indian plains.

The trail from Ali Bugyal splits in places, and a local shepherd may have to point you in the direction of the trail which descends steeply through the forest to the village of **Didana** (2450m). A further descent to the substantial bridge over Badni Ganga meets the main trail coming from Wan. A gradual ascent through pine, fir, oak and bamboo forest and past cascading side streams takes you to the ridge-top dhabas and the *GMVN hotel* at **Loharjang** (2150m). From here it is a short descent to the trailhead at **Mundoli** (1970m).

Getting Away

There is a local bus service from Mundoli to Debal. It takes two to three hours and costs Rs 15. Alternatively, jeeps are available. They are faster than the bus, and cost Rs 30 per seat. From Debal the overnight bus service direct to Delhi costs Rs 180. The service is irregular, however, so it is advisable to continue by local bus to Tharali, then on to Karanprayag for the daily bus service to Haridwar.

Alternatively, the bus service from Tharali via Gwaldam to Almora takes seven to eight hours and costs Rs 50. An overnight bus from Almora to Delhi costs Rs 110.

Almora

Almora (1650m) was founded some 400 years ago as the capital of the Chand rajahs of Kumaon. Like Mussoorie it affords uninterrupted views of the main Himalaya Range. It also is a convenient setting-off point for trekking to the Pindari Valley south of the Nanda Devi Sanctuary and to Munsyari and the Milam Glacier, a recently opened area east of Nanda Devi with a long trading history with Tibet.

Treks
Song to the Pindari Glacier
(introductory; 7 stages)
Munsyari to the Milam Glacier
(moderate; 7 stages)

History

The earliest exploration of the Nanda Devi region was from the south-east. In 1830 GW Traill, the first Deputy Commissioner of Kumaon, ascended the Pindari Glacier and crossed a high, glaciated pass (later named after him) that led to the upper Milam or Johar Valley. Exploration of the Johar Valley came later, in 1855, when Adolf and Robert Schlagintwent trekked the Milam Glacier before crossing into Tibet.

In 1905 Dr GT Longstaff, one of the world's leading mountaineers of the time, ascended the Milam Glacier during an epic season of climbing and exploring in the Nanda Devi region. During the late spring he ascended a col immediately to the south of Nanda Devi East. However the descent on the far side of the pass was considered too steep and dangerous, so his party returned to the Johar Valley before turning to the approach up the Rishi Ganga (out of Joshimath) in 1907.

In 1932 Hugh Ruttledge made an unsuccessful attempt to enter the Nanda Devi Sanctuary via a possible pass at the head of the Sunderdhunga Valley. The pass was crossed two years later in 1934 by Tilman and Shipton after they completed their exploration of the Nanda Devi Sanctuary. Their traverse over the Sunderdhunga Col was made from the north and was by no means straightforward, involving a technically demanding 2000m descent over two and a half days to the safety of the Sunderdhunga Valley.

When to Trek
The ideal time to trek in either the Johar or the Pindari valleys is during the pre or post-monsoon season. While the villagers from the upper Pindari Valley cross the low passes to Song for 10 months of the year (from mid-February till mid-December), heavy snow conditions preclude trekking to the Pindari Glacier until the beginning of May. The trekking season continues until mid-June, when the onset of the monsoon generally precludes trekking until mid-September. The post-monsoon season, from mid-September till mid-October, is an ideal time to trek before the onset of the first winter snows in the upper reaches of the Pindari Valley.

A similar pattern exists in the nearby Johar Valley, with the villagers and the local shepherds migrating up the valley towards the Milam Glacier from May onwards. While most of the Johar Valley is subject to the monsoon, the higher reaches, including the village of Milam, are beyond the influence of the heaviest of the rains that fall in July and August. From mid-September till mid-October the weather conditions become clear and sunny and the shepherds begin to make their way down to the villages of the Munsyari district, where they live throughout winter.

Trekking Agents
Almora Along the Mall there are several agencies, including Shivaya Trekking & Tours, Discover Himalaya Treks & Tours, High Adventure and Ridge & Trek. At best they can organise porters, but there is no shortage of porters in Song and Munsyari.

Song & Loharket While there are no recognised local agencies, the local porters will soon make themselves known. Alternatively, the manager of the UKD Tourist Rest House at Loharket seems to have plenty of contacts and can strike a fair deal.

Munsyari In the main bazaar you will find Panch Chuli Trekking, Nanda Devi Trekking and Devandra Jyoti Treks & Tours. All of these can assist with porters and local guides.

Accommodation Before & After the Trek
Almora There is no shortage of hotels on the Mall, and rooms are available even during the peak season as the town does not attract the numbers that visit nearby Nainital. The *Holiday Home* run by the Kumaon Mandal Vikas Niwas (KMVN) is a safe bet for the night with clean doubles for around Rs 400. The dining room has good vegetarian food and a sign insisting that 'self cooking is not allowed'!

Song There are no hotels or rest houses in Song. So if you want to spend the first night in a local lodge or rest house before commencing the Pindari Glacier trek you must head for Loharket, where there is a *PWD Rest House* charging Rs 100 per room and some lodges, including the *UKD Tourist Rest House*, charging Rs 50 per room.

Munsyari This is a picturesque town where you can spend a night or two before commencing the Milam Glacier trek. At present there are a couple of very basic lodges in the main bazaar. There is also the *Martolia Lodge*, run by a local retired police officer, Mr Martolia, who is a very considerate host. The lodge is two km from the bazaar on the road heading north-east towards the Johar Valley. It only has three rooms, but there is space to camp in the garden. Rooms are Rs 100 per double while camping is Rs 50 per tent. A *KMVN hotel* is also being constructed and will be open by spring 1997, with rooms for around Rs 500 a double.

Accommodation on the Trail
Pindari Glacier Trek There are *KMVN hotels* and *PWD Rest Houses* on the trek to the Pindari Glacier at Loharket, Dhakri, Khati, Dwali and Phurkiya. The PWD rooms are Rs 100 a double for foreigners and Rs 50 for Indian trekkers. A bed in the dormitories at

KMVN hotels costs Rs 50, while rooms are Rs 100 a double. There are private lodges at Dhakri, Khati and also at the village of Jyoti on the trek to Sunderdhunga.

Milam Glacier Trek There are rudimentary *PWD Rest Houses* at Lilam, Bodgwar and Milam. There are also private lodges at Lilam, Railkot and Martoli. At Milam there is the renovated *Deepu's Guest House* run by one of Nain Singh's grandsons, who lives there in summer. The house is at the upper end of the village, en route to the Milam Glacier.

Trekking Advice
Timing is all important if you are undertaking the Pindari Glacier trek. During the school holidays in May there can be over 100 students each day completing the stages to the glacier. They stay at the PWD or KMVN hotels, so there is little chance of a room, or time to collect your thoughts. If you have no option but to trek at this time, then bring your own tent and gear so you have the choice of camping away from the lodges/hotels.

There are far fewer trekkers to the Milam Glacier, although this may change with the recent changes in the trekking regulations. Nowadays there is no need to trek in a group or for the arrangements to be made through an agency. Neither do foreign trekkers need to apply for permission to the Ministry of Home Affairs in Delhi, or to the local magistrate in Munsyari; all they need is their passport. However, Indian trekkers, including any porters or staff from outside of the Munsyari region, need a special permit, which can be obtained in an hour or so from the local magistrate in Munsyari. Passports and permits are inspected at Milam by the Indo-Tibetan Police Force (ITBP).

Provisions
There is no shortage of tea stalls and lodges on the Pindari Glacier trek. Biscuits and basics can also be purchased, although fresh vegetables, fruit and luxuries including tinned food should be brought from Almora.

Food supplies in the Johar Valley, en route to the Milam Glacier, are less reliable. Indeed,

in 1996 it was a pleasant surprise to find that you couldn't buy a bottle of Coke or Limca, even in Munsyari. Buying kerosene was a problem; it has to be brought from Almora or Bageshwar, together with all luxury food items. On the trail, biscuits, dried milk and sugar are available from the local tea stalls and lodges, as well as potatoes and the very occasional egg. Other vegetables and fruit must be purchased in Munsyari.

Horsemen & Porters
Song & Loharket There is an ample supply of porters here, even during the high season in May; they each carry 25 kg and cost Rs 100 per day. Packhorses are an alternative and cost around Rs 130 to Rs 140 per horse per day. They cannot, however, be used on the trek to the Sunderdhunga Glacier.

Munsyari The porters here have yet to prove their reliability. Even after deals have been struck, there is no guarantee that they will stick to their word. The rates are worked out in terms of *paraos*, the local term for a trek stage. The problem is that some paraos involve just a few hours walking and you can sometimes cover two of these stages in a day. The current rate is Rs 75 per parao for carrying loads up to, but not exceeding, 20 kg. Add the commission to the local agent on top of this, and you can be in for a comparatively expensive trek. Horses are an alternative; budget on Rs 140 per parao.

Access
Song There are regular buses each day from Almora to Bageshwar. The drive takes three to four hours and costs Rs 45. From Bageshwar there are two buses a day to Song that cost Rs 16. The normal alternative is to hire a seat in a jeep; this costs Rs 20 and takes around two hours. A full jeep will be around Rs 250 to Rs 300. The jeeps will go beyond Song to the roadhead at Loharket, but for this leg they can only be hired on a full-jeep basis for around Rs 100 one way.

Munsyari The direct bus from Almora to Munsyari takes 10 hours and costs Rs 110.

UTTARAKHAND

Jeeps cost from Rs 800 to Rs 1000 and take around seven to eight hours.

SONG TO THE PINDARI GLACIER
Map: Uttarakhand Section 3 (pages 226-7)
Stage 1: Song to Dhakri
(Average walking time 6 to 7 hours)
The small bazaar at **Song** (1400m) is, at present, as far as buses and trucks can go, although jeeps can zigzag up the hillside for a further four or five km to the village of Loharket.

From above the main bazaar in Song, a well-marked stone trail ascends the two km to **Loharket** (1600m). The trail meets the roadhead near the *PWD Rest House*, while there is an adequate camp site close to the stream that flows through the village.

From Loharket the trail is, in places, being upgraded into a jeep track which continues to the *PWD Rest House* at **Dhukri** (1800m). From here it passes through an evergreen forest of quercus oak and horse chestnut before ascending to the small Hindu temple at **Taladhakri** (2300m). This is the halfway point on the ascent to the Dhakri Khal. One km beyond the temple there is a camp site (and a good stopping point if you commence the trek from Song at midday).

Beyond Taladhakri the trail winds up through meadows and rhododendron forest that bloom by the end of April. The gradient of the trail lessens towards the Dhakri Khal and there is a welcome tea stall just below the pass.

The impressive views from the **Dhakri Khal** (2830m) include Trisul, Devtoli, Maiktoli and Nanda Khat along the southern rim of the Nanda Devi Sanctuary, together with Nanda Kot rising high above the Pindari Glacier.

From the Dhakri Khal there is also an opportunity to gain uninterrupted views of the main Himalaya. Higher vantage points are reached by ascending the forested ridge south-east of the pass that leads to a series of bugyals where shepherds from the nearby villages graze their flocks throughout summer. The one hour ascent from the pass will be well rewarded with fine views of the Himalaya

that extend from Joshimath to the Panchchuli Range beyond Munsyari.

The meadow of **Dhakri** (2680m) lies just below the pass. A number of huts, including the *KMVN hotel* and the *PWD Rest House*, have been constructed in the centre of the meadow with three or four other lodges. These buildings are an unfortunate eyesore, and the nearby forest is being destroyed for construction and cooking. The water supply for the meadow is immediately west of the meadow, where there are alternative camp sites.

Stage 2: Dhakri to Dwali
(Average walking time 6 to 7 hours)
From Dhakri the trail descends steeply in places past a series of settlements and fields of potato and barley. Views up the Sunderdhunga Valley are impressive, including the huge ice wall at the head of the valley. After three or four km the trail diverts east and follows the contours through beautiful forest and meadow glades to the village of **Khati** (2250m), the largest village in the region. Most of the houses in the village have been fitted with solar panels, which eventually will be introduced to the other villages in the upper Pindari Valley. Khati is also the trekking-off point to the Sunderdhunga Valley.

One km beyond Khati the forest trail passes a *KNVN hotel* before winding high above the Pindari River. After five km the valley widens and the trail drops down to the valley floor. Here there are a few tea stalls beside a well-constructed wooden bridge over the Pindari River. Cross the bridge to the true right side of the valley and continue for a further four km to **Dwali** (2650m).

Dwali is above the confluence of the Pindari River and the river flowing from the Kafni Glacier. Cross the Pindari River by the wooden bridge just above the confluence of the two rivers and ascend to the *PWD Rest House*. Alternatively, there is a comfortable camp site immediately below the PWD Rest House, beside the Pindari River.

Stage 3: Dwali to Phurkiya
(Average walking time 2½ to 3 hours)
    This short stage is ideal for accli-

matisation before continuing to the Pindari Glacier.

From Dwali the trail ascends through mixed forest, past tumbling waterfalls, across residual snowfields (which remain until the end of July) and through flowered meadows. The peak of Nanda Khat appears at the head of the valley, while the tip of Nanda Devi East can just be seen.

Phurkiya (3250m) consists of a *PWD Rest House* and a *KMVN hotel* on the tree line. It also marks the point where the valley widens to a broad, U-shaped profile that extends to the Pindari Glacier.

Stage 4: Phurkiya to Pindari Glacier (Zero Point)
(Average walking time 3 to 4 hours)
Beyond Phurkiya the trail gradually ascends across a series of meadows set beneath the impressive flanks of Nanda Khat. The trail crosses some side streams and the assistance of a ski pole or ice axe is helpful, particularly early in the season when many of the gullies are still under snow. Following the spring snow melt, flocks of sheep and goats from the villages lower down the Pindari Valley are herded to these high pastures, where they remain until the temperatures begin to fall, which happens by mid-September.

The main shepherd encampment is about three km below the snout of the **Pindari Glacier** and is known as **Zero Point** (3650m). One km below Zero Point are a *PWD Rest House* and some lodges including one occupied by a friendly and informative sadhu who spends most of the year in this remote locality.

From the huts, the trail to Zero Point extends beside lateral moraine to where the Pindari River emerges from the glacier. From this vantage point the route to Traills Pass can be appreciated as well as unimpeded views of Nanda Khat, Changuch (6322m) and the formidable Nanda Kot at the head of the glacier.

While there is a steady stream of Indian students trekking to the Pindari Glacier in May and June, there are very few pilgrims. Given that the Pindari River is one of the main tributaries of the Ganges, this seems

surprising when one considers the thousands who trek to Yamunotri, Gaumukh, Kedarnath or Badrinath.

Stages 5 to 7: Return Trek to Song
The return trek to Song can be completed in three stages, the first back to Dwali, the second to Dhakri and the third to the roadhead, with time that day to continue by jeep or bus to Bageshwar and Almora.

Option: Sunderdhunga Glacier
(This option takes a minimum of three stages to complete.) If combining this option with a trek to the Pindari Glacier, it is necessary to return from the Pindari Glacier to the village of **Khati** (2250m). From Khati the trail heads steeply down to the Pindari River (2100m). There are two bridges to cross. The first crosses the Pindari River just above the confluence of the Pindari and the Sunderdhunga rivers, while the second crosses the Sunderdhunga River just above the confluence. The trail then remains on the true right side of the valley, ascending through mixed forest to the village of **Jyoti** (2450m).

Beyond Jyoti the trail winds high above the Sunderdhunga River with occasional glimpses towards the ice wall at the head of the valley. After four to five km the trail descends to the river bed. Until September 1995 the trail then crossed a meadow where villagers from Jyoti ran a couple of tea stalls throughout the season. However, after the floods in September 1995 most of the trail from this point to the alpine camp at **Sunderdhunga** was washed away. The new makeshift trail is hard to follow in places, including an initial strenuous ascent through the forest to bypass the Sunderdhunga River. Beyond this section the makeshift trail winds around the huge boulder fields across the river bed. It is estimated that it will take two to three seasons for the trail to be restored, and this should be taken into account when considering this option.

On reaching the camp at Sunderdhunga it is possible to continue to the sacred **Sukram Cave** and to the snout of the **Sunderdhunga Glacier** before returning to Jyoti and Khati.

MUNSYARI TO THE MILAM GLACIER
Map: Uttarakhand Section 3 (pages 226-7)

Stage 1: Munsyari to Lilam
(Average walking time 4 hours)
From the main bazaar at **Munsyari** (2290m) follow the road heading north-east towards the Johar Valley. The road is at present unsealed, while an alternative trail provides some short cuts to the roadhead just above the village of **Darkot** (1800m). From Darkot it's a steady descent to the Gori Ganga. The well-defined trail then follows the true right side of the river past a series of small villages. Here, some of the houses are constructed of bamboo, which provides some respite from the humid summer temperatures that reach the mid-30°Cs in the pre-monsoon season. There are also several tea stalls before the end of the short stage to the village of **Lilam** (1850m).

Stage 2: Lilam to Bodgwar
(Average walking time 6 to 7 hours)
From Lilam the main trail used to follow the Gori Ganga. However, during the heavy rains in September 1995 some of the trail was washed away so an alternative route needs to be followed for at least the next two seasons. This alternative trail climbs 1000m to a ridge high above Lilam before descending back down to the Gori Ganga to rejoin the main trail to Milam.

From Lilam ascend the trail past the ITBP camp to a small settlement (upper Lilam) where there is a small temple and a tea stall. The trail gradually winds up the open hillside and affords impressive views back to Munsyari. From early May onwards there is no end of activity as the shepherds from the Munsyari region lead their huge flocks of sheep or goats to the summer grazing pastures near Milam. At this time the goats are laden with saddlebags carrying potatoes, rice and seeds, or cement for construction.

The final 300m to the **Lilam Ridge** (2850m) goes up a narrow gully, and it is worth watching out for boulders occasionally dislodged by the flocks as they scurry up to the pass.

From Lilam Ridge there are panoramic views east towards the Panchchuli Range,

while to the north the steep gorges of both the Gori Ganga and its tributary the Rilam Gad indicate that the rivers are forging their way through the lower axis of the Great Himalaya. Just below the pass there is a bamboo tea stall, although the absence of a regular supply of water makes it difficult to camp here.

The trail descends first through rhododendrons and conifers and then through mixed forest of chestnut and bamboo to a small meadow overlooking the Gori Ganga River where remnants of the former trail direct from Lilam can be seen. Once down to the riverside you are back on the pre-September 1995 trail, and from here you ascend an impressive gorge where the waters of the Gori Ganga echo and thunder through an incredible series of rapids.

The trail through the gorge continues for four to five km up to the meadow of **Bodgwar** (2500m), which is nothing more than some shanty huts plus an ITBP Post and a *PWD Rest House*. If camping, it is advisable to continue for one km past the huts to a grassy ridge close to the main river.

Stage 3: Bodgwar to Martoli
(Average walking time 5 to 6 hours)
From Bodgwar the trail follows the course of the Gori Ganga through a further series of narrow gorges. Three km past Bodgwar there is a Hindu temple beneath a rock overhang. The trail then crosses a series of snow bridges that remain for most of season. Impressive waterfalls cascade down the cliff walls. After four or five km the gorge begins to widen, and after rounding a small meadow, the trail splits for a km or so. The higher and more substantial trail skirts high above a steep rock wall and is suitable for horses, while the lower trail, carved directly out of the rock face, is suitable only for trekkers and porters. This marks the upper limit of the Gori Ganga Gorge. Beyond here, the trail crosses a series of open meadows extending three or four km to the settlement of **Railkot** (3100m). Two km beyond Railkot the valley turns to the north and the first of the high mountain peaks beyond Milam can be appreciated.

Martoli (3430m) is on a grassy plateau high above the confluence of the Gori Ganga and the Lwanl Gad, the river flowing from Nanda Devi East. In its heyday the village would have supported several hundred people and included a school and some stores. This was a time when there was still a thriving trade with Tibet –which ended in 1962 when the border with Tibet was closed following the war between India and China.

Nowadays Martoli, like so many other villages in the upper Johar Valley, is practically deserted, its stone houses falling into total disrepair. The slate roofs on the houses have collapsed, while the once neatly constructed stone walls that enclosed the small gardens are in dire need of reconstruction. Even today only a handful of villagers make their way up the valley from Munsyari and the surrounding villages to spend the summer in Martoli or in the other villages between there and Milam.

Just above Martoli there is a small stone temple dedicated to Nanda Devi. The temple commands a view up the Lwanl Gad to the tip of Nanda Devi East and the peak of Nanda Kot. To the north, the peaks of Hardeol and Tirsuli can also be seen. Outside the temple is an impressive row of bells hanging from climbing rope attached to a prayer wall. Each bell was donated by a climbing expedition or a group of devotees from Munsyari to placate the goddess of the high mountains.

Beyond the temple there are several acres of conifer saplings planted over a decade ago by the Forestry Department. Other forestry projects are also being undertaken; much of the surrounding hillside would have suffered deforestation well before the borders with Tibet were closed.

Stage 4: Martoli to Milam
(Average walking time 4 hours)
This short and easy stage is one of the most spectacular for views of the high Himalaya, including the main peak of Nanda Devi.

From Martoli descend steeply to the bridge over the Lwanl Gad. The trail remains on the true right side of the valley for a further two km until it is opposite the settlement of **Burphu**

(3350m). Cross the solid wooden bridge over the Gori Ganga. Although the trail skirts below Burphu village, it is well worth the time to detour up the hillside as the village is one of the most active in this part of the Johar Valley.

Beyond Burphu several settlements dot the opposite side of the valley and are only occupied by a handful of shepherds from the Munsyari district from June until the end of September. One settlement in particular (that of Pachhu) attracts attention as the unmistakable profile of Nanda Devi and Nanda Devi East looms at the head of the Pachhu Valley. It is a magnificent sight in the early morning when the huge east face of Nanda Devi is visible.

Just beyond this vantage point, the trail to Milam continues past the settlement of Beiju, and from here it is a further three km to Milam (Mi Lam means 'man road'). The main settlement of Milam is just beyond the confluence of the Gori Ganga (which flows from the Milam Glacier) and the Goenka Gad (river), which flows from the north-east.

Milam (3450m) was the home of a number of the renowned Pundit explorers (see boxed text). It is also the last major settlement before Tibet. From Milam it is only one stage up the Goenka Valley to the base of the Unta Dhura, and the following day, after a series of three pass crossings (the Unta Dhura, the Jainta Dhura and the Kangri Bingri La), a trader or shepherd could be in Tibet.

In spite of the close association that the villagers of Milam have with Tibet, they are anxious not to be called Bhotia or Tibetan. The villagers trace their ancestry to the Rajput tribes who migrated from Rajasthan in the 12th century to settle in the hills of Uttarakhand. Later, at some time in the 16th century, they moved to the Munsyari region and established trading relations with Tibet that prospered for many generations until 1962.

HW Tilman's *The Ascent of Nanda Devi*, written in 1936, relates how trade was conducted each season. The local official from Tibet first visited Milam and checked that there were no endemic diseases in the valley before sanctioning the commencement of

UTTARAKHAND

UTTARAKHAND

The Pundits of the Johar Valley

The increasing importance of the Great Game in the 1860s made it imperative for the British to compile accurate surveys and gather political intelligence about the northern barriers of India and beyond, including the vast tracts of Tibet. There was no way, however, that imperial China would permit British survey officers to enter Tibet, let alone survey it. The Great Trigonometrical Survey of India Office (GTS), based in Dehra Dun, came up with the idea of training Indians who lived close to the Tibetan border and who were familiar with Tibetan customs and language to undertake the survey work on their behalf.

The villagers of the Johar Valley fitted the bill to a T. They had maintained trading relationships with Tibet for many generations and knew well the border regions where trade was conducted. In 1863 two educated young men were chosen to join the Survey. Nain Singh (Chief Pundit or No 1) and his cousin Mani Singh were sent for training in survey techniques at the Survey's headquarters at Dehra Dun. For two years the men were primed in the use of the sextant and the compass and the need to note the altitude by recording the temperature of boiling water. To calculate distance they were drilled to take exact steps and after every 100 steps to drop a bead in a modified Buddhist prayer wheel, which contained 100 rather than the traditional 108 beads. The prayer wheel was also modified to conceal their notes and calculations.

Nain Singh was the first to explore Tibet on behalf of the British. After a number of false starts (that resulted in his cousin Mani Singh retuning to Milam), he set off from Kathmandu in March 1865 disguised as a Ladakhi trader. On his journey he surveyed southern Tibet, including the Tsangpo Valley, Lhasa, Kailas and Manasorwar, before returning to Dehra Dun in June 1866. The following summer, in 1867, he was commissioned to return to Tibet with Mani Singh and another Pundit, Kailan Singh (designated GK). They left India by way of Badrinath and the Mana Pass, disguised as horse traders, and wandered in the vicinity of Kailas, confirming the source of the Indus and Sutlej rivers. This notable achievement gained due recognition for the Pundits and the Survey's work both in India and in the UK.

Once the courses of the Indus and the Sutlej were more or less determined, there was still much work to be completed on the course of the Tsangpo. This was Nain Singh's objective when he undertook his last journey in July 1874. Setting out from Leh, in Ladakh, he was to cross southern Tibet and the lower course of the Tsangpo as far as Assam to complete a journey of over 2000 km. Although he was not able to completely ascertain the lower course of the Tsangpo, it was a commendable effort. On returning to India, he enjoyed a comfortable retirement until his death in 1895.

Kishen Singh (AK), another of Nain Singh's cousins from the Johar Valley, also played an important role in the Survey. After undertaking his training in 1867, he embarked on his first important journey in 1872, exploring the ground between Shigatse and north of Lhasa. In April 1878 he returned to Tibet, travelling via Sikkim and Bhutan to Lhasa, before heading north to Mongolia. He returned south by a difficult route that took him along the lower course of the Tsangpo, before returning to Lhasa and eventually to Darjeeling in November 1882, after his family and the Survey had given him up for dead. His account mark was to add much to the knowledge of the northern regions of Tibet and the course of the Tsangpo below Lhasa.

A question mark still remained about whether the Tsangpo and the Brahmaputra in India were in fact the same river. The formidable terrain between the known course of the Tsangpo and the Brahmaputra had been the subject of considerable speculation, and was the objective for a number of Pundits, including the remarkable Kinthup, from Sikkim.

Leaving Sikkim in October 1878, Kinthup undertook an epic journey through Tibet that included being sold twice into slavery. In spite of these rigours he described the course of the Tsangpo as it rounded the huge peak of Namche Barwa (7745m) and the deep gorge country to within a short distance of the Indian foothills. However, on his return to India four years later, the lack of authentic details discredited his report. It was not until 1912, when the Tsangpo Gorge was finally explored, that Kinthup's report was finally given the recognition it deserved, just a few months before he died.

For more detailed accounts of the work of the Pundits, Indra Singh Rawat, a local surveyor from the Johar Valley, has written the detailed *Indian Explorers of the 19th Century*, published by the government of India in 1970. Interested parties are trying to establish a museum in Munsyari to record the travels of the famous Pundits from Milam. Contact Mr US Martolia (Retired Police Officer), c/- Post Office Munsyari, District: Pithoragarh, Uttar Pradesh, for details and to make donations. ■

trade. From then on, grains such as wheat, barley and rice were carried over the passes into Tibet and exchanged for salt, hardy Tibetan ponies and wool – the last, by far the most important commodity. By September, trade was completed and the villagers from around

Milam would return down the Johar Valley to spend the winter months.

Nowadays limited trade has resumed between Milam and Tibet, and one of the main roles for the ITBP in Milam is to check on smuggling.

Milam is as far as you are permitted to trek at present, although the ITBP will allow you to continue past the village for three km to a vantage point (3500m) where you can appreciate the size and extent of the Milam Glacier. This trail passes through high meadows dotted with sage, juniper, miniature gorse and briar roses high above the terminal moraine. At the head of the glacier the peaks include Rishi Pahar (6992m), Hardeol (7151m) and Tirsuli I (7074m), while the peaks along the northeast rim include Kholl (6114m), Nanda Gond (6315m), Nital Thaur (6236m) and Nanda Pal (6306m).

Stages 5 to 7: Return Trek to Munsyari

The return trek to Munsyari can be completed in three stages, the first from Milam back to Bodgwar, the second to Lilam and the third to Munsyari. Of course, if it were not for the detour over the Lilam Ridge, it would take only a matter of four hours to trek from Bodgwar to Lilam, allowing time that day to return to Munsyari.

Option: Nanda Devi East Base Camp

This option takes a minimum of four stages to complete. From Martoli allow two stages to reach the Nanda Devi East Base Camp. The trail follows the true right side of the Lwanl Gad for four km until it is opposite the small settlement of **Lwanl** (3500m).

This point is high above the confluence of the Lwanl Gad and the Shalang Gad, the tributary flowing in from the south-west and fed by the snows on the southern ridges of Nanda Kot. The trail then diverts along the true right side of the Shalang Gad with views up the valley to Shalang Dhura (5678m). In the early part of the season, cross the residual snow bridge over the tributary.

When the snow bridge collapses the villagers from Martoli and Lwanl construct a log bridge that suffices for the rest of the

season. Continue on the true left side of the valley to the settlement of Lwanl.

Beyond Lwanl continue up the Lwanl Gad before entering some spectacular gorge country. The trail at times skirts around side gullies and past rhododendron copses, which remain in bloom until the end of May, and at other times descends to the river's edge to avoid rocky overhangs. After four to five km the valley widens and affords views of the peak of Nanda Kot. Further up the valley the trail passes a series of moraine fields until it is opposite a sizable meadow – **Sartol Kharak** (3650m). Cross the Lwanl Gad here (early in the season by a snow bridge, later by a log bridge) to the true left side of the valley and an ideal intermediary camp.

The second, comparatively short, stage to the base of Nanda Devi East continues on the true left side of the valley to the meadow at **Naspanpatti** (3850m). A herd of bharal have been spotted on the cliffs above this meadow so (by association) there is always the chance of also sighting the elusive snow leopard, particularly at the end the season. Beyond Naspanpatti the trail ascends high above the terminal moraine engulfing the main valley floor before crossing some scree slopes just below the base camp.

Nanda Devi East Base Camp (4150m) is a delightful series of meadows. There is no shortage of camp sites from which to appreciate the peaks and the high snow ridges that virtually enclose this upper section of the valley. To the south a snow ridge links the imposing summit of Nanda Khat to Changuch. The lowest point on the ridge, to the northwest of Changuch, is **Traills Pass** (5312m). West of Traills Pass, the snow-capped ridge merges with the one striking north from Nanda Khat (6611m) before gradually rising to the imposing summit ridge below Nanda Devi East (7434m), the highest peak in the vicinity. Along this ridge lies the **Longstaff Col** (5910m), accessible only by a technical climb, and from which it is possible to peer into Nanda Devi Sanctuary.

From the base camp there are several options, including a two to three hour scramble up the snow ridges south-east of Nanda

UTTARAKHAND

Devi East. From a suitable vantage point there are unrivalled views of the gullies leading to the Longstaff Col and also the route leading to Traills Pass, the heavily crevassed pass linking the upper Lwanl Valley with the Pindari Valley.

Darjeeling

HISTORY

The district of Darjeeling was, until the beginning of the 18th century, part of Sikkim. In 1780 the Gurkhas invaded Sikkim as part of their plan to establish a vast Trans Himalayan empire. The British East India Company was drawn into the conflict, leading to the Gurkha wars. This resulted in the Treaty of Siliguri in 1817, whereby territory lost to the Gurkhas was restored to the rajahs of Sikkim on the condition that the British took control of their external affairs. It was during a local border dispute in 1828 that two British officers visited Darjeeling and recognised its potential as a hill station. This information was not lost on the authorities in Calcutta and in 1835 they pressured the rajah to grant them Darjeeling.

An agreement was reached and an annual payment made. However, the rajah was not totally comfortable with the agreement. In 1849 matters came to a head. The British Superintendent of Darjeeling and Dr Joseph Hooker, a renowned botanist, who were touring Sikkim with the permission of the rajah and the British government, were arrested by the Sikkim authorities. The British took this as an affront to their position and, after the release of the prisoners, they temporarily withdrew the rajah's stipend and annexed the area between the Sikkim border and the Indian plains. This effectively redrew the borders of Sikkim, cutting it off from the plains except through British territory, and at the same time gave Darjeeling direct access to the rest of British India.

From then on the development of Darjeeling was rapid. The newly completed road from the plains was upgraded and the small settlement expanded. The administrators from the East India Company, enjoying a break from Calcutta up at the hill station, were inspired by the magnificent views of Kangchenjunga. The tea plantations also thrived and a large number of workers were hired from across the border in Nepal. The Tea

Highlights – Darjeeling

Well-defined forest trails along the Nepalese border afford views of Kangchenjunga (8586m) and glimpses of Everest, Lhotse and Makalu.

Planters' Club was established in 1868, and the narrow-gauge railway was completed in 1882.

Darjeeling remained part of Bengal after 1947. However, in 1985, the Gurkhas and Nepalese mounted their own political group with the aim of making Darjeeling an independent hill state separate from Bengal. A compromise was eventually reached in 1988, which gave the Darjeeling Gurkha Hill Council a large measure of autonomy and a greater control over its local affairs.

GEOGRAPHY

The hill station of Darjeeling (2134m) is on the south-eastern rim of the Singali Ridge, which forms part of the Darjeeling Hills extending east towards the town of Kalimpong.

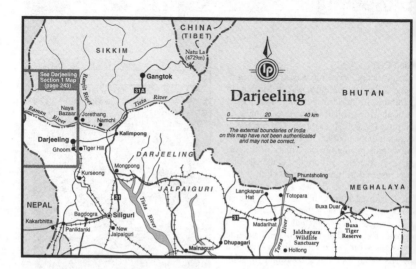

To the north-west of Darjeeling, the Singali Ridge constitutes the impressive Himalayan divide between Sikkim and Nepal. As it extends south, the ridge is also the border between Darjeeling and Nepal. The trek along this ridge between Mana Bhanjang and Phalut is described in this chapter.

Darjeeling's border with Sikkim is defined by the course of the Raman River. The headwaters of the river are just below the Singali La, the lowest point of the Singali Ridge.

CLIMATE

The huge cumulus clouds of the Indian monsoon build up by the end of May, and by early June, Darjeeling experiences the first of the continuous monsoon rains. July, with over 800 mm, has the highest rainfall of any month, establishing a pattern which continues until mid-September.

In the post-monsoon season the daytime temperatures vary around 10°C and the settled conditions make it an ideal time for trekking. Winter daytime temperatures fall to just above freezing, with snowfall common on the ridges for much of December, January and February. Daytime temperatures increase during March, and continue to rise to around 15°C to 20°C in the pre-monsoon season, which lasts until the end of May.

MAPS & BOOKS

For treks out of Darjeeling, the Air India trekking maps available from the Government of India Tourist Office provide a useful outline of the area's ridges and rivers. Guidebooks include *Sikkim, Darjeeling and Kalimpong* by Wendy Brewer Lama (1993) and *An Introduction to the Hill Stations of India* by Graeme Westlake (1993).

GETTING THERE & AWAY
Delhi

Indian Airlines and Jet Airways fly from Delhi to Bagdogra, near Siliguri, about 90 km from Darjeeling. The cost with either airline is US$156. Bookings are heavy, so try to make your reservation when buying your international ticket. There are many day buses from Siliguri and New Jalpaiguri to Darjeeling. The drive takes three to four hours and costs Rs 40. Taxis or shared jeeps are a faster alternative and cost Rs 100 per seat. Alternatively, the *North East Express* and *Brahmaputra Mail* trains operate from Delhi to New Jalpaiguri. They take about 36 hours and cost Rs 1042 in 1st class and Rs 288 in 2nd class. From New Jalpaiguri the *Toy Train* to Darjeeling costs Rs 185 and takes the best part of eight to 10 hours.

Calcutta
Indian Airlines flies three times a week from Calcutta to Bagdogra, while Jet Airways flies four times a week. Again, flights are heavily booked. The cost is US$65.

The *Kangchenjunga Express* runs from Calcutta to New Jalpaiguri and takes 10 hours. Alternatively, the *Darjeeling Mail* runs overnight and takes around 12 to 13 hours. The costs are Rs 461 in 1st class and Rs 168 in 2nd class.

Nepal
There are several bus companies in Darjeeling which operate daily services to Kathmandu. None of them run direct services and you will have to change buses at Siliguri. Buy a ticket as far as Siliguri, which will guarantee you a seat on the connecting bus to Kathmandu. The drive from Darjeeling to Siliguri takes four hours. It is a further one hour drive to the border, with one or two more hours to complete customs and immigration formalities at Kakarbhitta, the Nepalese border town. It is then a long and tiring 15 to 16 hour drive to Kathmandu. The bus costs Rs 250.

Note: there is no Nepalese consulate in Darjeeling, but a one week Nepalese visa can be issued at the border (US$15) and can be extended in Kathmandu.

SINGALI RIDGE
Treks
Mana Bhanjang to Rimbik via Sandakphu
(introductory; 3 stages)

History
The Nepalese villages on the Singali Ridge reflect the gradual migration of the Nepalese across the Darjeeling Hills over the last 200 years to Darjeeling, Kalimpong and Sikkim.

To the north of Phalut, the Singali La marks an important trade route between Darjeeling and the villages and towns of eastern Nepal.

When to Trek
The trekking season in Darjeeling is very similar to that in eastern Nepal. The post-monsoon season in October and November brings clear days and warm temperatures, particularly in the valleys. The daytime temperatures drop to around 0°C in December and January, although trekking from lodge to lodge can still make the trek enjoyable. The spring season, from March to May, has many attractions. The days are longer and the rhododendrons come into flower, remaining in full bloom until the first of the monsoon rains in early June.

Trekking Agents
Although there are a number of trekking agents in Darjeeling, most trekkers tend to go the youth hostel above Dr Zakir Hussan Rd to get information on the trek to Sandakphu and also to read the informative log of trekkers' comments. A limited supply of sleeping bags (Rs 25 per day), jackets (Rs 25 per day) and backpacks (Rs 15 per day) can be hired. Normally Rs 500 is required as a security deposit.

Himalayan Mountaineering Institute
The Himalayan Mountaineering Institute is about two km up from the town of Darjeeling. It houses exhibits from many climbing expeditions, and specimens of flora and fauna. It also contains a relief map of the Himalaya, which is of particular note if you are travelling on to Nepal or other parts of the Indian Himalaya. The Everest Museum next door contains equipment and books covering some of the postwar attempts on Everest. It has memorabilia of the famous mountaineer Sherpa Tenzing Norgay. There are also regular film shows and lectures.

Accommodation in Darjeeling
Like most Indian hill stations, Darjeeling has a wide variety of accommodation. This includes the *youth hostel*, above Dr Zakir Hussan Rd, which is popular with trekkers.

DARJEELING

The hostel is currently being renovated, and dormitory rooms cost Rs 25.

In the mid-range, Tibetan families run a number of hotels, including the *Shamrock Hotel*, close to the main bazaar, at Rs 300/550 a single/double, and the *Bellevue Hotel* on Chowrasta, where rooms are Rs 550/700. These are high-season rates (for May and June plus October); expect to pay about half that at other times of the year. If these places are full, there are plenty of other hotels nearby.

At the top end is the *Windermere Hotel*, on Observatory Hill, where a room with all meals costs US$70/100 a single/double. A little cheaper, but with a similar atmosphere, is the *New Elgin* hotel costing US$59/71. The *Darjeeling Club* above Nehru Rd, was the *Tea Planters' Club*, and has been recently renovated. The rooms, on a full-board basis, cost Rs 625/950.

Accommodation on the Trail

There is no shortage of houses and lodges on this trek to provide both meals and overnight accommodation. For instance, at the *Indira Lodge*, *Everest Lodge* and *Teachers Lodge* in Jaubari, a bed costs around Rs 30 per night, while the *Hotel Sherpa* at Rimbik provides good lodge-style accommodation for around Rs 50. There is no need for a tent unless continuing on the optional trek to Phalut.

Trekking Advice

The trek to Sandakphu is graded as introductory, but the walking conditions can become very warm and humid in May during the build-up to the monsoon. There are also a few places on the track where the trail splits. When in doubt, it is best to be patient as there is no shortage of villagers who will point you in the right direction.

Provisions

A wide variety of fruit, vegetables and other provisions can be purchased in Darjeeling. However, most people undertake this trek with the intention of staying in lodges, in which case all that is required is a few chocolate bars and other goodies to keep you going during the day.

Porters

Porters are generally available from Darjeeling or at Mana Bhanjang. Daily rates are around Rs 100.

Access

The bus to the trekking-off point at Mana Bhanjang costs Rs 35 and takes about two to three hours. En route you may have to produce your passport at the police checkpost, so keep it handy. The return from Rimbik costs Rs 50. This bus leaves at 7 am and takes six or seven hours to reach Darjeeling.

MANA BHANJANG TO RIMBIK VIA SANDAKPHU
Map: Darjeeling Section 1 (page 243)
Stage 1: Mana Bhanjang to Jaubari
(Average walking time 5 to 6 hours)
Mana Bhanjang is not the trailhead as a rough jeep track has been extended all the way to Sandakphu. However, you can avoid this track on some stages of the trek.

From **Mana Bhanjang** (2150m) there is a short, steep ascent for the first two km. The trail continues past several small settlements to the village of **Meghma** (2870m). Here the trail splits. Follow the route to the lodge at **Tonglu** (3020m), before continuing along the rhododendron-covered ridges to **Jaubari**, just inside the Nepal border, to gain your first uninterrupted views of the eastern Himalaya.

Stage 2: Jaubari to Sandakphu
(Average walking time 6 to 7 hours)
There is a sign outside the *Indira Lodge* at Jaubari outlining the route to Sandakphu. Essentially, the trail splits a number of times on this stage, and you may require directions from your porter or the local villagers at points where trails divert to other villages.

From **Jaubari** (2750m) descend to **Gairbas** (2620m) before a long, gradual ascent to the small lake and settlement at **Kali Pokhari** (2950m). Here there is a tea shop and lodge. From Kali Pokhari it is a two hour trek to **Bikhay Bhanjang** (Bhike; 3350m) from where it is a further hour up to the ridge and the trekkers' huts at **Sandakphu** (3580m).

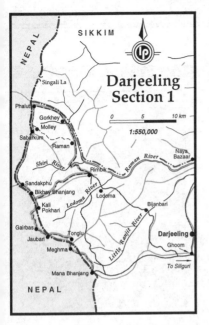

SIKKIM

NEPAL

Singali La

Phalut

Gorkhey

Molley

Sabarkum

Raman

Shiri River

Sandakphu

Bikhay Bhanjang

Kali Pokhari

Gairbas

Jaubari

Tonglu

Meghma

Mana Bhanjang

NEPAL

Darjeeling Section 1

0   5   10 km

1:550,000

Naya Bazaar

Raman River

Rimbik

Lodoma River

Lodoma

Bijanbari

Little Ranjit River

Darjeeling

Ghoom

To Siliguri

Sandakphu is the place to view the mountains. On a clear morning you can appreciate much of the eastern Himalaya. To the west, the peaks of Lhotse (8501m), Everest (8848m) and Makalu (8475m) are visible; while to the east of Makalu, the peak of Jannu (7710m) can be seen. Immediately to the north are the peaks along the Singali Ridge dividing Sikkim and Nepal, including Kokthang (6147m), Rathong (6679m), Kabru South (7317m), Talung (7349m) and, of course, the huge Kangchenjunga massif itself (8586m), the world's third-highest peak. To the east of Kangchenjunga, the sacred peak of Pandim (6691m) looms above the forested ridges of southern Sikkim.

Stage 3: Sandakphu to Rimbik
(Average walking time six hours)
From Sandakphu return along the trail down to Bikhay Bhanjang. From here follow the main trail as if returning to Kali Pokhari for one to 1.5 km. At this point, diverge from the main trail and head for a small hill with prayer flags on the summit before commencing your descent to **Rimbik** (2280m). The trail through rhododendron and coniferous forests is steep and muddy in places, and prone to leeches in the pre and post-monsoon period.

Option: Sandakphu to Rimbik via Phalut
This option takes three stages to complete. From **Sandakphu** (3580m) the trail continues along the ridge line to **Sabarkum** (3530m) a walk of four to five hours. There is no water on the ridge, and for food and lodgings you will have to descend to the village of Molley, two km down the valley. On the second day return to the ridge and complete the two hour walk to **Phalut** (3600m) to appreciate further views of the eastern Himalaya. It is debatable whether the views here are better than those from Sandakphu.

Directly across from Phalut to the north is the Singali La, an important trading pass between Sikkim and Darjeeling and their neighbour Nepal to the west. To the east, ridges drop steeply away to the upper reaches of the Raman River, which forms the border between Darjeeling (West Bengal) and Sikkim. There is a basic trekkers' hut at Phalut, but that's about it. You must bring your own tent and food for the night.

From Phalut it is an easy three hours down to the village of Gorkhey, where you have the choice of staying in the *Gurhka Hill Council Trekkers Hut* or in one of the private houses. The final stage can be completed in six to seven hours. The trail descends through the forest to the village of **Raman** (2560m) before crossing the Shiri River and past a few villages to reach **Rimbik**.

Getting Away
The bus leaves Rimbik at 7 am, costs Rs 50 and takes six to seven hours to complete the 65 km drive back to Darjeeling.

DARJEELING

Sikkim

HISTORY

Sikkim was originally populated by the Lepchas, a tribal people thought to have migrated from Assam in the 13th century. The Lepchas were essentially nature worshippers, moving from one forest clearing to the next as they spread throughout the valleys of Sikkim. With the migration of the Tibetans to Sikkim during the 17th century, the Lepchas were forced to move to the more remote regions of the country.

In 1641 the 5th Dalai Lama in Lhasa appointed Phuntsog Namgyal the first ruler of Sikkim. At this time the country included part of eastern Nepal, part of the Chumbi Valley in Tibet, some of the western valleys of Bhutan and, to the south, Darjeeling, Kalimpong and the territory down to the Indian plains.

Boundaries were altered as a result of the wars with Bhutan between 1717 and 1734. Sikkim lost much of the southern foothills, as well as Kalimpong on the important trade route between India and Tibet. More territory was lost after 1780, following the Gurkha expansion in Nepal. The boundaries were further realigned after the conflict between the British East India Company and the Gurkhas. The Treaty of Siliguri (1817) ensured that the territory lost to the Gurkhas was returned by the British to the rajah of Sikkim. In return, the British assumed control over Sikkim's external affairs and its trade negotiations with Nepal, Tibet and Bhutan.

The British annexation of Darjeeling is described under History in the Darjeeling chapter. Further British expansion led to the declaration of Sikkim as a protectorate in 1861, and a further delineation of its borders. The Tibetans, however, were becoming increasingly suspicious of British expansion and in particular regarded much of northern Sikkim as part of Tibet. In 1886 they invaded Sikkim to reassert their authority. The British resisted, and the powers of Sikkim's rajah were further reduced. In 1890 a separate treaty declared Sikkim a semi-independent

Highlights – Sikkim
Trails to the base of Kangchenjunga, luxuriant rhododendron forests, high yak pastures and huge glaciers. Magnificent views of the many 7000m peaks along the snow-capped Singali Ridge complement trekking in southern Sikkim.

state, administered by the rajah under the guidance of a British Political Officer. However, the northern boundaries of Sikkim had never been clearly defined, and it was not until 1902 that a Boundary Commission was established to determine the current borders between Sikkim and Tibet.

The British were keen to develop the country and encouraged workers from Nepal to settle in Sikkim. It was a development which continued after 1947, when India became independent, and Sikkim became a protectorate within the Indian Union. Indeed, in the early 1960s the Nepalese constituted 75% of Sikkim's population. During this time, Sikkim's rajah upheld a policy to prohibit further immigration and to restrict the rights of Nepalese to citizenship. Demonstrations followed, and the rajah sought refuge in India. India intervened, the rajah abdicated in 1975 and Sikkim became the 22nd state of the Indian Union.

GEOGRAPHY

The Kangchenjunga massif is on the main axis of the Singali Ridge – the mountain range forming the divide between Nepal and Sikkim. The massif includes the main peak (8586m), the central peak (8482m) and the south peak (8476m). To the east it is flanked by the Zemu Glacier, which feeds into the Zemu Chu and the Lhonak Chu, two of the main tributaries of the Tista River.

North of the Kangchenjunga massif, the Singali Ridge extends to Sikkim's northern border with Tibet. It includes such peaks as Nepal Peak (6910m), Kirat Chuli (7365m), Pyramid Peak (7123m), Dome Kang (7442m), Jongsang (7483m) and Lhonak Peak (6710m) close to the borders of Nepal, Sikkim and Tibet.

To the south of the Kangchenjunga massif, the Singali Ridge is equally impressive. It includes the main peak of Talung (7349m) at the head of the Talung Glacier, which feeds into the Talung Chu, another major tributary of the Tista River. Immediately south of the Talung peaks are Kabru North (7338m), Kabru South (7317m), Rathong (6679m) and Kokthang (6147m), while on a subsidiary ridge are Kabru Dome (6600m) and Forked Peak (6108m). These peaks provide an impressive mountain wall which encloses the Rathong Glacier and the Rathong River flowing south to Yuksam. At present this is the only region open to foreign trekkers, although there are plans to permit groups to trek the Zemu Glacier, and even the wild and desolate Lhonak Valley to the north of the state.

CLIMATE

Southern Sikkim comes under the influence of the north-east monsoon. In particular, the region south of Kangchenjunga and the main Himalaya Range is subject to heavy rainfall lasting from early June through till the beginning of September. During this time, the region experiences some of the heaviest rainfall in the Indian Himalaya, with up to 700 mm per month falling in July and August.

The post-monsoon season extends from the beginning of October until mid-November. Although the daytime temperatures rarely average more than 5°C, at altitudes above 3500m at this time the settled conditions are ideal for trekking.

The first of the winter snows fall by mid to late November, and snowfalls continue throughout the winter until early March. From mid-March onwards, the snows begin to melt on the mountain passes and the daytime temperatures begin to rise to between 10°C and 15°C. Monsoon clouds form by early May, with intermittent storms which last for a day or two, reflecting the gradual build-up of the monsoon. However, this should not preclude trekking at this time. The mornings are generally clear, and clouds do not build up until mid-morning. This is also the time when the rhododendrons and magnolias are in full bloom.

MAPS & BOOKS

For treks out of Yuksam, the Air India trekking maps provide a useful ridge-river outline of the area. Guidebooks include *Sikkim, Darjeeling and Kalimpong* by Wendy Brewer Lama (1993). For historical background at the turn of the century refer to *Sikkim & Bhutan* by Claude White (reprint 1984). For details of climbing expeditions in the region refer to *Exploring the Hidden Himalaya* by Soli Mehta & Harish Kapadia (1990), and *Himalayan Odyssey* by Trevor Braham (1974), plus the sections on Sikkim in *Abode of Snow* by Kenneth Mason (reprint 1987).

GETTING THERE & AWAY
Delhi

Indian Airlines flies three times a week from Delhi to Bagdogra, while Jet Airways operates a daily service. The cost of the flight is US$156. The *North East Express* and *Brahmaputra Mail* trains run from Delhi to New

Jalpaiguri, taking about 36 hours and costing Rs 1042 in 1st class and Rs 288 in 2nd class. The bus trip from Bagdogra (or nearby Siliguri) to Gangtok takes about six hours and costs Rs 50. Jeeps are faster and cost Rs 70 per seat.

Calcutta

Indian Airlines flies three times a week from Calcutta to Bagdogra, while Jet Airways flies twice a week. The cost is US$65. By train, the *Kangchenjunga Express* from Calcutta to New Jalpaiguri takes 10 hours, while the *Darjeeling Mail* runs overnight and takes 12

to 13 hours. The costs are Rs 461 1st class and Rs 168 2nd class.

Darjeeling

The bus service from Darjeeling to Gangtok takes around eight hours and costs Rs 90. Jeeps can also be hired for around Rs 900 per vehicle.

GANGTOK

Gangtok, the capital of Sikkim, is on a ridge above the Ranipul River. The views are spectacular, across to Kangchenjunga and the peaks on the Singali Ridge between Nepal

SIKKIM

and Sikkim. The town has gone through a period of rapid modernisation since 1975. However, time can be spent wandering the main bazaar with its array of handicrafts and Tibetan artefacts, or visiting the Institute of Cottage Industries just above the town. Also worth visiting is the Namgyal Institute of Tibetology, established in 1958 to promote the language and cultural traditions of Tibet. There is a comprehensive library, stocked with manuscripts brought from Tibet in 1959, together with many valuable *tankas* (Buddhist religious paintings).

Rumtek monastery is on the far side of the valley, opposite Gangtok and 24 km away by road. The monastery is the seat of the Gyalwa Karmapa, head of the Kargyupa sect of Tibetan Buddhism. The sect was founded in the 11th century, while the present monastic site was established in 1740. The main monastery is a recent construction, built in accordance with the design of the Gyalwa Karmapa's former monastery in Tibet.

YUKSAM & THE RATHONG VALLEY
Treks
Yuksam to Dzongri & the Guicha La
(moderate; 6 stages)

This route is, at present, the only one open for trekking in Sikkim. There are, however, plans to open some of the northern regions for trekking, so keep in contact with the Sikkim Tourist Office in Gangtok or Delhi for any changes in the regulations.

History
The trail to Dzongri has been followed by yak herders from the villages around Yuksam for many centuries. However, as the route does not pass through any villages (with the exception of the newly established Tibetan villages at Bakhim and Tsoska), the train over the Guicha La would not have been followed by local people on a regular basis.

Claude White, appointed in 1890 as the first Political Officer in Sikkim, was one of the first Europeans to cross the Guicha La. In 1890 he trekked from Dzongri over the pass to the Talung Glacier south-east of

Kangchenjunga. He also spent a number of seasons exploring the high mountain regions, including the Zemu Glacier and the Lhonak region, as part of the Sikkim-Tibet Boundary Commission in 1902.

In the interwar years, many expeditions trekked through Dzongri before attempting the peaks at the head of the Rathong Valley. However, following the Chinese occupation of Tibet in 1951, restrictions were introduced which even today only allow trekking in this region of West Sikkim.

When to Trek
Sikkim is subject to monsoonal conditions from June through till the end of September. There are therefore two distinct seasons. The pre-monsoon season extends from early April until mid-May, and the post-monsoon season, from early October to mid-November. The pre-monsoon season is best for the rhododendrons, while the post-monsoon season normally provides clearer views of the mountains. However, you should be prepared for inclement weather, as snow storms at higher altitudes can develop rapidly in both the pre and post-monsoon seasons.

Trekking Arrangements
The current regulations allow you to stay in Sikkim for only two weeks. A 15 day permit can be issued by the Sikkim authorities on your arrival in Delhi or Calcutta. Applications for permission to trek in West Sikkim should, however, reach the office of the Deputy Director, Sikkim Tourism, New Sikkim House, Chanakyapuri, New Delhi, two months before the date of the intended trek.

Essentially, if you want to trek in Sikkim you need to plan well in advance. Your arrangements must go through a local agency in Gangtok, recognised by the Sikkim Tourist Office, and you must have a minimum of four people in your group. The tourist office will organise all the paperwork for you, so send your passport details, visa number and photograph at least two months in advance. You should also forward a deposit at the same time. To date, trekking is restricted to the Yuksam-Dzongri area and a local guide

SIKKIM

must accompany you throughout the trek. Note: trekking permits are not necessary for Indian tourists.

Trekking Agents

A list of recognised agents can be supplied from the Sikkim Tourist Information Centre, Mahatma Gandhi Rd, Gangtok, Sikkim. A local agent recommended is Yak & Yeti Travels, Harka-Kala Bhavan, National Highway, PO Box 56, Gangtok 737101.

Accommodation in Gangtok

There are many small *hotels* on Tibet Rd just above the tourist office, while the *Hotel Chumila* below the GPO has been recommended and has rooms from Rs 100 upwards. The *Hotel Tibet*, on Stadium Rd, with singles/doubles for Rs 585/960, is a more expensive alternative. The up-market hotels, including the *Norkhill Hotel* and the *Tashi Delek*, cater mainly for organised groups. Expect to pay around Rs 1500/2000 a single/double, with meals included.

Accommodation on the Trail

The lodges and shelter huts on the trek to Dzongri include the *Forest Rest House* at Bakhim, costing Rs 25, and two well-maintained *lodges* at Tsoska with beds for Rs 30. At Dzongri there are *huts* maintained by the Sikkim government which charge Rs 50 per bed. *Government huts* have recently been constructed at Thansing and Samiti Lake. However, these huts, particularly at Dzongri, are often fully occupied by groups of porters or Indian students, and it is recommended that the trekking agency handling your trip provide tents so that you can be free to select a good camp site from which to savour the mountains in peace and quiet.

Trekking Advice

Acclimatisation is the most important consideration when undertaking the trek to Dzongri (4020m). To reach this altitude, it is imperative you take at least three or four days, either spending a rest day at Tsoska or Bakhim, or making an intermediary camp at Pethang (between Bakhim and Dzongri). If the itinerary set out for you by the local agent does not allow this much time, change it. Even after three stages you are still likely to experience the headaches and discomfort of adjusting to altitude, which will undermine your enjoyment of the trek.

Note that regulations in Sikkim require the use of a kerosene stove for cooking; you should insist that your local agent abides by this rule. There is also a constant need to check on the thoughtful disposal of garbage. Many camp sites show the effects of overuse with tin cans and waste discarded at random. Whenever possible, insist that the garbage is carried out in sacks for disposal at Yuksam.

Provisions

Food and provisions are generally provided by the agencies. However, a few luxuries such as chocolate and dried fruit can be purchased in Gangtok.

Horsemen & Porters

As with provisions, the hiring of porters or yaks is normally included in the arrangement with the trekking agency. However, for Indian trekkers visiting Sikkim, porters are normally available at Yuksam for around Rs 100 per day.

Access

From Gangtok, there is a daily bus service to Yuksam, which takes about eight to nine hours and costs Rs 90. There is also a daily bus service to the nearby monastery at Pemayantse, where you can spend the night before continuing to Yuksam the following day. Jeeps are a good way of getting around in Sikkim if you want to save time. From Gangtok they cost between Rs 800 and Rs 1000 to Yuksam via Pemayantse and Rumtek – very convenient if you are on a tight schedule.

YUKSAM TO DZONGRI & GUICHA LA

Map: Sikkim Section 1 (page 249)

Stage 1: Yuksam to Bakhim

(Average walking time 5 to 6 hours)

Yuksam (1760m), a former capital of Sikkim, is now no more than a village on a plateau with commanding views of southern Sikkim.

At the trailhead there are some small lodges, as well as a *tourism lodge* run by the Sikkim government and a camping area about 100m from the road. This is as far as foreign tourists can travel without a trekking permit.

The trail heads north through the village of Yuksam before entering oak and pine forest high above the Rathong River. The trail is well defined, with substantial bridges over the side rivers. Two words of warning on this stage: firstly, the number of midges make it necessary to wear long trousers and apply an insect repellent; secondly, the area abounds with leeches, so keep a box of matches handy to burn them off. Apart from one small clearing, there are no settlements en route. Just beyond the confluence of the Rathong and Prek rivers (the latter comes from the Guicha La), the trail descends steeply to a substantial bridge. There follows a 600m ascent up the forest trail to the small settlement of **Bakhim** (2750m), occupied by a family of Lepcha farmers. There is a *Forest Rest House* and a possible camp site, complete with a small spring, about five minutes below the settlement. From Bakhim, there are commanding views down the Rathong Gorge to Yuksam.

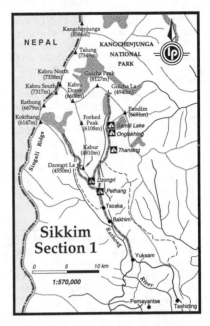

Stage 2: Bakhim to Pethang
(Average walking time 4 to 5 hours)
The trail from Bakhim heads up through grazing meadows, and past the first rhododendron and magnolia trees, to the village of **Tsoska** (3050m). It takes an hour to reach Tsoska, and for fit parties this is an ideal alternative for an overnight stay on the first stage, particularly during the Indian school holidays when the Forest Rest House at Bakhim tends to be crowded.

Tsoska is a comparatively new village, founded in the early 1960s when the Sikkim government granted this tract of land to Tibetan refugees who had fled over the border in 1959. The village consists of a dozen or so houses, a *gompa* (Tibetan Buddhist monastery), and rows of *chortens* (stone Buddhist monuments) lining the main trail.

Just above the village the trail splits. A small trail diverts towards the Rathong Valley

(see the first Option below), while the main trail continues up the ridge. It is steep in sections, and passes through magnificent rhododendron forests. There are over 400 flowering species in this region and many can be appreciated as they come into full bloom from mid-April to late May. The forest trail is well defined, with wooden boards over sections which could be very muddy after heavy rainfall.

Pethang (3650m) is a small clearing for camping, with a small hut for porters. The water supply is about 200m down the side trail leading to the Prek Valley.

Stage 3: Pethang to Dzongri
(Average walking time 2 to 3 hours)
From Pethang a steep ascent takes you to the upper limit of the conifers and the top of the ridge separating the Prek and Rathong valleys. Here there are wonderful 360° views. To the south you look down the valley and across the ridges beyond Yuksam; to the

north-east is the sacred peak of Pandim (6691m) on the far side of the Prek Valley; to the west, beyond the Rathong Valley, is the Singali Ridge; while to the north is the south face of Kangchenjunga (8586m), the world's third-highest peak.

The route along the ridge is covered with dwarf rhododendron bushes and leads to the open grazing meadows at **Dzongri** (4020m). The shelter huts constructed by the Sikkim government are just below the main yak-grazing area, while the best camp sites are one km further on in an open meadow. Dzongri is a vast, windswept grazing area where yaks from Yuksam and the surrounding villages graze from late March until early October.

From Dzongri, the views of the mountains along the Singali Ridge include Kokthang, Rathong and Kabru South, while Pandim and Jubonu (5936m) are two of the highest peaks on the east ridge side of the Prek Valley. The nearby **Dzongri Peak**, about 300m above the camp, is the best vantage point to view Kangchenjunga. Make sure to climb this peak in the early morning to gain fine views of Kangchenjunga and the surrounding peaks.

Option: Dzongri to the Rathong Valley

This option takes two to three stages to complete. To reach the Rathong Valley, head to the **Dzongri La** (4550m), a small pass to the west of Kabur Peak. It takes 1 1/2 to two hours to reach, with a steady ascent just before the pass. From here there are good views across to the Rathong Glacier and the peaks of Rathong, Kabru South, Kabru North, Kabru Dome and Forked Peak, which enclose the valley. It takes a further one to 1 1/2 hours to descend to one of the many camp sites (approximately 4100m) on the valley floor. The next stage takes you to the snout of the **Rathong Glacier** (4350m), with the option of ascending the moraine to the glacier. The third stage follows the trail down the Rathong Valley, before a very steep climb back up to Dzongri.

If time is at a premium, it is possible to trek over the Dzongri La, down to the Rathong Valley and return to Dzongri in one day. Allow a minimum of five to six hours and take your local guide with you, as the trail is difficult to follow in places.

Stage 4: Dzongri to Thansing

(Average walking time 4 hours)
From camp, head east from Dzongri to a series of cairns above the Prek Valley. From here, you can view Kangchenjunga and the entire Prek Valley as far north as the Guicha La. From the ridge there is a steep descent though rhododendron forest to the river bed. Head up along the boulder-strewn river bed to a bridge over the Prek River. The trail then leads to the meadows, camp site and trekkers' huts at **Thansing** (3930m). From the camp site there are uninterrupted views of Pandim and the east ridge of Kangchenjunga.

Option: Thansing to Guicha La

This option takes two stages to complete. From Thansing, it is a comparatively short two hour stage up the valley to Samiti Lake. The ascent is gradual, across grazing meadows to the huts at Zemathang and the snout of the Onglakhing Glacier. This is the base for climbing attempts on Pandim. It is also the beginning of the climb up the moraine to **Samiti Lake** (4200m) – the sacred source of the Prek River.

The huts at Samiti Lake provide a convenient base for climbing the nearby ridge separating the lake from Onglakhing Glacier. From the top of the ridge there are views of Forked Peak, the summit of Kabru North and Guicha Peak to the east of the Guicha La.

From Samiti Lake to the Guicha La will take about three to four hours. The pass is often shrouded in mist and cloud not long after sunrise, so an early start is necessary. The trail heads along the far side of the lake and through moraine before crossing a sandy section alongside the Onglakhing Glacier. From here, you can see the pass at the head of the valley. However, the trek through the lateral moraine is tiring – more so if there has been a recent snowfall.

From the **Guicha La** (4940m), marked with fluttering, colourful prayer flags, there are uninterrupted views of the awe-inspiring east ridge of Kangchenjunga beyond the extensive Talung Glacier. At present this is as far as the regulations permit you to trek. The return trek via Samiti Lake to Thansing will take three to four hours.

Stage 5: Thansing to Tsoska
(Average walking time 6 to 7 hours)
From Thansing, follow the trail back down to the Prek River to recross the bridge, then descend through the boulder field to the base of the climb back up to Dzongri. Here the trail divides. It is clearly signposted, with the upper trail leading to Dzongri and the lower trail heading direct to Pethang. This trail is too narrow for laden yaks, so if they are accompanying your group they will have to return via Dzongri and down the ridge to Pethang, along the route described in stages 3 and 4.

The lower trail gradually ascends above the Prek River, with views back to Pandim, through some of the finest rhododendron forest in the eastern Himalaya. From Thansing

it takes four to five hours to reach Pethang, and from here you are on familiar territory as you join the main trail back to Tsoska village.

Note: there are plans to open an alternative trail from Thansing down the true left side of the Prek Valley, directly to Tashiding monastery below Yuksam. It would take two stages to complete. Check in Gangtok about the current regulations.

Stage 6: Tsoska to Yuksam
(Average walking time 5 to 6 hours)
This stage is often hot and muggy after the rarefied climes of the Guicha La. It can be completed in a long morning with time to arrange onward transportation.

Getting Away
From Yuksam, there are local buses to nearby Pemayantse monastery. The daily bus service to Gangtok costs Rs 60. To reach Darjeeling you need to change buses at Gyalsing. Allow a full day for the journey.

SIKKIM

Glossary

Agni – the *Aryan* god of fire
Aryans – a people who migrated from Persia and Asia Minor to northern India between 2500 and 1500 BC

Bahairo – Hindu demon
Bakharval – goat herders from Jammu and Kashmir
bar – British term for pass sometimes still referred to on maps of Kashmir
beggar – system of forced labour'
Bodhisattva – one who almost reaches *nirvana*, but who renounces it in order to help others attain it
Bon Po – early animistic beliefs adopted in the northern Himalaya
Brahma – member of the Hindu trinity; referred to as the creator or the source of all existence
Brahman – member of the priest caste, the highest in the Hindu caste system
Buddha Jayanti – celebration of the Buddha's birth, death and enlightenment
bugyal – a high alpine meadow in the Garhwal region of Uttarakhand

chai – brewed tea (a mixture of tea, milk and sugar boiled together)
chang – barley beer brewed in Ladakh
chapatti – local bread baked on a dry griddle
charpoy – string bed
chola – woollen cloak worn by *Gaddi* shepherds in Himachal Pradesh
chorten – conical stone Buddhist monument, often containing relics and symbolising the natural elements
chowkidar – caretaker
chu – Ladakhi word for stream

Dalai Lama – spiritual leader of Tibetan Buddhists
Dalit – preferred name for India's Untouchable caste
dandy – a wooden platform or palanquin
Dards – people from Gilgit who introduced irrigation to the upper Indus Valley

darshan – prayers
Devanagiri – script of Sanskrit-based language
dhaba – local tea stall or restaurant
dhal – a lentil-based soup or main dish
dhal bhat – *dhal* with rice
dharma – the sacred law set out by the *Brahman* priests
dhobi – washerman/woman
dhura – term for a pass in some regions of Uttarakhand
Diwali – one of the most important Hindu festivals, including the worship of *Lakshmi*
Dogras – rulers from the hill stations of Jammu who established the state of Jammu & Kashmir
Drukpa – 17th-century Buddhist order supported by the royal families of Ladakh and Bhutan, often referred to as the Red Hat sect
dunga – local bridge built in Moghul style
durbar – royal court
Durrani – Afghan rulers who invaded Kashmir in the 18th century
Dussehra – Hindu festival commemorating the *Ramayana*

ferun – Kashmiri woollen cloak

gad – term for river in some regions of Uttarakhand
Gaddi – shepherds from Himachal Pradesh
gali – a type of pass characterised by a small defile in a mountain wall
Ganesh – elephant-headed god of wisdom and prosperity
Ganga – Ganges River; often used to name its tributaries, eg Gauri Ganga
garh – a fort in Uttar Pradesh
Garuda – the divine eagle, vehicle of transport throughout the universe for *Vishnu*
Gelukpa – followers of Tsongkhapa, often referred to as the Yellow Hat sect (now also referred to as the sect of the *Dalai Lama*)
Gita – sacred texts which set out the philosophical basis of reincarnation
gompa – Tibetan Buddhist monastery

Granth Sahib – *Sikh* holy book
Gujar – buffalo herders found in the foothills throughout Himachal Pradesh
gurdwara – Sikh temple
Gurkhas – military rulers from the Gorkha region of Nepal, who invaded the West Himalaya in the late 18th century

Harijan – former name of the Hindu caste referred to as Untouchables; see *Dalit*
Hinayana – the 'lesser vehicle' of Buddhism
Holi – colourful Hindu festival to mark the end of winter

Id-ul-Zuhara – an important event in the Muslim calendar commemorating Abraham's attempt to sacrifice his son
Indra – the Aryan god of the sky

jagir – the right to rule over, and collect taxes from, a tract of land or territory
Jai Mataji – Hindu chant, literally 'Victory to the Mother Goddess'
Jumla – pre-*Aryan* god worshipped by the people from Malana village in Himachal Pradesh

Kali – goddess of destruction, one of the forms of the consort of *Shiva*
kangri – a clay firepot used by Kashmiri people
Kargyupa – one of the earlier Tibetan Buddhist schools whose main centre nowadays is at Rumtek monastery in Sikkim
karma – the path through the cycle of rebirths determined by cause and effect
khal – term for a pass in Uttarakhand
Khampa – seminomadic Tibetan shepherds or herdsmen
kharak – high-altitude meadow in the Kumaon region of Uttarakhand
Koran – holy book outlining the precepts of the Muslim faith
Krishna – eighth incarnation of *Vishnu*
Kshatriyas – Hindu warrior caste
kund – term for lake in Uttar Pradesh

la – Ladakhi or Tibetan term for a mountain pass or the God of the pass

Lakshmi – consort of *Vishnu* and goddess of wealth
Lepchas – the original inhabitants of Sikkim
lingam – phallic symbol associated with *Shiva*

Mahabharata – Vedic epic containing over 10,000 verses describing the ancient battle between the Pandavas and the Kauravas
maharajah – king or ruler
Mahayana – 'greater-vehicle' Buddhism, a reformist school which focuses on broad compassion towards all sentient beings
Maitriya Buddha – the Buddha to come
mani wall – dry stone wall with many of the upper stones carved with Buddhist prayers
Marpa – noted Buddhist sage who wandered the Himalaya in the 11th century
mathas – seats of learning, established by *Shankara* in the 9th century
maya – the Hindu notion that the external world as we perceive it is an illusion
Mila-Repa – Buddhist sage of the 11th century, a student of Marpa
Moghul – Muslim dynasty of Indian emperors
Mons – early Buddhist missionaries from India who travelled to Ladakh
mosque – Muslim place of worship

Naga – benevolent half-snake, half-human being
Nandi – one of the major manifestations of *Vishnu*
Naropa – Buddhist sage who wandered the Himalaya in the 10th century
nirvana – the ultimate aim of Buddhist practice; release from the cycle of existence
nullah – river bed

Padmasambhava – Buddhist teacher who travelled the Himalaya in the 8th century
Pahari – hill people of Himachal Pradesh
paisa – smallest unit of Indian currency; 100 paise make a *rupee*
Pandava – one of the key families in the *Ramayana*
parao – local term for a trekking stage in the Kumaon region of Uttarakhand
paratha – local bread, cooked on an oiled griddle

Parvati – one of the forms of the consort of *Shiva*

Pathan – tribal group close to the Afghanistan border

puja – Hindu prayer session

pulao – savoury rice

puri – local bread, deep-fried

Raj Jat – important pilgrimage undertaken in Garhwal region of Uttarakhand

rajah – king

Rajatarangiri – 12th-century volumes which provided the definitive guide to Kashmir's early history

Rajput – Hindu warrior class; the royal rulers of Rajasthan

rakshi – rice wine

Rama – seventh incarnation of *Vishnu*

Ramadan – Muslim period of fasting, acknowledging the time when Mohammed had the *Koran* revealed to him in Mecca

Ramayana – the story of *Rama* and Sita (one of India's best-known legends)

rani – queen

Ravana – demon king in the *Ramayana*

Ringchen Brangpo – 11th-century Buddhist scholar said to have founded 108 monasteries in the West Himalaya

rupee – Indian unit of currency

sadhu – wandering Hindu holy man/woman

Saka Dawa – Buddha's birth and enlightenment, celebrated in the Tibetan calendar

Sakyamuni – the historical Buddha (also referred to as Gautama Buddha)

sar – Kashmiri term for lake

Shankara – noted 9th-century Hindu philosopher

Shia – Muslim followers of the son-in-law of the Prophet

shikara – boat similar in design and function to the gondola

Shiva – the Hindu destroyer and also the creator, worshipped in the form of the *lingam*

Shudras – Hindu caste of craftspeople

Sikhs – members of the religious body founded in the Punjab in the 16th century which drew on the best of both Hindu and Muslim traditions

sufi – Muslim holyman or mystic

sumdo – Ladakhi term for village

Surya – the Aryan god of the sun

tanka – Buddhist religious oil painting

Tantrism – cult embedded in magic and mystery adopted in some Hindu and Buddhist traditions

thach – alpine meadow in Himachal Pradesh

Thakur – titled rulers from Lahaul in Himachal Pradesh

tokpo – Ladakhi term for river

tongba – fermented millet mixed with boiling water, drunk in eastern Nepal and Sikkim

tsampa – roasted ground barley, often mixed with butter tea and drunk by Ladakhi and Tibetan people

Tsongkhapa – Buddhist teacher who established a major reformist school of Buddhism that was adopted by the *Dalai Lama*

Vago – the *Aryan* god of the wind

Vaishyas – Hindu cast of tradespeople

Varjrana – the Buddhist school which adopted Tantric practices often associated with *Padmasambhava*

Vedas – ancient set of hymns devoted to the Aryan gods

vihara – a Buddhist monastery

Vishnu – the preserver and sustainer; member of the Hindu trinity, along with *Shiva* and *Brahma*

wallah – worker or 'doer', eg dhobi wallah (washerman)

walli – the female equivalent of a *wallah*

Wesak – Buddha's birth and enlightenment, celebrated in the Hindu calendar

yatra – Hindu pilgrimage

Index

MAPS

TEXT

LONELY PLANET JOURNEYS

JOURNEYS is a unique collection of travel writing – published by the company that understands travel better than anyone else. It is a series for anyone who has ever experienced – or dreamed of – the magical moment when they encountered a strange culture or saw a place for the first time. They are tales to read while you're planning a trip, while you're on the road or while you're in an armchair, in front of a fire.

JOURNEYS books catch the spirit of a place, illuminate a culture, recount a crazy adventure, or introduce a fascinating way of life. They always entertain, and always enrich the experience of travel.

IN RAJASTHAN
Royina Grewal

Indian writer Royina Grewal's travels in Rajasthan take her from tribal villages to flamboyant palaces. Along the way she encounters a multitude of characters: snake charmers, holy men, nomads, astrologers, dispossessed princes, reformed bandits . . . And as she draws out the rarely told stories of farmers' wives, militant maharanis and ambitious schoolgirls, the author skilfully charts the changing place of women in contemporary India. The result is a splendidly evocative mosaic of life in India's most colourful state.

Royina Grewal lives on a farm in Rajasthan, where she and her husband are working to evolve minimal-impact methods of farming. Royina has published two monographs about the need for cultural conservation and development planning. She is also the author of *Sacred Virgin*, a travel narrative about her journey along the Narmada River, which was published to wide acclaim.

SHOPPING FOR BUDDHAS
Jeff Greenwald

Here in this distant, exotic land, we were compelled to raise the art of shopping to an experience that was, on the one hand, almost Zen – and, on the other hand, tinged with desperation like shopping at Macy's or Bloomingdale's during a one-day-only White Sale.

Shopping for Buddhas is Jeff Greenwald's story of his obsessive search for the perfect Buddha statue. In the backstreets of Kathmandu, he discovers more than he bargained for . . . and his souvenir-hunting turns into an ironic metaphor for the clash between spiritual riches and material greed. Politics, religion and serious shopping collide in this witty account of an enlightening visit to Nepal.

Jeff Greenwald is also the author of *Mister Raja's Neighborhood* and *The Size of the World*. His reflections on travel, science and the global community have appeared in the *Los Angeles Times*, the *Washington Post*, *Wired* and a range of other publications. Jeff lives in Oakland, California.

LONELY PLANET PHRASEBOOKS

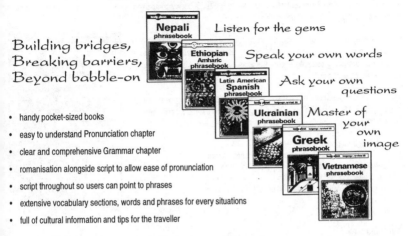

Building bridges,
Breaking barriers,
Beyond babble-on

Listen for the gems

Speak your own words

Ask your own questions

Master of your own image

- handy pocket-sized books
- easy to understand Pronunciation chapter
- clear and comprehensive Grammar chapter
- romanisation alongside script to allow ease of pronunciation
- script throughout so users can point to phrases
- extensive vocabulary sections, words and phrases for every situations
- full of cultural information and tips for the traveller

'...vital for a real DIY spirit and attitude in language learning' – Backpacker

'the phrasebooks have good cultural backgrounders and offer solid advice for challenging situations in remote locations' – San Francisco Examiner

'...they are unbeatable for their coverage of the world's more obscure languages' – The Geographical Magazine

---

Arabic (Egyptian)
Arabic (Moroccan)
Australia
  Australian English, Aboriginal and Torres Strait languages
Baltic States
  Estonian, Latvian, Lithuanian
Bengali
Burmese
Brazilian
Cantonese
Central Europe
  Czech, French, German, Hungarian, Italian and Slovak
Eastern Europe
  Bulgarian, Czech, Hungarian, Polish, Romanian and Slovak
Egyptian Arabic
Ethiopian (Amharic)
Fijian
Greek
Hindi/Urdu

Indonesian
Japanese
Korean
Lao
Latin American Spanish
Malay
Mandarin
Mediterranean Europe
  Albanian, Croatian, Greek, Italian, Macedonian, Maltese, Serbian, Slovene
Mongolian
Moroccan Arabic
Nepali
Papua New Guinea
Pilipino (Tagalog)
Quechua
Russian
Scandinavian Europe
  Danish, Finnish, Icelandic, Norwegian and Swedish

South-East Asia
  Burmese, Indonersian, Khmer, Lao, Malay, Tagalog (Pilipino), Thai and Vietnamese
Sri Lanka
Swahili
Thai
Thai Hill Tribes
Tibetan
Turkish
Ukrainian
USA
  US English, Vernacular Talk, Native American languages and Hawaiian
Vietnamese
Western Europe
  Basque, Catalan, Dutch, French, German, Irish, Italian, Portuguese, Scottish Gaelic, Spanish (Castilian) and Welsh

---

LONELY PLANET TRAVEL ATLASES

Lonely Planet has long been famous for the number and quality of its guidebook maps. Now we've gone one step further and in conjunction with Steinhart Katzir Publishers produced a handy companion series: Lonely Planet travel atlases – maps of a country produced in book form.

Unlike other maps, which look good but lead travellers astray, our travel atlases have been researched on the road by Lonely Planet's experienced team of writers. All details are carefully checked to ensure the atlas corresponds with the equivalent Lonely Planet guidebook.

The handy atlas format means no holes, wrinkles, torn sections or constant folding and unfolding. These atlases can survive long periods on the road, unlike cumbersome fold-out maps. The comprehensive index ensures easy reference.

* full-colour throughout
* maps researched and checked by Lonely Planet authors
* place names correspond with Lonely Planet guidebooks
  – no confusing spelling differences
* legend and travelling information in English, French, German, Japanese and Spanish
* size: 230 x 160 mm

Available now:
Chile & Easter Island • Egypt • India & Bangladesh • Israel & the Palestinian Territories • Jordan, Syria & Lebanon • Laos • Thailand • Vietnam • Zimbabwe, Botswana & Namibia

---

LONELY PLANET TV SERIES & VIDEOS

Lonely Planet travel guides have been brought to life on television screens around the world. Like our guides, the programmes are based on the joy of independent travel, and look honestly at some of the most exciting, picturesque and frustrating places in the world. Each show is presented by one of three travellers from Australia, England or the USA and combines an innovative mixture of video, Super-8 film, atmospheric soundscapes and original music.

Videos of each episode – containing additional footage not shown on television – are available from good book and video shops, but the availability of individual videos varies with regional screening schedules.

Video destinations include: Alaska • American Rockies • Australia – The South-East • Baja California & the Copper Canyon • Brazil • Central Asia • Chile & Easter Island • Corsica, Sicily & Sardinia – The Mediterranean Islands • East Africa (Tanzania & Zanzibar) • Ecuador & the Galapagos Islands • Greenland & Iceland • Indonesia • Israel & the Sinai Desert • Jamaica • Japan • La Ruta Maya • Morocco • New York • North India • Pacific Islands (Fiji, Solomon Islands & Vanuatu) • South India • South West China • Turkey • Vietnam • West Africa • Zimbabwe, Botswana & Namibia

The Lonely Planet TV series is produced by:
Pilot Productions
Duke of Sussex Studios
44 Uxbridge St
London W8 7TG UK

Lonely Planet videos are distributed by:
IVN Communications Inc
2246 Camino Ramon
California 94583, USA

107 Power Road, Chiswick
London W4 5PL UK

Music from the TV series is available on CD & cassette.
For video availability and ordering information contact your nearest Lonely Planet office.

PLANET TALK

Lonely Planet's FREE quarterly newsletter

We love hearing from you and think you'd like to hear from us.

*When...*is the right time to see reindeer in Finland?
*Where...*can you hear the best palm-wine music in Ghana?
*How...*do you get from Asunción to Areguá by steam train?
*What...*is the best way to see India?

For the answer to these and many other questions read PLANET TALK.

Every issue is packed with up-to-date travel news and advice including:

* a letter from Lonely Planet co-founders Tony and Maureen Wheeler
* go behind the scenes on the road with a Lonely Planet author
* feature article on an important and topical travel issue
* a selection of recent letters from travellers
* details on forthcoming Lonely Planet promotions
* complete list of Lonely Planet products

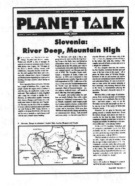

To join our mailing list contact any Lonely Planet office.

Also available: Lonely Planet T-shirts. 100% heavyweight cotton.

LONELY PLANET ONLINE

Get the latest travel information before you leave or while you're on the road

Whether you've just begun planning your next trip, or you're chasing down specific info on currency regulations or visa requirements, check out the Lonely Planet World Wide Web site for up-to-the-minute travel information.

As well as travel profiles of your favourite destinations (including interactive maps and full-colour photos), you'll find current reports from our army of researchers and other travellers, updates on health and visas, travel advisories, and the ecological and political issues you need to be aware of as you travel.

There's an online travellers' forum (the Thorn Tree) where you can share your experiences of life on the road, meet travel companions and ask other travellers for their recommendations and advice. We also have plenty of links to other Web sites useful to independent travellers.

With tens of thousands of visitors a month, the Lonely Planet Web site is one of the most popular on the Internet and has won a number of awards including GNN's Best of the Net travel award.

http://www.lonelyplanet.com

LONELY PLANET PRODUCTS

Lonely Planet is known worldwide for publishing practical, reliable and no-nonsense trav information in our guides and on our web site. The Lonely Planet list covers just about eve accessible part of the world. Currently there are eight series: *travel guides, shoestring guide walking guides, city guides, phrasebooks, audio packs, travel atlases* and *Journeys* – a uniqu collection of travel writing.

EUROPE

Austria • Baltic States & Kaliningrad • Baltic States phrasebook • Britain • Central Europe on a shoestring • Central Europ phrasebook • Czech & Slovak Republics • Denmark • Dublin city guide • Eastern Europe on a shoestring • Eastern Europ phrasebook • Finland • France • Greece • Greek phrasebook • Hungary • Iceland, Greenland & the Faroe Islands • Irelar • Italy • Mediterranean Europe on a shoestring • Mediterranean Europe phrasebook • Paris city guide • Poland • Pragu city guide • Russia, Ukraine & Belarus • Russian phrasebook • Scandinavian & Baltic Europe on a shoestring • Scandinavia Europe phrasebook • Slovenia • St Petersburg city guide • Switzerland • Trekking in Greece • Trekking in Spain • Ukraini phrasebook • Vienna city guide • Walking in Switzerland • Western Europe on a shoestring • Western Europe phraseboc

NORTH AMERICA

Alaska • Backpacking in Alaska • Baja California• California & Nevada • Canada • Florida • Hawaii • Honolulu city guide • Los Angeles city guide • Mexico • Miami city guide • New England • New Orleans city guide • Pacific Northwest USA • Rocky Mountain States • San Francisco city guide • Southwest USA • USA phrasebook

CENTRAL AMERICA & THE CARIBBEAN

Bermuda • Central America on a shoestring • Costa Rica • Cuba • Eastern Caribbean • Guatemala, Belize & Yucatán: La Ruta Maya • Jamaica

SOUTH AMERICA

Argentina, Uruguay & Paraguay • Bolivia • Brazil • Brazilian phrasebook • Buenos Aires city guide • Chile & Easter Island • Chile & Easter Island travel atlas • Colombia • Ecuador & the Galápagos Islands • Latin American Spanish phrasebook • Peru • Quechua phrasebook • Rio de Janeiro city guide • South America on a shoestring • Trekking in the Patagonian Andes • Venezuela

Travel Literature: Full Circle: A South American Journey

ANTARCTICA

Antarctica

ISLANDS OF THE INDIAN OCEAN

Madagascar & Comoros • Maldives & Islands of the East Indian Ocean • Mauritius, Réunion & Seychelles

AFRICA

Arabic (Moroccan) phrasebook • Africa on a shoestring Cape Town city guide • Central Africa • East Africa • Egyp • Egypt travel atlas• Ethiopian (Amharic) phrasebook Kenya • Morocco • North Africa • South Africa, Lesotho & Swaziland • Swahili phrasebook • Trekking in East Africa • West Africa • Zimbabwe, Botswana & Namibia • Zimbabwe, Botswana & Namibia travel atlas

Travel Literature: The Rainbird: A Central Africar Journey • Songs to an African Sunset: A Zimbabwean Story

MAIL ORDER

onely Planet products are distributed worldwide.They are also available by mail order from Lonely
Planet, so if you have difficulty finding a title please write to us. North American and South American
esidents should write to Embarcadero West, 155 Filbert St, Suite 251, Oakland CA 94607, USA;
European and African residents should write to 10 Barley Mow Passage, Chiswick, London W4 4PH;
and residents of other countries to PO Box 617, Hawthorn, Victoria 3122, Australia.

NORTH-EAST ASIA

Beijing city guide • Cantonese phrasebook • China • Hong
Kong, Macau & Guangzhou• Hong Kong city guide •
Japan • Japanese phrasebook • Japanese audio pack •
Korea • Korean phrasebook • Mandarin phrasebook •
Mongolia • Mongolian phrasebook • North-East Asia on a
shoestring • Seoul city guide • Taiwan • Tibet • Tibet
phrasebook • Tokyo city guide

Travel Literature: Lost Japan

MIDDLE EAST & CENTRAL ASIA

Arab Gulf States • Arabic (Egyptian) phrasebook • Central
Asia • Iran • Israel & the Palestinian Territories • Israel &
the Palestinian Territories travel atlas • Istanbul city guide
• Jerusalem city guide • Jordan & Syria • Jordan, Syria &
Lebanon travel atlas • Middle East • Turkey • Turkish
phrasebook • Yemen

Travel Literature: The Gates of Damascus • Kingdom of
the Film Stars: Journey into Jordan

ALSO AVAILABLE:

Travel with Children • Traveller's Tales

INDIAN SUBCONTINENT

Bangladesh • Bengali phrasebook • Delhi city guide •
Hindi/Urdu phrasebook • India • India & Bangladesh travel
atlas • Indian Himalaya • Karakoram Highway • Nepal •
Nepali phrasebook • Pakistan • Rajasthan • Sri Lanka • Sri
Lanka phrasebook • Trekking in the Indian Himalaya •
Trekking in the Karakoram & Hindukush • Trekking in the
Nepal Himalaya

Travel Literature: In Rajasthan • Shopping for Buddhas

SOUTH-EAST ASIA

Bali & Lombok • Bangkok city guide • Burmese
phrasebook • Cambodia • Ho Chi Minh city guide • Indonesia • Indonesian phrasebook • Indonesian audio pack •
Jakarta city guide • Java • Laos • Lao phrasebook • Laos
travel atlas • Malay phrasebook • Malaysia, Singapore &
Brunei • Myanmar (Burma) • Philippines • Pilipino
phrasebook • Singapore city guide • South-East Asia on
a shoestring •South-East Asia phrasebook • Thailand •
Thailand travel atlas • Thai phrasebook • Thai audio pack
• Thai Hill Tribes phrasebook • Vietnam • Vietnamese
phrasebook • Vietnam travel atlas

AUSTRALIA & THE PACIFIC

Australia • Australian phrasebook • Bushwalking in Aus-
tralia • Bushwalking in Papua New Guinea • Fiji • Fijian
phrasebook • Islands of Australia's Great Barrier Reef •
Melbourne city guide • Micronesia • New Caledonia • New
South Wales & the ACT • New Zealand • Northern Terri-
tory • Outback Australia • Papua New Guinea • Papua New
Guinea phrasebook • Queensland • Rarotonga & the Cook
Islands • Samoa • Solomon Islands • South Australia •
Sydney city guide • Tahiti & French Polynesia • Tasmania
• Tonga • Tramping in New Zealand • Vanuatu • Victoria •
Western Australia

Travel Literature: Islands in the Clouds • Sean & David's
Long Drive

THE LONELY PLANET STORY

Lonely Planet published its first book in 1973 in response to the numerous 'How did you do it?' questions Maureen and Tony Wheeler were asked after driving, bussing, hitching, sailing and railing their way from England to Australia.

Written at a kitchen table and hand collated, trimmed and stapled, *Across Asia on the Cheap* became an instant local bestseller, inspiring thoughts of another book.

Eighteen months in South-East Asia resulted in their second guide, *South-East Asia on a shoestring*, which they put together in a backstreet Chinese hotel in Singapore in 1975. The 'yellow bible', as it quickly became known to backpackers around the world, soon became *the* guide to the region. It has sold well over half a million copies and is now in its 8th edition, still retaining its familiar yellow cover.

Today there are over 180 titles, including travel guides, walking guides, language kits & phrasebooks, travel atlases and travel literature. The company is one of the largest travel publishers in the world. Although Lonely Planet initially specialised in guides to Asia, we now cover most regions of the world, including the Pacific, North America, South America, Africa, the Middle East and Europe.

The emphasis continues to be on travel for independent travellers. Tony and Maureen still travel for several months of each year and play an active part in the writing, updating and quality control of Lonely Planet's guides.

They have been joined by over 70 authors and 170 staff at our offices in Melbourne (Australia), Oakland (USA), London (UK) and Paris (France). Travellers themselves also make a valuable contribution to the guides through the feedback we receive in thousands of letters each year.

The people at Lonely Planet strongly believe that travellers can make a positive contribution to the countries they visit, both through their appreciation of the countries' culture, wildlife and natural features, and through the money they spend. In addition, the company makes a direct contribution to the countries and regions it covers. Since 1986 a percentage of the income from each book has been donated to ventures such as famine relief in Africa; aid projects in India; agricultural projects in Central America; Greenpeace's efforts to halt French nuclear testing in the Pacific; and Amnesty International.

'I hope we send the people out with the right attitude about travel. You realise when you travel that there are so many different perspectives about the world, so we hope these books will make people more interested in what they see. These are guidebooks, but you can't really guide people. All you can do is point them in the right direction.'
— Tony Wheeler

LONELY PLANET PUBLICATIONS

Australia
PO Box 617, Hawthorn 3122, Victoria
tel: (03) 9819 1877 fax: (03) 9819 6459
e-mail: talk2us@lonelyplanet.com.au

USA
Embarcadero West, 155 Filbert St, Suite 251,
Oakland, CA 94607
tel: (510) 893 8555 TOLL FREE: 800 275-8555
fax: (510) 893 8563
e-mail: info@lonelyplanet.com

UK
10 Barley Mow Passage, Chiswick,
London W4 4PH
tel: (0181) 742 3161 fax: (0181) 742 2772
e-mail: 100413.3551@compuserve.com

France:
71 bis rue du Cardinal Lemoine, 75005 Paris
tel: 1 44 32 06 20 fax: 1 46 34 72 55
e-mail: 100560.415@compuserve.com

World Wide Web: http://www.lonelyplanet.com